The Translatability of the Religious Dimension in Shakespeare from Page to Stage, from West to East

The Translatability of the Religious Dimension in Shakespeare from Page to Stage, from West to East

With Reference to *The Merchant of Venice* in Mainland China, Hong Kong, and Taiwan

Jenny Wong

FOREWORD BY
David Jasper

PICKWICK *Publications* · Eugene, Oregon

THE TRANSLATABILITY OF THE RELIGIOUS DIMENSION IN SHAKESPEARE FROM PAGE TO STAGE, FROM WEST TO EAST
With Reference to *The Merchant of Venice* in Mainland China, Hong Kong, and Taiwan

Copyright © 2018 Jenny Wong. All rights reserved. Except for brief quotations in critical publications or reviews, no part of this book may be reproduced in any manner without prior written permission from the publisher. Write: Permissions, Wipf and Stock Publishers, 199 W. 8th Ave., Suite 3, Eugene, OR 97401.

Pickwick Publications
An Imprint of Wipf and Stock Publishers
199 W. 8th Ave., Suite 3
Eugene, OR 97401

www.wipfandstock.com

PAPERBACK ISBN: 978-1-5326-3815-2
HARDCOVER ISBN: 978-1-5326-3816-9
EBOOK ISBN: 978-1-5326-3817-6

Cataloguing-in-Publication data:

Names: Wong, Jenny. | Jasper, David, foreword.

Title: The translatability of the religious dimension in Shakespeare from page to stage, from west to east : with reference to *The Merchant of Venice* in mainland China, Hong Kong, and Taiwan / Jenny Wong.

Description: Eugene, OR: Pickwick Publications, 2018. | Includes bibliographical references.

Identifiers: ISBN 978-1-5326-3815-2 (paperback). | ISBN 978-1-5326-3816-9 (hardcover). | ISBN 978-1-5326-3817-6 (ebook).

Subjects: LCSH: Shakespeare, William, 1564–1616—Religion. | Shakespeare, William, 1564–1616—Translations into Chinese. | Religion in literature. | Drama—Religious aspects.

Classification: PR3011 W66 2018 (print). | PR3011 (ebook).

Manufactured in the U.S.A.   05/25/18

Contents

Lists of Illustrations and Tables | vii
Foreword | ix
Acknowledgements | xi
Preface | xiii

1. Introduction | 1
2. History of Effects: Historical Overview of the Treatment of the Religious Dimension since the Early Twentieth Century | 40
3. Case Studies of *The Merchant of Venice* in Mainland China | 94

    Weinisi Shangren(威尼斯商人):the First Shakespearean Drama in China after the Cultural Revolution in 1980 | 94

    For the Heiress' Hand (豪門千金) in 2007 in Guangzhou, a Cantonese Operatic Version of *The Merchant of Venice* | 114

    Shylock(夏洛克): An Adaptation of *The Merchant of Venice* in Shanghai in 2010 | 134

4. Case Studies of *The Merchant of Venice* in Hong Kong | 149
5. *The Merchant of Venice* in Taiwan—*Bond* in 2009 | 186
6. The World behind the Text—Pre-understanding of Directors and Translators | 212
7. The Problems of Translating the Religious Language in Plays | 245

Bibliography | 279

Illustrations and Tables

Table 2.1 Comparison between Source Text and Laura White's Translation | 61

Table 2.2 Comparison between Shakespeare's Play Text and Charles Lamb's *Tales from Shakesepare* | 72

Table 3.1 Comparison between 1985 Production House Program and 2007 Production House Program | 120

Table 6.1 Theme Table on Religious Experiences | 217

Figure 1.1 Figure 1.1 Adapted Causal Model | 34

Figure 2.1 Nu Duo 女鐸, the Christian magazine for women that published the first full translation of *The Merchant of Venice* by missionary Laura White. (Source: Zhejiang Library, China) | 60

Figure 3.1 House programme of *The Merchant of Venice* 威尼斯商人 directed by Zhang Qihong in 1980, Beijing. (My own collection). | 98

Figure 3.2 Photo of *tianzhijiaonv* 天之嬌女 [Heaven's Proud Daughter] directed by Zhang Qihong in 1984 (Source: Guangzhou Cantonese Opera Troupe 廣州粵劇團) | 114

Figure 3.3 House programme of 豪門千金 [For the Heiress' Hand] in 2007. Producer Ni Huiying played Portia, who was featured in this house programme. (Source: Guangzhou Cantonese Opera Troupe 廣州粵劇團) | 122

Figure 3.4 Poster of *Haomenqianjin* 豪門千金 [For the Heiress' Hand] in 2007, produced by Ni Huiying. (Source: Guangzhou Cantonese Opera Troupe 廣州粵劇團) | 124

Figure 3.5 Poster of *Xia Luoke* 夏洛克 [Shylock], first staged in Shanghai in April 2010. (Source: Reflecting Drama Studio 心照工作室) | 141

Figure 4.1 House programme of *The Merchant of Venice* in Hong Kong in 2010, directed by Ko Tinlung. | 172

Figure 5.1 Photo of Shylock (left) with Portia (right) at the trial scene in *Bond* 約/束, 2010 in Taipei. (Source: Taiwan Bangzi Company 台灣豫劇團) | 210

Figure 5.2 Poster showing the major characters of *Bond*. (Source: Taiwan Bangzi Company 台灣豫劇團) | 210

Figure 5.3 Poster of *Bond* 約/束 staged in 2009 in Taipei, featuring the ring on Portia's hand, signifying a marriage bond. (Source: Taiwan Bangzi Company 台灣豫劇團) | 211

Foreword

As scholarly interests move from comparative literature to world literature, so the questions and demands of translation become ever more complex and necessary. Not least, as cultures meet and sometime clash the matter of religion and religious language is sensitive and sometimes untranslatable. Jenny Wong's new book addresses these issues as a play of William Shakespeare is translated and performed in three different but closely related cultures of Eastern Asia, those of contemporary Mainland China, Taiwan and Hong Kong.

The Merchant of Venice is a particularly sensitive and difficult play. It is rooted in religious questions and divisions between Christian and Jew in Renaissance England, centering upon the complex figure of Shylock. Language is burdened with theological significances that have the capacity to blend into another culture and take on social or political aspects that shift the sense and meaning of the play, sometimes in unexpected directions. This book is a fascinating exercise in exploring the task of translation as more than simply a linguistic matter but far broader as the play moves away from the written page onto the stage and its actors.

Wong's research includes profound exchanges with directors and audiences in the three cultural fields that are her concern. This cannot exclude literary explorations in theology and language in the transference of Shakespeare's drama from Elizabethan English into contemporary Chinese. At many different levels she challenges assumptions about translation, and about the complexities of religious shifts between cultures as the Christian tradition seeks expression in the China of today. This is a book that will be of interest to many people in the fields of translations studies, comparative religion, stage production and literature.

David Jasper
Glasgow
August 2017

Acknowledgments

THE IDEA OF THE translatability of the religious dimension in literature dawned on me while studying my Master of Arts in Christian Studies at The Chinese University of Hong Kong Divinity School of Chung Chi College (DSCCC). Hence I must thank the faculty members at DSCCC, i.e. John Lai, John Yieh and Lo Lung-kwong for opening my eyes to the possibility of this interdisciplinary research at the time when I was so unsure of this academic pursuit.

Yet, this work would never have come to fruition without the academic prowess and wholehearted support of my chief supervisor Prof. David Jasper (University of Glasgow) and my second supervisor Prof. Noel Peacock (University of Glasgow). The fortnightly theological dialogue over the past four years proved to be an important intellectual journey that challenged my long-standing presumptions especially of the dichotomy between the East and the West. It is from them that I learned the qualities of a great mentor—encouraging you along when you are lacking confidence, giving constructive criticisms when you are feeling complacent.

I am indebted to many who have read my book in part or in whole. First and foremost, my thanks go to Donald Mackay who read the entirety of this work with an eagle eye for coherence and grammatical errors major and minor. I am particularly grateful to Charles Orzech (University of Glasgow) who read nearly all the chapters meticulously. To Billy Lee (University of Edinburgh) who introduced me to the methodology of interpretative phenomenological analysis (IPA), and to Joanne Ferrie (University of Glasgow) who encouraged me with positive feedback on my chapter on IPA drawing on her expertise as a sociologist. To the late Martha Cheung (Hong Kong Baptist University) whose sharp advice on the main theme of my research given at the Translation Studies Summer School 2010 in Hong Kong contributed to the present focus of the study. I deeply appreciate the invaluable feedback and suggestions offered by the following scholars (listed alphabetically) for select chapters:

Andrew Adam (University of Oxford), Liping Bai (The Chinese University of Hong Kong), Leo Chan (Lingnan University), Alexander Chow (University of Edinburgh), Ryan Dunch (University of Alberta), Werner Jeanrond (University of Oxford), Francis Jones (University of Newcastle-upon-Tyne), Jason Lam (Institute of Sino-Christian Studies), Wayne Liang (Hong Kong Baptist University), Willy Maley (University of Glasgow), David Peng (Taiwan Baptist Theological Seminary) and Mia Spiro (University of Glasgow).

In the data collection process, I am very grateful to my interviewees who, despite their busy schedules, were willing to sacrifice their precious time to participate in the interview process. They are: Rupert Chan, Ko Tin-lung, Lu Poshen, Ni Huiying, Perng Ching-Hsi, Jack Shu, Chris Shum, Daniel S. P. Yang, Bowen Zhang and Zhang Qihong. Special thanks go to Perng Ching-Hsi, who more than once generously sent me his articles and books. To Daniel S. P. Yang who was willing to talk about his research at a time when he was busily directing the Chinese version of *The Importance of Being Ernest* in Taipei in 2012 May. To Ko Tin-lung, who referred me to Hong Kong Baptist University (HKBU) to collect over a hundred theatre reviews of his production written by his students at HKBU, and Chris Shum, who helped locate the DVD recordings of *The Merchant*. The staff of Chung Ying Theatre Company, Central Academy of Drama, Shanghai Drama Academy, Hong Kong Repertory Theater, Guangzhou Cantonese Opera Troupe and Taiwan Bangzi Company were all very helpful in locating the house program, relevant theatre reviews and performance texts, for which I am particularly thankful.

Being a self-funded overseas student, spending over three years full-time without employment has not been easy. I must express my thanks for the support of Aaron Sam who, financially and prayerfully, supported my living in Glasgow. Numerous individuals welcomed me into their homes during my conference trips inside and outside the UK. Their hospitality and generosity will always be remembered. I am also indebted to the School of Critical Studies which offered me postgraduate research support awards nearly every semester to cover a large part of the travel expenses of my conference trips within the UK.

On a personal note, I am deeply thankful to my parents, especially my mother Chi Ka Lee, who was willing to tolerate my long periods away from home. Every time I came home, I would be spoiled with my favorite dishes and would be given space to focus on my own work. I also wish to thank all those who have prayed for the completion of my book: their prayer support has been an important source of my strength and perseverance. Last but not least, I must acknowledge my highest gratitude to Almighty God, who oversees everything, who cares for my every need, and has opened every door for me to carry out the research from start to finish.

Preface

THE RESEARCH IS A hermeneutic-cum-semiotic approach to the study of the translatability of religious language in a secular play, using *The Merchant of Venice* in China as a reference. Under the "power turn" or "political turn" in translation studies, omissions and untranslatability of religious material are often seen as the product of censorship or self-censorship in the prevalent socio-political context. But the theology of each individual translating agent is often neglected as an important contributing factor to such untranslatability. This book offers a comprehensive approach in tracing the hermeneutical process of the translators/directors as a reader and the situational process and semiotics of theatre translation, which altogether gives rise to the image of translated literature which in turn influences audience reception. This interdisciplinary study thus traverses the disciplines of translation studies, hermeneutics, theatre studies, and sociology.

In this book I argue that while translation theorists under the current "sociological turn" view social factors as the overarching factors in determining translation activities and strategies, I will show how the interaction between the translator's or the dramatist's theology and religious values interact with the socio-cultural milieu to carve out a unique drama production. Often, as one can see from my case studies, it is the religious values of the translating agents that become the overarching factor in determining the translation product, rather than social factors. This book further argues that the translatability of religious discourse should be understood in a broader sense according to the seven dimensions proposed by Ninian Smart, rather than merely focusing on untranslatability as a result of semantic and linguistic differences.

1
Introduction

SHAKESPEARE'S PLAYS HAVE LEFT a legacy in world theatre since their production 400 years ago. There has been no lack of adaptation and translation of Shakespeare's plays since their first appearance, giving Shakespeare's plays, in Walter Benjamin's terms, an afterlife, one that enriches the cultures to which they were translated (i.e. target culture), and renews understanding of the source culture when these translated plays are transported back to the English-speaking world.

In this book, I will look at the issues and problems of translatability of Shakespeare's religious discourse on the Chinese stage, with reference to *The Merchant of Venice* (henceforth referred to as *The Merchant*). Despite the common notion that all translations fail, I will argue that religious discourse, when understood in a broader sense according to the seven dimensions proposed by Ninian Smart, is translatable. I also argue that while translation theorists under the current "sociological turn"[1] views social factors as the overarching factors in determining translation activities and strategies, I will show how the interaction between the translator's or the dramatist's theology and religious values interact with the socio-cultural milieu to carve out a unique drama production. Often, as one can see from my case studies, it is the religious values of the translating agents, rather than social factors, that become the overarching factor in determining the translation product. By illustration from the ideological conflicts, I will show that decisions of adaptation of religious materials are primarily theological decisions, rather than merely market decisions or those arising out of censorship concerns.

What has prompted me to embark on this study is the general observation that religious and theological issues in Shakespearean plays have not been given full play on stage. While this observation is commonly found

---

1. Under the sociological turn, translations are viewed as socially-situated activities rather than pure linguistic activities.

in Chinese Shakespeare scholars such as Ruru Li, Alexander Huang and Murray Levith, the topic is at most mentioned briefly in one page or in a footnote. The current research gap prompts me to ask this primary research question: what leads to the suppression of these religious materials in Chinese Shakespeare? Why are they lost, omitted, subdued or adapted on stage? What makes them untranslatable? This study traverses various areas—religious discourse, religious translation, theatre studies, and Shakespeare. The problems of translatability of religious discourse in Shakespeare are different from the problems of translatability of sacred texts, because the religious material of the former is located in a secular text, a secular drama. In a broader sense, is religious discourse in a secular production translatable?

To answer this question, one needs to look at what is meant by religious material or religious texts, a term that is used throughout the book. The distinction between "religious" and "secular" language is a Western Reformation invention, where the development of legal system in the Renaissance period represents a move away from the existing religious society. So the use of religious language and concepts in Shakespeare's time becomes acute and distinctive. Shakespeare is of an age conscious of what "religious" means and how that relates to conflicts with the secular world, cultural world and social world. It is an era when people such as William Tyndale and Thomas Cranmer were burnt at the stake for a particular use of religious words. Accordingly, Shakespeare is intentionally making pointed use of religious language, by setting up notions such as law and grace and forced conversion. *The Merchant of Venice* is introducing an acute sense of both confessional religion and religious language. All this is very sharply understood because they are deeply Christian concepts which have no counterparts in the Jewish language. However, in the Eastern tradition, the demarcation between "the religious" and "the secular" in China is neither clear-cut nor definite, as illustrated in the argument over whether Confucianism is a religion or not a religion. As a philosophy, Confucianism does draw on the authority of heaven and contains ethical ideas such as virtues, and is considered in the Western traditions as having a strong religious dimension. For instance, the canonical historical records *Chunqiu* 春秋 (*Annals*) and its commentaries, which had a significant impact on Chinese historiography, are regarded not simply as historical texts but as quasi-religious.[2] Furthermore, the exclusive Western religious thinking especially in Shakespeare's time may be contrasted with the more pluralistic religious thinking in the Chinese traditions,

---

2. Yuri Pines argues that these classical texts that documents the history of China have a quasi-religious dimension, and finds that *Chunqiu* omits incidents not according to its political importance but according to its ritual importance. See Pines, "Chinese History Writing," 315–40.

where people can have Buddhist and Daoist dimensions at the same time, as the final chapter illustrates. When the sharp demarcation between "religious" and "secular" in Shakespeare is contrasted with the indefinite definition of the "religious" in Chinese traditions, the issue of translatability arises. As one can see in the case studies, where the "religious" dimension (represented by such elements as ethical values) in Shakespeare's performance text comfortably rests within the Chinese traditions, it is translatable. But when the "religious" dimension runs counter to the Chinese ethos, it becomes untranslatable. In contemporary China, such "religious" texts either become so toxic and unintelligible that they have to be done away with, or they morph into the political and sociological. As can be seen from the case studies in the later chapters, some of the speeches using the language of Christianity in the play were much subdued or simply omitted, or interpreted in sociological terms by directors. Specifically, when I look at the untranslatability of the religious texts in a secular production, I am particularly focusing my attention on the Christian dimension, because very often it is the Christian dimension that causes the untranslatability issue.

In defining "religious text," one also needs to review the problems of translating religious texts in order to understand its translatability in Shakespeare's plays across cultures. Victoria Harrison, in her review of the traditions of religious language, defines religious language in a broader sense by regarding it as a "language that is used either to serve a religious purpose or in a religious context, or both."[3] In her discussion, she draws our attention to the significance of the metaphorical aspects of religious language by referring to the approach by George Lakoff and Mark Johnson, who argue for the power of metaphors to create a new reality. While her view that religious language is primarily metaphorical sheds new light on the discussion of the nature of religious language, it does not fundamentally enrich the discussion of its translatability if only the metaphorical aspect is highlighted.[4] In order to broaden the discussion of the translatability and the definition of religious language in a secular play, I will draw on models

---

3. Harrison, "Metaphor," 127–145.

4. A review of the discussions of religious language shows that traditionally,,religious language is categorized into two broad types: cognitive (i.e. that gives out knowledge), and non-cognitive. Dan Stiver mapped out the three historical approaches to religious language: the negative way, the univocal way, and the analogical way. In general, the existing body of research characterizes religious language with the following attributes: metaphorical, symbolic, emotive, narrative. However, such definition is skewed on the semantics of language, without considering the religious dimension which extends beyond the above categories. As such, a broader view of religious language is needed to enrich the discussion of translatability of religious language. See Stiver, *The Philosophy of Religious Language*, 14–36.

in religious studies as well as translation studies in this interdisciplinary research. In the discipline of religious studies, I propose to redefine the scope of religious language, drawing on the seven dimensions of religion adopted by religious studies scholar Ninian Smart[5]—an ethical and legal dimension, a doctrinal and philosophical dimension, a social and institutional dimension, a practical and ritual dimension, an experiential and emotional dimension, a narrative and mythic dimension, and a material dimension. That said, can ethics be translated from one religious tradition to another? If the target culture has no knowledge of the Christian doctrine (such as the meaning of sin and salvation), how is the concept of sin being transferred in the case of Hamlet, who hesitated over the murder of King Claudius? In terms of social dimension, if a church does not exist in the target culture, or only a small percentage of the population has been to a church (i.e. in the early 1980s when China just opened up to the outside world), how is the religious setting being rendered (e.g. the religious setting of *Romeo and Juliet* and *Measure for Measure*)? How is Christian and Jewish identity being perceived differently when *The Merchant* or its adaptation was staged in postcolonial Hong Kong, or contemporary Communist China? Would the gesture of praying hands have any meaning in the target culture, who did not pray but burn incense to ancestors instead? As for the experiential dimension, could the mercy speech of Portia in *The Merchant* stir the emotions of the audience who are largely non-Christians? And how would the audience react to the forced conversion of Shylock to Christianity when their predominant Daoist philosophy advocates non-violence and non-coercion? In terms of narrative, can the audience understand the citation of the Old Testament Jacob's story in Shylock's speech? In the material dimension, how are symbols such as the cross and the Jewish robes presented on stage? As my case studies show, discussions on the translatability of religious language in Shakespearean plays in Chapter 7 will draw on this broadened view of religious language, with references to the case studies of *The Merchant* staged in Mainland, Hong Kong and Taiwan.

To study the translatability of religious discourse in Shakespeare, which is a sacred text located within a secular play, it would be necessary to review the translation tradition of sacred texts and theatre translation to achieve a meaningful analysis. The aim of the following section serves to review the current discussion on the (un)translatability and problems of translating sacred texts, which can be categorized in the following areas:

---

5. For a comprehensive study of Ninian Smart's seven dimensions of religions, see Smart, *The World's Religions* 1998.

language diversity, socio-cultural and political, hermeneutic, metaphorical, cultural, literary value, semantic, institutional problems.

Literature Review

(Un)translatability and Problems of Translating Sacred Texts

Lamin Sanneh's groundbreaking work on the translatability of Christian scriptures centers on the connection between pluralism and translation.[6] To him, "pluralism is the direct and inevitable offshoot of translatability," which is the source of "success of Christianity across cultures," rendering itself "compatible with all cultures."[7] Quite unlike predecessors who recognize the absolutism in word-for-word scriptural translation, Sanneh takes translation beyond the "narrow, technical bounds of textual work,"[8] such that the scope of translation covers not just the language but the culture, such as rituals and norms, because to him, language is such an intimate, articulate expression of culture and language is synonymous with culture. Recognizing a flexible approach of translatability of Christian scriptures inevitably creates the tension between fostering pluralism and resisting with exclusivist cultural ideology among believers. The translatability of Christian scriptures recognized by Sanneh is an important notion in this book; without such translatability across cultures (as opposed to the un-translatability of the Quran), discussion of translatability of Christian discourse in Shakespeare will become futile.

In the translation of non-Christian sacred texts, Kate Crosby[9] pointed out that the vast range of languages that Buddhist scholars needed to acquire (such as Sanskrit, Pali, Tibetan and Chinese) when texts were translated into many different languages as Buddhism spread throughout Asia can constitute a problem in translation. It requires scholars to possess the knowledge of different languages in making editorial decisions in order to compare different versions of a text.[10]

---

6. See Sanneh, *Translating the Message*, 1989.

7. Ibid, 50–51.

8. Ibid, 3.

9. Crosby, "What Does Not Get Translated," 45.

10. This happens to the translation of the Bible where biblical translators are adept in the original languages, i.e. Hebrew for the Old Testament and Greek and Aramaic for the New Testament, and sometimes Latin to understand the Vulgate Bible in the Catholic tradition.

Some languages are considered more "sacred" than the others, for example, Latin being considered the only legitimate medium for the Bible by the Council of Trent in the Catholic church as a means to counter the vernacularization of the Protestant Reformation. As such, during the Spanish colonization of the Tagalogs of the Philippines from the late sixteenth to the early eighteenth century, Vicente Raphael showed that Castilian, a vernacular, state language whose grammatical structure is constructed in terms of Latin, stands as the mediating language between Latin (the sacred language) and Tagalog. Within this socio-political context, certain Latin or Castilian key terms were left untranslated by missionaries to maintain the purity of such Christian concepts and names (as in Dios, Cruz, Virgen, Jesus, Maria), as Vicente Raphael[11] pointed out in his groundbreaking work "Contracting Colonialism." Although conversion of the natives was recorded, Raphael pointed out that the natives, bombarded with so many untranslatable terms, were shocked. Rather than understanding the concept of salvation in translation, these converts who themselves confessed, upon hearing the sermons, that they were merely responding to the "specific intervals" in the priest's voice and not to the meaning of it, because the foreign sounds of those untranslatable terms were tied to the colonial authority which they sought to obey.[12] Jose Mario C. Francisco, from a cultural point of view, shows that the Catholic notion of the capital sin of sloth was translated from the Spanish "pereza" to "laziness" under the American rule of the Philippines, in accordance with the American government strategies that worked hand in hand with the Protestant missionary efforts to combat the stereotypical laziness of Catholic Filipinos, brought about by Spanish rule.[13]

Semantically, the undeveloped technical terminology in the target language creates barriers for scripture translators. This can be seen in the translation of Buddhist texts,[14] and in the case of Bible translation in China in the Nestorian period, Buddhist concepts are borrowed for translating Christian terminology. For example, God is translated as "佛 Buddha," Sin as "罪業 karma." In the nineteenth-century translation of *Pilgrim's Progress*, churches are translated as "寺 (temples) " and missionaries as "僧伽 (monks)."

In terms of literary value, Katharina Reiss[15] proposed that where the aesthetic dimension of language, the author, as well as the form of message, is foregrounded (i.e. carries an expressive function), the target text should

---

11. Raphael, *Contracting Colonialism*, 28.
12. Ibid,116-121.
13. Francisco, "Translating Vice into Filipino," 104–118.
14. Crosby, "What Does Not Get Translated," 46.
15. Reiss, "Text types," 72–75.

transmit the aesthetic and artistic form of the source text, using the perspective of source text author. Sacred texts carry an expressive function under this classification. But the literary value of a sacred text could be compromised when its respect for its authority overrides the respect for its aesthetics, rendering a translation too literal for the general reader. Buddhist ritual texts and manuals of instruction may repeat the same few words a thousand times.[16] Likewise, the Union Version of the Chinese Bible, whether it is the first edition (1919) or the latest edition (2010), is criticized by literary scholars as lacking in literary quality as seen in the King James Bible.[17]

The metaphorical nature of religious discourse has been widely discussed in the existing body of research.[18] The problems of this metaphorical nature arise from the failure to recognize how much the language is figurative,[19] making it hard for readers to distinguish between the symbols and a literal statement. Ricoeur claimed that indirectness, characteristic of religious language, is necessary, where the irrational act of evil could only be expressed by means of the indirect language of symbolism.[20] Because metaphor says what has not been said before and cannot be said in any other way, metaphor is irreducible to literal language, in I.A. Richards' terms.[21] This "irreducible concept" is echoed by Ricoeur, who believes metaphors generate new meanings if they are not reduced to the commonplace, opening up new avenues of interpretation. Anders Jeffner[22] cites three theories that justify the use of untranslatable indirect statements in religious language. The interaction theory argues that religion gives us knowledge of another kind of reality, and metaphorical or indirect statement helps one to see new aspects of empirical reality, and makes one aware of its relation to a transempirical reality. The theory of circumstantial metaphors shows that some untranslatable metaphorical religious sentences are statements containing

16. Crosby, "What Does Not Get Translated," 47.

17. In view of the awkwardness of the archaic language of the Union Bible translation, literary scholar Feng Xiang 馮象, a non-Christian, re-translated the Torah which gained critical acclaim outside of the Christian circle, while Christian scholars criticized his translations as full of mistranslations. See Zhang Da Min 張達民. *WenxueQixiangyuXueshuJiaxiang—Ping Feng Xiang Yizhu de Xinyue* 文學氣象與假象, 2010 Sep 26—Oct 24.

18. For a comprehensive discussion on the nature of religious language, see McFague, *Metaphorical Theology*,1982). Soskice, *Metaphor and Religious Language*, 1985; Stiver, *The Philosophy of Religious Language*, 1996; Fawcett, *The Symbolic Language of Religion*, 1970; Ricoeur, *The Symbolism of Evil*, 1967.

19. Donovan, 7.

20. See Ricoeur, *The Symbolism of Evil*, 1967.

21. Stiver. *The Philosophy of Religious Language*, 114–115.

22. Jeffner. *The Study of Religious Language*, 20–21.

a circumstantial metaphor, where the metaphor "indicates a situation in which the religious experience can be achieved," such as "God is in his holy temple." Thirdly, the theory of analogy that draws the relationship between God and something in the world explains the cognitive function of untranslatable metaphorical statements about God. In Paul Tillich's terms, symbols must be characterized by indirect or metaphorical statements, because it is only when symbols are located in the fictitious that one can see that they are true statements. Thus, religious symbolic sentences are untranslatable and irreducible to their literal meaning.[23]

The Bible contains a number of metaphors such as referring to God as "shepherd," Jesus as "vine" etc, which are often translated into the same image in the target culture. The most notorious example of un-translatability of metaphors is "four corners of the earth." How are translators to distinguish whether this is metaphorical or realistic? In the end, this literal translation eventually leads to the condemnation of Galileo who proposed that the Earth is round while the Vatican insisted on the literal reading of the translation. Another problematic example is the translation "Love God with all your heart." What will happen if Inga people, i.e. people in the Andes in Colombia come across this phrase, when they do not see the heart as the seat of emotion? If this is translated literally, it certainly cannot produce new meanings and open new ways of seeing the referents if they have a totally different understanding of heart from the original writers. The translators at Wycliffe Bible Society translated it as "love God with all your liver" as the closest equivalent to generate the same effect on the readers[24].

The hermeneutical task of sacred text translation can be seen not only in the "term question," i.e. the translation of the word "God" in the Chinese Bible,[25] but more recently the hermeneutical problem has become an issue in the feminist movement, most aptly seen in a feminist interpretation of the word "helper" in Genesis 2:18. Feminist theologian Phyllis Trible[26] elaborated on the Hebrew meaning of "helper" or "helpmate" which should carry the meaning of "companion" in Hebrew. Woman, in this sense, does not assume an "assistant" role, but one who corresponds to the other half on

---

23. Ibid.

24. See Fortosis, *Multilingual God*, 2012.

25. In 1843, fifteen missionaries met in Hong Kong to discuss revising the Chinese Bible translations, including the word "God." Opinions were split regarding whether the term should be translated as "神, lit. shen," or "上帝, lit. shangdi." Among the opponents of "shen" is James Legge, a British missionary who pointed out that "shen" is a created being and subordinated to Di, i.e. the Lord. See Legge, *James Legge, Missionary and Scholar*, 1905.

26. See Trible, *God and the Rhetoric*, 1978.

an equal basis. That said, being a "helper" does not necessarily imply inferiority, because the use of help, as appears in Psalm 33:20 and other verses, corresponds to the meaning of "protect" and even "save."

Translations in modern English versions range from "helper" to the more neutral term "companion," but the Chinese translations do not evolve significantly over the years. New translations do try to be gender-inclusive by using the phrase "brothers and sisters," but in the case of Genesis 2:18, the new translation (Today's Chinese Version) in 1992 still highlights the assistant role of women, which reads "I will make for him an assistant corresponding to him." The translation in the recently published Revised Chinese Union Version is just the same as the earlier Chinese Union Version (1919), the canonized Bible translation in the Chinese community, which reads, in back translation, "I will make him a spouse to help him." The Chinese Catholic Studium Biblicum reads, "I will make him a helper corresponding to him." In Lu Chenzhong's version, "I will make a helper as his spouse." Wong[27] cited an example where an elder from a fundamentalist church brought in his patriarchal pre-understanding in reading Genesis 2:18. In the wedding sermon he urged that the bride should sometimes look stupid because her role, according to the Bible, was to "help" her husband rather than to look intelligent.

John Lai, using André Lefevere's framework on patronage and ideology, shows how the translation of religious tracts by William Milne was subject to the ideological control of the Religious Tract Society (RTS) in nineteenth century China. Milne proposed a liberal approach to tract translation, where "something should be omitted, and something added" as more suitable for "heathen readers." This ran contrary to the firm conviction of RTS which preferred literalism in the translation of religious tracts. In a letter to RTS, Milne apologised for his liberal approach to translation.[28] The institutional influence in Bible translation can be seen in the translation of the Chinese Union Versions (CUVs), under the patronage of the British and Foreign Bible Society (BFBS), the largest Chinese Protestant Bible translation project initiated by the western Protestant churches in the nineteenth century.[29] In this journal article, George Mak illustrates how the BFBS served as a controlling factor of the translation of the CUV by examining the BFBS's financial support to the translation project, conferment of honorary titles on the translators and the influence of ideology on the translators' choice of Greek text as the basis for the CUVs New Testament translation. Not only

27. Wong, "Text of Submission," 2011.
28. Lai, "Institutional Patronage," 53.
29. Mak, "Laissez-faire or Active Intervention," 167–190.

did BFBS provide financial support to the project, it also built up a good relationship with the missionary organizations in China through granting honorary titles to their missionaries who served in the translation project, which paved the way for its reception. As the patron of the translation project representing two-fifths of the project cost, BFBS also "tried to press for the translators to follow the Textus Receptus as much as possible" for fear of losing the financial support from King James Version supporters. The pressure from BFBS did have a certain effect, as shown in Mak's textual analysis of the Mandarin CUV Gospel of John. He found that the translators finally decided to follow the Textus Receptus on eight occasions among the forty-five deviations between the Textus Receptus and the Greek text underlying the RV in the 1907 version. As seen from the above examples, both Lai and Mak use the sociological framework in translation studies in their analysis to show that translation is a socially-situated activity.

(Un)translatability and Problems of Translating Religious Discourse in Literature

However, theories or discussions on them while serving as useful pointers, are not sufficiently universally applicable to our present discussion of religious discourse in literature. This is because translation of sacred texts, a widely discussed subject, has strategies different from translation of the sacred into the secular, that is the religious discourse in literary works. Although both types of translation require religious knowledge, translating sacred texts require faith and faithfulness—one could hardly imagine a Muslim translating the Bible, or a Christian translating the Quran. The fact that it is sacred more often than not dictates the need for giving a close rendition of the text, which assumes a higher authority than in other forms of literature.

The need for faithfulness in sacred text translation has a long-standing tradition. St. Jerome (AD 348–420), a Roman born into a wealthy Christian family, was the first to translate the whole Christian Bible into Latin (subsequently known as the Vulgate) which was the most widely read Bible in Europe in the eighth and ninth centuries. He was known as the patron saint of translators, who relied not only on the Greek Septuagint but also on original Hebrew texts in the translation process. While he was among the first in the Western translation tradition to advocate a sense-for-sense translation, this applied only to the translation of learned texts except for the Bible, which should be translated word-for-word "so as not to violate the sacred mystery immanent in the very words of Scripture."[30] Now I not only admit but freely announce that in translating from the Greek—except of course in the case of the Holy Scripture, where even the syntax contains a mystery—I render not word-for-word, but sense-for-sense. In Epistle 57 to Pammachius (a.k.a. *De optimogenereinterpretandi*), St Jerome supports "saving and serving the source text, its meaning and force, by accepting the necessity of linguistic difference."[31]

Martin Luther, whose aim was is to translate the Bible into the common language of people, developed the concept of translating the Bible to reach the mass public and demanded that special attention be paid to the vernacular of the people in that period. Yet, in his translation into the common language, Luther attached more importance to the literal approach than to a "free translation" when presented with a dilemma of doctrinal interpretations:[32]

> ... when essential theological "truths" were concerned, Luther would sacrifice this principle of intelligibility [i.e. translating freely] and revert, for doctrinal reasons, to word-for-word translation.[33]

That is, word-for-word translation takes priority where theological truths are concerned.[34] While Eugene Nida's theory of dynamic equivalence born out of his involvement with missionaries applies to Bible Societies such as Wycliffe Bible Translators and is highly regarded in China as a practical translation theory, it does not gain much currency among Christian translators in the Chinese society which places much emphasis on the authority of the Bible, and hence the need for faithful translation.[35]

Religious discourse in literature, on the other hand, has a different localization from religious discourse in sacred text. The latter is localized in the world of believers, who believe that Bible is the source of authority.[36] The Bible, though written by men, is inspired by God, and is infallible. This traditional view of the infallible, inerrant Bible is still prevalent among churches today, despite the rise of contextual theology which holds that the

---

30. Copeland, *Rhetoric, Hermeneutics, and Translation*, 51.
31. Ibid., 45.
32. Kirk, "Holy Communicative?," 90.
33. Poltermann, "German Tradition," 418–428.
34. Kirk, "Holy Communicative?," 90.
35. Chong, *Study of the Phenomenon of Authoritativeness*, 2000.
36. For the authority of the Bible, see the discussions in Strange, *Authority of the Bible*, 2000; Graf, *Authority of the Bible*, 1984; Donovan, *The Study of Religious Language*, 68–74.

text should be read in historical contexts. Religious discourse in literature, however, is located in the fictitious world, the authority of which is subject to deconstruction by individual readers. Drawing on Ricoeur's argument of the third root of the hermeneutic problem in Christianity, just as the New Testament, written and interpreted by the witnesses, i.e. believing community, is a text to be interpreted, the religious discourse in Shakespeare should be considered an interpretation within an interpretation,[37] a text interpreted by the believing community which is then interpreted by the writer, and lastly by readers. In the modern age, the author ceases to assume authority, but according to Michel Foucault, Man and God dissolve into the text, which becomes an authority unto itself; forms of authority cease to impose laws, while the concept of originality of the text breaks down.[38] Martin Heidegger, in his fundamental work *Being and Time,* argues that the text does not offer a proof nor is it conclusive, but illustrates a process of de-centering, allowing the language to speak for itself. It is true that both the Bible and Shakespeare cannot escape such deconstruction and de-centering of authority. But when the localization of Shakespeare's text is not in the world of believers who mostly see it as the truth, its authority is at best derived from it as a classic,[39] which David Tracy[40] described as exerting a previous claim upon us.

The treatment of religious discourse in literature is still under-researched. In both the West and in China, discussion mainly points to issues of power and politics, over and above other factors leading to untranslatability. This is known as the "power turn" that focuses on why and how translation can participate in political and ideological struggles, to effect change as an agent of activism.[41]

In this framework, religious issues within a drama are often the subject of manipulation and re-writing in order to conform to the predominant ideology and socio-cultural conditions. In China, from late Qing period

---

37. The third hermeneutic problem requires one to go back to the witness character of the Gospel. As the kerygma is expressed in a witness and stories told by the confession of faith of the community. People in the modern world are hearers to the witnesses and can believe only by interpreting the New Testament which is itself already an interpretation. While the New Testament serves to decipher the Old, the New Testament is to be understood and interpreted. Since the New Testament does not contain just individual witnesses but comprises witnesses located in a believing community, to decipher the Scripture we need to decipher the witnesses too. See Ricoeur, "Preface to Bultmann," 1974.

38. For a discussion of deconstruction and translation, see Gentzler, *Contemporary Translation Theories,* 144–180.

39. See Bassnett, "An Introduction to Theatre Semiotics," 47–55.

40. See Tracy, *The Analogical Imagination,* 119.

41. See Tymoczko and Gentzler, *Translation and Power,* 2002.

to contemporary Communist era, Christian references in Shakespearean works are often marginalized, if not lost, at the receiving end. This can be related to the long-standing tradition that theatres are a mirror of social issues. In 1942, *Hamlet* was staged by the National Drama School in Sichuan, whose purpose was reportedly to prompt a spirit of resistance to the Japanese invasion.[42] The pragmatic function of foreign literature translation has long been advocated in its history. For example, during the Anti-Japanese war from 1937–1945, foreign literary works that promoted patriotism were translated. Mao Zedong reinforced this didactic function further in his "Talks at the Yan'an Forum on Literature and Art" in 1942, which has impacted the history of Chinese drama to this day. Mao emphasized that literature and art should always serve the political agenda, to ensure that the politically correct agenda was being followed.

Under this "power turn," Martha Cheung[43] applied Michel Foucault's theory of discourse as a starting point in analyzing the translation of *Uncle Tom's Cabin* by Lin Shu, the first scholar who introduced Shakespeare, and is also considered a nationalist reformer who upheld Confucian teaching and considered translation as a means of speeding up modernization and strengthening of China. Lin's translations are considered by Cheung's "ideological manipulation of the religious material of the source text," echoing Foucault's theory of discourse which sees that language and knowledge are intimately linked with ideology and power. Taking a sociological approach, she concluded that Lin exercised "knowledge management" in his translation of Christian content in Uncle Tom's Cabin, and introduced concepts including "knowledge management," "subversion," "containment" and "censorship/self-censorship" in establishing the framework of understanding translation and culture. In her conclusion, the translation product shorn of Christian references thereby aims to undermine "the ideological force of Christianity penetrating through various channels in the nineteenth century," because "Christianity is the pioneer for imperialism, with both concepts supplementing each other [. . .] Christianity penetrates, in a peaceful manner in China in a hope to broaden its cultural dominance; imperialism invades China by force and violence, possibly bringing about the loss of nation. Thus the two translators in *Uncle Tom's Cabin* used strategies on censorship and subversion as resistance." Perhaps inspired by Cheung's manipulation approach, Ding Dagang also concluded that American missionary Laura White exercised "knowledge management" in her translation of

---

42. See Huang, "Shakespeare on the Chinese Stage," 2004.
43. For more detailed discussion, see Cheung, "The Discourse of Occidentalism?," 127–149.

Silas Marner into Chinese in 1913, through retaining all Christian content but omitting narratives irrelevant to Christianity.[44]

Using a sociological approach to translation, Maria Goreti Monteiro[45] shows how the "zero translation" of Daniel Defoe's criticism of Catholicism in Robinson Crusoe in the Portuguese translation can be traced back to the life of the translator Henrique Leitao, suggesting that the omissions were due to self-censorship by a man who had experienced previous conflict with the Portuguese Inquisition. He was imprisoned three years by the Inquisition and released in 1781. Maria's textual analysis shows that he omitted texts which presented a religious problem. For instance, he deleted the text when Robinson is teaching Friday about the role of the devil in man's life, and also the part where the Bible is described as the only means to obtain redemption and salvation, which is in contrast to Catholic teaching that God's forgiveness is obtained through confession.

Jean Tsui followed on the footsteps of Martha Cheung and other Chinese translation scholars in situating the untranslatability of Christian discourse in Lin Shu's translation of *Tales from Shakespeare* in the context of power and ideology. She cited a few tales that domesticated the religious element into a Daoist framework: thus in the *Tempest*, the magician Prospero becomes a Daoist priest who studies Daoist scriptures alongside occult books, using Daoist registers to contain the elements and exorcise the spirits. In *Romeo and Juliet*, which is originally set in a Catholic framework, Lin gave the religious terms a Daoist touch: prayer becomes "blue paper prayer" (*qingci* 青詞), a "shrine" becomes a Daoist altar (*tanzhan* 壇玷), "Saints" turned into Daoist Deities (*mingshen* 明神). In other tales, Jean showed that the plot and characterisation changed to highlight filial piety which is a Confucian value in China. Tsui offered an explanation of the above by linking Lin's political agenda to his translation discourse—that his translation revealed "a new vision of the West," which "was not very much different from Old China." Lin Shu was a "reformer who took up translation on a political agenda and consciously manipulated this very medium to express his reformist ideal."[46]

John Lai[47] illustrated the loss in translation by situating the translation of *Pilgrim's Progress* in the context of nineteenth-century China. In his textual analysis, William Burns adopted a domestication strategy where the biblical allusions were translated into the semantic framework of Confucianism or

---

44. Ding, "Laura M. White's Translation of *Silas Marner*," 231–240.
45. See Monteiro, "Choosing Not to Translate," 65–74.
46. See Tsui, "Rewriting Shakespeare," 66.
47. Lai, "On the Translation Strategies," 73–97.

Daoism to ease the understanding of readers who had little knowledge of Christianity. For example, "to render the Cross" is translated into "正道/正路 (to walk the paths of righteousness)," "treasures in Egypt"(Hebrews 11:24–26) becomes "世間的財寶 (treasures of the world)," "(pagan) religion" is translated as "事鬼神 (contacting the ghosts)," "burden" translated as "任 (ren)," meaning obligation in Confucian terms, and the biblical allusion "avenger of blood" (Deuteronomy 19:12) is omitted. Lai reckoned that such domestication could be seen as a way of facilitating reader reception. As Chinese readers became more familiar with Christianity and the Bible half a century later, other translators such as Xi Hai (西海) kept the religious resonance intact in subsequent translations.

Note that the above studies focus on literary translations, i.e. religious translation on the page, but not translation on the stage. Despite their detailed textual analysis that situates the translated text in a historical context, the analysis is still text-based. Faithfulness or fidelity is evaluated against the text, rather than the embedded meaning of certain paralinguistic codes in the narratives, which is part and parcel of the creation of meaning in theatre production. Additionally, what is lacking is the voice of the translators who were already historical figures and could not offer their own explanation of the deletions. Their interpretation of the text, or "pre-understanding" in Heidegger's terms, is important in shaping their translation, but their hermeneutics are often neglected under the "power turn" in translation studies, which tends to view the political as the overarching factor in shaping a translation. Even when their interpretation is discussed, it often only appeared sporadically in translators' prefaces, which proved to be insufficient in elucidating the world of thinking, or the "world behind the text," in Ricoeur's hermeneutical terms. Additionally, apart from socio-political factors that vitiate these translations, other situational factors might be at work in the translation process. Apparently, textual analysis as a means of explaining untranslatability of religious discourse is not sufficient in the study of theatre translations, which involves a network of agents including directors, actors and translators, who all together make decisions regarding the selection and appropriation of text, i.e. "the world of the text." A text-based approach also lacks the empirical base for understanding the effects these omissions have on audience reception, a part which most theatre and translation researchers have found it hard to gauge. Given this existing research gap, a comprehensive approach that combines a socio-cultural, situational, hermeneutical and semiotic study of the theatre translation is thus necessary to give a full view of the translatability of religious discourse, and hence this study. Because of the lack of translators' discourse in illustrating their interpretations in reading a play, I have included individual interviews with translating agents in this book to fill the research gap.

As far as I am aware, adequate study of the treatment of the religious dimension in Chinese theatre has not yet been carried out. Among the few scholars who have attended to such questions is Alexander Huang who in his monograph made sporadic remarks on the omission of religious material in *The Merchant*, without further elaboration. Ruru Li[48] mentioned that the director Zhang Qihong of the 1980 production of *The Merchant* altered or deleted lines on the problems of religion or race, on the ground that these lines were opaque for Chinese audiences. Li compared the similarities between this omission approach to Lin's construction of Shakespeare's tales as "fantasies," as both tried to "seek familiarity and similarity in Shakespeare rather than emphasizing the difference."[49]

(Un)translatability of Shakespeare's religious discourse in other cultures

In other cultures, similar to the Chinese context, deletion or omission of religious material is often described by these scholars as a matter of censorship or self-censorship. Aoife Gallagher in his article "Pasternak's Hamlet: Translation, Censorship and Indirect Communication"[50] demonstrates how the complex character of Hamlet is reduced to that of a one-sided Soviet-style hero to conform to the conventions of translation in Soviet times, including a simplification of plot and modification to reflect Soviet ideology. Some critics argued that Boris Pasternak's translation left out the unheroic characteristics of Hamlet which conflicted with his conception of a "Christ-like" Hamlet. Sameh Hanna[51] in his doctoral thesis records that Mutran was criticised by his contemporaries for his choice of classical Arabic through frequent use of archaic lexicon and obsolete structures in translating Shakespeare's plays. However, Mutran's strategy in the choice of classical Arabic should be understood in the context that Syrian Christian scholars tried to use pre-Islamic Arabic to dissociate the language from Islam, maintaining that Arabic is not the private property of Muslims but also of Christian Arabs. The use of pre-Islamic Arabic is an attempt to forge unity among Arab nations for a homogeneous, collective identity through undermining

---

48. Li, *Shashibiya*, 17.
49. Ibid.
50. Gallagher, "Pasternak Hamlet," 119–131.
51. Hanna, "Towards a Sociology of Drama Translation," 2006.

all other forms of identity. As a result, in Mutran's translation, Othello's Christian identity was treated as a background.

Given the current gap in the study of translatability of religious language in literature in general, and drama in specific, this research brings together under one umbrella the domains of study of translatability of religion, and more precisely, of the sacred text in secular plays, theatre translation and translation pathways from page to stage. Apart from the present discussion on the relationship between one's theology and religious experiences and religious translation, what is important is to introduce both a hermeneutic turn and semiotic turn to the present research, on the premise that every stage production is an interpretation, and every drama translation is an intersemiotic activity. Borrowing from the strong philosophical and hermeneutic foundation underlying the study of religious translation can strengthen the theoretical base of theatre translation, which makes necessary the following review of the interaction between hermeneutics and translation studies, and between theatre translation and semiotics.

Hermeneutics, Theology and Translation

How important is the contribution of hermeneutics to translation studies? Despite the fact that important translation theories such as Lawrence Venuti's domestication versus foreignization theory comes from the hermeneutic tradition of Frederich Schleiermarcher, the hermeneutical turn to translation studies is currently less discussed compared to the "cultural" turn or "socio-cultural" turn, whose roots can be traced back to the development of the hermeneutic theories of Heidegger and Hans-Georg Gadamer. As such, given the hermeneutical framework that shapes this current research, and the current research gap on the relationship between hermeneutics and translation, a brief overview of their interrelationship becomes imperative. Hermeneutics is said to derive its meaning from the name of the Greek god Hermes, a messenger to interpret and communicate the messages of the gods to humans. From the etymology, hermeneutics and translation are invariably linked. Hermeneutics, as a term, is derived from the Greek word ἑρμηνεύω, which means translate or interpret. While the word origin cannot be traced, the word hermeneutics was first mapped into the discipline of philosophy in Aristotle's work *On Interpretation*, in which he explores the connection of language to idea. He defined hermeneutics as a "concern with linguistic action on things." In Aristotelian terms, hermeneutics is a praxis. His emphasis on practical application forms a model for basic theoretical problems of hermeneutics and influenced the definition of hermeneutic used by Hans-Georg Gadamer.[52]

Hermeneutics applies to a broad range of works from oral tradition to texts and rituals, whether religious or not, although from its early beginnings hermeneutics was concerned with the interpretation of scriptures. Moses interpreted the Ten Commandments and Jewish law to Israelites after his encounter with God in Mount Sinai. Hebrew rabbis interpreted the Torah by making connections between passages where the same word appears. Two major strands in hermeneutics developed that reflected the difference between Greek philosophers and Hebrew rabbis. While Hebrew rabbis stressed the preciseness of the Bible, where every form and shape carries a significant meaning, Christian Greek philosophers adopted an allegorical approach continuing from the time of Clement (d.ca.214) to Origen. Two main lines of Christian hermeneutical method prevailed—literal and allegorical—until medieval times when they were further subdivided into four approaches—literal, allegorical, moral and anagogical, although the latter three subdivisions sprang from the allegorical sense. The authority of scripture came into question with the emergence of these subdivisions. Such categorization was revolutionized in the Reformation Era where Martin Luther, a scholar and a Bible translator into German, brought attention back to the authority of the text itself in the form of *sola scriptura*. By translating into the vernacular, he aimed to "express the Word of God, as codified in the Bible, in the language of the common people."[53] It is from his translation strategies that one sees the meeting of both disciplines—hermeneutics and translation—where one's hermeneutical approach bears on its translation method. When faced with difficulties in scriptural interpretations, Luther would opt for word-for-word translation.[54] From the early Christian church community to the Reformation era, one could see a movement from allegorical interpretation to fine scrutiny of texts in the form of literalism or formal correspondence.

Several figures are important in the study of how the two disciplines crossed paths. The German pietist Friedrich Schleiermacher reckoned that there are two hermeneutic principles that can be universally applied to all texts—psychological interpretation and grammatical interpretation. The former describes the interplay between the reader and the text which allows for personal interpretation. The latter serves to provide the rules which counter-balance the psychology. To him, every problem of interpretation is

---

52. Copeland, *Rhetoric, Hermeneutics and Translation*, 18.
53. Kittel and Poltermann, "German Tradition," 421.
54. Ibid.

a problem of understanding. The two hermeneutic principles he proposes serve to avoid the problem of misunderstanding between the author and the text. From this hermeneutic a more comprehensive approach to the texts is achieved, emphasizing the interplay between text and author as well as textual analysis.

As a translator, Schleiermacher went on further to propose a two-way approach to translation. His treatise "Ueber die verschiedenen Methoden des Uebersetzens" (*On the Different Methods of Translating*) is hereby quoted at length to show how he progresses from hermeneutics of language to translation theory:

> Every person is, on the one hand, in the power of the language he speaks; he and everything he thinks are but a product of the same. Anything outside its boundaries cannot be thought by him with full determination; the shaping of his concepts, the way and the extent to which they may be linked to one another, are pre-programd by the language in which he is born and raised; his intellect and imagination are bound by it. On the other hand, however, any free-thinking, intellectually independent person creates his language. How else would it have changed and grown from its primitive beginnings to its consummate development in science and art? [. . .] But the translator proper, who wants to truly bring together two completely separated persons, his writer and his reader, and who wants to help the latter understand and enjoy the former as correctly and completely as possible without making it necessary for him to step outside his native tongue, what course is he to follow? In my opinion, he can take one of two approaches. The translator can either leave the writer in peace as much as possible and bring the reader to him, or he can leave the reader in peace as much as possible and bring the writer to him. The two approaches are so totally different from one another that one or the other must be followed as strictly as possible; any mixing will necessarily produce a highly unreliable result, and the writer and reader might miss each other altogether. The difference between the two methods and their opposing natures are immediately apparent. In the first case, you see, the translator tries to let his own work substitute for the reader's lacking comprehension of the original language. He tries to impart to the reader the same image, the same impression he gained from his knowledge of the original language of the work, such as it is. He thus tries to transport him to its location, which in all reality, is foreign to him. If, however, the translation is intended to make the Roman author, for example,

speak as a German would have spoken and written to a German, the translation does not so much merely bring the author to meet the translation, since even to him he will speak Latin rather than German, but rather moves him directly into the world of the German readers and changes him into one of their own; this, precisely, is the second case[55]

This quotation is an extraordinary example that illustrates the nexus between translation studies and hermeneutics. Schleiermacher, who has been advocating the inter-relationship between the author and the text, extends his argument by bringing together the reader, the author and the text together via translation. A translator can choose either to bring the reader to the author by introducing foreignness to the translation, or to bring the author to the reader by cultural adaptation. What lies at the heart of this polarization is still the entanglement between author and text.

This translation theory continues to have a far-reaching impact up to the present day. Lawrence Venuti, a translation scholar in the twentieth century, recharacterized this dualistic concept as the much-quoted concept of foreignization versus domestication, which is the close equivalent of "bringing reader to author" versus "moving the author forward towards the reader."[56] Many translation scholars follow in the footsteps of Schleiermacher, as Douglas Robinson noted:

> these later theorists typically dualize translation and assign overtly moral charges to the two choices: either you domesticate the [source] text, cravenly assimilate it ... or you foreignize it ... and so heroically resist the flattening pressures of commodity capitalism. [57]

Despite such a polarization seemingly on an equal standing, Schleiermacher preferred foreignizing to domesticating, because he believed that readers would be attuned to cultural diversity.[58] But this observation merits further empirical evidence, because in a lot of aboriginal cultures, indigenous residents of low literacy would find it hard to comprehend the translated works with foreignness. In the same treatise, Schleiermacher proposed another revolutionary concept. He differentiated between the translation of artistic texts and texts relating to natural sciences on one hand, and technical translation of pragmatic texts on the other hand and set different

---

55. Schleiermacher, "On the Different Methods of Translating," 49.
56. Kirk, "Holy Communicative?," 94.
57. Ibid.
58. Ibid.

judgement standards to qualify different text types. The former requires more from the hermeneutic capabilities of the translator than does a mode of communication.[59] Secondly, he proposes a faithful translation of philosophical texts versus a domestication approach to comedies. A paraphrase of the former, he believes, "can and will never appear to have been composed originally in the same language."[60] The genre of comedies, however, is closest to social conversation, where "lightness and naturalness in grace are its principal virtues." His comments, while insightful, do not resolve the issue of translatability of the religious, philosophical texts in a comedy, i.e. *The Merchant*. But his classification nonetheless gives us some pointers as to why the religious dimension is fluid, unstable and easily subject to manipulation suppression, because one has to consider the "gracefulness and naturalness" of the speeches in the play.

The impact of Schleiermacher does not just end here. His hermeneutic of individuality between the author and the text is reflected in von Humboldt's translation theory which became a center of thought in the late eighteenth to early nineteenth century. To him, "language is, as it were, the outer appearance of the spirit of a people; the language is their spirit, and the spirit their language; we can never think of them sufficiently as identical. How they actually conjoin with each other in one and the same source, beyond reach of our conception, remains inexplicably hidden from us. "[61]

Schleiermacher's hermeneutical translation theory left its footprints in the translation of Shakespeare, especially in early twentieth-century China. However, as the textual analysis of scripts shows, translation strategies are not unidirectional, as Schleiermacher or Venuti theorized. More often than not, translators have adopted a mix of strategies in the same translation, moving from domestication to foreignization as they have seen fit. Both Schleiermacher and Venuti preferred foreignization to domestication (considered a violent act of English imperialism by Venuti). In terms of my book, however (i.e. relating to the play-texts), I will show that foreignization of terms is not always preferred by dramatists, who see performability as the ultimate goal of theatre translation.

The next influential figure who discusses the interpretative aspect of translation is Martin Heidegger. Under the influence of Schleiermacher and informed by Dilthey, Heidegger "saw the act of understanding as an attempt to recreate the creative process of the writer and artist,"[62] and emphasized

---

59. Schleiermacher, "On the Different Methods of Translating," 43-44.
60. Ibid, 60.
61. Losonsky, *Humboldt. On Language*, 46.
62. See Heidegger's elaboration in Cross and Livingstone, *The Oxford Dictionary of*

reading as a social activity through "reliving the experience" on the basis of "empathy." This takes us to the dimension where Dasein, "the thing that is because it is there," comes into authentic being when it is comprehended, i.e. translated.[63] To Heidegger every translation is interpretation, and every interpretation is translation. As such, translation is influenced by the translator's pre-understanding. Such existentialist interpretation socializes the contexts, so that the reader can have a means of sharing the author's expressions and experiences. Hans-Georg Gadamer, his student, moved one step further in such social contextualization. Gadamer proposed a "fusion of horizons" in his formulation of a new hermeneutical event. That is, if the hermeneutical bridge is built to span the temporal difference, and if one has to inquire behind the text into the horizon of meaning—i.e. into the historical situation so that the interpreter can project the historical horizon—then one needs to investigate the historical continuity between the present and the past situation so as to link the interpreter's present to the historical situation of the text.[64] In addition, by reflecting on the linguisticality of transmitted tradition, Gadamer views understanding as mediated by the essential content of the text. But this content is brought into language in the text only within the totality of a horizon "which is not the interpreter's horizon of the present, but is rather connected with the particular historical situation within which the text originated."[65] Reflection on the relationship between the interpreter and the text requires one to reflect on the historical differences between their horizons bridged by means of a fusion of horizons. That is, there is no escape from history as one reads and interprets the text.

In the context of this book, Gadamer's "historically shaped consciousness" is important in understanding the directors' and translators' approach in interpreting Shakespeare, because from the case studies one can see how their reading of Shakespeare is shaped by their tradition and pre-understanding, conditioned by their own individual and socio-cultural environment. Their interpretation cannot be divorced from a history of effects. To Gadamer, such pre-understanding should not form the basis of prejudice against them, but rather the basis of comprehension. Gadamer likened the hermeneutical process to the experience of play, such that the text, or Shakespeare's play in this case, controls the game, but not the reader. Whether it is directors or translators, they cannot control the meaning of the play, rather, the play's meaning is created publicly in each new performance,

---

the Christian Church, 1997.

63. Ricouer, "Existence et herméneutique," 313.
64. Pannenberg, "Hermeneutic and Universal History," 129.
65. Ibid, 130.

and the audience's experience also forms part of the meaning, because "a complete change takes place when play as such becomes a play. It puts the spectator in the place of the player. He—and not the play—is the person for and in whom the play is played."[66] In the production of Shakespeare's plays, the dramatists first encounter a fusion of horizons with the original text. In turn, the audience's horizon is fused with Shakespeare's horizon which was mediated by the dramatists. In the end, the meaning of the play cannot be controlled, but in Heidegger's terms, the language of Shakespeare "speaks for itself." The audience's experience in turn informs the producers and new meanings are created.

What does Gadamer say about translation? In *Truth and Method*, he reckons that translation preserves and transposes the meaning into a different context. To him, every translation is already an interpretation.[67] This is what Gadamer says in *Truth and Method*:

> Here the translator must translate the meaning to be understood into the context in which the other speaker lives. This does not, of course, mean that he is at liberty to falsify the meaning of what the other person says. Rather the meaning must be preserved, but since it must be understood within a new language world, it must establish its validity within it a new way.[68]

It follows that it is never sufficient for the translator of a text just to reawaken the original process in the writer's mind; rather, it is necessarily a re-creation of the text.[69] Since translation, however faithful it is, can never close the gap between the two languages, Gadamer describes translation as a "highlighting" act, where translation is clearer than the original and where compensations are made to resolve the ambiguity of some original expressions.[70] In order to highlight what is important in the original, this inevitably involves "playing down" or "entirely suppressing other features."[71] This is especially true in theatre translation, because the director and translator together tend to highlight certain narratives while downplaying others within a limited timeframe on stage. Hence the pluralistic interpretations underlying the play text are reduced to the director's interpretation. For instance, sympathy for Shylock, or the cruelty of Christians, is made more explicit in some stage productions. As such, translation, like all interpretation,

---

66. See Gadamer, *Truth and Method*, 110.
67. Ibid, 402.
68. Ibid.
69. Ibid, 404.
70. Ibid.
71. Ibid.

is a "highlighting act."Gadamer goes on to conclude that "All performance is interpretation. All interpretation is highlighting,"[72] because every performance has its own emphasis.

Gadamer further introduced the concept of spirit (*Geist*). Translation moves from the spirit of the original words to the spirit of the target expression. Such concept of spirit found resonance in many other translation scholars, including Chinese translator Lin Shu who proposed the dualistic proposition of attaching to form versus to spirit.

Gadamer's hermeneutic of "fusion of horizons" is echoed by a growing trend of translation theories which promote engaging with the text's historical horizons. The hermeneutic discussion on social contextualization of texts provides significant input to translation studies research as it sets forth a trend for situating translated texts in social and ideological contexts in the work of scholars such as André Lefevere, Theo Hermans, Lawrence Venuti. Among them, Susan Bassnett, a proponent of a "cultural turn" in translation, argues for a cultural turn to examine translation in its cultural, historical and ideological contexts,[73] which "could offer a way of understanding how complex manipulative textual processes take place: how a text is selected for translation [. . .] what role the translator plays in that selection, what role an editor, publisher or patron plays, what criteria determine the strategies that will be employed by the translator."[74] Thus, a hermeneutic turn of translation studies, and in this case, the study of Shakespeare's translation, requires one to trace the historical approaches to understanding Shakespeare in order to find out the causes for the present adaptation of Shakespeare's religious language in China, which is the focus of the present research.

Translation has in the past too often been viewed as a purely linguistic activity,[75] it is against this backdrop that Bassnett argues that:

> translation does not happen in a vacuum, but in a continuum, it is not an isolated act, it is part of an ongoing process of intercultural transfer. Moreover, translation is a highly manipulative activity that involves all kinds of stages in that process of transfer across linguistic and cultural boundaries. Translation is not an innocent, transparent activity but is highly charged with significance at every stage.[76]

---

72. Ibid, 418.
73. Bassnett and Lefevere, *Translation, History and Culture*, 1990.
74. Bassnett, "The Translation Turn in Cultural Studies," 123.
75. Bassnett and Trivedi, *Postcolonial Translation*, 6.
76. Ibid. 2.

> Historical situations apparently form a part of the larger system of texts and people including those who produce, support, promote, oppose and censor the translation.[77]

Following Gadamer's hermeneutic tradition, Paul Ricoeur, a prolific philosopher whose work profoundly influenced philosophers as much as linguists, built on the notion of pre-understanding and developed his threefold mimesis theory in the formation of narratives, which can be suitably applied to the present study. Mimesis 1 (prefiguration) encompasses a pre-understanding by the reader of "the world of action, its meaningful structures, its symbolic resources and its temporal character."[78] It represents the pre-narrative context that shapes the reader's worldview. Three aspects of pre-understanding, or practical understanding as he terms it, characterizes the prefiguration of a text: semantic understanding (recognizing actions and its circumstances, i.e. the structure of incidents), symbolic understanding (recognizing the implications of roles, social norms and customs etc.) and temporal understanding (recognizing the consequences of actions). That is, to understand and appropriate a narrative, one needs to have a pre-understanding of the above, which is grounded in human action. This is what he calls the "world behind the text." Mimesis 2 (configuration) is the stage where various elements of a narrative are joined together to form a meaningful whole, the construction of a world of text encompassing elements such as style and genre through the act of reading. Mimesis 3 (refiguration) is the "intersection of the world of the text and that of the listener or reader," a stage that corresponds to Gadamer's "application" in hermeneutics. It is through refiguration that a text is appropriated and becomes a part of the reader's experience. That is, creating a "world in front of the text." Rather than being progressive, this theory is circular in nature.

Ricoeur's threefold mimesis has application in areas of religion and popular culture. It can be applied in this study as it summarizes the thinking process of a number of directors and translators, who had a pre-understanding conditioned by their different locations. For instance, those who received Western education read *The Merchant* differently from those who had not. Those who have had unpleasant experiences with Christianity would read the characters differently from those who are neutral. These directors and translators then construct a world of text as they read through the play, and form opinions on how the play should be structured and sequenced: what characterizes a hero (i.e. Antonio) or heroine (i.e. Portia), what the play symbolizes (i.e. whether it represents the contrast between

---

77. Lefevere, "Why Waste Our Time on Rewrites?," 237.
78. Ricoeur, *Time and Narrative*, 1:54.

Catholicism and Protestantism, or between Judaic justice and New Testament mercy). The construction of a text-world is manifested in the adaptation of the narrative structure, the choice of symbols, the stage setting and mise-en-scene. In Mimesis 3, he or she becomes inspired and transformed by the text world which becomes a part of his/her experience. These dramatists often found great inspiration from the play, and might try to identify with the characters in the play. In most cases, they could draw a parallel between the play and issues in society at large, such as identity. The threefold mimesis theory can likewise be applied to the audience who, as the present study shows, came to the play with preconceptions of Christianity, constructed a world of text on their own and later had their perceptions changed towards the religion. In the end, Ricoeur proposes that interpretation of a text culminates in the self-interpretation of a subject who understands himself better,[79] differently or simply begins to understand himself. On the other hand, understanding of text is not an end in itself; ultimately the goal is to mediate the relation to the self, i.e. self-understanding.[80] In the Chinese tradition which attaches importance to the social-pragmatic function of theatre, the notion of the "application" stage has found resonance with directors and translators, who mostly see social relevance as an important criterion for good theatre—as later chapters will show.

Do the hermeneutic theories discussed above have a bearing in contemporary translation studies? The answer is yes, but their application is still under-researched outside the realm of biblical translation. One most notable extension of the hermeneutical theory is in George Steiner's (1929–) influential book *After Babel* (1975), in which occurs a chapter on 'The Hermeneutic Motion'. In it he proposes a fourfold appropriative transfer of meaning for translators. His hermeneutic turn of translation theory still ranks as one of the few that traverses the disciplines of hermeneutics and translation, and one that is read by both philosophers and literary scholars. Heidegger and other hermeneuts seemed to have left their footprints on Steiner's translation theory. The first step is trust, "all understanding, and the demonstrative statement of understanding which is translation, starts with an act of trust."[81] He then explains to the readers that this reflects a convention which "derives from a sequence of phenomenological assumptions about the coherence of the world."[82] This leads one back to Ricoeur's interpretation of Bultmann's hermeneutical circle: "to understand a text,

---

79. Ricoeur, *Hermeneutics and the Human Sciences*, 142–143.
80. Ibid.
81. Steiner, *After Babel*. 312.
82. Ibid.

it is necessary to believe in what the text announces to me, but what the text announces to me is given nowhere but in the text. That is why it is necessary to understand the text in order to believe."[83] Trust, or belief, is a decisive factor in the translatability of religious texts, as manifested in Martha Cheung's examples,[84] where omission in the translations of *Uncle Tom's Cabin* reveals the ideological conflicts between the translator and the text. As the case studies of *The Merchant* show, directors who are sceptical of Christianity or doctrines of Christianity have expended effort towards eliminating religious discourse.

The second move is aggression, which is incursive and extractive in nature.[85] Steiner relates this to Heidegger's notion of understanding "as an act, on the access, inherently appropriative and therefore violent, of Erkenntnis to Dasein."[86] He is cognizant of Heidegger's contribution to show that "understanding, recognition, interpretation are a compacted, unavoidable mode of attack."[87] In this appropriative manner, the text in the other language becomes thinner.

The third movement is incorporative, of importation and of embodiment. However, this embodiment is not made into a vacuum, as the native semantic field is crowded with assimilation and domestication, as in the case of Martin Luther's Bible. When the native matrix is already disoriented, such import will not find a community.[88] The native community will react to naturalize or expel this force, as in the case of European romanticism that strikes back as an attempt to resist the import of French eighteenth-century goods.[89] After the importation of translation, there may be cases of imbalance where the native societies with ancient epistemologies of ritual and symbol may lose their sense of identity after assimilation.[90] Steiner reminds the readers of the Heideggerian notion "we are what we understand to be" in this hermeneutic stage, as one's own being is modified and transformed by such appropriation.[91] Societies with ancient beliefs may be "knocked off balance and made to lose belief in their own identity," as in the case where the natives in New Guinea worship what airplanes bring in.

83. Ricoeur, "Preface to Bultmann," 389.
84. See Cheung, "Re-reading of Lin Shu," 24:2.
85. Steiner, *After Babel*, 313.
86. Ibid.
87. Ibid.
88. Ibid, 315.
89. Ibid, 315.
90. Ibid, 316.
91. Ibid. 315.

The fourth move aims to restore the balance, where genuine translation will equalize the forces. When the translator, the exegete and the reader are faithful to the author's text, it restores the imbalance caused by his appropriative comprehension. Equilibrium is achieved. This wraps up the translation process as a hermeneutic of trust, of penetration, of embodiment and of restitution. The above four moves are not unfamiliar to China's theatre scene, where Shakespeare was introduced as an icon that brought fundamental changes to the forms of traditional theatre. When Shakespeare was appropriated by local dramatists, they counter-reacted, omitting materials including religious, sexual and political which they found aggressive to the culture. A balance is restored when one sees the mushrooming of Shakespearean performances in traditional operatic forms, which I will present in later chapters.

After Steiner, Douglas Robinson remains one of the few influential translation scholars whose writings bear the marks of the hermeneutic approach. Such hermeneutic approach to translation has not become the mainstay of translation theories, though it did open to us a new model to classify translations beyond the distinctions between literalism, free imitation, formal and dynamic equivalence. One common ground that seems to link the disciplines of translation and hermeneutics in the twenty-first century is the trend towards pluralism of interpretations. David Tracy, a supporter of such pluralism, believes that it is "unlikely that there will be a unity based on any particular interpretation of the Christian message." In this new paradigm, the key lies not in a "common hermeneutical enterprise" but in establishing "mutually critical correlations" where "every theological act of interpretation already involves some correlation of the two constants." Such pluralistic interpretation of the text thus invites a pluralistic approach to translation that is not characterized by the dualistic faithful-versus-free translation, but often a mix of approaches to suit the norms, ideology and agents at work.

Theatre Semiotics, Theatre Studies and Translation

Traditionally, there is a distinction between theatre translation and drama translation. The former relates to translation of performance text for performance, the latter relates to translation of the dramatic text for publication. Susan Bassnett defined the relationship between the dramatic text and the performance text as one of a dual tradition, which "corresponds to a split in theatre between what might be termed for present purposes the commercial and the aesthetic. In the case of the former, the eventual performance was crucial; in the case of the latter, what mattered was the creation: if a text could be read and would be judged according to aesthetic criteria for literature." Such dual tradition exists to this day: literary scholars who take a text-based approach in studying drama translation comment on the translation of rhetorical devices, proper names, the meter, and genre. Simon Chau,[92] for example, is among these scholars who commented on the Chinese translations of Shakespeare in terms of poetics and stylistics. Faithfulness is an important criterion against which the quality of drama translations is evaluated.[93] For literary Shakespeare translators such as Liang Shiqiu, whose translation is considered faithful but not performable, what is important is the creation of a text that can be judged according to aesthetic criteria.

A sociological turn among translation scholars is emerging—Sameh Hanna draws on Pierre Bourdieu's concepts of field and habitus to provide sociological insight into Shakespearean translations in Egypt, where struggle is seen between two groups of producers of drama translation: a group which used classical Arabic in translation in order to achieve dissociation from the manipulation of market forces, and another which paid more attention to the demands of the market.[94] Jean Tsui in her dissertation situates Lin Shu's translation of Shakespeare in the context of the early twentieth-century political environment to show that Shakespeare's translations are used as a strategy for reaffirming nationalist ideals. But the current sociological turn in the study of theatre translation is mainly based on the text largely because the translations under study were produced decades ago before the existence of audiovisual recording, as such, the religious adaptation on stage (i.e. the semiotic turn) is not taken into account, which calls for a semiotic approach to this study.

In the discipline of semiotics, semioticians such as Patrice Pavis tend to move beyond the text-based discussion of the script. This is not surprising as semiotics grew out as a reaction against 'textual imperialism', in Patrice Pavis' terms: the text "has been restored to its place of one system among the systems of the whole of the performance,"[95] rather than the most important system. He suggests that "theatre translation is never where one expects it to be: not in words, but in gesture, not in the letter, but in the spirit of a culture, ineffable but omnipresent" and "that a real *translation* takes place on the level

---

92. See Chau, *Studies on the Chinese Translations*, 1981.

93. For discussions on the faithfulness of drama translations, see Bassnett 1985; Lindsay, *Between tongues*, 2006.

94. See Hanna, "Towards a Sociology of Drama Translation," 7.

95. Patrice Pavis' reply to five questions on theatre semiotics, published in *VS*, September-December 1978, quoted in Bassnett, "An Introduction to Theatre Semiotics," 47–55.

of the *mise en scène* as a whole."[96] Such comments have attracted the criticism of Susan Bassnett[97] who argues against any notion of performability, to the point of inviting scholars to limit their investigations to two main streams of study only: a historiography of theatre translation and a further investigation into the linguistic structure of existing theatre texts. In the midst of growing attention to the performability[98] of translated text, Susan Bassnett has discredited the notion as "dangerous" by virtue of undermining the importance of the translator. She cites the example of the National Theatre in London which attaches the name of a famous playwright to the translation produced by a less well-known bilingual translator, because this marketing tactic could draw in a larger crowd. To sum up, those from the field of performance or theatre studies are more interested in examining the process of performance of the translated text, in how the performance is domesticated, in the interrelationship of performance and text, whereas those in translation studies are more interested in studying the translatability of the text.[99] As a general observation, theatrical practitioners focus more on the practical side of the translation of theatrical text than translation scholars, citing factors such as authority of director, authority of the text, dynamics among actors and directors, financial factors, performability and audience expectations as contributing to the final image of the translated script.[100] In the field of Chinese Shakespeare studies, Ruru Li and Zhang Xiaoyang joined the league of other dramatists in moving away from a text-based approach to a performance-based approach in studying Chinese Shakespeare.[101] The polarization between drama translation and theatre translation is, according to Hanna, a result of "the struggle between the two groups of translating agents who are positioned on both sides of the field of drama translation (which covers both literary translation and theatre translation)." When theatre translation is more dominant in the field than literary translation, the former, which is

---

96. Pavis,"Problems of Translation for Stage," 25–44.

97. See Bassnett,"Translating for the Theatre," 99–111.

98. The term "performability" is not solidly defined, nor has consensus been reached regarding its importance as a criterion in evaluating theatre translation. David Johnson sees "performability" as a reason for "creative struggle" (2004:25) of a translator. Eva Espasa sees "performability" as a collaborative process that engages in the ideological and power struggles inherent in the performance or production process. (Krebs 2007:29).

99. Lindsay, *Between Tongues*, 3.

100. For discussions on the practical side of theatre translation, see Zatlin, *Theatrical Translation*, 2005; Johnston, *Stages of Translation*, 1996; Upton, *Moving Target*, 2000.

101. See Li, *Shashibiya*, 2003; Zhang, *Shakespeare in China*, 1996.

more market-oriented, will exert its influence on the translation strategies in the field of drama translation.[102]

Why a text-centered approach is not adequate in this current study of religious adaptation? How then does the study of semiotics enrich our understanding of theatre translation, and the meaning-making of the religious dimension in the play? Erika Fischer Lichte, in her study of theatrical code,[103] classifies signs according to the following categories: sounds, music, linguistic signs, paralinguistic signs, mimic signs, gestural signs, mask, hair, costume, stage conception, stage decoration, props, lighting. Such a repertoire of signs denotes what occurs in a theatre when an actor, representing a sign, the spectator looks on. As such, in my case studies I will study how these signs are used in translating the dramatist's interpretations from page to stage.[104]

Under this semiotic turn, the theatrical text is not the pure, authoritative written text defined by literary critics who insist on the need for remaining faithful. It is not concerned with locating meaning as in hermeneutics, but with the relationship between signs.[105] Shakespeare's text is not a sacred text that assumes ultimate authority, but one that is constituted by two media: the actor and the surrounding space.[106] Such a semiotic turn provides important insights into my study of religious text in theatre, because it strikes a balance to the definitive meaning-making notion born out of the tradition of hermeneutics, which is rooted in the interpretation of the authoritative biblical text. A semiotic turn is also in accordance with the Chinese theatre tradition, where it is the actors and gestures, not the text, that are central to the play. As such, a third way that is neither purely text-based nor purely sign-based is necessary in the study of cross-cultural translation from page to stage. Roman Jakobson sees translation as falling into three main categories: interlingual translation, intersemiotic translation, and intralingual translation. Theatre translation of Shakespeare into Chinese is, in Jakobson's definition, both an interlingual translation and an intersemiotic translation, and hence the need for both textual and semiotic analysis. The third way of studying the translatability of religion from page to stage will be a combination of hermeneutic, semiotic and social sciences approach that incorporates the above theories.

102. See Hanna,"Towards a Sociology of Drama Translation," 81.
103. Lichte, *The Semiotics of Theatre*, 1992.
104. Ibid, 13.
105. Pavis, *Languages of the stage*, 13.
106. Lichte, *The Semiotics of Theatre*, 180.

Translatability of Religious Discourse in the Chinese Theatre Translation—A Semiotic-cum-Hermeneutic Turn

I hereby propose a third way, drawing on the causal model for translation studies proposed by Andrew Chesterman[107] to discuss the translatability of religious discourse in the Chinese theatre translation of *The Merchant*. The causal model is the richest of the three main research models for translation studies, namely the causal, the comparative and the process model. The comparative model deals with charting equivalences and relations between source language and target language, or between translated texts and parallel texts.[108] The process model sees translation as a dynamic process, representing a change of state over a time interval, which is useful in analyzing sequential relations between different phases of the translation process. The causal model proposed by Andrew Chesterman fills the gap between the first two models, which does not see translation explicitly as an effect, nor does it help to explain why the translation looks the way it does.[109] Simply put, the comparative model deals with the "what" question, the process model deals with the "how" question, while the causal model deals with the "why" question.

The causal model is useful in explaining translation causes and effects, and can be used in explaining the cause for the loss of religious material in the theatre translations, especially in describing the effects of "ideology" on a translation product. The levels of causation include cognitive (translation act), situational (the translation event) and socio-cultural. The model is expanded below:

Socio-cultural conditions (norms, history, ideologies, languages . . .)

Translation event (skopos, source text, computers, deadline, pay . . .)

Translation act (state of knowledge, mood, self-image)

Translation profile (linguistic features)

Cognitive effects (change of cognitive or emotional state . . .)

Behavioral effects (individual actions, criticism . . .)

Socio-cultural effects (on target language, consumer behaviour, discourse of translation, status of translators . . .)

---

107. Chesterman, "A causal model for translation studies," 15–28.
108. Ibid.
109. Ibid.

Basically, the causal model encompasses the other two research models, as the time element in the process model is inherent in any cause/effect relation. The comparison between source texts and target texts will also be present in such causal conditions of the translation.[110] However, this causal model has three limitations. It is basically text-based. Secondly, by situating the translation in socio-cultural conditions, it tends to view the social as the overarching factor in shaping a translation, which is not so in some of our cases, where one's religious values may be the topmost criterion in displacing religious material. Thirdly, it should be noted that the above causation model is linear.[111] In reality, conditions may not only have top-down effects, but also these effects may go in the other direction to exert influence on the causes. Socio-cultural conditions including the predominant ideology may directly affect the cognitive condition of the translator, i.e. his/her ideology in translation.[112] But socio-cultural conditions are not always the predominant level of conditions that influence individual ideologies; sometimes, the latter can operate independent of the socio-cultural conditions at large, as my case studies will show. Sabrina P. Ramet's theory on the interaction between religion and politics can be used to understand this phenomenon.[113] Ramet pointed out that the religious doctrine can be shaped by the political ideology, while at the same time the former can reinforce ideological transformation. The translation profile, cognitive effects, Behavioral effects and socio-cultural effects can in turn influence the situational conditions (i.e. theatre company's recruitment of translator) and cognitive and interpretative conditions (i.e. director's interpretation of the play). I would like to modify the model by incorporating the hermeneutic approach as well as the semiotic approach, as follows:

110. Ibid.
111. Lee,"Translators as Gatekeepers," 2010.
112. Ibid.
113. See Ramet, "Sacred Values and the Tapestry of Power," 3–20.

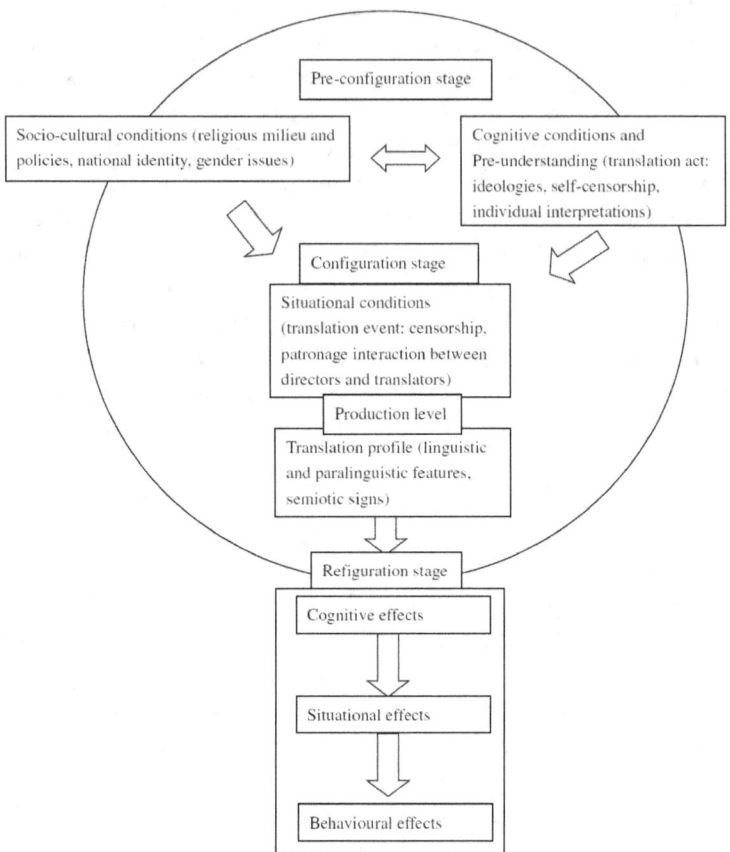

Figure 1.1 Adapted Causal Model

Upon modification, unlike Chesterman's model where socio-cultural conditions dictate cognitive conditions, i.e. individual ideologies, here in my version, the socio-cultural conditions interact with cognitive conditions, which are, in Ricoeur's terms, the world behind the text that shaped the pre-understanding of directors and translators (pre-configuraiton stage). The situational conditions correspond to the world of the text being created (configuration stage). The source text is first interpreted by the translator and director, who interacted under some situational conditions. They could be in line with each other in a horizontal relationship, or are in a vertical relationship where the translator is either submissive to the director's authority, or the director who is less well known than the translator pays due respect to the latter. After this hermeneutic stage of Shakespeare's text is the production level, according to Erika Fischer Lichte,[114] during which the text is translated and produced not only interlingually but also semiotically. Semiotic signs include sounds, music, mimic signs, gestural signs, mask, hair, costume, stage conception, stage decoration, props, lighting, among others. For instance, the Cantonese operatic version of *The Merchant* is set in Macau rather than in Venice under the leadership of Ni Huiying in 2007. This marks the transition from page to stage. The application or refiguration stage is where directors and audience reflect on how the show can be applied, and ultimately achieve self-understanding. This corresponds to the cognitive, behavioral effects of the performance. In Ricoeur's terms, this is the world in front of the text.

The causal model is particularly relevant in analyzing Shakespearean translations in China, because the plays under examination traverse different time periods, from the 1980s to the present day. The comparative model forms the basis of textual analysis as I compare the several translations of a particular scene using a critical discourse analysis approach.

In the modified causality model, the socio-cultural conditions that affect the religiosity of the play include the religious milieu and Christian sentiment, religious policies, issues of identity, homosexuality and gender. Ideologies of individual translators and directors, i.e. the cognitive and interpretative conditions may be influenced by what happens in the society at large, but independent artists often try to break free from pre-set ideologies to carve out their own style and voice, and thus develop a unique interpretation that defies the mainstream interpretations. Such a modification from previous theory is important, because as case studies in the later sections show, one's theology can lead to a translation and adaptation that defies the prevalent social conditions. Interviews are thus conducted with translators and directors to tease out their interpretative process, which will be discussed in Chapter 6. These two conditions on the other hand influence the operations of theatre companies, their choice of play and translators and the dynamics between directors and translators, and the role of translator and the capital he/she possesses in the habitus (translation field). The situational conditions interact with the cognitive conditions, because translators and directors do work alongside one another and seek consensus in interpretations, as my interviews show. The above conditions give rise to a translation

---

114. Erika Fischer Lichte establishes that the constitution of the theatrical text is a process of interpretation and a process of creating meaning, which occurs on two levels: the production of the text and the reception of the text. The production level is concerned with the situational process whereby a text is produced by a collective, a director and various actors, as well as the stage, costume and mask designers. See Lichte, *The Semiotics of Theatre*, 180–196.

that is unique in this socio-cultural context. The play, when staged, in turn will arouse emotions (which can be more positive or more negative towards Christianity), leading to criticisms in theatre reviews and further socio-cultural effects, e.g. sentiments for or against Christianity and the Jewish nation. Textual analysis is conducted to study the conditions that give rise to the translatability of religious discourse in *The Merchant* in China, Hong Kong and Taiwan. While the modified causation model provides the larger framework within which the play scripts and productions are analyzed, textual analysis, or more specifically, discourse analysis, is needed to subject these texts to close scrutiny.

Discourse analysis is characterized by its attention to language as social interaction. The analysis of discourse, the use of language in social life, is an important concept in the field of critical linguistics.[115] Behind the concept of discourse analysis is the importance it attaches to ideology. Fowler defines discourse as "speech or writing seen from the point of view of the beliefs, values and categories which it embodies; these beliefs (etc.) constitute a way of looking at the world, an organization or representation of experience— "ideology" in the neutral, non-pejorative sense."[116] For Norman Fairclough, discourse analysis "can be understood as an attempt to show systematic links between texts, discourse practices, and sociocultural practices.[117] Simpson suggested[118] that ideology refers to "taken for granted assumptions, beliefs and value systems shared collectively by social groups." The production of a drama, being a socially interactive process reflecting the values and beliefs in a culture is a suitable ground for discourse analysis.

Important in Fairclough's work is his notion of naturalization through which certain discourse types lose their ideological character. In other words, "the apparent emptying of the ideological content of discourses is, paradoxically, a fundamental ideological effect: ideology works through disguising its nature, pretending to be what it isn't ."[119] Simply put, ideology works most effectively when it erases itself. The omission of religious discourse in Shakespeare's plays throughout Chinese history will be discussed in Chapter 2.

---

115. Deacon et al., *Researching Communications*, 146.
116. Hawthorn, *A Glossary of Contemporary Literary Theory*, 48.
117. Fairclough, *Critical Discourse Analysis*, 16–17.
118. Simpson, *Language, Ideology and Point of View*, 5.
119. Fairclough, *Language and Power*, 76–77.

INTRODUCTION

Methodology and Outline

This study marks the first longitudinal and latitudinal study of the translatability of Shakespeare's religious language in China. Longitudinally, I will present the pathways of translations that shaped the pre-understanding of directors and translators by first giving a historical overview of the translation of religious discourse in *The Merchant* since the first introduction of Shakespeare in China in 1904 in Chapter 2. Textual analyses of certain excerpts will be conducted to illustrate their (un)translatability. Such overview will be triangulated from time to time by reference to other Shakespearean plays to give a more complete picture of the literary and translation scene. This analysis will be followed by seven case studies of *The Merchant* in Chapter 3, 4 and 5, which cover Chinese Shakespearean productions in Western spoken dramas, and Sinicized Shakespeare productions conforming to the conventions of traditional Chinese drama, such as yueju 粵劇 (Cantonese Opera) and yuju 豫劇 (Bangzi Opera). These case studies represent the latest productions since the opening up of China after the Cultural Revolution. They show a cross section of the plays staged in various parts of the Greater China in the same period, while at the same time trace the development of translation of Shakespeare's religion in the same place across different time periods. Chapter 6 aims to fill the research gap in the current text-based translation research on the translatability of religious dimension using a phenomenological approach by investigating the lifeworld, i.e. the world behind the text of the translating agents. Interviews are conducted with directors and translators of each play to flesh out the situational translation process as well as their hermeneutic process and theological position. The interview transcripts are studied using the interpretative phenomenological analysis (IPA) approach which focuses on using lived experience of interviewees and is about understanding people's everyday experience of reality in order to gain an understanding of the phenomenon in question. Knowledge of the lifeworld of these translating agents will shed light on how individual ideologies interact with Shakespeare's text that give rise to the final product. In Chapter 7, the problems of translatability of Shakespeare's religious language will be studied based on the expanded notion of religious language drawing on Ninian Smart's model of seven dimensions of religion. Questions of translatability across different time periods and cultures and across Hong Kong, Taiwan and China will be discussed. The research breaks new ground in that it traces the hermeneutical process of the translators/ directors as a reader and the situational process and semiotics of theatre translation, which altogether gives rise to the image of translated literature which in turn influences audience reception, supported by empirical data.

The study thus traverses the disciplines of translation studies, hermeneutics, theatre studies, and sociology.

Studying Shakespeare's translations in Greater China (including Hong Kong and Taiwan) serves as a good starting point for approaching the hermeneutic turn and semiotic turn of translating religious language in literature. Shakespeare's popularity and impact as seen in both the literary translations and stage productions give additional importance to the present research. The popularity of Shakespeare's plays also increases the availability of abundant resources on both literary and stage translations, together with the associated reviews and reception of performances. It is posited that the use of case studies from *The Merchant* is representative in the study of translatability of religious discourse in literature, because of its richness and density, such as Portia's mercy speech, its narrative on Judeo-Christian conflicts, and issues of Jewish and Christian identity. The fact that the story of the pound of flesh is included in the secondary school curriculum in China and Hong Kong and enjoys a high recognition throughout the generations make *The Merchant* arguably a valid choice for this study.

There are limitations in the discussion of Chinese Shakespeare, however. This is not a book on the historical development of Shakespearean productions in China in general, but specifically about the translatability of the religious dimension in Shakespeare's plays with reference to *The Merchant*. Thus, matters of interest in academia about the future trend of intercultural Shakespeare will not be of primary concern in this book. Moreover, I will focus on the religious dimension that relates to the Christian references, themes, biblical narratives and vocabulary in this play. The pagan thoughts, myths and allusions inherent in this play are not the focus in this study and will not be discussed.

The performance text of the various productions under study form the primary materials of my research. While three performances are available either as a VCD or published book available in public libraries, the remaining scripts are not published. Extra efforts are spent in contacting and visiting different troupes in Hong Kong, Taiwan and Mainland to obtain the needed script. Since this is a hermeneutic-cum-semiotic approach, only productions whose video-recordings can be accessed are included in this study.

In the end, this book seeks to re-define the concept of translatability. Francis Jones[120] proposed that "an ideal translation is no translation at all," that is, to achieve exact translation is next to impossible. In the context of

---

120. Francis Jones made this comment at the "First Durham Postgraduate Colloquium—Theoretical Frameworks and Methodologies: Research in Translation Studies" on 25 January 2013, University of Durham.

translating Shakespeare's religion, how do we define translation? Every stage production is an act of translation. In that case, un-translatability is still a form of translatability on stage, religious discourse and concepts that are not translated are, in fact, translated, but to a different form, assuming a different identity, which I will discuss in later chapters.

Jan Assmann argued that if translation is possible then there is no need of conversion, because "if all religions basically worship the same gods there is no need to give up one religion and to enter another one. The possibility only occurs if there is one religion claiming knowledge of a superior truth. It is precisely this claim that excludes translatability."[121] This proposition rings true in the translatability of the doctrinal dimension of religious discourse. Terms such as salvation and mercy can be understood in a different tradition, but the underlying Christian doctrine is inevitably lost in the translation. Having said that, the un-translatability of the doctrinal dimension does not mean that other aspects of the religious language are not translatable. In the final analysis, the book addresses the question—is translation conversion? Contrary to Assmann's argument, various scholars have used the analogy of conversion to help people in understanding translation. The intricate relationship between translation and conversion will be discussed in the final chapter of the book.

---

121. Assmann, "Translating Gods," 31.

2

History of Effects

Historical Overview of the Treatment of Religious Dimension since Early Twentieth Century

Before studying the various theatre translations of *The Merchant* in contemporary China, Hong Kong and Taiwan, it is important to review the traditions of translatability of the religious dimension of Shakespeare's works into Chinese since their first introduction which have informed the pre-understanding of directors and translators of the contemporary Chinese Shakespeare stage. In this chapter, instead of merely giving a descriptive textual analysis of the relationship between the source text and the translations, I situate the translation products in the socio-cultural and political context of the period, examine its interaction with the individual ideologies of translators, and juxtapose the development of the translation discipline against the development of the Chinese stage. From the examples in this chapter, I seek to demonstrate that apart from the sociocultural conditions that shape the translation products, one's theology plays an important role in modifying the influence of the predominant socio-political trend. This gives rise to varying translation products in the same period—renditions of Lin Shu 林紓 and Bao Tianxiao 包天笑 show that cultural norms are part and parcel of the toning down of Christian discourse, while Laura White, a Baptist missionary in the early twentieth century, gives full play to the religious references. While translations of *The Merchant* comprise the main body of discussion, translations of the religious discourse of other Shakespeare plays will also be studied together to give a broader perspective of its translatability. The Chinese translations cited are back translated into English by myself, unless otherwise specified.

Translation of *The Merchant of Venice* in the Early Twentieth Century

Historically, the early part of the twentieth century was a critical time in China during which two ideologies met—the traditional Chinese values rooted in Confucianism competed with the importation of Western modernization. Confucian *literati* expended efforts on asserting traditional Chinese values, whereas other intellectuals sought to abolish Confucian values, feudalism, together with superstitions. They campaigned for the importation of Western ideas, including science, democracy, equality and freedom. Politically, people in this period witnessed the overthrow of the Qing Dynasty and the establishment of the New Republican Era in 1911. The May Fourth movement that took place on 4th May, 1919 led by students and intellectuals called for a new mindset, which saw the overthrowing of Confuciansim with Western ideals of democracy and science. Ideologically, this marked a period of intense ideological conflicts when the downfall of traditional values also led to the displacement of other religious traditions, during which Buddhism was considered a philosophy rather than a religion, Christian miracles were considered unscientific and Christianity was identified with foreign imperialism.[1] Culturally, vernacular language replaced the elegant, classic style as the predominant literary style during the new cultural movement starting 1919. It is thus worth noting how the translation strategies varied in the hands of different translators representing different ideologies.

Lin Shu's Translation of *Tales from Shakespeare*

Shakespeare's work was first introduced to China by Lin Zexu 林則徐 (1785–1850), governor-general of the Hubei and Hunan provinces and a key figure in halting the opium war. Shakespeare was first cited in Lin's translation of the *Encyclopedia of Geography* (1843).[2] However, he became widely known in China when Lin Shu published the *Yinbian Yanyu* (吟邊燕語; 1904), his translation of Charles and Mary Lamb's *Tales from Shakespeare* (1807), a collection of prose adaptations of Shakespeare's plays written primarily for children. Although Lin did not speak English and did not read the original plays, he worked in collaboration with his interpreter Wei

---

1. See Chow, *Theosis, Sino-Christian Theology*, 24.

2. The manuscript was finished in 1839 but not published until 1843, after the Opium War, when it appeared under the title 海國圖志 (*Haiguotuzhi*).

Yi (魏易) who provided an oral account of the stories. When published, Lin's translations were set out as prose texts.

Lin Shu's lack of English did not hinder him from translating Western literature; he was a prolific translator and one of the first to make many of these texts available in China.[3] Indeed, Lin has been acclaimed as the most influential twentieth-century Chinese translator, completing 184 works in total.[4] In Shakespeare's case, however, Lin did not translate directly from the original plays but from Charles and Mary Lamb's adaptations. This may be because Lin was less concerned with the original texts than with incorporating Shakespeare's heritage into the existing Confucian tradition, thus giving Shakespeare a contemporary and cross-cultural touch.

As well as being a Confucian literatus, Lin Shu was a political reformer who campaigned for change in China. During the Qing Dynasty, China faced a significant influx of Western ideologies. Reformers accused the Chinese of 'sharing a narrow world view, obstinately opposed to change, allowing her past to dominate her present, and being over-enthusiastic about gods, fairies, ghosts and demons' (識見局，思想舊，泥古駭今，好言神怪).[5] Lin Shu, however, did not share this opinion. In his preface to the *Yinbian Yanyu* (吟邊燕語), he tried to bridge the gap between Western and Chinese literature by emphasizing that both made use of the 'supernatural', introducing the supernatural aspects of Shakespeare to the Chinese audience as a way of highlighting the importance of Chinese traditions, and stressing that these traditions should not be eradicated in the midst of the 'wholesale importation of Western values (全盤西化)' that was taking place. Lin wrote:

> Shakespeare's sonnets and tales, which rival those of Du Fu, a renowned Chinese poet, point to supernatural forces and spirits. . . . it is evident that famous people in the West recite Shakespearean tales in their homes; . . . literati and women shed tears upon listening to these stories without dismissing them as old-fashioned, or blaming them for upholding supernatural forces. Why? Good politics and religion can influence literature. Politics and education should be beautified through literature. On the other hand, literature, however beautiful, does not benefit politics and education. Thus Westerners are busy at politics and education to empower the country and military against the invasion of enemies, while they seek pleasure through literature.

---

3. He was a leading figure in early translation history in China and regarded as on a par with another reputable early translator, Yan Fu, who translated, among other works, Thomas Huxley's *Evolution and Ethics*.

4. Chan, *Twentieth-Century Chinese Translation Theory*, 16.

5. Cited in 林紓、魏易譯 [Lin Shu], 吟邊燕語 [*Yinbian Yanyu*], 1–2.

> Even though R[ider] Haggard's and Shakespeare's works are regarded as old-fashioned and reliant on the supernatural, civilized men do not see them as obstacles . . . The English seek out what is new for better government, but would never discard their Shakespeare.[6]

Here Lin offered a sociological sketch that situated the translator in the early twentieth century. While the West was regarded by some as engulfing much of the Chinese cultural scene, Confucian literati such as Lin Shu were reasserting the values of time-honoured Chinese heritage.[7] Lin's translations have been seen by scholars as a way of defending Confucian tradition and Chinese values. Robert Compton asserts that these principles were 'vibrant and alive in Lin's mind and spirit', and that Lin believed himself to bear the responsibility of 'preserving the best of what had been created in the past'.[8] In her close textual analysis of Lin's translations in the *Yinbian Yanyu*, Jean Tsui takes a similar view, arguing that *Yinbian Yanyu* is 'an expression of Lin's reformist enthusiasm in the midst of a swiftly changing political scene torn by diverse opinions and heated debates'.[9] Lin presented Shakespeare's tales as something familiar to Chinese culture, domesticating or naturalizing them as works expressing a world view recognizable to Chinese readers, containing stories of spirits, gods and monsters.[10] On the book's cover, he categorized these tales as stories of gods and spirits, a category which was familiar and appealing to the Chinese audience. The title of each story reflected the main plot rather than representing a literal translation of the title: thus *The Merchant of Venice* became the *Rou Quan* 肉券 (*Contract of the Flesh*), and was included as the first story in the collection.

Although Lin's translation of *The Merchant of Venice* was not his earliest, its popularity surpassed all his other translations. A. Ying (阿英) noted that although Lin's translation was not the first, it was to be preferred to others because 'it attracted the attention of many readers at the time'.[11] The popularity of Lin's translation of *The Merchant of Venice*

---

6. Ibid. 3.

7. Lin Shu's *Yinbian Yanyu* and his translation of other Western literature show evidence of Confucianization, i.e. giving the characters in Shakespeare a Confucian twist.

8. Compton, "A Study of the Translations of Lin Shu," 99.

9. Tsui, "Rewriting Shakespeare," 99.

10. Lawrence Venuti sets out two translation approaches: domestication versus foreignization: the former refers to adopting a fluent translation to ease readers' reception, the latter refers to the retention in the target text of cultural and linguistic references from the original.

11. Compton, "The Translations of Lin Shu," 200. In 1961, Ying had reprinted a

resulted in its being reprinted as a separate text eleven times between 1905 and 1935, in addition to the three editions of the *Yinbian Yanyu*.[12] A new project launched in 2001 to render all Shakespearean plays in prose recognized Lin Shu's significant achievement.[13] In 1999, the former Chinese Premier Zhu Rongji (朱鎔基) even referred to *The Merchant of Venice* in his response to a question regarding the bankruptcy of Guangdong International Trust and Investment Company when, after the Second Plenary Session of the Ninth National People's Congress, he recalled the story of 'A Pound of Flesh'—Lin's version—which he had read in high school, and related it to the bankruptcy case.

Lin's translation was also popular with dramatists. In July 1913, the National Renewal Society (*Xin min she*; 新民社) staged *Rou Quan* (*Contract of the Flesh*), a version of *Merchant of Venice* dramatized from Lin's *Yanbian Yanyu*. The production, the first professional performance of Shakespeare in Chinese, was well received and became an immediate box office success.[14] It was followed by other productions such as *Othello*, *Hamlet* and *The Taming of the Shrew*, which were staged in 1914 and 1915, also using Lin's translations.[15] The popularity of Lin's translations both in print and on stage was due to his creation of a 'fantasy world', as Cao Yu (曹禺; 1910–96) described it, or to their exotic plots, which were just like 'fairy tales', according to Guo Moruo (郭沫若; 1892–1978).[16] A synopsis of Lin's translation of *The Merchant of Venice*, also under the title *Contract of the Flesh*, was included in an anthology of plays edited by the acclaimed director Zheng Zhenqiu (鄭振秋).[17] In the 1930s, Lin Shu's translation was exported to colonial Hong Kong and adopted by the acclaimed Cantonese opera master Ma Shizeng (馬師曾), who directed the *Yi Bang Rou* (一磅肉; *A Pound of Flesh*) as a Cantonese opera adaptation. The story was staged again as *A Pound of Flesh* in 1953, starring the Cantonese opera diva Hong Xiannu (紅線女).[18]

---

collection of translations of Western novels from the late Qing Dynasty: A. Ying (Qian Heng Cun), ed., *Wan Qing Wen Xue Cong Chao* [*Translations from Foreign Literature*], 1961.

12. Li, *Shashibiya*, 16.

13. Tu An [屠岸、方平譯], *Xin Shashibiyaquanji* [新莎士比亞全集; *New Shakespeare's Works*], transl. Fang Ping (Taipei, 2000).

14. 鄭振秋 [Zheng Zhenqiu], 新劇考證百齣 [*Xinju kaozheng bai chu*; *Textual Criticism on a Hundred Spoken Drama Plays*] (Shanghai, 1919), 1–29.

15. Huang, *Shakespeare on the Chinese Stage*, 79.

16. Li, *Shashibiya*, 16.

17. Zheng Zhenqiu, *Xinju kaozheng bai chu*, 1.

18. Yi, "Shakespeare in Guangdong," 197–208.

Lin either omitted or adapted the religious language in Shakespeare's plays, as has been noted sporadically by contemporary scholars. However, such discussions have been limited to comparing the source and target texts. Thus Alexander Huang noted the omission of Christian references from Lin Shu's translations of the Lambs' *Tales from Shakespeare* but did not elaborate further.[19] Tsui compares Lin's translations of the Christian connotations in *Romeo and Juliet* and *The Tempest*, and notes the extent of Daoist interpretation in Lin's translations.[20] For instance, Friar Lawrence in *Romeo and Juliet* becomes a Daoist priest, residing in a monastery, who is interested in thaumaturgy. Prospero in *The Tempest*, in Lin's rendition, studies Daoist scriptures and practices such as 'Shaman's steps', a type of ritual walk or dance performed during the Daoist liturgy. This 'conventionalization' strategy of translating Christian concepts rendered Shakespeare's works familiar to Chinese.[21] It also helped to reinforce traditional Chinese culture and values, since Shakespeare was seen employing supernatural forces in the narratives. Tsui pointed out that '[Lin's] conventionalization is more than just a cultural shift: by using Daoism to replace Christianity, still a dominant religion in the West at the time, the translator had ventured to find the native religion a place in modernity'.[22]

Religious Material in *The Merchant of Venice* and in Charles and Mary Lamb's *Tales from Shakespeare*

Since Lin was translating Shakespeare through Lamb's version rather than directly from Shakespeare's script, one may ask, first of all, how different is this version from Shakespeare's version. Before I move on to discuss Lin's rendition, it is important to take a brief look at the presentation of religious material in Shakespeare's play text and its re-presentation in the Lamb adaptation, on which Lin's translation was based.

As John Milton suggests, abridgement gives adapters "an opportunity to leave out insalubrious elements that may not be accepted in translations

---

19. See Huang, "Lin Shu, Invisible Translation and Politics," 55–65.
20. Tsui, "Rewriting Shakespeare," 41–8.
21. 'Conventionalization' is a term coined by Frederic C. Bartlett in *Remembering: A Study in Experimental and Social Psychology* (Cambridge, 1932), 280; he proposed using the term to describe a process of cultural exchange whereby 'cultural materials coming into a group from outside are gradually worked into a pattern of a relatively stable kind distinctive of that group'. The conventionalization process involves four major principles: assimilation, simplification, retention and social constructiveness.
22. See Tsui, "Rewriting Shakespeare," 41–8.

destined for distribution."²³ It reduces the complexity of a classic novel. In Lamb's adaptation of *The Merchant* in *Tales from Shakespeare*, an English children's book that simplified the story line to suit children's needs, Lamb has omitted two story lines—the runaway of Jessica and her Christian lover Lorenzo, and the choice of the three caskets. According to the preface, the aim of such simplification is to interest children in the story, to "supply them with a clear and definite outline of the main argument, omitting such episodes or incidental sketches of character as were not absolutely necessary to its development."²⁴ Sex jokes in the last act were omitted for the above reason. The theme of Judeo-Christian conflict can still be seen, though in a much toned-down manner. Of the two important speeches that exhibit Christian references in the original play, Shylock's famous speech "hath not a Jew eyes" was omitted, only Portia's "mercy speech" was kept. In fact, Antonio's identity as a Christian was only indirectly referred to when Shylock says "O father Abram, what these Christians are." An observant reader might be able to infer from the first sentence in the story "He was a usurer who had amassed an immense fortune by lending money at great interest to *Christian* merchants" (my emphasis) that Antonio was one of the Christian merchants mentioned. Gone is Shylock's line "I hate him for he is a *Christian*" (my emphasis). Instead, it is Antonio's interest-free loans that create Shylock's distress. Although "Christian" as a predicate or a noun appears less frequently (i.e. 6 times in *Tales* versus 19 times in the play text) as a result of the above reduction, compensation is given at some points to show the quality of Christian, as a comparison table (Table A) on p.87-91 [X-ref] shows.

Such deletion of religious references is what John Milton describes as "loss of sacredness," which is a common characteristic of factory translation, i.e. translation with certain industrial characteristics.²⁵ As Walter Benjamin put it, in the age of mechanical reproduction, the contemporary possibilities of reproducing the object "destroy the ritualistic and magical elements surrounding the original."²⁶ Adaptations and condensed translations become standardized products, giving rise to a homogeneous, inoffensive text where "stylistic differences and idiosyncrasies of experimental authors are erased."²⁷

23. Milton, "Translation Studies and Adaptation Studies," 51–58.
24. Lamb. *Tales from Shakespeare*, 6.
25. See Milton, "Translation Studies and Adaptation Studies," 53.
26. See Benjamin, 217–251 in Milton, "Translation Studies and Adaptation Studies," 53.
27. Ibid.

Lin's Domestication of Christian Content

Lin's domestication strategy aimed to make Shakespeare a familiar voice for a Chinese audience rather than a foreign 'other'. How did this affect the translation of the religious aspects of the plays? Lin produced a paragraph-by-paragraph translation of the Lambs' texts (which were themselves simplified versions of the plays), preserving plot and characterization but omitting what he deemed to be less important details. In the resulting translation of *The Merchant of Venice*, the complexity of the play, including the relationship between Jews and Christians and the conflicts between them, was downplayed.[28] Shylock was depicted as a cruel moneylender, while Antonio was described as 'generous'. Almost all the direct speech in Lamb's text was translated by Lin, but the Lambs' versions of the narrative removed the story line relating to Jessica's running away and the casket scenes, and Lin did so too. Some additions can be seen to conform to Chinese values and customs. Antonio was addressed as an 'elder'—a title of respect in Chinese—by his friends, including Portia. In the court scene, Portia's beauty was emphasized by Lin even more strongly than by Shakespeare, in accordance with common expectations of a beautiful female protagonist in Chinese novels: when Portia is disguised as the apprentice lawyer Balthazar, 'people at the court saw the lawyer's beauty and were stunned'.[29]

In the Lambs' version, Shylock's attack on Christians in his infamous speech had been reduced to an attack addressed to Antonio. In Lin's translation Shylock addressed Antonio as 'Roman' rather than using the pronoun 'he', as the Lambs had done.

> [The Lambs' text] On this, Shylock thought within himself: 'If I can once catch him on the hip, I will feed fat the ancient grudge I bear him. He hates our Jewish nation; he lends out money gratis; and among the merchants he rails at me and my well-earned bargains, which he calls interest. Cursed be my tribe if I forgive him!'
>
> [Lin's translation] 歇洛克自念，彼羅馬人視吾猶太人遭黎直狗耳，今幸見貸，非重窘之不足洩吾憤.
>
> [My back translation] Shylock murmured, 'That Roman sees us Jews as cut-throat dogs. Now that he needs to borrow money, I must embarrass him heavily to vent my anger.'

---

28. See Shapiro, *Shakespeare and the Jews*, 1996, for discussion of the complexity of the play.

29. See Lin, *Yinbian Yanyu*, 3–4.

The hatred is here felt between Romans (personified by Antonio) and Jews. That Lin could use 'Roman' to stand in for Christian suggests that Christians were considered to be not much different from Romans, both being a foreign—potentially imperialist—'other' to the Chinese audience.[30] It also suggests an exotic character to Shakespeare's tales, which facilitated their reception during the early twentieth century, when the spread of Western ideologies in China prompted an interest in European and American culture. Adaptations of Antonio's identity occur not only in Lin's work, but also in the translation by Bao Tianxiao, a contemporary of Lin, who changed Antonio's nationality to British.[31] In these versions of the play, the Christian-Jewish conflicts in *The Merchant of Venice* became conflicts between Romans or Britons and Jews. Religious conflicts no longer took center stage in the play.

Similarly, Portia's 'mercy' speech in the trial scene was reduced in Lin's translation. In Lamb's version the speech closely resembled that of the full text. The five uses of the term 'mercy' in the original play are all retained in the Lambs' text. The Christian principle of 'mercy triumphing over justice' is evident from the modified speech:

> [The Lambs' text] [Portia] spoke so sweetly of the noble quality of mercy as would have softened any heart but the unfeeling Shylock's, saying that it dropped as the gentle rain from heaven upon the place beneath; and how mercy was a double blessing, it blessed him that gave and him that received it; and how it became monarchs better than their crowns, being an attribute of God Himself; and that earthly power came nearest to God's in proportion as mercy tempered justice; and she bade Shylock remember that as we all pray for mercy, that same prayer should teach us to show mercy.
>
> [Lin's translation] 顧為人須尚慈愛，君不過欲得錢耳，即索比多金為子者，於法亦善，何為誾誾爭此塊肉？"反復伸理至數百次，歇洛克屹然不為動，堅請如約。
>
> [My back translation] You should be kind. What you want is just money, if you ask for more money as interest the law is still obeyed. Why do you insist so much on taking this flesh? She pleaded several hundred times to Shylock, who was unmoved and insistent on executing the bond.

---

30. See van Kooten, "Christianity in the Graeco-Roman World," 3–37.

31. See 包天笑 [Bao Tianxiao], 女律師, ['The Lawyeress'], 女學生. [*Female Student Periodical*], 1911.

The Christian concept of 'mercy over justice', an important theme of this play, has been reduced to a simple utilitarian emphasis on economic terms. Mercy has important Christian overtones, where divine mercy refers to the forgiveness of one's sins through Christ's sacrifice (e.g. Eph. 2: 4–5). This is a reciprocal concept: just as God is merciful to people, so believers should exercise mercy towards others: 'Be merciful, just as your Father is merciful' (Luke 6: 36 NRSV). Mercy is used to temper justice:

> Do not judge, and you will not be judged; do not condemn, and you will not be condemned. Forgive, and you will be forgiven; give, and it will be given to you. A good measure, pressed down, shaken together, running over, will be put into your lap; for the measure you give will be the measure you get back. (Luke 6:37 NRSV)

Portia, alluding to the Lord's Prayer, asked Shylock to show mercy regarding Antonio's trespasses, in accordance with the Sermon on the Mount: 'for if you others their trespasses, your heavenly Father will also forgive you' (Matt. 6:14 NRSV). In its secularized meaning, mercy is 'the quality of care for another, willingness to make an effort, even at great sacrifice, to ease another's pain, readiness to forgive, eagerness to help'.[32] This quality of mercy was translated as *ci ai* (慈愛) by Lin, meaning kindness and benevolence. As such, mercy was not mentioned as an attribute of God, neither was the idea of justice translated. The biblical concept of 'mercy over justice' suffered from a shift to an emphasis on kindness and a utilitarian application.

Lin's translation contains just two references to 'Christian', compared with the six times it appears in the Lambs' version of the play. The lines where 'Christian' is still mentioned in the Chinese translation have negative connotations. It is the Christians who are suspicious, and it is a Christian whom Shylock's daughter, Jessica has married against her father's will.

> [The Lambs' text] Shylock, hearing this debate, exclaimed: 'O Father Abraham, what suspicious people these Christians are!'

> [Lin's translation] 歇洛克聞二人言,呼曰:'阿伯拉罕乎(此猶太始祖,猶太人動輒呼之者)!不圖基督教中人乃亦妄測乎人至此乎?'

---

32. There are three Hebrew roots that are frequently translated 'mercy', which carry the meanings of (1) the kind of love which is mutual and dependable; (2) the 'womb's love', i.e. the love of mother for a child; and (3) 'grace' or 'favor', i.e. a free gift. The New Testament builds on the Old Testament conceptualization, and three Greek roots underlie the English translation of 'mercy': mutuality, sympathy and the major weight of the physical feeling of mercy. For a full description of the theology of mercy, see Komonchak et al, *New Dictionary of Theology*, 650–2.

[My back translation] Shylock, hearing their conversations, exclaimed: 'O Father Abraham (this is an Israeli ancestor, an expression frequently used by Jews), what suspicious people these Christians are!'

[The Lambs' text] For Antonio knew that the Jew had an only daughter who had lately married against his consent a young Christian named Lorenzo, a friend of Antonio's . . .

[Lin's translation] 安東尼曰:吾無須此。彼猶太人有女嫁基督教人,歇洛克怒不予以奩具 . . .

[My back translation] Antonio: I don't need that [Shylock's estate]. The Jew has a daughter who has lately married a Christian. Shylock was so angry that he had disinherited her.

Apart from making fewer references to 'Christian', there is also a notable change in the plot. In Shakespeare's play and in the Lambs' adaptation, Antonio required Shylock to become a Christian as a condition of reducing his financial penalty. Lin removed this requirement, and left Shylock only having to surrender his wealth, giving half to the state and entrusting Antonio with the other half, to be passed to Jessica on her father's death. As will be discussed below, the requirement that Shylock must convert was also edited out of later Chinese productions, including the immensely popular Beijing production staged between 1980 and 1986 by director Zhang Qihong.

The sanitizing of the Christian content, however, can be contrasted with the retention of the Jewish heritage in Lin's text. The foreignness of this Shakespearean tale is introduced occasionally through transliteration or change of narrative style. Lin transliterated Daniel, the Old Testament prophet, as *Dan Nier* (但尼而) but with an addition, which reads: 'Daniel, a good Jewish judge' (但尼而者, 猶太良有司也). The introduction of foreign concepts through supplementation is also seen in an earlier example, where a parenthesis is added after the translation of Shylock's expression 'O Father Abraham' which reads: 'this is a Jewish ancestor, an expression frequently used by Jews'. This addition serves to remind the Chinese audience of Abraham's—and with him Shylock's—Jewishness. Jews had a long history of settlement and acclimatization in China,[33] and Shylock's Jewish identity would make him a more familiar 'other' to the Chinese audience, closer to Chinese traditions than the unfamiliar British or Roman 'other' with negative, imperialistic connotations.

---

33. See Shapiro, *Jews in Old China*, 1984.

The popular reception of Lin's version and the impression of Shakespeare as recounting fantasy stories of spirits can be attributed to his narrative style. Lin was the first to introduce changes in the narrative structure of Chinese literary works to suit a revised poetics. Before him, Chinese literary narratives began each chapter with a couplet relating to the chapter content. Lin changed this style by introducing the foreign custom of prose chapter headings, which was then followed by his contemporaries. Lin had a distinctive elegant literary style known as *wenyan* (文言). This was a classical style used before the vernacular movement; it was peppered with colloquial terms, which may explain its popular reception. *Wenyan* was the predominant style among literati but, when punctuated with colloquial terms, Lin's semi-classical literary style appealed to both the intellectuals and the masses, who found the pure *wenyan* form difficult to understand. His style was commended by the then renowned scholar Qian Zhongshu (錢鍾書; 1910–98) as a form of '*wenyan* that is more [for the] layman, casual and flexible'.[34] A number of well-known literati and dramatists were heavily influenced by Lin's works, such as Cao Yu, who hailed him as the Shakespeare of the Orient:

> One of my favorite Western playwrights is Shakespeare, and my fondness of Shakespeare's plays started from reading Lin Shu's *Tales* when I was [a] little boy. As soon as I was able to read the original English, I was eager to get hold of a Shakespeare play, because Lin's translation of Shakespeare's fantasy world was so fresh in my young mind.

Guo Moruo, a prominent dramatist and literary figure in the twentieth century, commented: 'I was unconsciously influenced by this book [*Tales*]. I read *The Tempest* and *Romeo and Juliet* in the original when I grew up, but it seems that Lin's way of telling these stories as fairy tales was more appealing'.[35] As noted above, Lin described the *Tales* as '*shenguaixiaoshuo* (神怪小說)', stories of spirits and gods, a genre familiar to Chinese readers. The titles of the plays are translated neatly into polysyllabic terms that render them poetic. For instance, *Merchant of Venice* was translated as *Rou Quan* (*Contract of the Flesh*); *Hamlet* was rendered as *Guizhao* (*The Ghost's Command*); *Macbeth* as *Guzheng* (*Witchy Omens*). All these Chinese titles highlight the supernatural aspect of the plays.

By using a narrative that emphasized spirits and gods, and in a classical literary style, Lin successfully introduced Shakespeare, the foreign 'other',

---

34. Qian, *Lin Shu's Translations*, 36–37.

35. The translations of the quotations of Guo and Cao are taken from Li, *Shashibiya*, 16.

under a familiar Chinese guise. In this respect Lin was reflecting the approach to translation later identified by Lefevere. According to Lefevere, one of the three factors in determining the acceptance of texts is the dominant poetics, which may include genres and the relationship between literature and the social system. As such, some literature, in this case tales of spirits and gods, will be more readily accepted because these tales are operating within a system that recognizes it.[36]

Omissions and modifications are not infrequent in Lin's other translations. He was criticized by contemporaries for distorting the text. Qian Zhongshu, for instance, judged that Lin's 'misrepresentations' were the result of a 'willful act'.[37] However, Lin was not the only literatus in that period who transformed religious themes in literary works. Translators in the late nineteenth and early twentieth centuries were often seen as agents for social change, and rewriting of the original text was not uncommon among them. Yan Fu (嚴復; 1853–1921), who translated T. H. Huxley's *Evolution and Ethics* in 1898, added extensive commentaries on the notions of 'natural selection' and 'survival of the fittest'. His translation exerted significant influence among reformists such as Liang Qichao (梁啟超; 1873–1929) who were advocating social progress and change. Liang used classical Chinese even in the midst of the vernacular movement in China in order to address an elite audience with the aim of persuading them of the quality of Western literature.[38]

Translation as a form of rewriting was a typical approach in early twentieth-century China, where remaining faithful to the source text was not considered the most important criterion. Rather, translation was used to introduce ideas from the West in order to enrich Chinese culture. The range of literary genres was broadened as a result to include political novels, educational novels, science fiction and detective stories, all of which had hitherto been unknown. In order to facilitate reception among Chinese readers, the text was sanitized or domesticated: place names and people's names were often 'sinicized'. Lawrence Wong suggested that this was done from necessity rather than choice: owing to the lack of knowledge about the West amongst readers, the translator often could not bridge the gap between

---

36. Lefevere, "Why Waste Our Time on Rewrites?," 215–43.

37. Qian, "The Translations of Lin Shu," 112. Lin's efforts in influencing reader response are evident not only in his rendering of religious material but also in the translator's prefaces in various works. According to Martha Cheung Pui-Yiu, Lin exercised 'knowledge management' in his translation of Christian content in *Uncle Tom's Cabin*: Cheung, "The Discourse of Occidentalism," 127–49.

38. Pollard, *Translation and Creation*, 15.

the two cultures, even when they themselves fully understood the meaning of the source text.[39]

Bao Tianxiao's Translations

While Lin Shu was among the first to translate Shakespeare's stories, the first public performance of *The Merchant* by the East City Girls' School in Shanghai (*cheng dong nvzixue tang* 城東女子學堂) in early 1913 was not based on this translation, but on the version translated by Bao Tianxiao (1912), a contemporary of Lin Shu. It was published in a feminist magazine *Female Student* (*nvxue sheng* 女學生), an internal school magazine which promoted women's education among the students.[40] Bao was a well-known journalist in the late Qing period. He was a prolific writer, a teacher, an editor of educational materials and translated numerous novels. However, he admitted that his knowledge of foreign languages was limited. He studied Japanese for three months, English for six months and French for eight months.[41] He reckoned, "My level of English is not good enough to translate books. My level of Japanese is just enough (to translate), but I cannot understand the colloquial terms. That's why I don't like (to translate) Japanese autobiographies. Rather I chose (to translate Japanese) books that were translated from the West."[42] Given his limited English competence, it is very probable that his translation of *The Merchant*, known as *The Lawyeress* (*nvlushi* 女律師, is based not on Lamb's version but on Lin's Chinese translation.

While Lin's version is regarded as a re-writing that is heavily moralistic and infused with Confucian values, Bao's version is a feminist re-creation. The title of the translation—*The Lawyeress*—foregrounds Portia as the title character. The main story line highlights Portia's cleverness in outwitting Shylock, and her strong will to establish a girls' school. Alongside the importation of Western ideas in the early twentieth-century China was the emergence of female education brought about by Christian female missionaries who set up mission secondary schools and colleges for females in that period. The last decades of the nineteenth century witnessed the women's reform movements

39. Wong, *Reinterpreting Fidelity, Communicability and Elegance*, 222.

40. The magazine is published to supplement knowledge outside of class. In the preface of the magazine, the editor mentioned three main objectives of the magazine in its inaugural issue: firstly, students will see this magazine just like a good friend that offers critiques, second, the magazine becomes a mirror to showcase the educational model to parents, third, those females who have yet to attend schools will become motivated. See Bao Tianxiao 包天笑, The Lawyeress 女律師, 3.

41. See Bao, *Memoirs of Chuanying Tower*, 187–190.

42. Ibid, 207.

in China whereby Christian women became the first group of Chinese women to address issues of footbinding, concubinage, health care etc.[43] Such Christian women's reform activities occurred alongside the socioeconomic change of women's status in China in general, where a small percentage of women studied overseas and brought back new ideas of womanhood that facilitated the social reform. With the opening up of educational opportunities for Chinese women in the 1890s, female education became more and more acceptable, and Christian girls' schools that offered Western science subjects and English became the destination for women from well-off families. The women's reform gained support from well-known *literati* such as Liang Qichao, who wrote articles to advocate the establishment of girls' schools and anti-footbinding movements.[44] Bao himself supported anti-footbinding movements and the establishment of girls' schools. In his *Memoirs of Chuan Ying Tower*, he touched upon women's liberation, " . . . at that time people were advocating women's education and anti-footbinding practices. Some foreign churches also set up women's colleges. We *literati* wrote about the liberation of women from time to time."[45]

Against such a background, one can understand the change of plot in Bao's translation. The genre was modelled on a script, and included four scenes. The script began with Portia's criticism:

近來世界上，有件極不平等的事。諸位知道是甚麼事?便是我們女子沒有參政權。我想二十世紀中，這參政權也不能讓男人獨佔。所以我急急想辦個女子政法學堂。只是辦學堂，第一要有經濟，沒有錢如何辦得。不免和我哥哥商量去者。[46]

Back Translation:

Recently there is something very unfair happening in the world. Do you know what this is? It is us women having no political rights. I think in the twentieth century, such political rights should not be owned by men. Thus I want to set up a girl's college on politics and law quickly. However, to set up a school, the

---

43. See Kwok, *Chinese Women and Christianity*, 101–102.

44. See Liang, "Changshenvxuetang qi," 20-30, cited in Kwok, *Chinese Women and Christianity 1860–1927*, 106.

45. See Bao Tianxiao 包天笑, *Chuanyinglouhuiyilu* 釧影樓回憶錄 [Memoirs of Chuanying Tower], 240. While Bao seemingly advocates liberation of women in China, Chen Hong-Shu in her PhD thesis points out that Bao's philosophy carried the baggage of traditional Confucian ideas on women's chastity and status. See Chen, "Translation and Manipulation," 2010.

46. See Bao, *Memoirs of Chuanying Tower*, 104.

first thing is to have economic conditions. Without money how can we set it up? I should discuss this with my elder brother.

The quest for equality of the sexes is underlined by her maid's quibble about the need to change to men's costumes in her disguise as the lawyer, "我不曉得以前，是那一個作俑，分別了男女的衣服，害得鮑姑娘東借衣服，西借帽子，比了演莎士比的詩更忙呢。 [I don't know in the past who initiated this idea—making a distinction between men's and women's clothes, giving me the trouble to borrow clothes and hat elsewhere.]" What underlies this comment is not only the resentment over the distinction of clothes, but also the need to disguise in a man's cloak in order to exert influence in the public domain.[47] In terms of characterization, Portia became the younger sister of Bassanio, rather than his lover. Setting up a girls' school became the main reason for asking Antonio's help in borrowing from Shylock. It was also Portia's idea to suggest Bassanio in asking Antonio for help, who was described by Portia as "very helpful (很熱心)."

Throughout the script, there is no mention of Christianity and Christian identities. Shylock's Jewish identity is maintained and he is addressed as a Jew in dialogues. Shylock is depicted as the money-sucking foreign other who is a tycoon in Venice but is hated by the Briton who treats the Jews as a dog and describes the Jews as people from a fallen nation.

> 洛克:可恨那英國人，待我猶太人，如同狗一般輕賤。又說我們是亡國之民。可知猶太人眼中，只知道有錢，卻並不知道有甚麼國。[48]

Back Translation:

Shylock said, "That Englishman treated us Jews as unworthy dogs, and said that we are people of a fallen nation. However, in Jew's eyes, we care only about money, but won't care about our nationality.

Clearly, the description of Israel as a fallen nation and Shylock's lack of national identity is in contrast with the strong Jewish identity embodied in Shakespeare's or Lamb's text. On the other hand, Bao's description of the Jew reinforces the image of the wandering Jew common in literature.[49] It is obvious that the above speech by Shylock is adapted from the "Hath not a Jew eyes" speech. What was originally the Judeo-Christian conflict was adapted

---

47. For a detailed feminist interpretation of Lin Shu's and BaoTianxiao's translation, see Luo, "The Construction of Translation Literature," 105–132.

48. See Bao, *Memoirs of Chuanying Tower*, 105.

49. See Malcolm and Malcolm, "(Re) Locating The Jew," 154.

to conflicts between Briton and the Jews. In other words, an equivalence was drawn between the Christians and Britons. Under this characterization, Shylock was reduced to a materialistic figure, whose materialism was further reinforced by dismissing the idea of establishing a school as stupid, saying, "Who on earth will borrow money for the sake of setting up schools? If I have the money, why not use it for myself instead of building a school? There is such a fool on earth. (世界上有借了錢辦學堂的理麼？我有了錢，不會自己用，拿來辦學堂？世界上有這種笨人。)"

This is then followed by Antonio's criticism of the Jews as "without a nation":

你們猶太人，是沒有國家的，那裏懂得，人家為了辦學堂，把性命都不要的，也有列。

Back Translation:

You Jews have no nation, how will you understand that someone has sacrificed her life in order to establish a school.

Antonio, on one hand, was despising the Jew's rootlessness, while on the other hand he (who is English in this story) was commending the martyr spirit of a Chinese female principal Hui Xing who swore to commit suicide if the school closed down. She did fulfil her promise in December 1905 when the school stopped operating due to lack of funding.[50] This racial conflict is exemplified not only between Antonio and Shylock, but also demonstrated in Bassanio's hatred towards Shylock. Bassanio sees Shylock as an Other upon hearing that Antonio is taken to jail when he could not pay the debts on time, "猶太人可惡，猶太人可惡，到底非我族類，其心必異" (trans. The Jew is resentful, the Jews is resentful! He who does not belong to our ethnic group, his heart is different [from ours]). The anti-foreign sentiment displayed among Antonio, Bassanio and Shylock mirrored the anti-foreign sentiment existing throughout Chinese history which predates the time of Bao's writing.

The conditions for releasing Shylock, in the absence of conversion to Christianity as a requirement, became ten times the original loan, i.e. 10 thousand dollars, of which half was to be confiscated for the state, the other for setting up the school.

The defeated Shylock did not say "I am content," but became moralistic in tone, "tricks turned foul, gold turned iron. The rich people here . . . do not follow me Shylock."

---

50. See Luo, "The Construction of Translation Literature," 118.

Translation as a form of re-writing is a typical translation approach in the early twentieth century where fidelity to the source text is not considered the most important criterion in translation. Rather, translation is being used as a vehicle to introduce ideas from the West in order to enrich Chinese culture. The types of genres in literature were broadened as a result, including political novels, educational novels, science fictions and detective stories which had hitherto been unknown. On the other hand, in order to facilitate reception among Chinese readers, domestication strategy is employed from time to time. Place names and people's names are often "sinicized." Lawrence Wong[51] opined that owing to the lack of knowledge regarding the West among readers, the translator often could not bridge the gap between the two cultures even when the translator could fully comprehend the meaning of the source text. In addition, Chinese readers might still be resistant towards certain elements in the Western culture owing to their long-standing history.

In the past, translators in the late Qing dynasty period, i.e. late nineteenth century to early twentieth century are often accused of being unfaithful to the source text and making 'mistakes' owing to their ignorance of Western languages and cultures. Rather than making mistakes, the translators are manipulating reader responses, and in Lefevere's terms, their work should be "studied in conjunction with other forms of rewriting, and not on its own."[52] In fact, Lefevere further reminds us that such displacement of religious discourse in Chinese culture may be related to the homogeneity and the ethno-centricity of the Chinese culture. He opines that the Chinese culture "tends to see their own way of doing things as 'naturally', the only way"; and when this culture takes over elements from outside, "they will, once again, naturalize them without too many qualms and too many restrictions. When Chinese translates texts produced by Others outside its boundaries, it translates these texts in order to replace them, pure and simple. The translations take the place of the originals."[53] As I will illustrate with more examples later in this chapter, such manipulation and domestication strategy in Chinese translations of Shakespeare continued

---

51. See Wong, *Re-interpreting Fidelity, Communicability and Elegance*, 222.

52. André Lefevere in "Why Waste Our Time on Rewrites," writes, "If the study of translation is to be made productive for the study of literary theory and, especially, can no longer be analysed in isolation, but that it should be studied as part of a whole system of texts and the people who produce, support, propagate, oppose, censor them. Or, to put it differently, translation can be studied in isolation only if it is reduced to one half of one of the constraints under which it is produced: that of the locutionary level of language." See Lefevere, "Why Waste Our Time on Rewrites," 237.

53. See Lefevere, "Chinese and Western Thinking on Translation," 14.

until the beginning of the twentieth century when the Chinese system that ensured the political and cultural dominance of the language collapsed.[54] Rather than a pure linguistic transfer, translations in this period are under a political "cloak"—infidelity is not the first and foremost criterion for translators, rather the test is whether such translations can serve the social function of reviving the country.[55]

As one looks to the history of reformist movement and vernacular movement behind the omission of religious language in the early twentieth century, translation scholars have so far neglected the dominant aesthetic theory in the same period that might have a bearing on the translation approach. CaiYuanpei蔡元培, the founding principal of Peking University 北京大學, delivered a momentous speech in 1917 on "Aesthetic Education as a Replacement of Religion" (*Yi meiyudaizongjiaoshuo* 以美育帶宗教說).[56] He claimed that religion was only followed in the West as a tradition, and drew an analogy between religion in the West on the one hand, and on the other the traditional long robes of the Qing Dynasty that were still worn by people merely as a form of tradition in the post-imperialist period. He stated, " . . . overseas students saw the progress in the west and hoped to teach fellow countrymen on the basis of Christianity, after being misled by missionaries who told them all (progress) is attributed to religion. " He further argued that "when aesthetic education is subsumed under religion, it would be adversely influenced by religion, thus lacking its function to cultivate, leading to a shift to stimulate emotions instead. This is because regardless of which religions, each aims at expanding its own religion and attacking other religions . . . "

However, one should not assume that the domestication of religious material into Chinese culture is a feature of all other authors in the early twentieth century. I will illustrate in the following section that the translation strategies of religious themes are largely dependent on the individual translator's social situation, theology and hermeneutics, which interact with the prevalent social ideology during the relevant period.

---

54. Ibid,17.

55. See Meng and Li, *The Literary History of Chinese Translations*, 54.

56. The speech was delivered on 8 April 1917 in Beijing. Included in Cai , *Collection of Cai*, 30–35.

Laura White and Her Translation of
The Merchant of Venice (1914)

While Lin is the first known translator[57] of *Tales from Shakespeare*, Laura White produced the most complete translation of *The Merchant* in the early twentieth century.[58] An American missionary sent to China during the volunteer missionary movement in the late nineteenth century, she swiftly established, upon arriving to China, Huiwen Girls' University 匯文女子學堂 in Nanking in 1887, which saw rapid missionary growth.[59] Between 1890 and 1905, the number of American missionaries more than doubled, and by 1919 it had grown to 3,300.[60] Laura White's talent was appreciated by Welsh-born Baptist missionary Timothy Richard, who invited her to be the chief editor of *Nu Duo* 女鐸, the then first women's Christian magazine in China whose target audience were mainly Christians and women. Like Lin, who had to rely on local assistants in the comprehension of foreign texts, a number of Laura White's literary translation works were assisted by Chinese translators. These include *As the Twig is Bent* (1901), *Little Lord Fauntleroy* (1902), *Silas Marner* (1913–1914), *Sara Crewe* (1914), *Mrs Wiggs of Cabbage Patch* (1924), amongst others.[61] Some of these local assistants were her students. Though no assistance from local translators was indicated in the magazine regarding the translation of *The Merchant*, only her transliterated name Liang Leyue (亮樂月) appeared in print,[62] it is reasonable to assume that she translated the text with some help from local assistants. Her translation of *The Merchant* was published in series from 1914 to 1915 in *Nu Duo* under the title *The Story of Shedding Meat* (*Wan Rou Ji* 剜肉記). The translated script was later performed by her students at a graduation ceremony.

---

57. An anonymous translation of *Tales from Shakespeare* was published in 1904, one year before Lin's translation was published.

58. One third of the original play text was cut, according to Zhu Jing. See Zhu, *New Discoveries of Chinese Translation of Merchant of Venice*, 50–54.

59. The early part of the twentieth century saw rapid development of church activities in China through urban missions and in particular the establishment of mission schools. 66 percent of missionaries resided in big cities with over 50,000 population. In the 9 years from 1906 to 1915, the number of students in mission schools grew from 57,683 to 172,979. See Yang, *Christianity and Modern China*, 1994.

60. Such rapid growth demonstrated a late nineteenth-century American expansion. See Hunter, *The Gospel of Gentility*, 1984.

61. Song, *A Study on Chinese Fictions by Missionaries*, 179–189.

62. In other translations of Shakespearean plays published in *Nu Duo*, the translators were local Chinese.

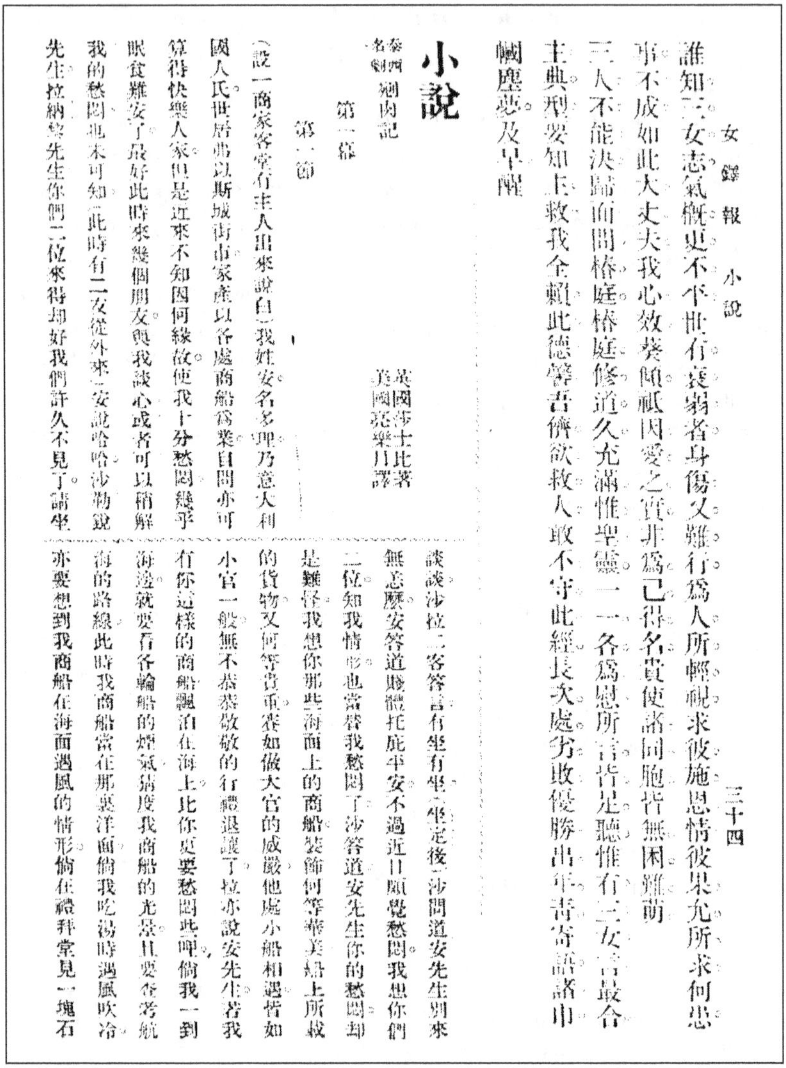

女鐸報 小說 三十四

誰知二女志氣慨更不平世有衰弱者身傷又難行爲人所輕視求彼施恩情彼果允所求何患
事不成如此大丈夫我心效葵傾祇因愛之實非爲己得名實使諸同胞皆無困難
三人不能決歸面問椿庭椿庭修道久充滿惟聖靈一一各爲思所言皆是聽惟有二女言最合
主典刑要知主救我全賴此德籍吾儕欲救人敢不守此經長大處劣敗優勝出年青寄語諸巾
幗塵夢及早醒

小說

泰西名劇 剜肉記

英國莎士比著 美國亮樂月譯

第一幕

第一節

(設一商家客堂有主人出來說白)我姓安名多理乃意大利
國人氏世居曲以斯城街市家產以各處商船爲業自問亦可
算得快樂人家但是近來不知因何緣故使我十分愁悶幾乎
眠食難安了最好此時來幾個朋友與我談心或者可以稍解
我的愁悶也未可知(此時有二友從外來)安說哈哈沙勒說
先生拉納客先生你們二位來得却好我們許久不見了請坐
談談(沙拉二客答言有坐有坐)(坐定後)沙問道安先生別來
無恙麼安答道賤體托庇平安不過近日頗覺愁悶我想你們
二位知我情形也當替我愁悶了沙答道安先生你的愁悶却
是難怪我想你那些海面上的商船裝飾何等華美船上所載
的貨物又何等貴重好如做大官的威嚴他處小船相遇皆如
小官一般無不恭恭敬敬的行禮退讓了拉亦說安先生若我
有你這樣的商船飄泊在海上比你更要愁悶些呢倘我一到
海邊就要看各輪船的煙氣猜度我商船的光景且要查考航
海的路線此時我商船當在那裏洋面倘我吃湯時遇風吹冷
亦要想到我商船在海面遇風的情形倘在禮拜堂見一塊石

Figure 2.1 *Nu Duo* 女鐸, the Christian magazine for women that published the first full translation of *The Merchant of Venice* by missionary Laura White. (Source: Zhejiang Library, China)

Domesticating or Foreignizing?

Laura White's translation is grounded in a different hermeneutic, ideology and literary style from Lin's. Upon close scrutiny of her translation, Laura

White's translation is not always domesticating or foreignizing. What is domesticated is the relationship between Antonio and Bassanio, which became uncle and nephew, serving to rationalize the sacrifice that is more common among family members than among non-family members in a traditional Chinese context. In terms of style, the foreignness of the play was emphasized, as the play is described as *tai xi* 泰西 (Western) famous drama, and the origin of the author and translator was printed—"written by English Shakespeare, translated by American Laura White." She kept the Western narrative structure of a script such as acts and scenes. All mention of Christian identity of major characters is retained, as opposed to Lin's reduction strategy. But in introducing a foreign concept or a biblical allusion, her strategy is not always foreignizing. For example, when Portia's intelligence is equated with that of the biblical prophet Daniel on three occasions, White would explicate it as "a clever and brave lawyer," without mentioning the name Daniel. This is in contrast to Lin's explication strategy, where the name Daniel is transliterated.

But in contrast with Lin's reduction, Portia's "mercy" speech is rendered fully in White's adaptation, if not expanded, as the following comparison shows.

Table 2.1 Comparison between Source Text and Laura White's Translation

Source Text	White's translation (my translation into English. JW)
Portia Then must the Jew be merciful.	**Portia** Then Shylock must be merciful.
Shylock On what compulsion must I? Tell me that.	**Shylock** Why must I be merciful? Tell me that.

Source Text	White's translation (my translation into English. JW)
Portia The quality of mercy is not strain'd, It droppeth as the gentle rain from heaven Upon the place beneath: it is twice blest; It blesseth him that gives and him that takes: 'Tis mightiest in the mightiest: it becomes The throned monarch better than his crown; His sceptre shows the force of temporal power, The attribute to awe and majesty, Wherein doth sit the dread and fear of kings; But mercy is above this sceptred sway; It is enthroned in the hearts of kings, It is an attribute to God himself; And earthly power doth then show likest God's *When mercy seasons justice. Therefore, Jew,* *Though justice be thy plea, consider this,* *That, in the course of justice, none of us* *Should see salvation: we do pray for mercy;* *And that same prayer doth teach us all to render* *The deeds of mercy.*(my emphasis) I have spoke thus much To mitigate the justice of thy plea; Which if thou follow, this strict court of Venice Must needs give sentence 'gainst the merchant there. (Lamb, 1807, p.151)	**Portia** No one can force the exercise of mercy, because mercy cannot be forced, just like gentle rain from heaven drop by drop it is out of nature, and is everywhere. Those who gives and those who takes receives benefits. it seems peaceful and yet it represents mightiest in the mightiest; If a king shows his mercy. This is more dignified than his crown; His crown shows only the force of temporal power, which leaves people in awe; But mercy saves the world from crisis; what binds people's passion;while power is man-made; Mercy is given by God; Power of the monarch is like God's power. *If mercy is used in justice, lenience restrains fierceness* *fierceness restrains lenience,* *as such it is not difficult to rule the world.* *you said one needs to rule by justice, one needs to know the world,* *if we rule everything by justice,* *no one can live.* *We pray day by day so as to receive God's mercy,* *so that God can induce our sense of mercy.* (my emphasis) I am speaking these words in order to induce your sense of mercy, but your heart is as hard as steel which cannot be induced.[63]

63. The Chinese translation of Portia's mercy speech by Laura White reads as follows:

世上無人可以勉強發慈悲，因為慈悲不能勉強的，如同細雨一點一點從天降下，出於自然。無處不到。這個慈悲施的受的兩方面都有益處，看似和平，卻是強中之強。一個國王倘能顯他的慈悲，比戴他冠冕還堂皇些，因為冠冕不過表明世上的權力使人懼怕。慈悲乃拯救世上的危難。結人感情，權力是人為的。慈悲是神賜的。國王的權如同上帝的權。若是能用慈悲在律法之中，寬以

The italicized sentences show where the explication takes place. It is intriguing to note that while White reduced one-third of the play script, the "mercy speech" is not in any degree reduced, rather elaborated. This is achieved through the use of rhetorical devices such as contrast and parallelism "If mercy is used in justice, *lenience restrains fierceness, fierceness restrains lenience*" (寬以濟猛,猛以濟寬), emphasis on prayer ("We pray day by day" 我們天天禱告) and repetition of God ("so as to receive *God's mercy*, so that *God* can induce our sense of mercy" 要得上帝的大慈悲, 亦無非要上帝激動我們共發慈悲的心). The emphasis on "mercy over justice" is achieved by the above rhetorical devices in accordance with Nevill Coghill's interpretation of the play in the Christian dimension—an allegory of justice and mercy, of the Old Testament and the New Testament. The theology of "mercy over justice" is expanded from one clause to three clauses. The concept of salvation, which refers to the "deliverance from the consequences of sin and admission into the joys of heaven,"[64] is not rendered directly, but domesticated into a non-Christian term "live" (活). "Mercy" is translated into "慈悲 ci bei" ten times throughout Portia's speech, a term derived from Buddhist texts and particularly associated with *The Great Compassion Mantra* (觀音大悲咒) but widely adopted in secular text. "慈悲 ci bei" is a polysyllabic word where "慈 ci" means the provision of happiness out of the Buddha's love of all living things, and "*bei* 悲" can be translated as the rescue of human beings from disaster. The Buddhist gods who advocate non-violence are known to show these qualities to all living beings. The frequent occurrence of this Buddhist term can be compared to Robert Morrison's Bible translation, where the term "mercy" has several translations: "*aijin* 哀矜"(sympathy)," *ailian* 哀憐" (sympathy), "*en ci* 恩慈" (grace), "*ren ci* 仁慈" (kindness), along with the more common term "*ci bei* 慈悲."[65] It is clear that White preferred to domesticate the Christian term into a Buddhist-turned-secular term to ensure wider acceptance among the public.

But the biggest difference between Lin's and White's adaptations lies in the final judgment of Shylock—not only did White retain the "forced conversion" of Shylock in the final verdict, she added a reason for the

---

濟猛,猛以濟寬,如此治天下就不難了。你說要按律行事,要知天下事,倘件件按律,恐沒有一個能活了。我們天天禱告無非亦要得上帝的大慈悲,亦無非要上帝激動我們共發慈悲的心。我現在講這話,也就是要激動你的慈悲心。

See White, "The Story of Shredding Meat," 5.

64. See Hassel, *Shakespeare's Religious Language,* 301.

65. To see how the word mercy is being translated into Chinese in the Chinese Bible in the 19th century, see Robert Morrison's translation of the New Testament in *Yesu jilishidu wo zhu jiu zhe xin yi zhao shu.* [Bible. New Testament] China, 1813.

conversion *"he should become a Christian to reduce his cruelty"* (要他做一基督徒以便改變他殘暴的惡性). In this translation, Christian salvation is interpreted in a moralizing or ethicizing Confucian framework, which has been the main orientation of Chinese Christianity.[66]

White's domestication strategy of the Christian term "salvation," and her explication strategy in suggesting that conversion to Christianity would reduce the cruelty of the Jew, should not be treated as coincidental. In combination, they effectively placed the emphasis on the present worldview. Salvation of the soul was not mentioned in her translation, as this was not in line with the Chinese pragmatic view with regard to issues of life and death. A well-known Confucius saying goes, "Before we know about life how can we know death 未知生,焉知死"? (Confucius Analects Book IX, Chap.XI). The adoption of a Confucian frame of reference in explicating Christian concepts is a common strategy among missionaries in China. In Ralph R. Covell's *Confucius, The Buddha, and Christ* (1986), he shows that many early Protestant writings quoted the above Confucian question as a way to introduce God's revelation in the Bible about the life to come.[67]

Conclusions for Early Twentieth Century Translations of Shakespeare's Religious Discourse

As Martha Cheung points out, omissions and changes reveal as much as they conceal.[68] I offer the following reasons for Lin's appropriation of Shakespeare's tale. First, forced religious conversion is a notion foreign to the Chinese culture, deeply influenced by Taoism and Confucianism, which emphasize social harmony and order. Buddhism, a major religion in China, relies on a system of rewards and punishments that is established by karma, or cause-effect relationship.[69] Secondly, concern for reception by readers may likely have constrained his rendition according to what was socially acceptable. In another of Lin's translations, *Uncle Tom's Cabin,* a novel that contains a number of religious references, he asked for understanding in the translator's preface from a putative "enlightened and educated" audience for his rendering of religious material. This he obviously did to disclaim being "won over by teachings of Christianity."[70] Another reason relates to the degree of

66. See Yang, "Ethicized Chinese-Language Christianity," 68–84.
67. See Covell, *Confucius, The Buddha, and Christ,* 94-96 for a discussion of the Confucian frame of reference in missionary writings in China.
68. Cheung, "The Discourse of Occidentalism," 131.
69. Robertson, *The Sociological Interpretation of Religion,* 87.
70. Cheung, "The Discourse of Occidentalism," 140.

religious freedom that existed under the pressure of the Confucian-oriented regime. In the aftermath of the First Opium War between China and Britain, foreign missionaries, under the Treaties of Tianjin and the Sino-French Convention of Beijing, were permitted to live, own property and preach in the interior of China. Lin's translation was situated in a period where Christianity was protected under the Treaties, which gradually changed to increased hostility towards churches by Confucianists. They sabotaged the reputation of Christians, attacked churches, and considered religions other than Confucianism as evil. These Confucianists suggested that Christians should be registered and their apartments and garments be labeled. Officials also risked losing their officer titles if they converted to Christianity.[71] In 1905, Huang Zicai 黃梓材 wrote that officials and learners needed to worship at temples whether they were at work or at school. The government did not allow religious freedom, and churches and missionaries were often attacked.[72] Under such political pressure, it is not impossible that self-censorship took place, as rendering Western religious thoughts might have been a sensitive issue that might have provoked disquiet among audiences[73] Highlighting in his translation of *The Merchant of Venice* the exoticism, i.e. the demand for a pound of human flesh, a female lawyer, the suspense in the court, rather than the religious dimension of the story, could ensure a favorable reception of Shakespeare among the target audience. Stage performance in this period (1913-1929), based on such appropriation of foreign plays is known as *wenmingxi* 文明戲, which is a performance style that combines elements of Western spoken drama with traditional Chinese operas. Under this operative style, there is only a synopsis without the script. Most dialogues were by spelt out impromptu, except for a few lines specified. The director would gather the actors for a briefing of their sequence of staging and assign them suitable characters.[74]

71. See DeGroot, *Is there Religous Liberty in China?*, 148–150.

72. See Huang, *On the Separation of Church and State*, 14–15.

73. The treaties which remained in effect until 1943 prompted phenomenal growth of missionary enterprise well into the early 1950s. In the ten years between 1905 to 1915, the number of missionaries grew by 55 percent. On the other hand, the hostility towards Christianity increased, as was evident from the growth of anti-Christian pamphlets and tracts since the late nineteenth century, which finally culminated in the anti-Christian movement from 1922 to 1927. The meeting of the World Student Christian Federation in 1922 provided the occasion for the anti-Christian sentiment to materialize. An Anti-Christian Student Federation, founded in 1922, issued a manifesto denouncing an imperial alliance of Christianity and capitalism under American leadership. For more details, see Cohen, *China and Christianity*, 44–45; Hunter, *The Gospel of Gentility*, 1984.

74. See Wang, "The development of Shakespearean performances," 92.

Not only has Lin's re-writing succeeded in appealing to the masses, but his adaptation strategies with regard to Christian references have left an impact on the staging of *The Merchant*. From the 1910s to the 1980s, there were no Christian references in most of the stage performances of *The Merchant*. Bao Tianxiao, a popular novelist, published *Women's Lawyer* in 1911, an adaptation of *The Merchant*, which edited out the Christian references in the play, while the Jewish identity of Shylock was maintained. In 1914, *Rou Quan*, another adaptation based on Lin's translation that was staged in Shanghai, followed Lin's treatment of religious materials by omitting the Christian references while retaining Shylock's Jewishness. The after-life of the de-christianized translation of Lin Shu [*Rou Quan*] cannot be overstated. Well-known director such as Cao Yu and writer Guo Moruo had been profoundly inspired by this widely popular series of Shakespeare tales.[75] A parallel of such omission can be found in Zhang Qihong 張奇虹's production during which she attributed her deletions in the 1980 production to the search for conformity with the tastes of the local audience, as "the conflicts between Christianity and Judaism that took place hundreds years back, as well as the racial conflicts, are relatively remote for the Chinese audience."[76]

Bao Tianxiao's feminist approach in changing the plot and hence the translation is yet another manifestation of translation as re-writing and manipulation in the early twentieth century. André Lefevere in his first full presentation of his theory in "Why Waste Our Time on Rewrites," states that

> If the study of translation is to be made productive for the study of literary theory and especially, it can no longer be analysed in isolation, but that it should be studied as part of a whole system of texts and the people who produce, support, propagate, oppose, censor them. Or, to put it differently, translation can be studied in isolation only if it is reduced to one half of one of the constraints under which it is produced: that of the locutionary level of language.[77]

---

75. Cao Yu said, "One of my favorite playwrights is Shakespeare, and my fondness of Shakespeare started from reading Lin Shu's *Tales* when I was a little boy. As soon as I was able to read the original English, I was eager to get hold of a Shakespeare play, because Lin's translation of Shakespeare's fantasy world was so fresh in my young mind."Guo Moruo wrote: "I was unconsciously influenced by this book [Tales]. I read *The Tempest, Hamlet* and *Romeo and Juliet* in the original when I grew up, but it seemed to me that Lin's way of telling these stories as fairy tales was more appealing," quotations from See Li, 16–17.

76. Zhang, "Some Points in the Process of Implementation and Exploration," 280–287.

77. Lefevere, "Why Waste Our Time on Rewrites?, 237.

HISTORY OF EFFECTS 67

For Lefevere, the two constraints within the literary system that determines the image of a work of literature are ideology and poetics; patronage, on the other hand, is a control factor external to the system. Ideology had been defined as the "world view," of a certain society at a certain moment. Poetics is the dominant concept of what literature should be.[78] Patronage, which exerts influence outside of the system, represents "the powers (persons, institutions) which can further or hinder the reading, writing and rewriting of literature."[79] It represented individuals, groups, institutions, a social class, a political party, publishers, the media etc. [80] These are a regulatory body whose job is to maintain the literary system's ideology and poetics. Bao's advocacy for female education, under the patronage of the women's college *Cheng Dong NvXue* 城東女學 that funded the publication of the magazine *Female Student (nu xue sheng)*, gave rise to a re-creation of the narrative that highlighted the importance of women's education. Additionally, the change of characterization where Portia and Bassanio became sister and brother, and the change of reason for Bassanio's loan application, i.e. to help build a girls' school rather than to court Portia, may be the result of patronage control. In traditional middle schools in China, it is not uncommon to see the prohibition of developing relationships among students at a young age—a form of control which might be reflected in the move to delete the plot on courtship.

The negative depiction of Jews and Englishmen in the narrative suggest an inferior Other, where Jews had no sense of their nation, and were despised by Englishmen as people without a nation. Using Englishmen to stand in for Christians suggests that Chinese view Christians as Other, which goes hand in hand with their view of English imperialism.[81]

As for Laura White's translation, her approach is uniquely different from the predominant trend, where suppression of the Christian dimension was current among translators and publishers. Not only did she retain the theme of Judeo-Christian conflict, but also explicated the forced conversion by providing a reason for it—to soften Shylock's cruelty. All mentions of the Christian identity of major characters were retained. When one considers this treatment under Lefevere's notion of ideology and patronage, the target readers of the women's Christian magazine where White´s translation was

78. Ibid, 226–227.
79. Lefevere, *Translation, Rewriting and the Manipulation of Literary*, 15.
80. Hermans, *Translation in Systems*, 126.
81. In the aftermath of the First Opium War between China and Britain, foreign missionaries, under the Treaties of Tianjin and the Sino-French Convention of Beijing, were permitted to live, own property and preach in the interior of China, which further reinforced the image of Christians being connected with imperialistic power.

published, were mostly female Christians. The magazine was under the leadership of Timothy Richard, General Secretary of the Society of Diffusion of Christian and General Knowledge 廣學會 (later renamed as The Christian Literature Society for China). This provides an additional clue to the retention of religious references—her patrons were likely to support her strategies of insinuating Christian theology in her works. Her translation of "forced conversion" is by far the only Chinese translation that supplemented the reason for a conversion—to reduce the cruelty of Shylock. Explication could reduce the fear of an audience, who at that time mostly regarded Christianity as a hegemonic enterprise, associated with force and weapons. Such translation is at the same time a form of domestication. A Christian interpretation of this line suggests mercy to Shylock, because conversion would mean saving his soul. White domesticated the line to conform with the Chinese pragmatic worldview, where the present world has a higher status than the afterlife. White's approach might be influenced or directed by Timothy Richard's "practical" theology. Lauren Pfister[82] describes him as a "practical man driven by detailed plans and visions for the total renovation of the Chinese people under a broad vision of the Kingdom of God in Christ," with a "practical theology of missions." Among his writings which seek to educate the Chinese on the advantages of Christianity, he published a collection of essays under the title "Historical Evidences of Christianity for China" with a strong emphasis on the practical benefits that Christianity brings- these benefits include social benefits, intellectual benefits, political benefits, moral benefits, spiritual benefits and the present benefits offered to the imperial Qing empire. White's mixed translation approach in explicating, retaining and at the same time domesticating Christian references mirrored a controversial political environment in the Early Republican era that is both conducive and prohibitive to the spread of Christian message. The overthrowing of the Qing Dynasty by a Christian leader Sun Yatsen 孫中山 brought hope to church leaders and missionaries in China, as religious freedom was specified in the constitution of the provisional government in 1912—the first time that religious freedom was guaranteed in the history of China. But constitutional support for Christian work met with resistance from Confucian reformers who campaigned for the establishment of Confucianism as a state religion. The Confucian movement developed in direct competition with the movement for religious freedom. The Confucian movement supporters involved *literati* such as Liang Qichao and Yan Fu, who were contemporaries of Lin Shu. While tension existed between the Christian groups and Confucian

---

82. Pfister, *Re-thinking mission in China*, 1–45.

reformers, the missionary enterprise in the early Republican era enjoyed a more popular reception than before.[83]

Lin Shu and his collaborator Wei Yi, Bao Tianxiao, as well as Laura White, who worked in the period of the late Qing dynasty and early Republican era, represent different hermeneutic approaches which are uniquely reflected in their works. Lin Shu's domesticating approach in the reduction of religious material and in shaping reader response in the translator's preface in *YinbianYanyu* succeeded in popularizing Shakespeare by highlighting the common ground of the Chinese and Western cultures. Religious conflict or Christian concepts that were too alien or sensitive to the target audience were downplayed while highlighting the fantasy and romance. On one hand these themes are familiar to the audience, and on the other hand, highlighting such themes serves his implicit agenda to revive the spiritual traditions of China. As a Confucianist, Lin Shu might concur with his contemporaries that Christian thoughts conflict and/or compete with Confucian values. Ancestor worship is one area where Chinese see Christianity as competing with their Confucian traditions of filial piety, because even up to today, ancestor worship is seen by Protestant churches as equivalent to idol worship and is not accepted by some Protestant churches. Accordingly, to convert is to tear up one's roots, to run the risk of being seen as unfilial, and is therefore an obstacle to evangelization.[84] By using Shakespeare as a way to reassert Confucian thoughts, as textual analysis of his *Tales from Shakespeare* show,[85] the highlighting of these Confucian values inevitably implies suppression of the Christian references. By translating it into elegant Chinese that was meant mainly for the elite, his representation of Shakespearean plays influenced many literary scholars and reformers. Yet, retention of the cultural Other, i.e. Shylock the Jew, Antonio the Roman, the Western chapter headings, serve to preserve an exotic flavour in Shakespeare's tales, which facilitated its reception among Chinese who thirsted for Western knowledge amid the large-scale importation of Western ideologies in the early twentieth-century China. Lin Shu's translation not only constructed representations of English culture and shaped domestic attitudes towards the Western world, but simultaneously constructed a cultural identity in the target audience, and argued for the value of traditional Chinese literature. As Lawrence Venuti puts it: "As translation constructs a domestic representation for a foreign text and culture, it simultaneously constructs a domestic subject, a position of intel-

---

83. For an overview of the degree of religious freedom between 1900 and 1917, see Liu, "Religious Freedom," 247–270.

84. See Ying and Leung, *Chinese Ancestor Worship*, 85.

85. See Tsui, "Rewriting Shakespeare," 41–48.

ligibility that is also an ideological position, shaped by the codes and canons, interests and agendas of certain domestic social groups."[86]

For White, propagation of Christian literature and education was a missionary's primary concern. While her translation represents an abridged version of *The Merchant*, she elaborated aspects of Christian theology through rhetorical devices, such as parallelism ("if mercy is used in justice, *lenience restrains fierceness, fierceness restrains lenience*") and explication ("We pray day by day so as to receive *God's mercy*, so that *God* can induce our sense of mercy," "he should become a Christian to *reduce his cruelty*").

The above examples show that cultural translations of religious discourse in China does not represent a domestication/ foreignization dichotomy, nor is it a singular, one-way process. More often, it is a combination of both strategies, dependent on the strength of the forces of the dominant and dominated cultures. Lawrence Venuti argues that books translated into English follows the values of the target culture, domesticating the text and rendering the translator "invisible," while texts produced in the colonial culture serve to reinforce the ideology embedded in the colony.[87] In the above examples, Chinese is the dominant culture while Christian concepts represent the foreign Other. Instead of a total domestication in Lin's translation, a certain degree of foreignness is still retained. Similarly, in White's translation, the introduction of Christian Other follows both domestication and foreignization strategies, rather than a total foreignization to retain and revive all Christian terms and content, because its purpose is not to preserve the cultural differences between Chinese and Christian values which lead to texts that are "strange and estranging," [88] but to propagate Christian beliefs to the mass. A fluent translation strategy can serve this purpose as it "performs a labour of acculturation which domesticates the foreign text, making it intelligible and even familiar to the target language reader, providing him or her with the narcissistic experience of recognizing his or her own culture in a culture other [. . .], fluency leads to translations that are eminently readable and therefore consumable on the book market [. . .]"[89] In fact, White's domestication/fluent strategy reminds one of Eugene Nida's notion of dynamic equivalence. Eugene Nida states that, "A translation of dynamic equivalence aims at complete naturalness of expression and tries to relate the receptor to modes of behaviour relevant within the context of his own

---

86. Venuti, *The Translator's Invisibility*, 10.
87. Venuti, "Translation as Cultural Politics," 208–23.
88. Venuti, *Rethinking Translation*, 13.
89. Ibid, 5.

culture."⁹⁰ Laura White's translation strategy is an embodiment of Nida's philosophy as both seek to find ways to communicate the Christian message from an evangelical point of view. In fact, Nida's translation theory is developed from his observation and consultancy work among the community of Bible translators. His notion of dynamic equivalence is attached to an evangelical zeal and has had an important influence among Bible translators and missionaries. In *Customs and Cultures: Anthropology for Christian Missions*, he states that a close examination of successful missionary work inevitably reveals the correspondingly effective manner in which the missionaries are able to identify themselves with the people—"to be all things to all men"—and to communicate their message in terms which have meaning for the lives of the people.⁹¹

In *God's Word in Man's Language*, he states that "The task of the true translator is one of identification. As a Christian servant he must identify himself with Christ; as a translator he must identify himself with the Word; as a missionary he must identify himself with the people."⁹² Well before Nida's concept of dynamic equivalence had been proposed, Laura White knew how to identify with the Chinese audience through the domestication of certain Christian concepts, while at the same time retaining the Christian vocabulary inherent in the play.

Translation strategies in the early twentieth century are thus not limited to manipulation and re-writing strategies as described by most Chinese translation scholars. Nor is the issue about a binary position proposed by Western translation theorists as regards the opposition between Venuti's foreignization and domestication—between translating the letter or the spirit—or between Nida's formal equivalence and dynamic equivalence. What characterizes the translations of *The Merchant* at this stage relates to the prevalent socio-cultural conditions and the hermeneutics and motivation of an individual translator that shapes his or her translation. It is worth noting that, despite the suppression of the Christian dimension seen in Shakespearean works and other literary works in that period, Laura White's approach to retaining the religious language reminds one of how an individual writer's religious faith and theology may not be subsumed under the predominant societal ideology. The translatability of religious language in a secular work is thereby not easily predetermined or predicted by the socio-cultural and political forces, as is suggested by the manipulation school. One's theology can be a powerful dissident voice

---

90. Nida, *Toward a Science of Translating*, 159.
91. Nida, *Customs and Cultures*, 250.
92. Nida, *God's World in Man's Language*, 117.

that counteracts the predominant trend, which still rings true in the literary scene and theatre circles today, as my case studies in contemporary China will later show.

Table 2.2 Comparison between Shakespeare's Play Text and Charles Lamb's *Tales from Shakesepare*

Shakespeare's play text	Charles Lamb's *Tales from Shakespeare*
No mention	Shylock, the Jew, lived at Venice. He was a usurer who had amassed an immense fortune by lending money at great interest to **Christian*** merchants.
Act 1 Scene 3	
SHYLOCK [Aside] How like a fawning publican he looks! I hate him for he is a **Christian**, he hates our Jewish nation; he lends out money gratis; and among the merchants he rails at me and my well-earned bargains, which he calls interest. Cursed be my tribe if I forgive him!"	He hates our Jewish nation; he lends out money gratis; and among the merchants he rails at me and my well-earned bargains, which he calls interest. Cursed be my tribe if I forgive him!"
SHYLOCK O father Abram, what these **Christians** are,	Shylock, hearing this debate, exclaimed: "O Father Abraham, what suspicious people these **Christians** are!
ANTONIA The Hebrew will turn **Christian**: he grows kind.	Omitted
Act 2 Scene 3	
LAUNCELOT Adieu! tears exhibit my tongue. Most beautiful pagan, most sweet Jew! if a **Christian** did not play the knave and get thee, I am much deceived. But, adieu: these foolish drops do something drown my manly spirit: adieu.	Omitted
JESSICA If thou keep promise, I shall end this strife, Become a **Christian** and thy loving wife.	Omitted
Act 2 Scene 4	

Shakespeare's play text	Charles Lamb's *Tales from Shakespeare*
LAUNCELOT Marry, sir, to bid my old master the Jew to sup to-night with my new master the **Christian**.	Omitted

Act 3 Scene 1

SHYLOCK There I have another bad match: a bankrupt, a prodigal, who dare scarce show his head on the Rialto; a beggar, that was used to come so smug upon the mart; let him look to his bond: he was wont to call me usurer; let him look to his bond: he was wont to lend money for a **Christian** courtesy;	Omitted
SHYLOCK hath not a Jew hands, organs, dimensions, senses, affections, passions? fed with the same food, hurt with the same weapons, subject to the same diseases, healed by the same means, warmed and cooled by the same winter and summer, as a **Christian** is? If you prick us, do we not bleed? if you tickle us, do we not laugh? if you poison us, do we not die? and if you wrong us, shall we not revenge? If we are like you in the rest, we will resemble you in that. If a Jew wrong a **Christian**, what is his humility? Revenge. If a **Christian** wrong a Jew, what should his sufferance be by **Christian** example? Why, revenge. The villany you teach me, I will execute, and it shall go hard but I will better the instruction.	Omitted

Act 3 Scene 3

SHYLOCK To **Christian** intercessors. Follow not; I'll have no speaking: I will have my bond.	Omitted

Act 3 Scene 5

JESSICA I shall be saved by my husband; he hath made me a **Christian**.	Omitted

Shakespeare's play text	Charles Lamb's *Tales from Shakespeare*
LAUNCELOT Truly, the more to blame he: we were **Christians** enow before; e'en as many as could well live, one by another. This making **Christians** will raise the price of hogs: if we grow all to be pork-eaters, we shall not shortly have a rasher on the coals for money.	Omitted

Act 4 Scene 1

SHYLOCK These be the **Christian** husbands. I have a daughter; Would any of the stock of Barabbas had been her husband rather than a Christian!	Omitted
PORTIA One drop of **Christian** blood, thy lands and goods Are, by the laws of Venice, confiscate Unto the state of Venice.	' If in the cutting off the pound of flesh you shed one drop of **Christian** blood, your lands and goods are by the law to be confiscated to the state of Venice."
SHYLOCK I take this offer, then; pay the bond thrice And let the **Christian** go.	Omitted
DUKE That thou shalt see the difference of **our** spirit I pardon thee thy life before thou ask it: For half thy wealth, it is Antonio's, The other half comes to the general state, Which humbleness may drive unto a fine.	The duke then said to Shylock: "That you may see the difference of our **Christian*** spirit, I pardon you your life before you ask it. Half your wealth belongs to Antonio, the other half comes to the state."
ANTONIA So please my lord the duke, and all the court, To quit the fine for one half of his goods, I am content: so he will let me have The other half in use, to render it Upon his death unto the **gentleman** That lately stole his daughter Two things provided more, that, for this favor, He presently become a **Christian**;	for Antonio knew that the Jew had an only daughter who had lately married against his consent a young **Christian*** named Lorenzo, a friend of Antonio's, which had so offended Shylock that he disinherited her . . . "Get thee gone, then," said the duke, "and sign it; and if you repent your cruelty and turn **Christian**, the state will forgive you the fine of the other half of your riches."

*shows where the compensation takes place.

Translation and Translatability in the 1920s and Beyond

The 1920s and 1930s form an important phase in Chinese translation history in terms of translation output and theoretical discussions on translation.[93] In the literary scene, the appropriation approach was overtaken by the fidelity approach in this period, which in turn explains the translatability of the religious dimension in Shakespearean works as the textual analyses in a later section shows. China saw a renaissance of Shakespearean works, during which the most celebrated and ambitious Shakespearean translators, i.e. Liang Shiqiu 梁實秋 and Zhu Shenghao 朱生豪 came to the literary scene in this period, each translating between twenty and thirty Shakespearean works No understanding of the translatability issue will be complete without regard to the prevalent social-cultural conditions and translators' ideologies at that time, which will be illustrated with textual analyses of translated works from various well-known translators such as Gu Zhongyi 顧仲彝, Liang Shiqiu and Zhu Shenghao.

The Fidelity Turn of Chinese Shakespeare

Leo Chan Tak-hung describes this period as entering a phase of Chinese modernity. The early twentieth century China is often regarded as the first renaissance or first instance of "colonization"—colonization in the cultural sense. While Mainland China, unlike Taiwan and Hong Kong, has not been colonized, the term "colonization" is interpreted in a broader sense that transcends geographic locations. The concept of colonization is important in understanding the interest in embarking on full-scale translation of Shakespearean works by different scholars in this period. Hu Shi 胡適, a renowned literary scholar who encouraged Liang Shiqiu to translate Shakespeare, believed that Western literature was superior to Chinese literature and thus should be recognized as *the* standard.[94] In the Chinese literary vacuum, Western literature should be translated because it "constituted a serious inquiry into 'human nature' and that as such it would alleviate the nation's 'spiritual poverty' and remedy the people's 'human shortcomings'."[95] Not only did China face the threat of Western imperialism at that time, but also the imperialistic force of Japan, who laughed at the backwardness of China without having complete works of Shakespeare translated, as a later section shows. In Franz Fanon's term, China had entered the second

---

93. See Chan, *Twentieth Century Chinese Translation Theory*, 15.
94. Hu, "The Making of a Theory of Literary Revolution," 40–54.
95. Shen, "Thoughts about the past year and plans for the new," 219–220.

phase in countering colonization—a period of recovering the pre-colonial past to develop national culture. In the face of the threat of two colonizers, Shakespeare was, on the one hand, a colonizing tool to which Chinese scholars could look to mimic the literary standards set by Western colonizers, while on the other hand it became a self-empowering tool for Chinese nationalists in building up national identity.

Moreover, debates in this period focus on the following aspects: nature and function of translation in the "new" China, the translation approach of foreignization, the use of Europeanized structures and expressions and the criterion of fidelity.[96] This new phase came after the May Fourth Movement in 1919, an anti-feudal movement among the intellectuals based in Beijing, one that challenges Chinese tradition and Confucianist values. The movement grew out of the New Culture Movement (1917-1921) whereby liberal intellectuals such as Hu Shi, Chen Duxiu 陳獨秀, Zhou Zuoren 周作人, and Lu Xun 魯迅, as well as students, campaigned against the anti-democratic influence of Confucianism on Chinese society, a movement that stressed the importance of democracy and science.

The translation scene was heavily influenced by theories proposed by these intellectuals. One of the most influential is Lu Xun (1881-1936), who went to great lengths in arguing for word-for-word translation over sense-for-sense translation. His translation was termed "stiff translation," which was heavily criticized for making no sense of the Russian litterateur Lunacharsky by Lu Xun's opponents including Liang Shiqiu (1902-1987), a well-known Shakespeare translator. Liang reckoned that Lu Xun's translations were not only "stiff translations," but "dead translations." Chinese theatre moved away from the period of *wenmingxi* characterized by impromptu acting without scripts to a phase of realism (1930-1949).[97] According to Chen Xianmo who was cast as Bassanio in the 1930 performance of *The Merchant*, "We were very serious in studying the script. Actors must be familiar with the script. Only after some rehearsals can we go on stage." In the history of Chinese drama, the 1930 performance was considered as the first formal stage performance of Shakespeare. The stage, under a realism approach, made use of fountain, garden, balcony, bridge and streets to simulate an authentic Western drama. Actors donned Western costumes, according to Yu youyun, the lady who was cast as Portia.

The heightened awareness of fidelity (as against the free translation approach) gave rise to a new form of Shakespeare translation that came close to the original Shakespeare. Gu Zhongyi's translation of *The Merchant*

---

96. Ibid,16.
97. See Wang, "The development of Shakespearean Performances," 93-94.

staged by the Shanghai Drama Society in 1930 was advertised as "faithful and elegant, every line actable on the stage." The performance based on this text was advertised as a "complete Shakespearean production."[98] The search for a faithful translation in the translation discipline developed alongside the search for realism on the Chinese stage, an appetite for the "real" foreign country on the Chinese stage, which was dependent on both the scenography as well as on the "authenticity" of the performance text.[99] Such convergence was not coincidental in this "cultural colonization" period which favored Western ideals as superior to the Chinese culture.

Ruru Li in her monograph *Shashibiya*[100] described the 1930 performance as "a serious production [. . .] [in contrast to] earlier Shakespeare performances," because it "used a complete translation text." The production was well received with a total of 4 performances staged in May 1930, and 15 performances in July the same year.[101] Gu himself described his translation in the translator's preface (1930) as follows," I translate what is in the script, and never delete, never add a word so as to comply with the fidelity rule. In addition, the original is so good that the translator is not willing to modify, thus I decide to translate word by word to retain its original flavor and style."

Being the most complete Shakespeare translated text at the time, Gu's strove to retain the religious language in accordance with the fidelity rule, though it was far from accurate—misrepresentations could be seen especially in areas where religious or biblical language was used. Among the 54 translation errors pointed out by Jichengzhi 紀乘之,[102] the following relate to translation of the religious dimension of the text:

i. Ash Wednesday was mistranslated as Christmas Day (聖誕日).

ii. Black Monday was translated literally into Chinese (黑暗的星期一) without reference to Easter.

iii. Or, as it (the merchant's ship) were, the pageants of the sea—pageants were erroneously translated as the Chinese Buddha.

iv. "It is a good divine that follows his own instruction"- this is domesticated as 能遵照自己的教訓而行的只有聖賢人做得到。 The

---

98. Xinyue 新月 [New moon magazine] 3: 1 (1930) 14; quoted in Shih, "Intercultural Theatre," 181.

99. See Huang, "Shakespeare on the Chinese Stage," 2004.

100. Li, *Shashibiya*, 26.

101. Meng, *Shakespeare in China-A Brief History*, 162.

102. See Ji, "Translation of *The Merchant of Venice*," 307–316.

Christian doctrine underlying the original line becomes a lesson, divine becomes a sage.

v. The reference to Jacob's story in Genesis 9:10 had been partly mistranslated. In "The skilful shepherd peeled me certain wands and, in the doing of the deed of the kind, he stuck them up before the fulsome ewes," the translator mistranslated "stuck them" as "holding up the male sheep with sticks (用木棒把公羊挑著站起)."

vi. If e'er the Jew her father come to heaven,
It will be for his gentle daughter's sake:
And never dare misfortune cross her foot,
Unless she do it under this excuse,
That she is issue to a faithless Jew.

The condition "if [. . .]" was not understood correctly, it becomes "if ever the Jew died for the sake of his daughter, she should not have any misfortune as long as she did not admit that she is the daughter of the Jew. 如果那猶太人為了他女兒的緣故，急急死了，只要她不承認是叛徒猶太人的女兒，她就沒有甚麼危險了。"

The major adaptation in this performance is the significant reduction in the number of acts so that change in stage setting need not take place so frequently. The scenes and acts after the adaptation are as follows:

Scene 1: Act 1 (Venice. A Street)& 2 (Before Shylock's home)

Scene 2: Act 1 (Belmont. A room in Portia's house)

Scene 3: Act 1 (Venice. A Street) & 2 (Belmont)

Scene 4: Act 1 (Venice. A court of justice) & 2 (Street in front of court)

Scene 5: Act 1 (Belmont. Avenue to Portia's home)

Under this faithful translation strategy and a realist stage setting, one would not be surprised to find that all the religious content was retained for performance. For example, Daniel the judge is rendered as *Dan Nier* 但尼爾. But this also left one wondering how much the audience understood of this content, given that no other commentary was included in the script, and that there were no articles on Shakespeare to inform the audience about the background to the play. Gu was one of only four contemporary translators who had translated Shakespeare, the others being Tian Han 田漢 (translator of Hamlet), Dai Wangshu 戴望舒 and Sun Dayu 孫大雨 (King Lear).

It should be noted that Shakespeare commentaries in the 1930s were few, a fact which posed challenges for translators in translating religious concepts. According to Ji Chengzhi, existing translations comprised *Hamlet* by Tian Han, *Macbeth* by Dai Wangshu, *King Lear* by Sun Dayu and *The Merchant* by Guzhongyi. Articles that introduced Shakespeare were limited to the translator prefaces in these works.

In the period between 1920 and 1940, the theatre had seen few Shakespearean plays despite the introduction of these new translations, as Shakespeare did not seem to offer a solution to the then socio-political situations—only five Shakespearean plays were staged.[103] As for the published translations, their target audiences were mainly scholars and students. Their impact on the general public was limited.[104] On the other hand, while professional theatre troupes seldom staged Shakespeare plays, non-professional staging could be seen in schools during which students benefited from learning drama techniques through Shakespeare.[105] Overall, Shakespeare's translated plays, whether in print or on stage, cannot be said to have attracted widespread attention.

After Gu there were two important and well-respected Shakespeare translators, both deserving attention and close textual analysis—Zhu Shenghao and Liang Shiqiu, who started translating Shakespeare in 1935 and 1931 respectively.

1. About Liang Shiqiu

Liang Shiqiu worked under the patronage of the well-known *literatus* Hu Shi who encouraged him to translate Shakespeare in the first place. A US educated scholar well-versed in English and American literature, he was the only Chinese scholar who completed the translation of all Shakespearean plays. His collection of essays became a required text for students in Taiwan, but was not widely circulated in China. This was related to his political stance—he fled to Taiwan after the Communist Party took over in 1949. He criticized the social function of literature proposed by Mao Zedong 毛澤東, and maintained that literary voices should continue to offer an independent view of society. During the civil war, he argued, in his capacity as editor of *ZhongyangRibao* 中央日報 (Central Daily) in Chongqing, China, that literature is unrelated to war, a view which was heavily criticized by well-known translator Lu Xun as the work of a "capitalist dog."[106] He was regarded as a liberal thinker—not standing with the Communist Party, or

---

103. Li, *Shashibiya*, 25.
104. He,"Shakespeare through Chinese Eyes," 6.
105. Ibid.
106. See Yan, *Research on Liang Shiqiu*, 11.

the Nationalist Party while in Taiwan, and he issued criticisms against the Mainland government. Mao Zedong criticized his works as "advocating capitalist." [107] However, he was criticized by Li Ao 李敖, a writer of popular acclaim, for remaining silent after relocating to Taiwan.

Liang in his *Literary Criticisms* (文學批評辯),[108] showed his disagreement with leftists over their Marxist interpretation of Shakespeare by laying emphasis on Shakespeare's insights into human nature. By translating Karl Marx's recommendation of Shakespeare, he criticized the argument that Shakespeare supports capitalism (see his post-translation note).[109]

There are two points worth noting in Liang's appraisal: 1) Shakespeare is a genius whose greatness lies in the broad application of his works to all human beings- spanning royal families, aristocrats and the general public, who all find a place in his works. Some say Shakespeare is a capitalist—they should read Shakespeare's works and read the above passage by Karl Marx. 2) Shakespeare is not a protagonist for one party, his arts hold up a mirror to reflect nature.

Liang's translation strategy was faithful to the original, characterized by his "thick" translation (in Appiah's[110] terms) e.g. his use of commentaries to supply information on culture-bound allusions or biblical references.[111] While his translations are faithful, they are not considered performable. His translations were rarely performed in China or Taiwan after his relocation to Taiwan, for political reasons aforementioned and for lacking performability. In fact, only three of his translations were staged so far, namely *The Merchant of Venice* (1937 and 1948), *Othello* (1938) and *Hamlet* (1942). When his translation of *The Merchant* was staged in 1937, it was an act of support by Yu Shangyuan 余上沅, an influential theatre practitioner, to Liang's translation project. However, his version underwent substantial omissions when performed in 1937 among the first graduating class of Nanjing Theatre Academy which he founded in 1935. This is Liang's comment on the stage performance, "*The Merchant* was successful, using my translation, and was substantially reduced by Shangyuan. Omitting scenes and redundant words are necessary to comply with modern drama."[112]

107. See Mao, *Selected Works of Mao Zedong Volume 3*, 855.
108. Liang, "Talks on Literary Criticism," 133–134.
109. Liang, "Shakespeare on Money," 626–631.
110. Appiah, "Thick Translation," 808–819.
111. For studies on Liang Shiqiu's translation under institutional patronage, see Bai, "Poetics, Ideology and Patronage in Translation," 2004.
112. Liang, *Liang Shiqiuwenxuehuiyilu.*, 367.

Later, it was Taiwan publisher Far East (*yuan dong* 遠東) that published Liang's collection of Shakespeare's translations in 1967, and Beijing published his collection only in 2002. No translation of his was ever staged in China after he fled to Taiwan in 1949.

Liang is well versed in the Bible. In *A Few Books that Influenced Me* 影響我的幾本書,[113] Liang said that Jesus Christ taught about charity and the need to share wealth with others. He interprets *The Merchant* not only as a play on Judeo-Christian conflicts, but about the oppressor and the oppressed.[114] He considers that Shakespeare portrays Antonio and other Christians as un-Christian—as those who were not loving towards their enemy—Shylock. He believes that Shakespeare would only be ironic about Christians if his aim was to depict Shylock's enemies as representing Christians. Liang's insight was rare in this period when Shakespeare commentaries were few and far between. His commentaries show that his translation project was well-researched.

Liang's example illustrates the role that institutional patronage and poetics played in the marginalization of an important translation that most faithfully retained the religious language among his contemporaries. Directors and adapters such as Zhang Qihong and Ni Huiying 倪惠英 who relied heavily on Chinese translations to understand the play, inevitably turn to other, more easily accessed and more performable translations than Liang's, which are also translations that retain fewer religious references and annotations. As such, the reduction of religious language occurred at the preconfiguration stage, even before the adapters interpreted the play.

The translations more often used by Mainland directors will be discussed in the following section.

2. Zhu Shenghao

Zhu Shenghao served as English editor after graduating from Zhi Jiang University 浙江大學 in Hangzhou. He began translation of Shakespearean plays in 1935 and continued until his death. He admitted in his translator prefaces that he was not satisfied with the stiff translation of Shakespeare's works earlier,[115] and, with fluency as his primary criterion, he would skip translating culture-bound materials which might not be understood by readers.[116]

---

113. See Liang, *yashe sanwen*, 81.
114. See Liang, *weinisishangren*, 6.
115. See Chau, *Chinese Translation of Hamlet*, 23.
116. See Fong, "Dramatists and Drama Translation," 296.

Unlike Liang who was prompted by Hu Shi to translate Shakespeare, Zhu translated Shakespeare on his own initiative. The 1930s was a time where Japanese occupied the North East part of China. Zhu said to his wife Song Qingru 宋清如 in a letter:

> Do you admire national heroes? My younger brother said if I successfully finish translating Shakespeare, I will become a national hero. This is because some foreigner said China is a nation without culture, not even Shakespeare has been translated.[117]

His patriotic drive urged him to embark on a decade-long translation project until he died of fatigue after translating over twenty of Shakepeare's works. His younger brother Zhu Wenzhen 朱文振 further confirmed the patriotic drive of Zhu in his translation of Shakespeare:

> He started translating Shakespeare in 1935 spring . . . in those days, Japanese imperialism in oppressing Chinese was rampant. And it is the Japanese who laughed about Chinese culture, saying that it was so backward that not even a Shakespearean collection had been rendered into Chinese. Thus, I believe that his decision to translate Shakespeare arose not only out of personal interest, but also to fight for the Chinese nation under the oppression of Japanese imperialism in China.[118]

In terms of translation strategy, Zhu's translation was considered fluent and smooth. His translation of *The Merchant* (1947) was commended by the well-known playwright Fang Ping (who later proof-read his translation of *The Merchant*) in preference to the following three translators in terms of fluency and appropriateness:[119] GuZhong Yi (1930), Liang Shiqiu (1936) and Cao Weifeng 曹未風 (1946).

During the translation process, Zhu originally referred to Liang's translation published earlier (1936), but later gave up as he did not want to be influenced by Liang's style. At times he criticized Liang's inaccuracies in translating *The Merchant*. In his letter to his wife Song Qingru, he explained his translation process of *The Merchant*:

> *The Merchant* is a great literary piece, without too many obstacles to comprehension. But the original sentence structure was compact which made translation time-consuming. I read

---

117. See Wu and Zhu, *Biography of Zhu Shenghao*, 108.

118. For more details on Zhu's life, see Wu and Zhu, *Biography of Zhu Shenghao*, 1990. The quote is cited in p.107–108. Also, see Zhu, *Letters by Zhu Shenghao*, 2003.

119. See Fang Ping's translator preface in *The Merchant of Venice*, Shanghai: Ping Ming Chubanshe, 1959.

Liang's translation while working on my translation as a start for convenience sake, but in the end I suffered; this is because after reading another's translation, one cannot but be influenced by it. Sometimes in order to avoid plagiarism, I need to make a different translation. In the end, I feel restricted, and my translation cannot be consistent and smooth.[120]

Theologically, Zhu, although once cast as Holy Mary during a Christmas performance at middle school, was not particularly fond of Christians. He noted, "I despised this year's Christmas. Compared to previous Christmas, we have to sing 'Glory to heaven. Peace and good will to earth,' which is boring. Matters such as YMCA, distributing candies to unpriviledged kids—these Christians need to become very kind, but all are hypocritical. I dislike Buddhism more than Christianity, but despised Christians more than Buddhists."[121]

Has the translators' theological stance affected their translation products? How have their approaches to translation led to a difference in treating religious materials? Below is a comparative analysis of the translation of the Mercy speech by Zhu Shenghao and Liang Shiqiu that sheds light on the above.

Source text:

> The quality of mercy is not strain'd,
> It droppeth as the gentle rain from heaven
> Upon the place beneath: it is twice blest;
> It blesseth him that gives and him that takes:
> 'Tis mightiest in the mightiest: it becomes
> The thronèd monarch better than his crown;
> His sceptre shows the force of temporal power,
> The attribute to awe and majesty,
> Wherein doth sit the dread and fear of kings;
> But mercy is above this sceptred sway;
> It is enthroned in the hearts of kings,
> It is an attribute to God himself;
> And earthly power doth then show likest God's
> When mercy seasons justice. Therefore, Jew,
> Though justice be thy plea, consider this,

---

120. See Zhu, *Letters by Zhu Shenghao*, 306–7.
121. See Wu and Zhu, *Biography of Zhu Shenghao*, 48.

> That, in the course of justice, none of us
> Should see salvation: we do pray for mercy;
> And that same prayer doth teach us all to render
> The deeds of mercy. I have spoke thus much
> To mitigate the justice of thy plea;
> Which if thou follow, this strict court of Venice
> Must needs give sentence 'gainst the merchant there.

Zhu's translation:

> 慈悲不是出於勉強,它是像甘霖一樣從天上降下塵世;它不但給幸福與受的人,也同樣給幸福與施與的人;它有超乎一切的無上威力,比皇冠更足以顯出一個帝王的高貴;御杖不過象徵著俗世的威權,使人民對於君上的尊嚴凜然生畏;慈悲的力量卻高出於權力之上,它深藏在帝王的內心,是一種屬於上帝的德性,執法的人倘能把慈悲調劑著公道,人間的權力就和上帝的神力沒有差別。所以,猶太人,雖然你所要求的是公道,可是請你想一想,要是真的按照公道執行起賞罰來,誰也沒有死後得救的希望。我們既然祈禱著上帝的慈悲,就應該按照祈禱的指點,自己做一些慈悲的事。

Back translation:

> Mercy is not something that can be forced,
> just like gentle rain from heaven and scattered on earth.
>
> Not only does it give blessings to those blessed, but also gives blessings to those who gives.
>
> It has an overwhelming power, and befits the king's majesty more than his crown;
>
> The staff in his hands merely shows the secular authority, so that people are awed,
>
> but mercy, higher than the power; it is deep within the king's hearts, it is a virtue belong to Shangdi (God), if the law enforcer can season mercy with gong dao (the way of fairness), there is no difference between human power and God's divine power. So, Jew, what you ask is gong dao, but think about it, if we carry out reward and punishment based on gong dao, then, no one has the hope for salvation after death. We pray for God's mercy, and should pray according to the prayer's instructions, that we do some merciful deeds.

Liang's translation:

慈悲不是勉強的，它像是甘霖自天而降:它有雙重的福佑，它
賜福給那施者和受者:
它在最有威權的人手裏是最有威權的:它比皇冠
更適宜帝王的身份，它的寶杖是人間威權的象徵。
這威權既是帝王尊嚴的標記，才即是帝王所以令人敬畏的緣由;
而慈悲卻在王權之上，它佔住國王的心頭，
它是上帝的象徵，以慈悲調劑法律的時候帝王是最近似上帝了。
所以，猶太人，你要求的雖然只是公平，但是要想想，如果真要
公平，我們死後誰也不能獲救。所以我們祈禱慈悲，而這一
番祈禱也教訓我們要做慈悲的事。

Back translation:

Mercy is not something that can be forced,

just like gentle rain from heaven and scattered on earth.

It gives double blessings: it blesses those who give and those who take.

It is upheld in the hands of the most authoritative:

it shows the status of monarch better than his crown;

The staff shows the secular authority. This authority symbolizes the king's majesty, which is what makes the king venerable. but mercy is higher than the power of the king; it resides deep within the king's heart, it symbolizes Shangdi. When mercy seasons the law, it is when the king is closest to God. So, Jew, what you ask is fairness, but think about it, if we insist on fairness, no one will be saved after death. That's why we pray for mercy, and this prayer teaches us to do merciful deeds.

The major difference lies in the translation of key terms and sentence structure. Zhu is inclined to elaborate the concepts over a longer sentence to facilitate comprehension, while Liang's translation is more compact. For example, "And earthly power doth then show likest God's When mercy seasons justice" was elaborated as "no difference between man's power and God's divine power" by Zhu, while Liang kept the original meaning. Both translated mercy with "*ci bei* 慈悲," i.e. a localized Chinese term with Buddhist connotations. Despite the slight lexical difference in the translation of "justice"—Liang's being "*gong ping* 公平" (i.e. fairness), Zhu's being "*gong dao* 公道" (i.e. way of fairness), the reference to the Christian theology of mercy and justice is retained. Lastly, on the term salvation, both translators elaborated it as life after death. Zhu elaborated the line "none of us should see salvation" as "none of us have hope for salvation after death," Liang, on the other hand, had a closer equivalent to the original "none of us would be saved after death." In conclusion, in terms of smoothness, Zhu's translation was preferred to Liang's.

In terms of translatability of religious discourse, Zhu's strategy is a hybrid one, which aims to bring the writer to the reader, but at the same time manages to keep the religious flavour with sometimes explicit concepts such as "salvation." This strategy gained him popularity among Chinese dramatists who considered performability as the supreme criterion in theatre translation. Liang's strategy is mostly foreignizing and sometimes domesticating, compensated by way of commentaries. Such kind of thick translation (i.e. with footnotes) was not popular with directors, who do not put footnotes on stage. As can be seen, both translators had kept religious discourse in the translations in accordance with the trend of "understanding authentic Shakespeare." Although one could hardly establish that their theological positions shaped the religious references of the translation products in print, one can be certain that, in these two examples, it is the patronage and poetics (i.e. performability) that give rise to the popularization of one translation (i.e. Zhu's) over the other, and hence the religious translation used in the former.

1950s and Onwards

Shakespeare began to receive wider attention from the public after the establishment of the Communist Party and until the Cultural Revolution. In the 1950s, playwrights from USSR, which was in an amicable relationship with China, were invited to establish modern theatre in China and to teach at theatre academies. They used Shakespearean plays as well as Russian plays as teaching materials for students. Karl Marx's high recommendation of Shakespeare further enhanced its acceptance. In 1956, after the publication of the full collections of Shakespeare's translations by Zhu Shenghao, the cinematic versions of *Hamlet*, *Othello* and *Twelfth Night* were put on stage, leaving a widespread influence of Shakespeare in China nationwide. The Shakespearean commentaries were mostly around realism and humanism, so as to "learn from Russian stage performances, and establish the relationship between performance, translation and research."[122] On the other hand, this kind of leftist approach, using Shakespeare to serve political purpose, influenced the research orientation of Shakespeare's scholarship in China.[123] The Chinese translations of Russian commen-

122. Ling, *Report on Shanghai Shakespeare Research*, 34.
123. See Li, *History of Critique of Chinese Shakespeare*, 37.

taries on Shakespeare became the reference readings of foreign language departments of universities[124]. Until the nineties, Shakespeare's research in China was still under the influence of Russian methodology, highlighting the humanism aspects of Shakespeare but neglecting their theological aspects. Take Hamlet as an example, Shakespeare was introduced through the purely humanist approach.[125] For instance, Shakespeare in Russia sees Hamlet's struggle as a conflict between the humanist approach and his weaknesses, rather than a theological perspective when Hamlet ponders on the Christian concept of sin and murder.

During the ten years of the Cultural Revolution, Shakespeare was labelled capitalist, and was absent from schools and theatres and publication circles. The plan for publishing full collections of Shakespeare had been abandoned. It was after the Cultural Revolution that Shakespearean performances mushroomed—in fact, the number of Shakespeare plays staged after 1980 accounted for 90 percent of the plays staged between 1913 to 2000.

Fang Ping's Translations

During the period under Marxist influence came Fang Ping 方平 and his new collection of translations starting in the 1950s. He published his translation of *The Merchant* in 1977. While not as prolific as his predecessors in terms of translating Shakespeare's works,[126] he is considered an authoritative figure in Shakespearean research and well connected in literary circles. Like many Chinese in this period, his first contact with Shakespeare was through Chinese translation, by Liang Shiqiu and Sun Dayu, before he read the English scripts and started translating, according to his interview with Southern Daily (*NanfangRibao* 南方日報). Upon graduating from high school, Fang was editor in several well-known publishing houses in Shanghai, including *ReminWenxue* 人民文學 publishing house, and became professor at Shanghai Normal University, and visiting professor at Peking University and Qingdao University. He was the second president of the China Shakespeare Research Institute, and editor of the book *ShashibiyaYanjiu* 莎士比亞研究 (*Shakespare's Research*), as well as a council member of the China Translators' Association. Starting 1993, he embarked on the enormous task of revising and editing all Chinese translations of Shakespearean plays by

---

124. Ibid, 32.
125. Ibid, 59.
126. Fang Ping translated 21 Shakespearean works and co-translated 3 other titles which are included in his collection of Shakespeare's translations. In comparison, his predecessors Zhu and Liang translated over 30 works.

Zhu Shenghao which was published in 2000. He was an honorary member of the Hong Kong Translation Society in 2001. What is significant about his translation of *The Merchant* is that its performability was preferred by directors and was later used by troupes in Beijing, Shanghai and Sichuan. In the 1980 production, Zhang Qihong based her script on Fang's translation after comparing his and Zhu's work. Additionally, apart from translating *The Merchant*, Fang was a prolific theatre critic and published articles on Shylock in 1979[127] before the production was staged. In this sense, Fang possessed higher cultural capital in the translation of this particular play than Zhu who did not have any scholarly output apart from being the translator of over 30 Shakespearean plays.

On the matter of performability, Fang Ping commented that stage effects were his primary concern in translating the plays: "literary translation is about rolling out the paper, translating silently in a room, but translating Shakespearean plays are different, some "accompanying sounds" will ring in your ears, as if you can hear it, and see the "accompanying visions," as if you see the person." [128] He said in the epilogue to the new Shakespearean translations which he edited that translating Shakespearean plays into verse involved giving more attention to the artistic forms of language, and the inter-relationship of form and content; and not stopping at the superficial representation (or repetition) of a language, but emphasising the equivalence of discourse, emotions, image etc. between source text and target text.[129] Although Zhu, his predecessor, mostly translated Shakespearean plays into prose, Fang's new translations served to challenge this approach by attempting his best to keep the original form of each play in his re-translations, i.e., whatever is verse in the play text was translated into verse, whatever is prose was translated into prose, thereby keeping the tempo and rhythm as closest to the Shakespearean text as possible.

How did Fang, an influential translator among dramatists, interpret *The Merchant*? He argued that Shakespeare is a capitalist, humanistic writer who showed favor to Antonio, one who represented capitalism and associated with the upper echelon in Venice. Fang claimed that Shakespeare beautified Antonio as a generous, righteous, gung-ho, self-sacrificial "royal merchant," leading to a schizophrenic character. He was a gentle, "white-glove wearing" merchant who deep down was a dirty soul, an exploiter.[130] For Fang, capitalist merchants like Antonio and money lenders are birds of

---

127. See Fang, "*Lun Xia Luoke* 論夏洛克 [On Shylock, 213–233."
128. See Fang, *New Shakespeare Translations*, 5.
129. Ibid, 692–700.
130. Ibid, 232.

a feather who exploit the labour force. This Marxist, atheist ideology can be aptly seen in the following quotation:

> The calculating, greedy nature of usurers unreservedly highlights the ugly, profit-oriented nature of capitalist class, inciting resentment of the upper class industrials and capitalists. These people on one hand want to engage in acts like "pirates," on the other hand they want the fame and reputation of a righteous man. Merchant Antonio's "righteous" anger towards money-lender Shylock should be interpreted this way.[131]

Citing the history of the medieval church that "indoctrinated people with those 'so-called heaven and hell, God and devil' anti-movement doctrines" and which conspired to suppress the protests of the oppressed against the feudal rule, Fang believed that Antonio scolded the money-lending business of the Jews under the name of "old-fashioned" Christian doctrines. "(Antonio) rode on the anti-semitic waves fanned by feudal churches and cruelly humiliated those 'chou' or filthy money-lending Jews." The purpose, he claimed, was to oppress this money-minded Jew to a point where Shylock could never climb up from his lowly social status under any conditions or situations to compete with him. [132]

In his Marxist interpretation, the pound of flesh is a symbol of capitalist exploitation. "Behind the stage, in our real life, the capitalists use the creed upheld by money-lender Shylock as their creed, repeating Shylock's speech to defend their bloody sin; but in this comedy on stage, they curse Shylock as a "devil," "inhumane" wolf, just because Shylock has made that speech and upheld that creed. This makes us think that they (capitalists) are on the same horizon as those Jews. Seeing through their tricks, their conspiracy, we can feel that in this capitalist world that rationalizes exploitation, the play is full of comedic irony."

Despite this Marxist interpretation, Fang Ping's literary translation kept all biblical allusions intact during the translation process without omission.

In one example in Shylock's speech:

> "These be thy Christian husbands! I have a daughter;
> Would any of the stock of Barabbas
> Had been her husband rather than a Christian!"

---

131. Ibid, 220.
132. Ibid.

Zhu Shenghao generalized the biblical allusion "stock of Barabbas" to "強盜的子孫" (offsprings of pirates), and Fang translated the biblical allusion literally, supplemented by annotation.

However, in Portia's mercy speech, through which the Christian notion of mercy and justice was prominent, Fang adopted a domestication strategy as follows:

> "慈悲，並不是強逼硬求的東西，它象甘
> 霖一樣，從天而降，灑落到人間。它給人雙重的祝福
> 祝福那施主，也賜福給受施的人。它，萬王之王所
> 奉行的王道，它比皇冠更昭示了帝皇的身份。
> 而帝皇手裡的節杖不過是象徵著世俗的威權，
> 讓人望而生畏⋯
> 可是慈悲，卻高於王權的勢焰；它，
> 供奉在帝皇的內心深處，是替天行道，象徵了上帝的
> 宏恩。人間的權威跟上帝的天道最接近，若是王法裡
> 滲透著慈悲的德性。所以，猶太人，你要求的雖說是
> 王法，可是想一想，依著王法執行賞罰，那我們中間，
> 誰還能得救？"

Back translation:

> Mercy is not something that can be forced,
>
> just like gentle rain from heaven and scattered on earth.
>
> It gives double blessings: it blesses those who give and those who take receive benefits.
>
> It is a rule upheld by king of thousand kings,
>
> it shows the status of monarch better than his crown;
>
> The staff in his hands merely shows the secular authority, so that people are awed,
>
> but mercy, higher than the power of the crown; is hidden deep within the king's hearts, it exercises the way on behalf of heaven, it symbolizes God's great grace. Human power is closest to heaven's way of God, if mercy is infiltrated in the nation's law. So, Jew, what you ask is the nation's law, but think about it, if we carry out reward and punishment based on the nation's law, then, who can be saved among us?

In Fang's rendition, some Christian terms, when translated, carry Buddhist and Confucian undertones. For example, "him that gives and him that takes" becomes "*shizhu* 施主" and "*shoushi de ren* 受施的人." "*shizhu* 施主"(Dānapati) is a Sanskrit translation that means a patron or lay monastic supporter, usually a wealthy donor and the archetype of the Buddhist layman. Secondly, the term Christian "mercy" is translated into a Buddhist term "*ci bei* 慈悲," which is a polysyllabic transeme, meaning both kindness (*ci* 慈) and sympathy (*bei* 悲), a quality of Buddhist gods which emphasize non-violence to all living beings. A parallel is also drawn between mercy and a benevolent policy based on kindness (*ren* 仁) and righteousness (*yi* 義), as in 萬王之王所奉行的王道. Earthly power is translated as "exercising the (just) way on behalf of heaven" (*ti tianxingdao* 替天行道). The mercy that is "enthroned within the heart of kings" is translated into "*gong feng* 供奉," an act of offering to Gods which involved the offer of incense and cooked meat as sacrifice.[133]

Lastly, "when mercy seasons justice" becomes "mercy is infiltrated in the law." No mention of justice can be seen in the translation. What the Jew asks for is executing the nation's or the king's law (*wangfa*, 王法), rather than the quality of justice. The use of the term "the king's law" embodies the Confucian concept where the emperor is mandated by Heaven, accordingly, his rule carries the heavenly quality of justice. Mercy, which originally was placed on the scales with justice as an antagonistic pair, became a quality infiltrated in the rule of a nation. The allegory or competing balance between the two Christian qualities is simply lost in the translation.

In China, there were no other translators achieving the canonical status of Liang and Zhu in the 40 years that followed their translation, until Fang Ping's new collection of translations came on to the literary scene. Zhu's translation was more commonly staged than Liang's in China, and exercised its influence up to the contemporary period. In the period between the end of the Cultural Revolution and 2001, 66 Shakespearean plays were staged, with Zhu Shenghao's translation being used 25 times, Fang ping 3 times, and Ying Ruocheng 英若誠 twice. Liang Shiqiu's translations were on stage four times, but not after he fled to Taiwan. Of these 66 plays, 26 were adaptations in different operatic forms—Cantonese opera, *Kunju* 崑劇, *Hangmeixi* 黃梅戲, and even Tibetan.[134] Some were sarcastic about social issues, some were rendered close to Western style, for instance, the 1980 *Merchant of Venice* which I wish to study in detail.

Zhu, adopting a more easily accessible translation, was able to help the public understand the religious terms without substantial effort. At the same time, Liang's translation which used mainly foreignization as strategy and supplemented religious terms through detailed footnotes was not widely circulated in the Chinese theatre. In theatrical terms, this was due to its

---

133. Other than laying out offerings to serve the Gods and spirits, the act of *Gongfeng* also involves an enshrinement of the images or pictures of ancestors and spirits.

134. Ruru Li compiled a table on the types of Chinese Shakespearean productions during that period. See Li. , *Shashibiya*, 2003.

lack of "performability"; the popularity of Zhu over Liang was compounded by the institutional patronage of the government. Zhu's patriotic drive was highly commended by Mao Zedong, who described Zhu as one who "used all his life to martyr for gaining pride for this nation in the enterprise of translating Shakespeare," a "persistent hero."[135] Liang, on the contrary, was criticized by Mao as "advocating capitalism." Ideologically, he did not conform to Communist thinking and fled to Taiwan when the Communist Party took over in 1949. It was the Taiwan publisher Far East (*yuan dong*) that published Liang's collection of Shakespeare's translations in 1967, and Beijing published his collection only in 2002, i.e. 20 years after the first post-Cultural Revolution production of *The Merchant* by Zhang Qihong. Liang's influence on the literary scene impacted on the written translation, rather than on the stage.

Discussion and Conclusion

From this historical overview, one can see that the (un)translatability of religious discourse in Shakespeare's works in print hinges on the following factors: socio-political, semantic, cultural, and ideological. Contextualizing the translations in the then socio-political environment is important in understanding why Shakespeare was brought into China in the first place, how the literary scene welcomed Shakespearean translations, and how the fidelity turn favored the retention of religious language. In terms of socio-political untranslatability, even when Liang tried hard to remain independent of ideological control, in the end the adoption of his translations could not escape the institutional patronage in the process. Despite the fact that no religious resonance was filtered out by means of censorship or self-censorship in his works (which included detailed footnotes on religious terms), they were not picked up by directors in China such as Zhang Qihong who produced *The Merchant* in 1980, owing to problems with regard to performability and institutional patronage. Socio-political untranslatability is most apparent when there is a competition of ideologies –for example, in Fang Ping's translation, the Confucian or Buddhist ideology clouds out certain Christian concepts. The semantic problems faced by Gu were not surprising in the 1930s when Chinese scholars educated in the West were few and far between. As regards the cultural dimension, the Christian concept of mercy which bears the meaning of forgiveness could not be fully translated into the Buddhist term "慈悲 *ci bei*," which bears the meaning of kindness and compassion. In terms of ideological untranslatability, the loss of religious

---

135. See Wu and Zhu, *Biography of Zhu Shenghao*, 302.

language in Lin's translation testifies to the fact that his approach in reviving Confucianism inevitably eliminates the foreignness and imperialism that Christian references bring.

Despite these challenges to translatability, one can see that the strong emphasis placed on a "faithfulness" strategy in literary circles since 1920s left a legacy in the retention of religious discourse. One can find a parallel in contemporary theatre circles in post-colonial Hong Kong, where the staging of "authentic Shakespeare," highlighted in program notes and advertisements, often leads to the retention of the religious language and plot of *The Merchant*. However, translatability of religious language on the page did not necessarily lead to translatability on the stage, which is a more dynamic process that involves more agents than in literary translation. For the above literary translations, the translator is the main agent, plus the institution that supports the work behind the scenes. In theatre translation, as the case studies in the following chapters will show, actors, directors and translators are subject to ideological, socio-cultural, political, economic forces that affect translatability more fundamentally. Even when the translations retaining religious language were read by directors, in the end they had the ultimate decision to cut or to keep. The theatre becomes a site of ideological manipulation and theological manifestation which sees substantial adaptation of the religious content at the hands of translators and directors. The clouding-out effect of Christian content by competing ideologies is even more apparent in the theatre translations. We shall see more clearly in the next chapter how the Marxist influence led to a downplaying of theological concepts. Accordingly, a more sophisticated model drawing on both translation studies and religious studies is needed to explain the phenomenon. Therefore, in the case studies in Chapter 3, I draw on a modified version of Andrew Chesterman's model to show how other conditions interact to shape the translation of the religious dimension, while in the final chapter I draw on Ninian Smart's model on religious dimensions to redefine the scope of untranslatability.

Since Taiwan and Hong Kong followed different pathways in the importation of Shakespeare and its effects on interpretation by directors, translators and audience, the development of the treatment of Shakespeare's reception in these two regions will be discussed in more detail in Chapter 3.

3

Case Studies of *The Merchant of Venice* in Mainland China

IN THIS CHAPTER, I will illustrate, with the use of case studies from Mainland China, how the religious contents are adapted and translated using the translation model I developed in Chapter 1—i.e. a semiotic-cum-hermeneutic turn adapted from Andrew Chesterman's model. I will show how socio-cultural conditions interact with the translation agent's ideology, which may concur with or counter the prevalent conditions. In the section on socio-cultural conditions, I set the production not only in the context of political environment, but also of the religious milieu of the place in order to trace the interaction with both the dominant ideology and the individual's theology in arriving at the final shape of the product. Socio-cultural conditions include topics such as taboos, gender and sexuality, as these all have a bearing on the director's characterization and directorial emphasis. Such interaction in turn gives rise to a displacement or adaptation of religious content in the performance text and the subsequent mise-en-scene on stage. The translation process does not end on the page as such, but continues as actors' bodies become sites of translation that communicate the director's interpretation of the religious dimension to the audience.

Weinisi Shangren (威尼斯商人): The First Shakespearean Drama in China after the Cultural Revolution in 1980

Socio-cultural Conditions

As Shakespeare performances ceased during the Cultural Revolution, *The Merchant* became the first Shakespearean play brought on to the Chinese stage. In fact, the early 1980s saw a revival of interest in Shakespeare, including its being the first Western literature that was reintegrated into the curriculum of post-secondary education, and the formation of the first Chinese Shakespeare Center in 1984 and the Shakespeare Society of China in 1995 by playwright Cao Yu.

There are three reasons behind the rise of Shakespeare in the early eighties: first, China in the early eighties had just come out of a feudal system and political turmoil; Chinese could thus strongly identify with the "reform consciousness" underlying Shakespeare's works. It was also a period of transition which was close to that of Elizabethan England, characterized by a youthful, glorious and radical cultural temperament[1]. Secondly, in the post revolution era, the Chinese were drawn to the humanistic optimism in Shakespeare. They could walk out of the shadow of distorted ideological values and appreciate individuality and humanity in Shakespeare's works. Thirdly, they hoped to reconnect to the world theatre for new insight and revitalization after being cut off from the world stage during the period of the Revolution[2]. During that time, only a few model revolutionary dramas remained on stage, where class struggle must be expressed sharply. Villains must be portrayed as brutal and without gentleness, while heroes must show revolutionary optimism and faith in Mao's concept of communism. Such stereotyped characters are a far cry from the Western approach which prefers a less black-and-white perspective.[3] The complexity in the characterisation in Shakespeare's plays caters to the appetite of the audience in the early eighties.

The scholarly reception of *The Merchant*'s translation was tinged with Marxist ideals. Contemporary commentators quoted Karl Marx's citation of Shylock's speech at the court in his famed writing *Capital*. Marx believed that the scene is a criticism of capitalist laws.[4] Despite the fact that churches began to reopen in 1978 during Christmas, i.e. after the Cultural Revolution, the government still exerted stringent control on religious affairs in the early eighties, and agreed with the Marxist ideology that equated religion with opium until the mid-eighties. In 1982-1983, an anti-spiritual pollution campaign was launched against the *literati* circle, and religious material in literature was suppressed in this period. In the early eighties, taboos existed in the arts and literature circle. There is no explicit state censorship of theatre productions, but there were two main sensitive areas in the media that

1. Shih, "Intercultural Theatre," 200.
2. Hu, "Notes on Directing *Twelfth Night*," 128.
3. Mackerras, *The Chinese Theatre in Modern Times*, 172.
4. Wu, "Post-Symposium Afterthoughts of *The Merchant of Venice*," 54–57.

invited censorship: explicit description of sex and sensitive political issues.⁵ In the publishing sector, censorship might take several forms, including deletion, attenuation, mis-translation, denunciation in the text, the title or the preface, and disclaimers.⁶ In the production of *Measure for Measure* in 1981, over five hundred lines on sex, religion and politics were deleted, according to the director Ying Ruocheng 英若誠.

Meanwhile, 1980s saw the importation of feminist ideas from the West to China, and the 1990s saw feminist writings mushroom.⁷ In the post-Mao era, women's awakening-consciousness in China had been significant.⁸ In the eighties, feminist writings such as *On the Same Horizon* (by Zhang Xinxin), *Ark* and *Mid-age Years* showed the difficulties and challenges of women in their pursuit of individual values. Whatever struggles the female characters went through, they still lived in the bondage of a patriarchal society.

In 1980, Zhang directed *The Merchant*, the first Shakespearean play in China after the Cultural Revolution. Its popularity could be demonstrated by over two hundred performances during the period from 3 September 1980 to 13 August 1982. The production was later re-run in 1986. In total, over 500 performances were recorded between 1980 and 1986. The 1980 production won a First Class award in acting and in directorship granted by the Cultural Ministry of PRC. The early eighties was a historically critical time, as people in China saw the shift of regime from the "dark age" of the decade-long Cultural Revolution where human values were highly suppressed, to the adoption of an "open-door" policy spearheaded by Deng Xiaoping.

Situational and Cognitive Conditions: Translation Process

Is Zhang's translation a product of negotiation /or collaboration with the translator? Since Zhang did not read English well, the translation process is reduced to a choice of translation version among two published translations, one by Fang Ping, a director and her contemporary, and the other by Zhu Shenghao. There was no negotiation with the translator. Zhang made her selection on the basis of performability of the translation—whether the lines were easily performed by actors and understood by the audience. Zhang chose Fang Ping's translation over Zhu Shenghao's translation and

---

5. Chang, "Censorship in Translation," 229–40.
6. Ibid.
7. Xi, "Review of the Characteristics of Feminist Writings," 47–50.
8. Li, "Women's Consciousness and Women's Writing," 299.

made extensive modifications to render it more colloquial and performable. Zhang's interpretation of the play was thus based solely on Chinese translations, as she could not read the English play text. The two Chinese translations that Zhang read did not suppress the religious content.

When Zhang Qihong decided to stage *The Merchant*, she consulted experts and did extensive research on economics, history, religions, literature and reviews regarding the play, and read the translated texts over and over, but she was still puzzled over a number of questions, including whether the play should be staged as a comedy or a tragedy, what to cut in the 5 acts 25 scenes, and how to treat the religious and racial conflicts. After discussions with theatre colleagues, she involved Cao Yu, a renowned playwright, the "Shakespeare of the Orient" as the artistic director.[9] Cao Yu, familiar with the expectations of Chinese audiences and a translator of *Romeo and Juliet*, decided that *The Merchant* should be a comedy[10] and the production was staged as a romantic comedy.

The decision to delete lines on religious conflicts was not an individual one, but out of collaborative discussions with Wang Jingyu, who was cast as Shylock.[11] He explained that the biblical allusions on the one hand could enrich the character of Shylock as a Jewish money-lender, but on the other hand the audience might not understand the allusions, and the purpose of enriching the character would be defeated. Removing the religious conflict could enhance audience reception without impeding the central theme of *The Merchant*. After the deletion, the conflict between Antonio the capitalist and Shylock who represented money-lenders under the feudal system would be even more prominent.[12]

9. See Zhang, "The Artistic Ideas of Director," 1.
10. See Wu, "Post-Symposium Afterthoughts of *The Merchant of Venice*," 55.
11. Wang, "Debates on the Characterization of Shylock," 61–62.
12. Ibid.

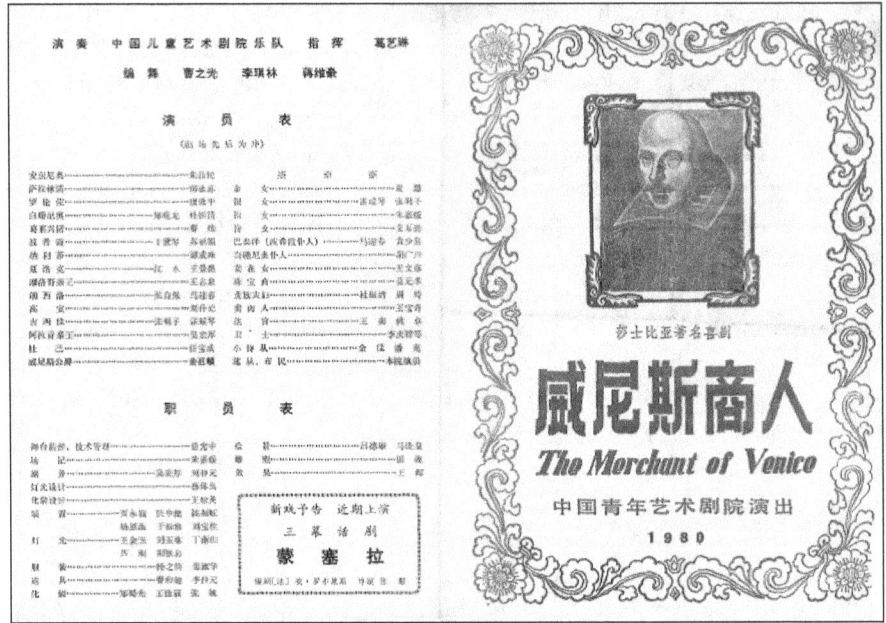

Figure 3.1 House programme of *The Merchant of Venice* 威尼斯商人 directed by Zhang Qihong in 1980, Beijing. (My own collection).

Zhang Qihong chose the published translation of playwright Fang Ping from among other literary translators for its comprehensibility, according to Zhang in an interview.

Translation Profile

Zhang adopted a "Western style"[13] production—Chinese actors and actresses wore wigs and Western costumes. While it attempted to be faithful to the text in terms of the character, time, locale and customs of the Shakespearean play, the Christian references were virtually removed from the script.

---

13. Other than "western style" productions, Shakespearean plays are often "sinicized" in China, i.e. the stories are reset in ancient China and the characters bear Chinese names and observe Chinese customs.

Biblical allusions

In the two-hour performance, besides the removal of the Christian identity of Antonio and other Christians, all biblical allusions disappeared altogether. Daniel, an Old Testament prophet whose name is used to describe Portia's clever judgment in the court scene in Act 4, has been generalized and translated to "a clever judge." The story of Jacob and Laban in the Old Testament, cited by Shylock in Act 1 as a way to indicate how he could match Jacob's cunningness[14] is deleted to avoid audience's confusion.[15] The only translated reference to Christianity occurs in the following lines spoken by Antonio in Act 1:

> The devil can cite Scripture for his purpose. An evil soul producing holy witness.

But inclusion of such would not have left a clue to the audience because, in the original text, these lines follow Shylock's citation of the biblical story of Jacob and Laban. When the story is omitted, even keeping the succeeding lines would not have made sense. The only time where the term "Christian" appeared was in Lancelot's remark when Jessica planned to run away with the Christian Lorenzo. But as all other mentions of Christian identity were dropped, the one-time mention of Lorenzo's Christian identity did not contribute to the interpretation of the Christian-Judeo conflict.

The removal of the allusions seems to have weighed less significantly in defining and shaping character than the reduction of the Judeo-Christian conflict originally explicit in the play. The reason for Shylock's hatred towards Antonio, as in Shylock's speech in Act 1 Scene 3, "I hate him for he is a Christian" was removed from the translated version. In the celebrated speech of Shylock in Act 3 Scene 1, the reason for Antonio's humiliation of him underwent a mutative shift: the Jew in "just because I am a Jew" became "just because I am a money-lender." By removing Christian and Jew as the reason for their mutual hatred, no religious conflict could be established between the two. Although the elopement of Jessica and Lorenzo was kept, the storyline became different with the deletion of Lorenzo's Christian identity. Shylock was infuriated because of the monetary loss with Jessica's running away, not because she ran away with a Christian, as implied from Shakespeare's play text.

---

14. See *Modern Language Notes*, 1947, for commentary on the inclusion of this biblical story in Shakespeare's text.

15. Wang, "Debates on the Characterization of Shylock," 61.

Zhang defended her omission in two ways: that racial and religious conflicts are not essential to the understanding of the plot, and that the audience might not find such Shakespearean themes relevant.

> In assessing the meticulousness of a production, we should not focus on whether the director can "reproduce" the play, but on whether he could give full play to the writer's intention, to the substance of the script, and on whether the main themes are explored in-depth. Based on these criteria, we inevitably deleted conflicts that are not essential to the main theme. For instance, scenes on religious conflicts (between Jews and Christian), racial conflicts are deleted or downplayed, retaining only three soliloquies of Shylock. We retain all the speeches that praised the Jews, and keep the Jewish costumes on stage to give a real sense of the historical background. In the original play, the author objectively describes religious conflicts and racial conflicts. But we reckon that religious conflicts and racial conflicts are not the essential conflicts in this play. They do not constitute the main theme according to Shakespeare.
>
> ... Owing to the differences across time periods, countries and races, another reason we undermined the storyline on religious and racial conflicts is that we want to let the Chinese general audience understand what it is about *The Merchant* of Venice. The conflicts between Christianity and Judaism that took place hundreds of years back, as well as the racial conflicts, are relatively remote for the Chinese audience. In order to let the Chinese audience have a clear understanding of Shakespeare, I undermine these non-essential conflicts while at the same time not jeopardizing the spirit of the original play.[16]

The two points made by Zhang in explaining her reduction and omission of religious material deserved further scrutiny. Contrary to the common conception that deletion of religious material in this period is out of censorship, what lies behind her interpretation of religious material as non-crucial is related to her ideology, which will be discussed in further detail in the Chapter 6. Now in her seventies, Zhang spent five years in Moscow studying directorship in the late nineteen fifties, and had taught at the Central Drama Academy for 20 years upon returning from Moscow. It should be noted that for decades, directors in China had been under the influence of experts from the USSR who were invited to work in China in the 1950s.[17] Until the

---

16. Zhang, "Some Points in the Process of Implementation and Exploration," 285–286.

17. Chinese drama practitioners used Caucasian makeup such as blonde wigs and

1990s, the USSR remained a popular place to which Chinese scholars and professionals were sent by the Chinese government. Sending these people from one Communist regime to another was considered politically safe, as they would be subject to similar ideology. While Zhang opined that students from the Stanislavski School were not taught Marxism nor a Marxist interpretation of plays, the prevalent Marxist ideology that pervaded the eighties in China nonetheless showed its footprints in her directorial notes. She sees the conflicts between Antonio and Shylock as a conflict between "Shylock the feudal exploiter and Antonio the emerging capitalist."[18] The view that Shylock is the exploiter and Antonio the capitalist had its parallel in the ethos of the literary translator of this production Fang Ping, whose Marxist, atheist stance in his critiques have been examined in the previous chapter, although Fang was more skeptical of Antonio's character as a capitalist than Zhang, who read him as a generous good man. Additionally, Zhang argued that it is questionable that the audience in the eighties would agree with Heinrich Heine's interpretation of Shylock as an oppressed Jew and his categorization of *The Merchant* as a tragedy, despite the fact that this interpretation might be appreciated in the nineteenth century when Jews were subject to oppressions and accusations.

Interpretation of Shylock

In Zhang's views, Shylock is a "greedy, selfish, cruel" money-lender who wants to "control the economic lifeline of the whole of Venice." These are the reasons for his taking revenge, she argued. "Although Jews were oppressed in history, his cruel soul should not be covered because of this ethnic oppression. Nor can his cruel exploitation be justified and sympathized because of such ethnic oppression."[19] His revenge is more driven by personal hatred, Zhang claimed. Zhang interpreted Shylock's revenge from a utilitarian perspective, which stemmed from Antonio's interest-free loans and thus affected his money-lending business. She believed that the verdict passed by the Duke on Shylock, requiring him to hand over "all" of his estate to his daughter Jessica[20] was a "merciful" decision and reflected Shakespeare's

---

prosthetic noses and read Shakespeare under the influence of the Russian school. For more discussion on these stage effects, see Li, *Shashibiya*, 2003.

18. Zhang, "Some Points in the Process of Implementation," 4.
19. Ibid.
20. Zhang actually rewrote this scene as half of Shylock's estate would be confiscated while the other half will be handed over to Antonio as a trustee. Strangely, Zhang did not mention the "forced conversion" here. I will discuss this "omission" in later sections.

intention to be kind and merciful. She reckoned that as a comedy, Shakespeare's intention was to satirize such a cruel portrayal of Shylock, but not inviting others to sympathize with or forgive him.

Main Theme

Like other contemporary directors trained in the Russian school, Zhang adopted a humanistic view in her production and read Shakespeare as "the essence of humanistic ideals and aesthetics."[21] She particularly highlights the character of Portia, who is "clever, intelligent, wise," a "giant" representing the Renaissance, an embodiment of "truth, kindness and beauty." In her eyes, Jessica is "beautiful and courageous"; Antonio, Bassanio and Gratiano are all "classics of humanistic ideals." It is through this perspective that she made the deletions and reductions in religious and racial conflicts. Including and highlighting such conflicts might not do justice to the Jewish nation, as Shylock's image was not noble, and his behavior "cruel." His image is one of "business-oriented, exploitative, inhuman loan shark," who cannot represent the Jewish nation. In order to counterbalance the negative image of Shylock as a Jew, she retained the references where Jews were praised.[22] She reckoned that "ethnic oppression is not the main theme of *The Merchant*," and should be treated as a background. If conflicts and emotions arising from such were emphasized in this play, then Shakespeare would not have listed it as a comedy.

The Merchant is highly relevant to contemporary society, she believed. "We really need honest merchants, and truth, kindness and beauty are the perennial qualities that we need: The humanistic ideal in *The Merchant*, genuine friendship, the kindness of Antonio who is willing to rescue his friend. I think not many could do that these days. Such is needed, very much needed."[23] In fact, her emphasis on "truth, kindness and beauty," or zhen-shan-mei (真善美) in Chinese, has been a perennial theme in Chinese theatre.[24] For instance, Zheng Tusheng describes Shakespeare's works as "the highest model of zhen-shan-mei in all world literature."[25] Why is this theme considered a perennial theme and is especially highlighted (which

---

21. Ibid.
22. Zhang, "Some Points in the Process of Implementation," 285–286.
23. According to my interview with Zhang Qihong on 2nd August 2010.
24. See Zheng, "Truth, Goodness and Beauty," 149–162., where Zheng lists twelve virtues of "truth, kindness and beauty" that in his view are compatible with Marxism-Maoism.
25. See Zheng, "Recent Situations of Chinese Shakespeare Scholarship," 310–314.

inevitably suppresses the religious dimension)? The answer to this, I would say, is a theological one. The three words zhen-shan-mei embody the essence of Chinese traditional philosophies—Confucianism, Buddhism and Daoism. While Buddhism places the emphasis on kindness and compassion, Daoism truth of nature, the ultimate goal is the attainment of beauty. Contemporary Chinese philosopher Li Zehou 李澤厚 describes the philosophy of Daoist philosopher Zhuangzi 莊子 as tantamount to aesthetics[26] so rather than seeking religious experience as the basis of a philosophy of life, the attainment of aesthetics is the guiding principle towards an ideal human life: no calculation of interests, right or wrong, reward or punishment, and dissolving the boundaries of material and self, host and guest, others or self. Since aesthetics rather than religion is the final goal of life, Li points out that Zhuangzi does not seek to resolve the fear and sorrow arising from death, nor does it seek the painful sacrifice of present life to reach redemption of the soul.[27] Li further proposed that China has a culture of joy in contrast to the culture of sin in Western civilization[28] and that joy specifically points to the achievement by effort rather than a reflex reaction. This implies that the Chinese stress the making of effort in the attainment of joy through education and learning. Such joy as attained through learning is specified in the first line of the Analects: 學而時習之，不亦悅乎? [Is it not pleasant to learn with a constant perseverance and application?] Liu Xiaofeng 劉小楓, a contemporary influential scholar on philosophy, argued that despite the fact that Confucianism has a culture of anxiety, especially over matters of the state, in the end, the achievement of joy is emphasized as the final, highest destination in human life, as exemplified in the saying: 先天下之憂而憂，後天下之樂而樂 [Be the first to worry about the troubles across the land, the last to enjoy universal happiness].[29] This pursuit of joy is reflected in the optimistic character of Chinese people and is deeply entrenched in the culture. In this connection, it is not hard to detect that topics such as conflicts and sin are less popular in traditional Chinese theatre.

Zhang's emphasis on these three elements: truth, kindness and beauty, is inherited by her successor Ni Huiying, which will be discussed later in this chapter later.

26. See Li, *History of Chinese Thoughts*, 193. The aesthetics proposed by Zhuangzi can be exemplified in his statement from Zhuangzi's Zhibeiyou 知北遊 [Knowledge Rambling in the North]: 天地大美有三: 一曰形之美，二曰道之美，三曰德之美 [the beauty of heaven and earth has the following three qualities: first is the beauty of form, second is the beauty of the nature's way, third is the beauty of virtue]

27. Ibid.

28. Ibid, 316.

29. See Liu, *Salvation and Easy Wandering*, 176.

Racial issues

The weakening of the Jewish identity of Shylock was necessary, according to actor Wang Jingyu. He reasoned that the reduction is a response to the time Jews have suffered enormously in history, and were persecuted in the Second World War. "We assume, if Shakespeare were still alive, that he with his humanistic spirit, probably would not wish to highlight the Jewish identity of Shylock and go on to humiliate him."[30]

Secondly, the deletion of religious and racial conflicts, Wang argued, should not be simplified and generalized. The characterisation of Shylock did not change with the deletion of the Judeo-Christian conflict, he is still the moneylender full of emotions and complexity. He is still the same person as the one who grinned at the signing of the bond of flesh, he who was devastated by the loss of daughter and money, he who vented anger against Antonio's humiliation in his celebrated speech.

But it is Portia's mercy speech that saw a significant loss in Christian ideology inherent in it. As Fang Ping's translation already had the allegory of mercy and justice removed, one can no longer see a close equivalent of justice, which mutated into "king's rule." The Lord's Prayer that teaches people the deeds of mercy has been mutated into" 心地的善良顯示出靈魂的美好 (A kind heart shows a good soul)." No prayer was mentioned, but the kindness of heart, as the following translation shows:

> 仁慈並不是什麼可以強求的東西，它，像甘露一樣從天而降撒落到人間。它是萬王之王所奉行的王道，它比皇冠更昭示了帝皇的身份。而帝皇手裡的節杖不過是象徵著世俗的威權，讓人望而生畏，可是仁慈卻高於王法的威力，它象徵著上帝的鴻恩！所以夏洛克，心地的善良顯示出靈魂的美好。我說這番話無非是想勸你別堅持那法律的立場，要是你說一不二，那麼威尼斯的法庭執法無私，只好把這商人拿來判罪。

Kindness is not something that can be forced.

It is like gentle rain falling from heaven and scattered in the mortal world.

It is the king's way upheld by the king of kings.

It shows the monarch's identity better than a crown.

The staff in the hand of the monarch is but a symbol of temporal power,

that leaves people in awe.

30. See Wang, "Debates on the Characterization of Shylock," 62.

But kindness is above the authority of king's ruling-it symbolizes the great grace of God.

So Shylock, kindness of heart can show the beauty of soul.

I say these words so as to plead with you not to insist the legal requirement.

If you insist, then the court of Venice is just and can only give sentence against him.

Zhang's translation cannot be seen as translation—it should be regarded as adaptation where Portia's long speech is condensed to only ten lines. The condensed speech, it should be noted, is more memorable. Zhang's version, based on Fang Ping's translation, retained some of the Chinese idiomatic expressions in Fang's translation, such as "king of kings 萬王之王" and the use of parallel expressions such as "kindness of heart 心地的善良"and "beauty of soul 靈魂的美好." However, the idea of salvation and prayer to God, retained in Fang's translation, were totally omitted from Zhang's version. The only religious connotation retained is the "great grace of God 上帝的鴻恩," an adaptation of "an attribute of God." According to Nevill Coghill,[31] who saw *The Merchant* as an allegory of Justice and Mercy, Shylock who lived by the law and denied mercy should perish by the law. The only way out is to become a Christian, which to him, is a punishment; but to Christians, a mercy. The dichotomy of mercy and justice, a Christian concept embedded in the source text, is lost at the receiving end under the reduction strategy of Zhang. Without mentioning justice, the emphasis of Portia's speech is placed on mercy alone, a quality Portia asked of Shylock. The audience on the receiving end would simply interpret Portia's speech as a plea to Shylock, but would not relate to the Christian concept that God's mercy is above justice and leads people to salvation.

Below is another example showing how the religious dimension was lost in Shylock's "hath not a Jew eyes" speech.

夏洛克：提起他，那安東尼奧！這個破落戶！現在他再也不敢到市場上來露臉了吧！這個叫花子！你看他平常在市場上穿得多麼威風啊！我叫他留心留心他那份借據吧！他罵我是吸血鬼，我叫他留心留心他那份借據吧！他放債不要利錢，他大方，我叫他留心留心他那份借據吧！

朗西洛：哎，我的老東家，如果他到期無力償還，我擔保您不會向他要那一磅肉吧。

葛萊興諾：一磅人肉要它幹嘛！

---

31. Coghill, "The Theme of The Merchant of Venice," 108–112.

朗西洛：是呀，幹嘛！

夏洛克：幹嘛？拿它來餵魚，給魚吃，魚不吃至少可以讓我那復仇的心好有點東西消化消化，他侮辱我，破壞我，叫我損失了幾十萬兩銀子！看見我虧損了，他就挖苦我，我要是賺了他就笑我，跟我的生意買賣搗蛋。在我的朋友面前潑我的冷水，到我的冤家那裡煽動他們復仇的火焰！這一切！這一切！都為的什麼呀！為的什麼呀！就因為我是猶太人！猶太人怎麼了？猶太人沒有眼？不生手？沒有五官四肢沒知覺沒骨肉之情沒血氣了嗎？猶太人不是一樣的要吃飯嗎，不是一樣要生病，生了病不是一樣要醫治的嗎？我們不是一樣夏天感到熱冬天感到冷？你們要是用針刺我們，我們不是一樣也會流血？你們要是胳肢我們，我們不是一樣也呵呵呵笑嗎？你們要是用毒藥謀害我們我們不是也會死的嗎？那麼，要是你們侮辱了我們難道我們就不報仇了嗎！不！既然在別的地方我們都跟你們一樣，那麼在這一點上也是不分彼此的！要報仇啊！要報仇！要報仇！

回音人：要報仇要報仇要報仇！

夏洛克：你．．．．你是誰！

回音人：我和你一樣

夏洛克：你也是猶太人？

回音人：不！

夏洛克：那，你也放高利貸？

回音人：我們那裡叫放印子錢！

夏洛克：那麼他們也破壞你侮辱你跟你的生意買賣搗蛋！

回音人：對，他們也用毒辣的手段對待我！

夏洛克：啊，那我們就照著他們的榜樣學，不壓倒他們我們就不甘休！

回音人：不甘休！

夏洛克：不甘休！

回音人：不甘休！不甘休！不甘休！不甘休！不甘休！

Shylock

Mentioning him—that Antonio! That bankrupt! Now he dare not show his face in the market. That prodigal! Look how confidently he dressed in the market. I have him to look to his bond! He called me a vampire! I have him to look to his bond! He lends money without charging interest, he is generous. I have him to look to his bond!

Launcelot[32]

Ah, my lord, if he forfeit, I am sure you will not take his one pound of flesh.

Gratiano

What is the use of one pound of flesh?

Launcelot

Yes, what use?

Shylock

What use? To bait fish, feed fish, even if fish does not take it, at least my revengeful heart has something to digest. He mocked at me, sabotaged me, made me lose hundreds of thousands. Seeing my losses, he scoffed at me. If I gained, he laughed at me. He thwarted my businesses. He took me down in front of my friends. He roasted me in front of my enemies. All this! All this! Why? Why? Just because I am a Jew! Have not Jews eyes? No hands? No organs and limbs and without senses without family bonding, without passion? Don't Jews eat rice just as others, get sick just as others, and need medical treatment in sickness just like others? Don't we feel hot during summers, feel cold during winter? If you prick us, do we not bleed? If you tickle us, do we not laugh? if you poison us, do we not die? If you insult us, do we not take revenge? No! If we are like you in the rest, we will resemble you in that. Revenge! Revenge! Revenge!

Phantom man: Revenge! Revenge! Revenge!

Shylock: Who are you?

Phantom Man: Same as you.

Shylock: You are also a Jew?

Phantom Man: No!

32. Salarino's line has been taken up by Launcelot in Zhang's production. In fact, the character of Salarino did not appear in Zhang's production, possibly with the intention of reducing the number of characters.

Shylock: So, you also lend money at high interest?

Phantom Man: We call this lending "stamped money."

Shylock: So do they sabotage you, insult you, and thwarted your businesses?

Phantom Man: Yes, they also ill-treat me!

Shylock: Arh, so we learn from their example. We won't give up unless we overtake them!

Phantom man: Won't give up!

Shylock: Won't give up!

Phantom Man: Won't give up! Won't give up! Won't give up! Won't give up! Won't give up!

In Shylock's long speech, Zhang simply substituted all mentioning of Christians with "you"—creating an antagonism between Jews and non-Jews, rather than Jews and Christians. As a stagecraft, the use of "you" would engage with the Chinese audience more, which creating an issue of reception where "you" might simply be interpreted as Chinese to the audience. "Christian courtesy"[33] in Shylock's speech was not seen, disappeared, or rather, this was paraphrased as "lend money without charging interest 放債不要利錢." The translation did not mention the Christian revenge if a Jew wrong a Christian as in the source text, and did not mention the villainy Jews were treated by Christians[34] The separation of the Christian identity from Antonio avoids the label of hypocritical Christian on Antonio, thus reinforcing his image as a great hero.

Zhang's reduction of Christian terminology was later compensated by an additional touch to the original play—an appearance of a phantom man who echoed what Shylock said. The phantom represented a Chinese counterpart of Shylock, a moneylender in the Ming Dynasty, who was sympathetic with Shylock's situation. This touch avoided the need to address the conflicts and historical relationship between a Christian and a Jew. The inner suffering of Shylock was reinforced through this dramatic effect, according to Chinese Shakespeare scholar Zhang Xiao Yang. This in

---

33. The source text reads: He was wont to lend money for a Christian courtesy; let him look to his bond.

34. The source text reads: If a Jew wrong a Christian, what is his humility? Revenge. If a Christian wrong a Jew, what should his sufferance be by Christian example? Why, revenge. The villainy you teach me I will execute—and it shall go hard but I will better the instruction.

turn brought the Chinese audience closer to and in greater sympathy with this Jewish protagonist. In an interview, Zhang Qihong admitted that such Chinese-Jewish dialogue had historical reference, as Jewish and Chinese had come into contact through trade in the past centuries.[35]

Defending her omission of religious conflicts and racial conflicts, she disputed the idea that such treatment would "generalize," "simplify" or "romanticize" the play. Shylock is still a complex character who is at times sorrowful and joyful, who shows love and hatred towards his daughter, who is at times kind and at times cruel to his enemy, and who experiences great pain at the loss of money and ring, but great joy at Antonio's fiasco. "How can the deletion of 'Christian' and 'Jews' affect the complexity of a person's character and inner self? Both images of Shylock have their characteristics [. . .] some audiences watched not just once, but twice. Through their responses, Shylock becomes, as Chernyshevsky said, 'a living person with reddened cheeks.' A lively, complex character is created."[36] Her humanistic-cum-Marxist interpretation of the play left a deep impact on the reception of this play throughout the eighties. Reviews of this play in that period centered around the conflict between a bourgeois and a capitalist exploiter.

Forced Conversion

Omitting all references to Christianity inevitably led to the omission of Shylock's "forced conversion" at the trial scene. Zhang's treatment of "forced conversion" reflects not only the predominant ideology that disapproves of forced conversion which disrupts social harmony, but also her own. Behind her consideration for audience expectations lies her resistance to the idea of Christian forced conversion, as "everyone should have freedom of religion." Her resistance will be studied in more detail in Chapter 6.

Gender Issues

Just as interesting as what was deleted is what was added or modified. In this two-hour production, one third of the scenes are dedicated to Portia's selection of husband. Zhang gave Portia a special place in the play by personifying the gold, silver and lead caskets in her selection of husband. The large portrait of Portia's late father hanging on the wall of Portia's room suggested the bondage of patriarchal society on Portia who is trying to break away in

---

35. Zhang, *Shakespeare in China*, 128.
36. Ibid.

pursuit of liberation. In the usual productions, the three caskets were laid on the table to be chosen by suitors of Portia. However, in order to highlight Portia's wisdom and liveliness, three ladies in different costumes holding out their respective caskets danced in front of the suitors. The gold casket was held by a glamorous lady in golden costumes, while the silver casket was held by a fine lady in silver. The lead casket was held by a modestly-dressed lady executing a grave dance. She was positioned towards the back of stage. Her modesty highlighted Bassanio's nobleness. The addition aptly illustrated the adage of "all that glitters is not gold"[37] Another addition to the play is that this lead casket lady was later married to Lancelot in the last act. Three pairs of lovers were wedded on the same day, enhancing the liveliness of this romantic comedy.

Portia as a wise lawyer has been a likeable character in the eyes of Chinese women since her introduction in the early twentieth century and has been a role model for female directors and producers alike. Zhang admitted in the interview that she liked Portia, who was clever and unconventional. She cleverly thought of a way to liberate herself from the bondage of her family to choose her lover. In the casket scene, the hint made by Portia pointing to the correct casket made by Portia in her song to Bassanio is made explicit in her production, which can be seen from Zhang's translation totally different from Fang Ping's:

Source Text (Act III):

Tell me where is fancy bred,

Or in the heart, or in the head?

How begot, how nourished?

Reply, reply.

It is engender'd in the eyes,

With gazing fed; and fancy dies

In the cradle where it lies.

Let us all ring fancy's knell

I'll begin it,—Ding, dong, bell.

假如是要找到她，

假如是要找到她，

---

37. See Lin, "The Light of the Ideal Dimension," 22–24.

不要被那妖豔的光彩蒙住了眼睛

不要被那華麗內心蒙住了你的眼睛

If you find her, If you find her, Do not have your eyes blinded by the glamorous glory

Do not have your eyes blinded by the fancy heart.

This feminist interpretation of the play is evidenced by the synopsis in the house program, which sees Portia being portrayed as the lead character:

> This story took place in the second half of the 16th century in Belmont, a city in Italy. There lived a beautiful and clever lady known as Portia. Her rich father left three boxes—gold, silver and copper. Only one box contains the portrait of Portia. Whoever picks this box can marry her. Portia was in love with the handsome and able Bassanio. However, she could only comply with the bond imposed by her father [. . .]

The highlighting of gender issues inevitably gives rise to the suppression of other themes, in particular the religious dimension. Such highlighting of gender can be seen in her predecessor Bao Tianxiao's production, and was carried forward to her successor Ni Huiying's Cantonese operatic production, which will be studied later.

Cognitive and Behavioral Effects

Judging from the record number of performances, Zhang's omissions made sense to the box office. Her deletions condensed the play to slightly over 2 hours. Such treatment of religious material, however well-received by the audience, invited criticisms. Reviews are mixed regarding the omission of the Judeo-Christian conflict and the simplification of Shylock's character. At the post-performance symposium held on 23 Oct 1981, attended by the director of the play, theatre critics and drama scholars, the majority agreed that the simplification of Shylock's complex character was partly due to the deletion of religious and racial conflicts. Dr Zhang Long Xi argued that "it [the deletion of lines on the religious conflicts between Shylock and Antonio] fundamentally alters Shakespeare's intention which is unacceptable."[38] Drama scholar Zhang Longxi believed that the Judeo-Christian conflict is less opaque when staged in the UK and America as there is a large Jewish population in these Western countries, but in China, this is not the case. So

---

38. Sun, *Who's Butterfly?*, 65.

Shylock should not be given a black-or-white portrayal, but his complexity should be retained. The current portrait simplifies his character.[39] This view was echoed by Song Yan, who opined that such a deletion on one hand highlights the conflict between Antonio as the emerging bourgeois and Shylock the loan shark under the feudal system, while on the other hand, reduced the many facets of Shylock's character to just one level. Retention of religious and racial conflicts, she thought, might restore the complexity of Shylock's character. Director Sun Jiasou did not agree to portray Shylock only as a money-lender but deleted the references to racial and religious oppression that might win him sympathy. If the German poet Heinrich Heine, who showed sympathy towards Shylock and the humiliation suffered by the Jew, was still alive, Sun asked, would one see sympathy in him? Other performers of the China National Youth Art Theatre nonetheless agreed with her theatrical approach, because the storyline between a Jew and a Christian was not meaningful to the Chinese audience. Whether it is a Jew or a Caucasian, they are aliens, or the "other" to the Chinese.[40]

The personification of three caskets was highly commended by critics. All reviews mentioned these additional scenes as an important storyline,[41] which livened up what used to be the most static, boring episodes.[42] The highlighting of Portia with the addition of such scenes, however, weakened the original plot of the pound of flesh.[43] The effects of omitting religious and racial conflicts plus the emphasis on liberation gave rise to a romanticized production.

Zhang's approach to this romantic comedy was considered bold by a considerable conservative audience. Audiences went away recalling that "there is kissing on the stage."[44] The Beijing Evening Post published a letter from an official on 7 September 1980 who was disturbed for weeks after watching the production. He criticized the production for being "harmful to public morals" because performers embraced and kissed each other in front of such a big audience."[45] His letter created a stir among the audience—a majority disagreed with him, but still there were dozens of letters

---

39. See Wu, "Debates on the Characterization of Shylock," 56; Zhang ,"On Shylock," 57–60.

40. Ibid.

41. See Lin, "The Light of the Ideal Dimension," 24.

42. Ibid.

43. Wu, "Debates on the Characterization of Shylock," 56.

44. See Li, *Shashibiya*, 2.

45. Ibid.

that concurred with him, expressing concern that certain lines involving sex jokes in Act 5 were "vulgar and dreadful."[46]

Socio-cultural Effects

The performance of this production—highly acclaimed by both spectators and critics—left a significant socio-cultural impact. Theatre critics agreed that this performance in the eighties led to the following effects: 1. It was conducive to restoring and establishing an ethos where friendship and love should entail self-sacrifice. The pure love and friendship championed by Shakespeare four hundred years ago can cultivate noble thoughts, especially in a corrupt society; 2. It was conducive to increasing knowledge among young people of humanistic writers and their works during the renaissance period, helping them to understand the early capitalist society and historical conditions, people and ethos during that period; 3. It was conducive to the development of theatre in the country. Shakespearean plays have structures similar to Chinese traditional drama (xiqu): the quick pace in Elizabethan drama and the detailed portrayal of characters can inspire the development of Chinese dramas.[47] The impact of this production prompted Prof. Zhu Guangqian, professor at Peking University, to send a letter of commendation to the post-performance symposium. Anticipating its positive impact on future productions, he said: "*The Merchant of Venice* opened a new chapter for Shakespearean plays in our country's theatre." Attendees at the symposium agreed that more "elaborate, foreign and ancient" plays should be staged.

The treatment of certain scenes in this production, especially the personification of the three caskets with three ladies holding each casket in the gold, silver and lead costumes were followed by other Mainland productions. Daniel Yang, who watched Zhang's production, did take reference from Zhang and included this personification in this production in 1984 in Hong Kong, which will be discussed in a later section.

How has Zhang's production with subdued religious content impacted on the interpretation of latter day directors? As the following case study shows, this de-christianization process is seen in a Cantonese adaptation of *The Merchant* in 2007, known as Hao men qianjin 豪門千金, or *For The Heiress' Hand*, produced by an actress under Zhang's directorship in the 1980s.

46. Ibid.
47. Wu, "Debates on the Characterization of Shylock," 57.

For The Heiress' Hand (豪門千金) in 2007 in Guangzhou, a Cantonese Operatic Version of The Merchant of Venice.

Socio-cultural Conditions

Adapting Shakespeare into Cantonese opera is not a totally new concept, but can be seen as a survival strategy for traditional theatrical formats seeking to cope with the emergence of new media. In the 1930s, when movies were threatening the existence of Cantonese opera, foreign or Japanese theatre productions were translated and adapted into Cantonese opera, for example *One Thousand and One Nights* became *Prince of Thieves* (賊王子 Zei Wangzi). The first Cantonese operatic version of *The Merchant* can be traced back to the 1930s directed by the Cantonese opera master Ma Shizeng 馬師曾, based on the story of the pound of flesh in Lin Shu's translation of *Tales from Shakespeare*. Later, in the 1950s, he put on another adaptation known as *The Merchant of Venice*, this time using Western costumes. In 1983, Zhang Qihong and Hong Xiannu, an icon in Cantonese opera history until the 1990s, together staged *The Heaven's Proud Daughter* (天之驕女), highlighting the wisdom of Portia as the title character. A parallel can be drawn between the early twentieth and the early twenty-first century, both of which have seen the continual adaptation of traditional operatic forms through blending with foreign theatrical formats as a way of survival in the face of new media.

Figure 3.2 Photo of *tianzhijiaonv* 天之嬌女 [Heaven's Proud Daughter] directed by Zhang Qihong in 1984 (Source: Guangzhou Cantonese Opera Troupe 廣州粵劇團)

Whether it is the story of the pound of flesh, or Zhang Qihong's *The Heaven's Proud Daughter*, the history of past interpretations has informed this current production. The good-and-evil dichotomy, plus the suppression of religious discourse in these earlier plots, left its footprints on the producer's line of interpretation. He continued to see Shylock as a "heartless" villain, and religious conflicts as a side issue of the play. Worth noting is the fact that the producer Ni Huiying 倪惠英 was cast as Portia under the directorship of Zhang Qihong in the 1983 Cantonese adaptation. Zhang sees Portia as one who "knows how to liberate herself from the family bond to find the love of her life," and one who is brave and clever in disguising herself as a lawyer (or, more specifically, as an apprentice to a barrister from Hong Kong) to save her husband—a manifestation of female dignity and wisdom in Shakespeare's portrayal. Consciously or unconsciously, Ni continued this feminist interpretation in this new adaptation.

As to the state of censorship in this period, while it is not explicitly stated that theatre productions have to be censored, the fact that theatre troupes in China are supported by the state helps one to understand the importance of making productions that are "officially approved." The Government has supported the ongoing survival of Cantonese opera through bulk purchase of tickets to be distributed to party officials. The fact that the producer herself is a senior party member may help explain her viewpoint that "religion" is not an important issue in this play.

The Religious Fever in the Early Twenty-First Century

Compared to the post-Mao era thirty years back, the religious policy in China has evolved substantially and vastly loosened in the past ten years. Since the open-door policy was instigated under the leadership of Deng Xiaoping, a softening in the control of religious activities gave rise to a more vibrant religious milieu with mushrooming activities. In 2004, there were over 16,000 Protestant churches, 32,000 meeting points. 70 per cent of them were built within the previous years.[48] Protestants numbered 14 million in 2004, up from 5-6 million in 1993. It was estimated that the number of Protestants had risen to approximately 50 to 60 million by 2010.

The publication of *On Religion under Socialism* in 2003 by the Religious Affairs Bureau which analyzed the relationship between religion and socialism was highly commended as a big step forward in asserting the compatibility between religion and socialism, and in promoting religion as a harmonious factor in a society. Religious Bureau head Ye Xiaowen

---

48. Leung, "China's Religious Freedom Policy," 894–913.

summarized five new directional shifts in China's religious work which reasserts the positive force of religion.[49]

Parallel to this resurgence of religious activity is the economic progress since the reform and open-door policy. This is by no means accidental. Modernization is dependent on foreign aid which in turn is related to the country's human rights record. Money from the West would not flow to a country which had no religious freedom.[50] But in order to maintain control of religious activity, Communist Party officials have the controlling power in the religious establishments, rendering local religious leaders a minor role.[51] The resurgence was interrupted by setbacks as a result of changes in policy and regime throughout this period. In the 1990s, a new set of measures put in place included requirement for registration of religious groups with civil authorities to be approved by the Religious Affairs Bureau. Religious groups and activities were also required to be free from "foreign control" according to Article 36 of the Constitution of the People's Republic of China where "foreigner" was defined in Document No. 144 (1994) "Guowuyuan guanyu zongjiao huodong changsuo guanli tiaoli" ("Regulations from the State Council on managing religious activities") as anyone not a Chinese national, such as overseas Chinese, Chinese in Hong Kong, Macau and Taiwan, and Chinese living in China but holding foreign passports.[52] Even to this day, foreigners (including people from Hong Kong) are not permitted to be involved in religious gatherings with locals to prevent infiltration from outside of China. It is only since 2001 that religion has been recognized for

---

49. The five forces are:
   1. See believers as insiders, as a positive force rather than backward, negative force;
   2. shift the emphasis on religion as an exploiting factor in controlling the public's spirit in the social hierarchy to a matter-of-fact assertion of religion's positive and negative factors in the socialist society that needs adjustment and restraints;
   3. from a critical approach in the revolutionary period to emphasis on unity among believers in this construction period;
   4. see religious works as public and societal affairs management rather than mental, political and internal affairs, and undergo the path of institutionalization and standardization;
   5. shifting religious works from departmental and territorial to belonging to the party-wide and bureau-wide levels.

   For details, see Ye, "New Collections on Socialism," 13–15.
50. Leung, "China's Religious Freedom Policy," 903.
51. Ibid.
52. Ibid, 909.

the first time by the then head of state Jiang Zemin as a stabilizing force in the society.[53] During the era of the new leader Hu Jintao, the model of "stabilization" and "management through legal regulation" is still in effect. The importance of "harmony" was asserted in the revised constitution (2004), where "no one can carry out activities that cause disruption to social order, harm the physical health of citizens or hinder the national education system" [任何人不得利用宗教進行破壞社會秩序、損害公民身體健康、妨礙國家教育制度的活動。] But the religious stance of the government remains ambiguous, swinging from one extreme to the other, relaxing and tightening control when it sees fit, and differently across provinces and cities. For example, the Sichuan earthquake in May 2008 prompted the government to welcome Christian organizations in rebuilding efforts, but the revival of Christian activities was short-lived as some organizations were later found to be unreliable. Some provinces have more stringent control on religious policies. For example, according to the Hainan provincial religious affairs management ordinance, Article 39 requires religious groups to obtain prior approval from religious affairs department at the municipal level or above if they propose to organize training sessions or religious learning activities. In Gansu province, Article 20 of the provisional regulations of religious affairs management requires that religious activities should be "small-scale, local and scattered," a principle not recognized in other provinces nor in the Constitution.

Has the greater degree of religious freedom been reflected in the *literati* circle? Does implicit self-censorship still exist? In the trial scene of *The Merchant* which is translated and included in the Chinese language textbooks of the secondary school curriculum, a course book shows that Antonio's forgiveness upon Shylock's conversion was omitted. A teacher criticised this treatment as leaving students the impression that Shylock was not treated humanely and mercifully as the Christians had promised.[54] What may be the reasons behind the omission of Antonio's "forced conversion" in educational materials at a time of religious tolerance in the twenty-first century? "Forced conversion" remains a sensitive, untouchable issue as one refers to Article 36 of the Constitution of the People's Republic of China which was promulgated in 1982 and basically remained unchanged thereafter, which states that no forced conversion is allowed:

---

53. Ibid, 910.
54. Diu, "A Tail that Should Not be Cut Off," 40.

no national authorities, societal groups or individuals can force citizens to believe or disbelieve a religion, and cannot discriminate against citizens who are believers or non-believers.[55]

In 2004, the Religious Affairs Ordinance (ZongjiaoShiwuTiaoli 宗教事務條例) was passed at the State Council's 57th Standing Committee meeting, and publication of religious material was within the terms of reference of the ordinance. All material relating to religious content should be in accordance with the requirements set out in the Publication Management Ordinance (ChubanGuanliTiaoli 出版管理條例), which should not include the following materials which:

- Damage the harmony between believers and non-believers;
- Damage the harmony among religions and the harmony within a religion;
- Discriminate against or humiliate believers or non-believers;
- Promote radicalism in religions;
- Work against the self-reliance, self-management principle of religions.

The forced conversion mentioned by Antonio as a condition for pardoning Shylock's life exemplifies the religious conflicts between Judaism, represented by Shylock, and Christianity represented by Antonio. In that sense, the plot may disrupt the harmony among religions. Such "forced conversion" can be interpreted as a humiliation or discrimination against Jews, and may be viewed as "radical," causing uncomfortable feelings by the audience who are mostly unbelievers.[56] Why harmony is more than once emphasized in the above Ordinance? Ying Futsang believed that what concerns the government most is the disruption of harmony may lead to religious conflicts that in turn disrupt the unity and stability in society.[57]

55. Additionally, until 2005, the state prohibited the propagation of religious thoughts to children under the age of 18. In 2005, the Department of Diplomacy allowed parents to propagate religious thoughts to their children, and children under 18 can participate in religious activities. Despite the relaxation of religious control, provinces may not adhere to such guidelines to the same degree. In Urghurs, for example, parents are not allowed to bring children to religious activities, nor can the children participate in prayer meetings. The new religious policy has not yet been effectively communicated downward, leading to gaps of communication and self-censorship in times of uncertain interpretation of the regulations. It came as no surprise that omission is seen in the religious material in children's literature.

56. In fact, some commentators believed that such lines may cause discomfort among audience and might be the reasons for its deletion in Zhang Qihong's 1980 production. See Ji. "Discussions on the Directorship of *The Merchant of Venice*," 302–306.

57. See Ying, "New Wine and Old Wineskin," 2006.

The suppression of religious content in publications at a period of so-called "religious fever" seems to anticipate the untranslatability of religious dimension in other areas, which I will show in the Translation Profile section in this chapter.

Situational and Cognitive Conditions

About producer, actress and interviewee Ni Huiying—she was the chair of the Guangzhou Cantonese opera troupe from 2001, and became chair of the board of directors in 2009. Being both producer and actress who was cast as Portia, she had the leading influence in the interpretation and directorship of the production. The idea of adapting *The Merchant* into Cantonese opera occurred to her after she was cast as Portia in the Cantonese operatic version of *The Merchant* directed by Zhang Qihong and Hong Xiannu 紅線女 in 1986. This was a decision driven by market forces, and also by her belief in Shakespeare's universality. Here is what she said in an interview:

> In the process of performance, I heard a lot of commendations from the audience [of the 1986 production], but I also heard comments that it did not look familiar to them, because Cantonese opera is a very localized, down-to-earth form of art. Cantonese opera has its unique aura, and costumes. At that time I had a thought of localizing it, [as] I believe Shakespeare belongs to everyone.

Impressed with Shakespeare's social relevance, and the play's sharp and poignant portrayal of human nature and characterization that transcends time and space, she sought to "stand on the shoulders of the Bard" to create and spread to China the humanity embedded in Shakespeare.

The casting for the production is a strong one—Ni Huiying, cast as Portia, is an award-winning actress and had been in the industry since 1970s; Guan Dongtian 關棟天, cast as Antonio, a well-respected Peking Opera actor, while Li Junsheng 李駿聲 who, cast as Bassanio, is also a household name in Cantonese opera. Numerous press releases were published before the performance in major newspapers in the Guangdong area, testifying to marketing effort as well as media support. Not only did the production gain media support, its rehearsal ceremony was well attended by the Propaganda Department of Guangzhou Municipal Government, and the leading officials at the Cultural Bureau, underlining the official support it attained.

The adaptation process took 5 years, starting in 2000. The first draft, rendered by the veteran dramaturg Qin Zhongying 秦中英 and under

Ni Huiying's leadership, came out as a period play, with Portia cast as a duchess. However, the cultural differences between the East and the West left Ni to wonder about its practicability, which leads one to consider the cognitive process.

The main line of interpretation of this production is "good versus evil, good begets good, and evil begets evil," as she described. Her involvement in *The Merchant* when she was cast as Portia in the Cantonese adaptation of *The Merchant* in 1985, known as 天之驕女 *Heaven's Proud Daughter*, could shed light on how she arrived at this interpretation.

A comparison of the two scripts in the 1985 and the 2007 productions shows that the script in the later production was re-written largely on the basis of the earlier version. The later production should be described as an adaptation of *Heaven*, but this was not mentioned anywhere in the house program or in press interviews. Both plots feature a single characterization of the villainous Shylock and the heroic Antonio. Portia was the title character, rather than *The Merchant*, reflecting the preference of the then director—Zhang Qihong for a feminist interpretation in the 1980 production of *The Merchant*.

Both house programs describe Portia's beauty and intelligence in the synopsis, and foreground her over and above other lead characters, as shown below:

Table 3.1 Comparison between 1985 Production House Program and 2007 Production House Program

1985	2007
In the Medieval times a duke passed away in Belmont in Italy, leaving a wealth of property and his only daughter Portia (Bao Xiaya 鮑西婭). Portia is clever, beautiful and intelligent, and is hailed as "the Heaven's proud daughter."	A tycoon in Guangzhou left his only daughter Portia (Zhu xiya 朱西婭) who was beautiful and clever, and had been educated overseas. She followed her father's will to openly advertise for a husband. The news spread to Macau and attracted a number of tycoons and foreign merchants to come for the contest.
Portia and Bassanio (Ba saniao 巴薩尼奧) from Venice met in the spring as they were horse-racing, and were attracted to one another. Although they were in love, Portia could not take control of her marriage. Her father left three boxes-gold, silver and lead. Whoever chose the right box (the one that contained her portrait) could marry her	

1985	2007

1985

On the day of selection, many aristocrats and dukes came and were attracted to the gold and silver boxes. Only Bassanio who was genuinely in love chose the lead box under the guidance of Portia, and the two were married.

Bassanio was a distressed aristocrat, and originally he could not afford the wedding gifts. His good friend Antonio (An Dongniao 安東尼奧) helped fulfil his wish and borrowed 3,000 ducats from the high-interest money lender Shylock (Xia Luoke 夏洛克) for a period of three months. If he failed to repay at maturity, he would have to let Shylock cut a pound of flesh from him. However the merchant ship was wrecked and his debt was due. Portia heard the news, but according to the law of Venice, Antonio could not be saved even if he repaid ten times of money back over.

Clever Portia disguised herself as a lawyer at the court and won the case filed by the cruel Shylock, and saved Antonio which gained the applause of the people. Then came the accident of the ring, which made Bassanio realize the solemnity and authenticity of love between husband and wife.

This is a play that promulgates truth, kindness and beauty, and condemns hypocrisy, evil and the ugly.

2007

The now distressed merchant's son Bassanio (Chang Yingzhi 常英志) met Portia while having a day out in spring, and was attracted to her. He went along for the open competition but had no money to purchase gifts. So he borrowed 3,000 ducats from his good friend the merchant Antonio (Li Andong 李安東). Antonio's merchant ships had yet to come back and she had no cash on hand. But he borrowed money from the Macanese loan shark (money-lender) Shylock (Xia Laoke 夏老克) in order to help his friend. Shylock was notorious for his cruelty, and specified in the contract that if the money could not be repaid on maturity, he would have the right to cut a pound of flesh from the borrower. Antonio agreed in order to help his friend.

Portia required her suitors to choose from among the gold, silver and lead boxes a box that contained her portrait in order to have the right to marry her, in accordance with her father's will. If they failed they could not marry. After a lot of hesitation, Bassanio chose the right box with the portrait. However, the bad news came that Antonio's ship had been wrecked by a typhoon, and so he could not repay on time. Shylock took him to the court in Macau and demanded his pound of flesh Portia asks Bassanio to carry the money to Macau first, while she thought out a strategy.

In the Macanese court, Shylock insisted on his pound of flesh. Portia disguised herself as a lawyer, taught Shylock a lesson with her wit and saved Antonio from the ordeal.

Another hiccup came as Bassanio lost Portia's engagement ring.

In the end, all's well that ends well.

Figure 3.3 House programme of 豪門千金 [For the Heiress' Hand] in 2007. Producer Ni Huiying played Portia, who was featured in this house programme. (Source: Guangzhou Cantonese Opera Troupe 廣州粵劇團)

Ni Huiying followed in Zhang's footsteps in this plot in the 2007 production, using Portia as the title character in *For The Heiress' Hand* (豪門千金). Portia, as Ni described, is "the wisest female character in all of Shakespeare's plays." The pathways of interpretation are as follows: the 2007 version is an adaptation of the 1985 Cantonese operatic version, which is in fact an adaptation of the 1980 production by the same director, Zhang Qihong, whose interpretation has been discussed earlier. Both the 1985 and 2007 dramatic scripts were rendered by the same dramaturge, Qin Zhongying, under the leadership of Zhang in 1985 and the leadership of Ni in 2007. The comparison of the scripts and house programs of the two productions allows one to see the sequence of interpretations that Ni Huiying underwent, which in turn forms her pre-understanding of *The Merchant*. Both productions omit the plot of the elopement scene of Jessica and her Christian lover Lorenzo, which is often regarded as the major cause of Shylock's revenge on Antonio. In both productions, Shylock's revenge and hatred towards Antonio is not due to the elopement of Shylock's daughter with Antonio's friend, nor to the Christian identity of Antonio (because all Christian references were omitted, including the line, "I hate him for he is a Christian"), but reduced rather to the single fact that Antonio the generous and righteous merchant lends money at low interest. The first act of both productions sees a righteous Antonio paying the interest on behalf of a debtor to Shylock who snatches the meat out of the debtor's hand to serve as interest. In the house program of *Heaven*, the play is portrayed as a promulgation of "truth, kindness and beauty," and a condemnation of "hypocrisy, evil and the ugly," which is later embodied in Ni Huiying's production. Both productions see Bassanio as a wealthy man who met Portia during a springtime activity and developed an affection for her which paved the way for his proposal not out of the need for paying debts, but out of genuine love. Shylock's portrayal as a money-sucking, cruel, heartless villain in Zhang's 1980 Western drama production, continued his villainous afterlife in Zhang's 1985 Cantonese operatic version, and later in Ni's production in 2007. Ni Huiying echoed Zhang's interpretation of a villainous Shylock as Ni described Shylock as "a slave to money who sees money as more important than his own life." When I interviewed Ni on her interpretation and adaptation process in January 2013, Ni cited Shylock's last line in the court scene in 2007 production to support her interpretation, "Shylock said, 'oh, I would rather wish that you took a pound of flesh from me', when the judge ordered the confiscation of his property. This is a very impressive portrayal of his character." Upon close scrutiny, this last line by Shylock in Ni's production in fact is taken from Zhang's Cantonese operatic production in 1985. Instead of just translating, "I am content," Shylock's greed is made more explicit in his final sentence in both versions. From the similarities between the two versions in 1985 and 2007, one could trace the influence of previous versions on a recent production. Perhaps the biggest difference that sets Ni's production apart from Zhang's 1985 production lies in Ni's localization strategy, as opposed to Zhang's Western style drama. Zhang, in response to my question why her Cantonese production did not use Chinese costumes, said that it was not her intention to localize, which would take much more effort.[58]

---

58. According to my interview with Zhang Qihong on 2ndAugust 2010 in Beijing.

124 SHAKESPEARE FROM PAGE TO STAGE, FROM WEST TO EAST

Another reason that belies the producer's motivation in introducing *The Merchant* into Cantonese opera is the hope of showcasing a melting pot of cultures. In this production, one sees a mix of Canton and the West at a historically critical moment—where old and new ideologies met in the late imperial, early Republican period. The producer has especially emphasized the equal exchange of cultures, as can be seen from the poster where Shakespeare shakes hands with Portia (see figure below), symbolizing the tribute paid to Shakespeare by the Chinese, while at the same time showcasing the Chinese culture and the uniquely inclusive Canton culture. It was five years after she met director Chen Xinyi 陳薪伊 before they could find a setting suitable for staging a hybrid of cultures—Guangzhou and Macau—as both places bear a marked geographical resemblance to Venice. These two are coastal cities which have been important trading ports for hundreds of years.

Figure 3.4 Poster of *Haomenqianjin* 豪門千金 [For the Heiress' Hand] in 2007, produced by Ni Huiying. (Source: Guangzhou Cantonese Opera Troupe 廣州粵劇團)

CASE STUDIES OF *THE MERCHANT OF VENICE* IN MAINLAND CHINA

The following quote from my interview with Ni below shows her agenda to promote Chinese culture through the production, "The Western legal system has its shortcomings—according to the rule-based Western culture, this contract of the bond is reasonable, because it is signed on mutual consent. However, this bond is unethical in the Chinese culture, especially as it concerns the taking of one's life. Thus, it is necessary to consider a cultural exchange between the East and the West for the development and enhancement of human thinking."[59] The respect for contract and the law in the West cannot be replicated in the Chinese culture, as Ni commented:

> The Western culture upholds the contractual spirit and the law, but the Chinese governance is based on humanity. Shylock is such a heartless being and wants to take another's life. From the ethical point of view, a bond involving "a pound of flesh" would arouse anger among [Chinese] people, and thus the bond would not be executed. It does not conform to the Chinese culture.

The producer's interpretation of the religious content apparently affected its translatability. Macau has over 400 years of missionary history since the Jesuit missionaries came in 1555, and it is where Robert Morrison—the first Protestant missionary to China—stopped over in 1807 before moving inland. This calls into question whether the omission of Christian discourse is necessary when the story is set in Macau. In the interview, Ni's response reflected the importance she attached to audience expectations: "I think [the bowdlerized version] is more suitable for the general audience. I think this [religious dimension] need not be mentioned. I think the so-called religion in the play is in fact about racial conflicts. In a 2-hour production, a lot of issues can hardly be clarified, and the audience would not understand." Is it the fact that the Chinese have a harmonious culture that led her to suppress conflict in this play? Ni admitted, "It (Christianity) is a religion that instigates conflicts." This once again illustrates the point that directorial decision on the translatability of religion is often an ideological decision. In Chapter 6 I will discuss the ideology and interpretation of different directors in more depth.

Translation Profile

The play is set in the early Republican period, i.e. early twentieth-century China. The names in the play have all been localized with a Chinese

---

59. The interview was conducted in January 2013 by myself, and the quotations were back translated from Cantonese to English.

surname—Portia became 朱西婭 (Zhu xiya), Antonio becomes 李安東 (Li Andong), Bassanio becomes 常英志 (Chang Yingzhi), Shylock becomes 夏老克 (Xia Laoke). Compared to *The Merchant* which is set in Venice and Belmont, their cultural equivalents become Macau and Guangzhou. Ni Huiying told me in the interview that when she and the director Chen Xinyi came up with the idea of these two places, both of them became so excited that they flew in from their own city to Macau the next day to confirm their intuition. Macau was a suitable substitute for Venice because it represents a blend of the East and the West, making the reception of the Western notion of the bond of flesh more plausible. Guangzhou, where the Chinese Portia is from, has been a busy trading port for hundreds of years and the starting point of the maritime Silk Road. The fact that the Ling Ding Ocean off the Southern China coast witnessed the recent excavation of the wrecked ship South China One (南海一號) reminded the producer of the shipwreck that came near to costing Antonio's pound of flesh.

When it comes to the treatment of religious material, the production omits the religious or racial conflicts, the Christian identity of characters was not highlighted, and Shylock became a moneylender pure and simple, not a Jew. When the suitors are asked to swear to God not to marry if they fail to choose the right box, 皇天 *huangtian* (emperor heaven) is used instead, a terminology that originates from *shijing* 詩經 (Book of Songs) referring to the creator God in ancient Chinese culture.[60] When Shylock describes Portia, the disguised lawyer, as Daniel, the Old Testament prophet in order to praise her wit, the Cantonese adaptation becomes Dhamapalas, or Protector of the Teaching, a Buddhist God who protect the religion, gods, monasteries and followers (護法神 *hufashen*). There is one occasion where the word Christian is not omitted but adapted in this production: in Act 1 Scene 3, Antonio says the following when Shylock agrees to lend money, "The Hebrew will turn Christian: he grows kind." The Chinese adaptation turns the word Hebrew to "demon Raksa" 魔鬼羅刹, a devil in Hindu mythology, and Christian to "Guan Yin 觀音," a female Buddhist Goddess popularly worshiped in China for her kindness and compassion. Despite the omission of religious language and conflicts, and despite the producer's dismissal of religious issues as unimportant, there is a religious term being used in the 2007 production at the court scene, immediately following Bassanio's righteous act of asking the judge to cut his flesh. Shylock commented, "This is the court which executes the law, not a school that teaches the Bible." The term Bible is used not as a way to recognize the

---

60. Jesuit missionary Matteo Ricci is the first who translated Christian God as 上帝, a word that originates from the Book of Songs. Even today, 上帝 is used to refer to Christian God in Christian books and the Chinese Union Version Bible in China.

merits of the religion, but is cited sarcastically by Shylock in dismissing the act of righteousness of Bassanio and Antonio.

What is interesting in this production lies not only in the contents being removed, but in the contents that are added to give a local taste to the production. With the deletion of Christian references, allusions to folk religion were added. In both versions when Antonio was presented with the bond of flesh, he described it as "閻王債 yanwangzhai," or debt of the God of Death, a local Chinese Buddhist God of Hindu origin, implying that Shylock was more villainous than the God of Death. In Act Four, a suitor (Huang Miaozhang 黃妙章) who self-acclaimed as "exceptionally talented and well-versed in literature" was ridiculed by suitor Cha Liangao (查良奧) as follows: "[if you are literate] Go to Guangxiao Temple and set up a fortune-telling booth." Fortune-telling booths are commonly seen outside temples whereby fortune tellers offer the often anxious temple visitors a prediction of their future. Fortune-telling can come in various forms, and in this play, the fortune telling technique requires the client to write a Chinese character. Allusions to folk religions, as discussed in Chapter 1, are not uncommon in Chinese translations of Shakespeare and other literature. Additionally, certain forms of Cantonese operas have traditionally been connected to folk religions—shengongxi (神功戲), literally meaning God's Work Theatre, a theatre that performs work for Gods. Traditionally the ShenGongxi stage is set in a direction towards the temple, so that the Gods in the temple could watch the performance. If the geographical constraints prevent the stage from facing the temple, a wooden frame that houses the God's statutes will be built instead. Actors are seen bowing on stage, not to the audience, but to Gods.[61]

The 2007 production uses the same mercy speech as used in 1985, which has been significantly shortened from the original Shakespeare which contains concepts of Christian mercy and prayer. One can see the Confucian influence which disapproves of the execution of the bond of flesh:

為善予人，為福於己，

兩頭法碼，一樣公平。

借債為解貧，放債圖利，

並非生死冤家，

何必取人性命。

結百世之仇。

61. Chen, *Hong Kong YueJuYan Jiu*, 18–19.

智者不為，仁者不取，

須知世情難料，

莫欺天道無聲。

望你收回十倍錢，

放他一條活路徑。

Back translation:

To help others, to do good for oneself,

Two measures, one fairness,

Loan is for relieving poverty, Money-lending makes profit,

Not lifelong enemies,

Why take a life,

And become enemies for hundreds of generations?

The wise will not do so, neither will the kind,

No one knows what the future holds.

Don't cheat the silent heaven.

Hope you can take ten times the loan as reward,

And give him a way to live.

In this shortened speech, one could see the emphasis on being "wise (智, zhi)" and "kind (仁, ren)," the two important criteria of being good according to the Confucius Analects 4.2: "仁者安仁，知者利仁" (The humane take comfort in ren, the wise profit from ren.) Doing good for oneself to accumulate prosperity is a Buddhist karmic concept. The notion "to be kind and gentle to others because God oversees" reminds one of the Chinese concept of the omniscient heaven, as in the saying, "天網恢恢, 疏而不漏" (the net of heaven will not miss anything).

In the 2007 production, Shylock came from Macau, a place now characterized by vices connected to gambling, including the business of loan sharks. However, the fact that Shylock was originally a foreign Jew in the play was not brought out in the production. Shylock, the other character who gained much sympathy with the audience with his identity as a foreign Jew, becomes Shylock the indigenous Macanese. Shylock's cold-bloodedness is further strengthened in terms of his relationship with Jessica, his daughter. When he is told by his servant that Jessica who took his money away for gambling cannot be found, all that concerns him is that his money is gone. Shylock said that if the money had not been taken from him, he "would not bother if she gambled from from dusk to dawn." This is in contrast to the original Shakespeare where Shylock was seen crying for the loss of his daughter whom he described as his "flesh and blood" in Act 2 Scene 8—"My daughter! O my ducats! O my daughter! Fled with a Christian! O my Christian ducats!" The humane side of Shylock is simply replaced by a greedy, cruel character.

In terms of the plot, a comparison between the 1985 version and the 2007 version reveals the similarities in the narratives, thus evidencing that the 2007 version is not a new adaptation, but an adaptation of an adaptation. Both Cantonese operatic versions highlight the love story between Bassanio and Portia, the conflict between the pursuit of wealth (characterized by Shylock) and the pursuit of righteousness, characterized by Antonio.

In both adaptations, the theme of righteousness over profit is highlighted in the added conflicts between Antonio and Shylock: A poor old man was unable to repay the loan, but used his last 50 cents to buy a pound of lamb meat to save his sick wife. His meat was snatched by Shylock who claimed it as interest on his loan. Antonio paid the loan and interest on the old man's behalf, while passers-by were scoffing at Shylock as the "bloodsucker." This has become a trigger point for Shylock's hatred of Antonio, no longer because "he is a Christian," but because of Antonio's generosity, as seen in the following soliloquy that appears in both versions:

夏老克：

想起那天在市場，

為了肉八兩，

人人罵我吸血鬼，

讚他仗義大方，

我高利貸，

他低利錢，

處處拆我的檔。

Shylock:
Think of that day in Rialto
For the sake of eight taels of meat
Everyone calls me blood-sucking demon
But hails him righteous and generous

I charge high interest

But he low interest

Under-cutting my market everywhere.

At the court scene of both versions, both Antonio and Bassanio were "vying for" penalty, each asking the duke to cut his flesh instead, which was described by the duke as embodying "profound righteousness and noble character" (厚義高風). Bassanio, who is usually regarded as a coward, became a righteous hero in this play. The following are the lines that appear in both productions:

安東: 依法，應割我的肉!

英志: 於理，應割我的肉!

安東: 割我的肉!

英志: 割我的肉!

Antonio (An Dong): Should cut my flesh according to the law!

Bassanio (Ying zhi): Should cut my flesh according to reason!

Antonio (An Dong): Cut my flesh!

Bassanio (Ying zhi): Cut my flesh!

It should be noted that the term "righteousness," or *yi* 義 appears more prominently throughout Antonio's aria in the 2007 version than in that of 1985, e.g.,「拼將血肉酬知己，仗義人間死亦香」(use blood and flesh to thank my friend, exercise righteousness on earth and death smells sweet).

In both productions, Bassanio and Portia had an encounter before Bassanio's proposal. This is different from the original Shakespeare's production, where Bassanio and Portia met only briefly before he came to Belmont for the marriage proposal. An additional act was added in both productions to romanticize the love between Bassanio and Portia. 80 percent of the lines in this act in the 2007 production came from the former adaptation in 1985. The only major textual difference lies in the localization of the geographic names in the two recited poems. The 2007 production uses plants and objects such as Red Bean which are typical plants in Southern China, while the earlier production uses names such as the Mediterranean Sea and the Alps. Both versions locate the encounter during springtime, and introduce the idea that their fathers had a business relationship. Portia was in a rider's suit and carried a fencing sword. They exchanged fencing techniques and recited poems as a way of courting. It was after this memorable encounter that Bassanio decided to court Portia. When the two met again at Portia's house, Portia showed affection and particular eagerness in her wait for Bassanio, such that if Bassanio could not choose the right box, she would not marry anyone else. This additional act not only romanticized the love plot, but also fundamentally changed Bassanio's characterization. He was seen to want to marry Portia not for the sake of paying off his debts, but out of genuine affection for her.

The highlight of the love plot between two major characters –Bassanio and Portia is in line with the traditional Cantonese operatic format, which gives emphasis to the two major characters –文武生 (*wenwu sheng*, a major male character), and 花旦 (*huadan*, a major female character), which together are known as "two major pillars 兩大柱" in Cantonese opera, among a total of "six major pillars."[62] The happy ending sees Antonio officiating at the wedding with Bassanio and Portia dressed in traditional Chinese wedding costumes. In fact, in the cover of the house program, the play is described as a "romantic comedy" in both Chinese and English, as romance and comedy are an important draw for the audience of Cantonese opera.

Semiotic Analysis

In the opening scene the backdrop shows the shaking of two hands—the Bard's and Portia's, a symbol of cultural exchange between East and West. The same symbol recurs in the theatre promotional poster. The backdrop later shifts to a street view of Macau where bilingual signposts can be clearly seen, again a representation of the meeting of the two cultures. Since Macau was leased to the Portuguese government in 1557, the place has seen a mixture of cultures, and was thus chosen as the setting of this production. In this version, other than Bassanio, Portia's suitors came from Arabia (Morocco) and Persia, countries which had long-standing trade links with China, though in the original version a suitor came from Spain.

Antonio, the merchant of Venice, becomes a merchant of Guangzhou, who borrows money from Shylock a Macanese. This change of characterization leads to a fundamental change in the portrayal of Shylock's villainous character, as has been shown in the textual analysis, Shylock is no longer an oppressed foreigner (Jew) who cannot do other businesses than moneylending. Shylock is an indigenous Macanese, a host, not an alien, in this host culture. This would render Shylock less sympathetic than the original portrayal as the Other in Venice.

---

62. See Chen, "Translating Theatre," 59–90.

The costumes in this production are culturally hybrid. The period costumes of the early republican period are used alongside Western costumes. Antonio (Li Andong) and Bassanio are seen in Western suits throughout. Antonio wears purple in the opening, a color of nobility in Chinese culture. In the court scene, Antonio and Bassanio are wearing beige, a light color used to signify "good people" in theatre. Portia shifted between traditional and Western costumes: she is seen in a rider's suit and hat at her first encounter with Bassanio, a device to show that the couple are Western educated. Later she is in bright red early republican costumes when she is at home waiting for the suitors. At the wedding, Portia and Bassanio, in their traditional bright red Chinese robes, are seen bowing thrice, a ritual to symbolize long-lasting marriage. Shylock (Xia Laoke 夏老克), wearing a tall black hat, is in black traditional Chinese long robe and pants, the dark color reinforcing his dark nature. At the court scene, he wears a black top imprinted with golden coins, an attire that symbolizes wealth. In sum, the change of costumes portrays a dynamic period in China under Western influence.

In terms of music, Cantonese opera is one of the most inclusive and all-encompassing among the 300-odd operatic forms in China. It is not uncommon to hear background music combined with Western or even Buddhist music. Since the 1930s, Western musical instruments such as saxophone, trumpet, guitar have been introduced. In the *Pound of Flesh* staged in 1952, for example, saxophone, violin and electronic guitar are used in the background music. What fundamentally sets the 2007 production apart from the 1985 production in the choice of music is the blending of traditional Chinese folk songs, melodies and Mozart's compositions in the former, a unique example of the versatility of Cantonese opera: whereas in the 1985, production, Cantonese operatic tunes are used. The fact that Guan Dongtian 關棟天, a Hong Kong-born Peking opera actor was enlisted to act the part of Antonio in the 2007 production is a first in the history of Cantonese opera, and one sees also the blending of the tunes of Peking Opera into Cantonese opera. It is uniquely this openness to foreign influences typical in Cantonese opera that makes it acceptable to watch a Shakespearean play in a Chinese setting. As early as the 1930s, a hybrid fantasy-musical comedy known as Western Costume Cantonese operas (西裝劇) began in southern China and Shanghai, and lasted until the 1950s in Hong Kong. It is such foreignness, using Western costumes and novel music, to name just a few examples, that appealed to the Cantonese-speaking Chinese audience living in different parts of China, Asia and America who lived in different geopolitical conditions.⁶³ It is interesting to note that, despite the foreign influence on Cantonese operas, such influence happens only at the semiotic level but not at the ideological level. Christian references, which were considered "foreign," were displaced in this cross-cultural negotiation.

Several theatre practitioners commented positively on this unique blend of music in 2007 production. Zhao Chengyan 趙承燕, China's Dramatists Association Chair, said that "the music that blends in Western elements does not overshadow the Cantonese operatic style—this blend is a promulgation of our Cantonese operatic tradition." Cui Wei 崔偉, China's Dramatists Association Research Director, commented that the use of Mozart's music augments the development of the characters and the plot.

Socio-cultural and Cognitive Effects

While Cantonese opera, like other forms of opera, faced the issue of declining interests among the younger generation, this production was re-run over 10 times in the university city of Guangzhou under a scheme "University students go to theatre," each attended by over 2,000 students. The production was also exported to Singapore, Shanghai and Hong Kong. It was the white collar types and the students who were most enthusiastic about the performance. University students need to pay only RMB1 to watch the show.

Theatre critics and party officials praised not only the production's unique blend of Chinese and Western cultures, but also the strategic promotion of Cantonese opera among the younger generation. Ji Guoping 季國平, Party office vice secretary for China's Dramatists Association reckoned that the promotion among university students was "forward-looking," and an important pointer for the development of opera. "We theatrical practitioners care not only for rural villages, but also for high-quality audiences who demand high-quality productions, and *Hao men qianjin* is a masterpiece orchestrated by Cantonese Opera Troupe."⁶⁴ Theatre critic Yi Hongxia 易紅霞 described the response of university students as "highly passionate and resonating with the play," with long queues awaiting for the autograph of actors, and bouts of applause and laughter were heard from time to time. The blend of Shakespearean language and Cantonese operatic language, together with the blend of spoken drama and Cantonese opera, were "revolutionary, a break-through."

63. Wang, *Remaking Chinese Cinema*, 82-112.

64. Ji's comments, together with the comments of theatre critics Yi Hongxia and He Jiqing, were printed on the house programme of the 2007 production.

The localization of setting gained critical acclaim, as He Jiqing 何繼青, deputy chair of Guangzhou Municipal Cultural Bureau, said, "the adaptation of Shakespeare's play to a Cantonese setting minimizes the historical and geographical distance [from the original production], allowing audiences to experience the special charisma of Shakespeare and an interpersonal relationship with his times."

Evidently, the localization efforts have paid off. Shakespeare becomes an important channel through which traditional operatic forms find continuity and renewed vitality. Such hybrid operatic form sparked off a debate between Cantonese opera purists and general audiences. Adeline Chia queried when the production was staged in Singapore, "whether modern opera compromised its stylistic conventions too much to win new audiences."[65]

Shylock (夏洛克) : An Adaptation of *The Merchant of Venice* in Shanghai in 2010

Background

Shylock is vastly different from the previous two productions and so I deem it necessary to provide more background information before launching into the socio-cultural conditions of the period. In April 2010, a small theatre in Shanghai staged three performances of *Shylock*, an adaptation of an English play *Shylock* which involves a one-man performance written, directed and played by Gareth Armstrong, a veteran performer with the Royal Shakespeare Company. He was inspired to put on this production after acting Shylock and being given John Gross's book *Shylock: Four Hundred Years in the Life of a Legend*.

Armstrong's adaptation is a sympathetic account of the character Shylock through the narration of his ally, Tubal, who appears only in one scene and referred to only once by Shylock in Act 1 Scene 3:

> What of that?
> Tubal, a wealthy Hebrew of my tribe,
> Will furnish me.

The choice of Tubal as the protagonist is, according to Gareth Armstrong, because no background information could be deduced from the play about Tubal, which rendered him a character to be manipulated, a chance to

---

65. Chia, "Cantonese Twist for *The Merchant of Venice*," 12 Feb 2014.

step from the periphery onto center stage.[66] He assumed that Tubal could be a silent witness in all of Shylock's scenes, "an omnipresent Tubal could hear each of Shylock's utterances, observe his relationships with other characters and solidarity, moments of dissent and, ultimately, moments of compassion for his kinsman." Armstrong's device of using Tubal is to do him justice and offer him deserved visibility, as illustrated from the quote below:

> Unlike many major characters, Shylock is not greatly given to soliloquy, and I found the solo speeches he does have were remarkably easy to reassign as 'asides' to Tubal. Shylock's references to Judaism are usually made in the plural, as 'us' and 'our', and these were even more credible as indicative of a companion on the stage. That Tubal's presence is not acknowledged in the stage directions I rationalized as merely bad editing. Shakespeare, after all, was long dead and unable to protest his absence when the First Folio was published.[67]

Shylock deviated from *The Merchant* considerably in the plot, where three main story lines were developed from Tubal's narration—a history of interpretation of Shylock, a history of Judeo-Christian conflicts, more specifically how the Jews suffered from persecution from the Roman Catholic Church, and the story of *The Merchant*. The gist of Il Pecorone, the primary source of *The Merchant*, was included in the opening to introduce *The Merchant*. The Judeo-Christian conflicts that were dubious in Shakespeare's *The Merchant* were intensified in *Shylock*.

Through the mouth and commentary of Tubal, Shylock became a humane figure. On more than one occasion, Shylock was referred to as the man who was constantly despised. "That's what was expected of Jews on stage—comedy and villainy."[68] Commentaries on each character were added in Tubal's narration. In the trial scene, Tubal commented on the Duke as being "partial" to Antonio, and was "threatening" Shylock. Portia's part in the trial was "fake," thus questioning the justice of the court. Tubal showed sympathy to his "ally" Shylock, saying that it was not easy to raise up a daughter as a single parent and as a despised Jew, that being strict towards a young daughter who misbehaves is understandable. Towards the end of the court scene, Shylock disappeared from the stage, and Tubal reminded the audience that he was probably re-united with Jessica, his only blood relative as he had lost Leah his dear wife. But it was the last line of the play that wrapped up his

---

66. Armstrong, *A Case for Shylock*, 72.
67. Ibid.
68. This is quoted from Gareth Armstrong's script for Shylock—shortened version for 75 min performance without intermission, p.6.

loneliness, reminding the audience once again that he had lost his wife's ring which was traded for a monkey. Shylock was no longer portrayed in front of the audience as a cruel villain, he missed his wife and he was the only tragic figure in the play amidst the happy ending and celebrations of Christians. Christians, on the other hand, became the murderers, drinking the blood of the Jews during the homicide in the twelfth century, and killing forty Polish Jews after WWII. Lorenzo was described by Tubal as a "lounge lizard" who took the initiative to tempt Jessica a premature teenager to run away. Lorenzo was accused of being a drunkard who received Jessica's stolen money.

In line with his sympathetic portrayal of the Jews, Armstrong has an eclectic background that renders him a suitable person to interweave different threads of interpretations. He is the youngest son of a Welsh preacher, whose whole life was dedicated to the Presbyterian Church of Wales. Armstrong himself attended church services as would be expected of an established Christian, but "faith was taken for granted."[69] Later in his college life, he attempted to enroll in a joint degree in Drama and Theology, only to find that he could hardly "get to grips with New Testament Greek" and finally gave up on it. The Bible was put aside for thirty years before he picked it up again for the sake of staging *Shylock*.

Armstrong's Shylock was a worldwide success, touring over thirty countries worldwide. His production was first introduced to the Chinese audience at Shanghai's International Arts Festival in 2008, which inspired Liu Lei, actor-cum-dramaturge, to adapt it for Chinese audience.

Box office for the 2008 performance in English was not outstanding[70] owing to the language barrier of Chinese audience, as only English, rather than Chinese, subtitles were available. But those who had a high level of English competence showed their appreciation for the play.

Socio-cultural Conditions, Including Taboos

In Shanghai where Shylock was staged, the religious milieu is more tolerant compared to other cities. It is a sending-out place of tens of thousands of overseas Chinese students. As a flagship city under China's open-door policy, expatriates in Shanghai grew from 40,000 in 1997 to over 100,000 in 2002, accounting for 0.6 percent of the city's population. It is expected that by 2015, expatriates may account for 10 percent of the city's population, who have different faiths. Some may have a faith that are beyond the five religions

---

69. Armstrong, 79.

70. According to the interview with *Merchant of Venice—Shylock*'s director Zhang Bowen on 5 August 2010 in Shanghai.

recognized by the government, namely, Catholicism, Protestantism, Islam, Buddhism, Taoism. Shanghai municipal often faced new requests regarding their religious life from foreign embassies and from expatriates. The religious tolerance in Shanghai explained this director's choice in staging Shylock, who believes that "religion is not a sensitive matter, but political issues are."

In the 2009-2010 National Human Rights Action Plan, China showed positive support for religious activities. According to the action plan, it encourages religious believers to launch social charitable activities, and explore the ways religions serve the society and the people. The government openly affirms the positive function that religious groups can bring to society, and supports registered religious groups in offering social service. Foreign faith-based aid groups that are on the register are allowed to offer service after coordinating with local authorities.

The religious milieu set the stage for the staging of *Shylock*, a play with more heightened religious undertones than *The Merchant*. Starting from 1990s, scholarly reviews on the play script of *The Merchant* in China shifted from the Marxist focus to a wide range of issues, including feminist interpretation of Portia, racial issues, biblical allusions in the play and its Christian interpretation. Portia's "mercy speech" was described as a "sermon"[71] and both Portia's and Antonio's Christian quality of mercy were emphasized. Shakespeare's Christian faith has been the subject of research, and biblical allusions and Christian prototypes in his plays including *Hamlet* and *Macbeth* aroused interest among *literati*. Liang Gong's (梁工) two-volume monograph on "Shakespeare and Bible" (shashibiyayu sheng jing 莎士比亞與聖經) published in 2005 was extensively cited in Shakespearean studies work, containing the biblical references of nearly every play. Discussions on characterisation are no longer single-dimension, complexity of each character is discussed—Shylock was no longer only a cruel villain, but a real human figure whose suffering began to gain sympathy from critics, who introduced the Jews to Chinese readers as the victims of racial discrimination and religious oppression.[72] Shylock is more seen as a tragic figure in a tragicomedy, rather than a villain in a comedy. Readings of this play and characters are contextualized to take account of the histories of the Jewish nation, development of Christianity, and cultural influence of the Bible. Interest in Christianity as an academic subject has grown tremendously in the past decade with the establishment of research institutes on Christianity in universities in China. Apart from appreciating Shakespeare in print, the BBC production's Shakespeare series arrived in China in the 90s and was

---

71. See Huang, "The Christian Dimension Embodied," 54.
72. Liu, "Shakespeare's Racial and Religious Discrimination," 81.

broadcast on cable TV. The audience could access Shakespeare more easily via the Chinese subtitles.[73]

In the scholarly reviews of the play in the past decade, association between Christianity and imperialism or Western forces is rarely seen. Marxist reading of conflicts between Antonio and Shylock along the lines of capitalist and feudal struggles gradually faded, but the humanistic interpretation of Shakespearean characters under the Marxist school is still apparent and dominant.[74]

Homosexuality, once a taboo during the Cultural Revolution, has gained higher visibility in the twenty-first century. Any deviation from the twentieth- century definition of sexually acceptable behavior would be labeled as "hooliganism."[75] Homosexual identities moved from "hooliganism" in Article 106 of the Criminal Law of 1979, to being accepted as a normal way of life.[76] Gay individuals were featured on TV shows *Let's Talk* in Hunan.[77] The first Beijing Queer Film Festival started in 2001, but was cancelled at the last minute as officials from the venue, i.e. Beijing University, were wary that this might be viewed as an encouragement of homosexuality. The fourth festival was held in 2009 in suburban Beijing in order to avoid government intervention and media attention.[78] Sex that was taboo on the stage in the early eighties has since become accepted in the theatre and public media. Radio shows including phone-in programs from couples on sex life have taken place since the nineties. Accordingly, it is not surprising to see suggestive scenes in this 2010 production which would otherwise have been considered bold in the eighties.

It is with this socio-cultural background that I orient my discussion of translation and adaptation strategies of Shylock in the following sections.

Situational and Cognitive Conditions

Liu Lei, while undertaking undergraduate studies (major in electronic and electrical engineering) at Shanghai Jiaotong University, was inspired

---

73. Not all dialogues were translated in the BBC series. A subtitle translator who now teaches at university told me that as a translator for the BBC Shakespeare series, he was interfered by the editor not to translate Antonio's "forced conversion," which was deemed by the editor as "too sensitive."

74. See Li, *History of Criticisms of Chinese Shakespeare*, 2006.

75. See Zhang, "The Rights of People with Same Sex Sexual Behaviour," 117.

76. Kong, *Chinese Male Homosexualities*, 155.

77. Ibid.

78. Ibid., 156.

by Gareth Armstrong's new perspective on the character of Shylock and his exceptional performance in *Shylock* at Shanghai Dramatic Arts Center from 28 June to 3 July 2005. In 2009 Liu, as an amateur dramatist, proposed to his friends the idea of staging *Shylock*. He enlisted a troupe at Shanghai Foreign Languages University to translate the script, which was further edited by himself, with input from director Karin Zhang Bowen. It was decided by Zhang that the one-man show in the original *Shylock* should be divided into three roles. Liu Lei would check the different meanings should he come across certain terms and translate them in a way understandable by the audience (i.e. domestication). The director and dramaturge came to the conclusion that the original play involving a storyline on the history of Shylock's interpretations should be deleted from the adaptation as it was too long and would hardly be comprehensible by the audience.[79] They agreed on the need to check the historical and religious background information contained in the script. With little budget and lacking manpower, each performer assumes various roles—Liu Lei the actor and dramaturge, the director is responsible for costumes and make-up. Both the director and dramaturge worked for Shanghai Dramatic Arts Center, but none of the crew underwent formal training in the Arts and Performing Academy. The training they went through was an informal apprenticeship as part of the annual drama festival of university students in Shanghai, during which participants would be provided with mentors to guide their performance. The troupe, known as Heart Light Workshop (Xinzhao Gongzuoshi 心照工作室) was finally formed in March 2010, and rehearsals began only two months prior to performance. As a non-professional troupe, they were not granted a performance license and they were not allowed to charge for admission. Since they were not an official troupe, no registration with the authorities was required. Only Officials from the cultural monitoring group will visit any performances they know of. It is this non-professional, non-fee charging nature that gave them a free hand to stage *Shylock*, a play steeped in religious connotations. Zhang said in an interview, "If [our aim] was profit-making, we certainly will not consider this theme. This is certainly not a profitable play, as no one is willing to buy tickets, or only a very small number. The box office will not be good."[80] Directing and performing a show free to the public was out of passion rather than driven by reward, director Zhang Bowen told me in an interview. In the end, the productions recorded over 80 per cent attendance. Attendees were mostly white collars. Of the

79. According to Liu Lei, the dramaturge, in the post-performance seminar on 31 May 2010, Shanghai.

80. According to the interview with *Merchant of Venice—Shylock*'s director Zhang Bowen on 5 August 2010 in Shanghai.

two performances, one was staged in a small community theatre known as Xujiahui Community Cultural and Activity Center in downtown, the other on campus of Zhejiang University in Hangzhou.

Did the director take into account in the adaptation process the likely audience reception of the religious dimension in the play? The director said, "During the rehearsal, we constantly asked what we should do regarding the religious part of the play. China is an atheist country, most people did not care about religious matters. But that is what this play is about. Some people may not accept it, but most of the audience accepted the religious discourse."

At first the director and dramaturge were not in agreement as to sympathy towards Jews, in the very beginning. Karin Zhang Bowen, who was invited to direct the play, did not like *Shylock* at first, finding him "wordy" and she herself is not interested in religion. Her perception changed when she played a role in a play to be performed in a Jewish Memorial Museum in Shanghai, which previously was a Jewish refugee camp during the Second World War. The play was about how Jews were persecuted, which moved the director to the point where she could finally find relevance between Chinese and Jews, who were once protected in Shanghai.

Liu Lei developed his sympathy when he found close resemblance between the tragic history of the Jews and of China. On the one hand, both are being persecuted, on the other hand, both are optimistic and resilient. He said during the post-performance seminar in May 2010:

> During the creative process, we asked, will Chinese audiences show interest in a play on Jewish destiny? How are the Jews related to us? I think, this play's intention is not about Jews, it is about the self-reflection of a nation. Jews are a race which I admire very much. They made a good life for themselves through their wisdom, a very positive attitude. But they suffered from 2000-year long persecution, the reasons behind which call for deep thinking on our part. We Chinese are also facing the issue of self-strengthening. I think, we should learn from the Jewish destiny.

Director Zhang added that the play is relevant to the people of Shanghai, a place exhibiting xenophobic attitudes. The crew thought about modifying the play to zoom in on the life of the Shanghainese: "They are particularly xenophobic, and on the Internet some people said something like, [non-Shanghainese] get lost. Why do the Shanghainese so discriminate against 'the others'? Out of jealousy, hostility to the rich, narrow-mindedness ... Shanghainese thought that 'the others' had thrown away their money." Zhang said.[81]

---

81. According to the interview with *Merchant of Venice—Shylock*'s director Zhang Bowen on 5 August 2010 in Shanghai.

Would they find the religious material in the play too sensitive for staging in China? Both the director and deputy director responded simultaneously in the interview that only political issues are sensitive but not religious issues, as China is an atheist country. The perception of this generation in Shanghai is not surprising: Shanghai has been a coastal area long subject to missionary influence. It was where the Shanghai Missionary Conference was held in 1890 during which Hudson Taylor appealed to 1,000 volunteers to join Chinese missions over the next five years. It was the headquarters of the China Inland Mission (now renamed as Overseas Missionary Fellowship) until 1950 after the victory of the Communist Party which labeled foreign missionaries as "foreign spies." At present, religious activities are widespread in Shanghai and state churches numbered over 80 in 2009.

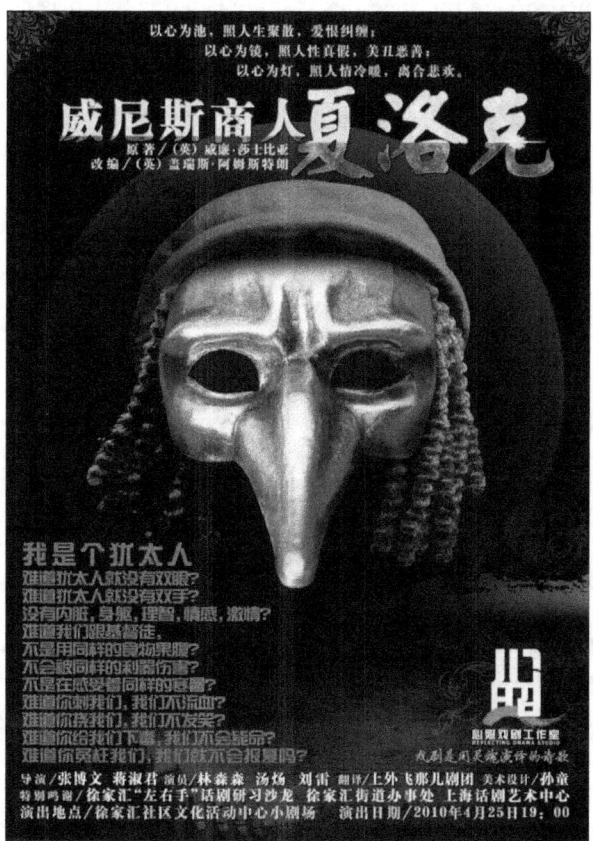

Figure 3.5 Poster of *Xia Luoke* 夏洛克 [Shylock], first staged in Shanghai in April 2010. (Source: Reflecting Drama Studio 心照工作室)

The religious and racial conflicts of the play were featured in the above poster, which cited Shylock's famous speech "hath not a Jew eyes" in the left hand side. The Venetian mask is covered with a red hat that is symbolic of the Jew who wears a red hat to distinguish him from other citizens.

Translation Profile

Treatment of Religious Material

As mentioned earlier, apart from deleting the section on the history of interpretations of Shylock, other lines depicting Judeo-Christian conflicts, the death of Jesus, and the origin of Christian hatred towards Jews, have been retained. So are the speeches that are laden with Christian concepts, including Portia's mercy speech and Shylock's "hath Jews no eyes" speech. Attention needs to be given to what is added in this Chinese Shylock.

Some lines on Shanghai's protection of Jews are added to domesticate the play, bringing the writer closer to the audience.

> 乙：好，現在我代表德意志帝國正式批准你移民國外申請，3天后啟程，目的地中國上海。
>
> 甲：中國上海，是當時唯一不需要簽證就能去的地方。1938年，全世界其他國家都對我們猶太人關上了大門。就在中國上海，我們才能夠僥倖的活下去。
>
> Tubal B: I now represent Deutschland to approve your migration application. Your journey will begin in three days, destination Shanghai.
>
> Tubal A: Shanghai China, the only place where no visa is required. 1938, when the whole world closed the door on us Jews. In Shanghai, China, we survived.

In another instance, Chinese identity was brought in to relate the humiliation of the Jews with that of the Chinese. Drawing a parallel has the effect of arousing the sympathy of Chinese towards a victimized ethnic group.

> 丙：不要指責莎士比亞同志嘛，你不能怪莎士比亞，這在歐洲已經是一個古老的傳統了，就好像在好萊塢劇場上，中國人都是那些扒手阿瘋子之類的。在歐洲也有這樣的傳統。在中世紀的舞臺上當人們演出聖經裡的故事，我們猶太人總是那個最壞的。

CASE STUDIES OF *THE MERCHANT OF VENICE* IN MAINLAND CHINA 143

Tubal C: Do not blame comrade Shakespeare [for depicting Jews as villains]. You cannot blame Shakespeare for following an age-old tradition in Europe. Just as in Hollywood films, Chinese are often given the roles of pick-pockets, lunatics or the like. In Europe a similar tradition exists. In medieval theatres when performers act out bible stories, we Jews are always the bad guys.

To add to the intensity of ethnic conflicts, lines about Korea's self-importance were added to make fun of their closest Chinese neighbors. The lines below did provoke laughter, but post-performance reviews showed their disapproval by saying the lines were too "odd" and "blunt."

丙：地理呀，一竅不通！從這點來說，莎士比亞他極有可能是個韓國人（笑）

丙：韓國人對於歷史和地理也是一無所知阿，他們堅持認為

甲: 屈原是我們韓國人。

乙: 孔子是我們韓國人。

丙：李白也是我們韓國人。

甲: 北京曾經是我們韓國的。

乙: 河南曾經是我們韓國的。

丙：上海將來也曾經是我們韓國的。

Tubal C: [Shakespeare] knows nothing of geography! From this, I guess Shakespeare is likely to be a Korean!

Tubal C: Koreans know nothing about history and geography, they insist that . . .

Tubal A: Quyuan[82] belongs to us Korean,

Tubal B: Confucius belongs to us Korean,

Tubal C: Li Bai[83] belongs to us Korean,

Tubal A: Beijing once belonged to us Korea,

Tubal B: Henan once belonged to us Korea,

---

82. 屈原 Qu Yuan (BC339-278) is a reputable poet and minister in the Warring Period who committed suicide to protest against the corruption of the era. His death is still commemorated nowadays as Dragon Boat Festival.

83. 李白 Li Bai is a well-known poet in the Tang Dynasty. The directors ironically connect these prominent figures in Chinese History to the Korean origins, as a way to show the arrogance of this nation.

> Tubal C: Shanghai in the future may sometime belong to us Korea.

As for the speeches and lines that closely resembled Shakespeare's *The Merchant*, the translation came mostly from the literary translation of Zhu Shenghao, who was known for naturalizing the content to bring the writer closer to the reader.

> 慈悲不是出於勉強,他是像甘霖一樣從天上降臨塵世,它有著高於一切的無上威力,比皇冠更能顯出帝王的尊貴,權杖不過象徵著族世的威權,是人們對於君上的威嚴凜然生畏,而慈悲的力量卻高於權利之上,所以,猶太人,儘管你要求的是公道,可是請你想一想,如果真的按照公道執行期上發來,誰也沒有死後得救的希望不是嗎?既然都祈禱著上帝的慈悲,那就請按照祈禱的指示,自己做一些慈悲的是吧。我說的這一番話,只是希望你能從你的法律立場上做幾個讓步,當然如果你堅持著原來的請求,那麼威尼斯的法庭將是執法無私的,只好把那個商人宣判定罪了。

> Mercy is not something that can be forced, just like gentle rain from heaven and scattered on earth. It is higher than the ultimate power, nobler than the king's crown, the staff symbolizing temporal force, so that people are awed by the king's authority. Mercy's force is higher than power. So, Jew, though what you ask is justice, think twice, if one operates solely according to justice, no one can have hope in life after death, isn't it? As we all pray for God's mercy, then in accordance with the instruction of prayer, do some merciful deeds. I say this in a hope that you will make some concessions on legal grounds. But if you insist on your original request, then the Venetian court is impartial and will pass judgment on the merchant.

While Fang Ping's translation was more popular in productions and adaptations of *The Merchant*, Zhu's translation, which had a higher circulation in print, was chosen this time. The result was a translation where the theology was made more visible, justice was translated to an equivalent term of justice or gongdao "公道" in Chinese, and the notion of "salvation" was explicated into "hope in life after death." A sympathetic tone was heavily displayed when the actor said "I am content," with his hat taken off and disappeared. I—am—content, three words were particularly lingered over to show Shylock's reluctance.

The open attitude towards homosexuality in the twenty-first century was reflected in a scene where Tubal and Shylock were seen caressing each other. The audience laughed at the treatment knowing that it was about homosexuality. But this issue was not further developed in the storyline later. As the earlier section noted, homosexuality is still considered taboo in the Mainland society, which is more conservative than Hong Kong or Taiwan on this matter. Sex scenes, on the other hand, are less of an issue: the gist of *Il Pecorone* in the opening act, including explicit depictions of sex scenes, was staged and provoked laughter among the audience.[84]

Cognitive and Behavioral Effects

In general, the audience's sympathy was not skewed towards the Jew after watching this sympathetic account of Shylock. During the post-performance seminar, a Christian attendee stood up and challenged the director's interpretation, saying that he was libeling against Christians. Her provocative challenge was noted by a few reviews, as such kind of "disharmony," as one reviewer put it, but this is relatively rare among Mainland Chinese theatre audience.

There were a handful of reviews that reflected negative sentiment towards Christians provoked by the play, seeing Christianity as lacking religious tolerance and hypocritical. The perception that Western imperialistic forces are linked with Christianity is still strong in China, as one reviewer pointed out, the conversion scene by Christians who "robbed the Jews off their property" reminded her of the Western powers that invaded China in the Qing Dynasty bringing together allied forces from eight countries. They burnt down some well-known artefacts including Yuan Ming Yuan, a monument in Beijing by these foreign troops.[85] "To survive, one must be suppressed [by external forces]," she said. This shows that despite the absence of such emphasis of the link between Christianity and Western power politics in contemporary scholarly articles on *The Merchant*, the general prejudice among the masses against Christianity cannot easily be shaken. Some audiences showed their lack of background knowledge of Christianity

---

84. The first story of the fourth day in *Il Pecorone* (written at the end of the fourteenth century and was printed in 1558) is very close to *The Merchant*. It opened with the Florentian merchant's son Giannetto, who set sail to Alexandria and discovered a beautiful bay owned by a widowed lady. She made a law that whoever arrived must sleep with her, and if he could enjoy her, he must take her for wife. If not, he would lose everything. Giannetto was poisoned to deep sleep for the first two times while in her chamber, but won her upon his third arrival.

85. See *Qishimeiyouhuairen*. 其實沒有壞人 [In fact there are no villains]. Web. 1 June 2010. <http://cando360.com/>

and Judaism, questioning why Shylock as a Jew could cite stories from the Old Testament, which is not surprising in an atheist country.[86]

On the other hand, there are reviews that painted an objective picture of religion, as the following comment shows:

> Religion itself is not an issue. It's not that Christian doctrine asked people to kill, to hate, they are all driven by human sins. Now, Christianity does not persecute pagans or show hatred. Human ideas are progressing. Today people reach consensus on "forgiveness." The law protects us with freedom of religion, people's mentality began to change. History will not repeat itself. Christianity teaches us to be forgiving, rather it is the atheist that lacks "forgiveness."[87]

Audiences were particularly receptive to parts that were of relevance to their culture. The two lines on Shanghai's protection of Jews were noted by a few reviews, showing that relevance plays an important role in leaving an indelible impression on the audience.

Socio-cultural Effects

The play has given rise to heightened awareness of Jewish history among the audiences. The strong reaction observed in some Christian audiences showed that when the balance was tipped and skewed towards one party, regardless of how victimized they were, this would cause audience reception to shift to the weaker force, this time it is Christianity that was misrepresented and suppressed. In fact, in the re-run of the production in Shanghai in 2012 and 2013, the emphasis on religious conflicts was subdued to avoid negative audience reaction, when the play became a commercialized production rather than a free-for-all performance.[88] This de-emphasis is exemplified in the omission of the speech "hath not a Jew eyes" in the latest promotion poster. The phenomenon is well summed up in an online review at http://cando360.com as follows:

> As to the content, the introduction of too many historical episodes skewed the author's intention. As we know, the selection of text is the most

---

86. See *He zhongguoren tan zongjiao-wo hen xinwei*. 和中國人談宗教-我很欣慰 [Talking to Chinese about religion—I feel pleased]. Web. 1 June 2010. <http://cando360.com/>

87. The above quote, along with some other audience reviews, are supplied by dramaturg Liu Lei.

88. The admission fee in 2013 production ranged from RMB100-150. According to a review by an audience, religious materials were reduced.

direct form of expressing [the producer's stance]. The selection of historical data should be a serious, responsible enterprise: it is next to re-creation. One-sided representation would naturally raise the question "why are you biased against Christianity? Too much information will lead to overload of expression that suffocates audience's thinking, just like a form of indoctrination, thus weakening the work's power and reducing it to a documentary—oh, Jews are sympathetic. This will weaken the original intent.[89]

Conclusion

In this chapter, I have conducted textual analyses of three productions of a Shakespeare play in different time periods in Mainland China over a span of thirty years. Situating the text analysis against the background of various socio-cultural conditions, as well as individual and prevalent ideologies, I sought to show that different generations favor different theologies, leading to varying translation and adaptation strategies of the religious discourse in the play. The end of the Cultural Revolution marked the beginning of the Second Chinese Enlightenment (1980s-1990s), as it was termed, which witnessed the revival of debate on culture and religion in a period of cultural fever (*wenhua re* 文化熱) and religious fever (*zongjiao re* 宗教熱).[90] The cultural fever explains the revival of interests in Shakespeare and the immense popularity of *The Merchant* as the first play post-Cultural Revolution. However, both Zhang and her successor Ni, in the midst of relaxed religious censorship, did not break free from the Marxist-Maoist interpretation of religion, which forms the primary reason for the untranslatability of the religious dimension rather than any political pressure exerted on the dramatists. Moreover, their humanistic reading of the play—putting emphasis on the traditional Chinese ethics of "truth, kindness and beauty"—is based on the traditional Confucian and Daoist philosophies which uphold aesthetics and joy as the ultimate goal in human life, under the Chinese "culture of joy." In that context, forced conversion, ethnic and religious conflicts are themes to be suppressed and considered irrelevant, while romance and the victory of good over evil are highlighted. The younger generation, however, tends to break free from such Marxist or Confucian interpretation. Their

89. See *Ni manyi ma—Xia Luoke.* 你滿意嗎-夏洛克 [Are you content—Shylock]. Web. 7 June 2010. <http://cando360.com/>

90. See Chow, *Theosis, Sino-Christian Theology*, 21–40 for a discussion on the Second Chinese Enlightenment. The second Chinese enlightenment is different from the first, i.e. May Fourth movement in that faith and religion is part and parcel of this second enlightenment, while in the May Fourth period, traditions, faith and the supernatural were labelled as stumbling blocks to modernization of society.

hermeneutical approach views religion with openness. To the young directors of *Shylock* in 2010, "religion" is no longer viewed as a sensitive issue, but something that can be openly discussed in the post-performance forum. Rather than emphasizing on the perennial theme of zhen-shan-mei (真善美) in traditional Chinese productions, the team chose an adaptation that highlights conflicts and suppression. The initial lack of interest in religious topics shown by director Zhang Bowen was transformed radically after her being involved as a cast member in a production on the persecution of Jews, which led to her hermeneutical shift in highlighting the sympathetic Jew in *Shylock*. Her change of mind testifies to Hans Georg Gadamer's insight— "because of the many experiences he has had and the knowledge he has drawn from them, one is particularly well equipped to have new experiences and to learn from them."[91] The theologies of various directors will be under further scrutiny in Chapter 6 to provide additional illustrations of the bearing that their theologies have on the interpretation and treatment of the religious dimension in these productions.

Having discussed cases in Mainland China, I will, in the next chapter, turn to Hong Kong, a place which has attracted less attention in Shakespeare scholarship[92] but whose vastly different religious milieu serves as a point of contrast with the above cases and is thus worthy of attention.

---

91. Gadamer, *Truth and Method*, 355.

92. Adele Lee points out that there is a neglect of Shakespeare on film in Hong Kong owing to the following reasons: non-Asian critics turn their attention more to Western Shakespeare than to Asian Shakespeare, the domination of discussions on traditional Chinese operatic versions of Shakespeare, the fact that Hong Kong is a cultural desert, and the link between Shakespeare and British colonisation in Hong Kong. See Lee, "The Bard Onscreen in Hong Kong," 459–480.

4

Case Studies of *The Merchant of Venice* in Hong Kong

Background

THIS CHAPTER COVERS THREE productions staged in Hong Kong during the period from 1984 to 2010, traversing two eras from the end of the colonial era to the post-colonial era. These productions in Hong Kong serve as markers for comparison with their Mainland counterparts in the same period as discussed in the previous chapter, as the drama translation scene and its reception were vastly different from the post-Mao era in the Mainland. Accordingly, I will begin this chapter with a brief overview of Shakespearean productions in Hong Kong, which will be followed by a case-by-case analysis of the three productions using a model modified from Andrew Chesterman.

In contrast with the introduction of Shakespeare into Mainland China through the Lin Shu's confucianized adaptation, performance of Shakespeare in Hong Kong was a product of colonialism. Shakespeare was introduced not via translation, but as an English play mainly for the British expatriates, the only garrison of seven hundred in Hong Kong when the British government withdrew their troops.[1] The earliest production was *Shylock* or *The Merchant of Venice Preserved*, a burlesque written by F. Talfourd, performed by the Hong Kong Amateur Theatrical Society in 1867.[2] The production was re-run in 1871: a review of which appearing on 29 April 1871 noted, "*The Merchant of Venice* was repeated with very great effort; Shylock being even better than on the last presentation, and the other actors fully equal to their previous admirable playing. It is needless to say that the

---

1. See Wong, "The 'Cooking Stove' vs. the 'Chinese Takeaway,'" 293.
2. See Wong, "Situating in Another Context," 27–40.

Spanish dance was loudly encored." The performance was shown to an elite, English-speaking audience able to pay for a seat in the City Hall Theatre in the mid-nineteenth century.

Shakespeare appreciation is considered a colonial product because it was brought in as a required subject in the secondary school curriculum in 1882. Furthermore, the Oxford Local Examination, an examination for all students in Hong Kong in the late nineteenth and early twentieth centuries that could grant them admission to universities in the United Kingdom and America, included Shakespeare as part of English studies. Comparison with the inclusion of Shakespeare in the Shanghai-based St. John's University curriculum in 1877 shows that prescription in secondary school ensured a much more widespread reception. Later, in 1888, Shakespeare became an independent subject in the entrance examination of the Chinese Imperial Maritime Custom Service, which further exemplifies the role of Shakespeare under the colonial rule. This meant that students who wished to carve out a career in the civil service needed to be acquainted with Shakespeare. British advocacy for Shakespeare in education can be further demonstrated in the Teaching of English in England by the Board of Education Report, published in 1921, which states that "Shakespeare is an inevitable and necessary part of school activity because he is our greatest English writer."[3]

As Dorothy Wong notes, from the available examination scripts available at the Hong Kong Examination Authority, Shakespeare was a compulsory part of English studies between 1950 and 1968.[4] But this mandatory requirement disappeared towards the end of colonial rule when the use of the Chinese language was gradually emphasized in the 1960s.[5]

Such institutionalized study of Shakespeare paved the way for a widespread and positive reception of Shakespeare in Hong Kong. Shakespeare was first known to students through Charles Lamb's *Tales from Shakespeare*. As with school education in the Mainland, the trial scene had been a favorite in the secondary school curriculum. Among the different Shakespearean plays, *The Merchant of Venice* occupied a special position. In 1958, the trial scene of *The Merchant of Venice* was included in two compulsory papers in the General English examination, which was the first time that Shakespeare was introduced in its original form rather than as a tale. One of my interviewees recalled the story of *The Merchant of Venice* appearing on the

---

3. For a detailed examination of Shakespeare education in Hong Kong under the colonial rule, see Wong, "Shakespeare in Hong Kong," 39.

4. Ibid, 293.

5. A correlation can be seen between the status of English language and the study of Shakespeare in Hong Kong during colonial rule. Ibid, 39.

education television channel, a government sponsored channel broadcast to students during class time.

In contrast with the Mainland experience, readers and audiences in Hong Kong had for a long time been exposed to Shakespearean plays not through its Chinese translation, but in English. The first complete translation of *The Merchant* appeared in 1914-1915 in a Christian women's magazine Nu Duo in Shanghai, but it was only in 1964 that saw the first Cantonese presentation of *The Merchant*. This was staged by the Dramatic Society of the United College of the Chinese University of Hong Kong at City Hall Theatre from 2 April to 4 April, nearly a century after the first Shakespeare performance in English in Hong Kong.

The different approaches to the Chinese translation of Shakespeare across the political divide can be explained by the differing ideologies prevailing on the two sides. Shakespearean plays in Chinese were promoted by scholars who saw urgency in the importation and translation of Western ideals (including Shakespeare and Thomas Huxley) to strengthen national power. This was achieved through stage performance among mass audiences starting in the 1920s,[6] through translation into literary texts by Lin Shu in the early twentieth century, and other scholars such as Zhu Shenghao and Liang Shiqiu who emerged later. Across the border, Hong Kong, under the colonial rule, saw no such urgency to translate Shakespeare as a way of popularizing it among the masses. Appreciation of Shakespeare remained in the form of high culture among the English-speaking elite, as secondary school education which promoted Shakespeare remained a luxury until 1978 when primary and junior school education became available free of charge.

The difference caused by Western education, plus the variety of spoken dialects, explains the different translation styles used by translators on the two sides of the border. On the Mainland, directors relied on the language competence of Shakespeare literary translators like Zhu Sheng Hao and Fang Ping who achieved a canonical status. Most of the mainland drama translations are based on these literary translations but with improved performability. It was the director who picked an existing translation without engaging a separate translation. In Hong Kong, translators derived their interpretation of the play not only from the existing translation, but also from the annotated English play. They would make out a separate translation in order to reflect the different lexicons of Cantonese. People in Hong Kong like to pride themselves on a high level of English competence, a result of

---

6. The first full Chinese stage performance of Shakespeare was Hamlet in 1921. See Meng, *Shakespeare in China*, 1994.

the "de-nationalizing" policies of the colonial government that privileged English rather than Chinese as the official language. This probably explains why translators preferred to read the English script rather than the Chinese translation, which was given a lower status. The difference in reading and interpretation processes gave rise in Hong Kong to a different interpretation of the religious material in *The Merchant*. The prolonged exposure to Shakespeare and the Western culture under the colonial rule, and the consequent differences in interpretation, could probably explain the phenomenon in Hong Kong where no one or two translators were canonized as *the* Shakespeare translator: instead, there were different translators for different Shakespearean productions on stage. In *The Merchant*, at least four different Cantonese translations were used. That means that the religious element in the play was subject to various degree of adaptation or manipulation as a result in these different interpretations.

Christianity in Hong Kong

Hong Kong has enjoyed a strong Christian presence since the occupation of Hong Kong by the British government in the nineteenth century. Protestant and Catholic missionary organizations such as the London Missionary Society, Basel Mission, Lutheran, Baptist Mission, Maryknoll Sisters, Columban Sisters, have been active in establishing Christian schools, which presently represent nearly half of the total number of local schools in Hong Kong. Missionaries not only exerted influence in religious education but worked hand in hand with the government in promoting government-sponsored, high-quality secular education for the Chinese population. James Legge, an Anglican missionary from the London Missionary Society, for example, was chairman of the Board of Education and helped found the Central School, the first secular school in Hong Kong in 1860 which still exists as one of the most prestigious secondary schools in Hong Kong. With the help of government subsidies, missionary schools obtained the much needed funding to expand locally. In fact, the government worked in partnership with Christian schools and entrusted churches with the provision of education to the refugees in the 1950s, mainly because they shared the government's anti-Communist ideology. The government's support for Christian schools was thus able to counteract the influence of atheistic Communism.[7] In contrast with the Mainland, where most students did not know about the Christian faith, few people in Hong Kong rarely had not heard of Christianity.

7. For an overview of the church-state relations in Hong Kong, see Leung and Chan, *Changing Church*, 26.

Knowledge of Christianity was widely disseminated through the availability of Christian media and publishers, churches, Christian schools and other Christian organizations. These Christian schools were initially a product of colonialism as this former British colony granted missionaries free access after China's defeat in the Opium War. The disciplined management of missionary schools, an emphasis on an English-speaking environment through the presence of English-speaking missionaries, plus a subsidized tuition fee by the government, earned them a good reputation and they became very popular among parents. Under the current allocation system, kindergarten children could be allocated more credits towards gaining entry to primary schools if their parents were Christian. Some parents reportedly applied to be baptized just for the sake of paving a way for their children's schooling. The name and fame of Christian schools successfully attracted the crème of the community who graduated to become influential leaders in society. The situation continues when the two highest ranking officials in Hong Kong, Donald Tsang, Chief Executive of Hong Kong Special Administrative Region in 2002-2012, and Wong Yan Lung, the second Secretary for Justice of Hong Kong in 2005-2012, are Catholic Christian and Protestant Christian respectively and openly support Christian activities.[8] The result of such an institutionalized and close relationship between the Hong Kong educational system and missionary activities effectively bound secular education to a strong non-denominational Christian world-view.[9]

In terms of social development, the Hong Kong government has entered into a mutually beneficial partnership with the church, which accepted the government's invitation to provide social services from the 1950s onwards. The churches helped the government solve social issues caused by the influx of refugees from the Mainland, and at the same time helped protect the authority and colonial rule of the government in the face of pro-nationalist and pro-Communist forces in Hong Kong during those times of political turmoil. On the other hand, because of the privileged position that the churches enjoyed, they were able to fulfil the mission of serving the people of Hong Kong and preaching the gospel. Unlike Communist China which used to associate Christianity with imperialism in a negative way, Christian ideology permeated in Hong Kong through institutionalized Christian education and social development.[10] Hong Kong is also known for its freedom of expression among different religious

---

8. Wong Yan Lung officiated at the Christian vessel Doulos opening ceremony in Sept 2007, while Donald Tsang went for morning prayer at the Catholic church and visited the King James Bible exhibition in April 2011.

9. See Wong, "Christian Missions," 1996.

10. See Leung and Chan, *Changing Church and State Relations*, 146.

groups. There are approximately thirty Christian publishing houses, and Christian programs are broadcast in mainstream media broadcasting companies, including Television Broadcasts Limited (TVB), Asia Television Limited (ATV), and Radio Television of Hong Kong (RTHK). Other than the abundance of Christian actors and actresses such as Qiao Hong (喬宏) have been seen giving thanks to God at different TV and film award presentation ceremonies without being negatively depicted by the media or attracted any complaints.[11] It is thus worth noting that against this background of freedom of expression and positive impression of Christianity, how Christian references were suppressed in some productions in Hong Kong, which will be discussed later in this chapter.

The Shakespearean Scene in Hong Kong

Shakespeare productions grew in professionalism as well as budget from the 1970s onwards. The first stage of Shakespearean productions was in the 1970s when Cantonese Shakespearean productions in Hong Kong were mostly adaptations. Lacking resources and funding, productions tended to be truncated. In 1977, Hamlet was staged by the Hong Kong Repertory Theater where over 50 per cent of the play was omitted. It was set in the period of the Southern Han Dynasty, and the architecture on stage was inspired by the Tang Dynasty. The names of characters and titles were adapted to reflect the period. Later productions suffered similar omissions, with Macbeth (1980) being cut by half. The second stage of Shakespearean productions saw more professional directorship and stage design: lines were not deleted as drastically as in the first stage. It was also a time of active cultural exchange prior to the end of the colonial era. Overseas directors, such as Daniel Yang who was US educated, Glenn Walford of Hong Kong Repertory, Colin George of the Hong Kong Academy for Performing Arts, Bernard Goss and Chris Johnson of the Chung Ying Theater were enlisted in presenting Shakespeare in Cantonese. *Twelfth Night* was presented by Chung Ying Theatre Company in 1986 under the directorship of Bernard Goss; Othello was directed by US educated Dr Joanna Chan in 1986; A Midsummer's Night's Dream by Bernard Goss in 1988; The *Comedy of Errors* by Colin George of the Drama School of the Performing Arts in 1986, Daniel Yang directed *Much Ado About Nothing* in 1990. Only *The Tempest* in 1989 and *Measure for Measure* in 1986 were directed by local Chinese directors, namely Sam Lam and Ying Ruo Cheng from Beijing respectively. These directors played a significant role in deciding the translation strategy,

---

11. Ng, "The Role of Religion in Hong Kong Society," 3–20.

and translator Rupert Chan once lamented that the ending of *Twelfth Night* was deleted by Goss without informing him. *The Merchant of Venice* in 1984 belonged to the second stage and was the first most complete Cantonese production[12] of the play. The third stage began in the 1990s when an international standard of local production was reached.[13]

The Merchant of Venice in 1984

In the early eighties after Zhang's production in the Post-cultural revolution in Beijing, Hong Kong Repertory Theatre, the first government-funded theatre company in Hong Kong, put on six performances of *The Merchant of Venice* in January 24-29 1984, which were re-run in May 1–10, 1984. Although both Yang's and Zhang's productions were situated in the same time period, their difference in the treatment of religious material deserves discussion.

About the Translator/Director

Prof. Daniel Yang, director and translator of the production, is a contemporary of Zhang. He is the first American-educated Chinese to graduate with a PhD from the drama department. He has experience in directing and teaching in both the West and the East. Born in 1936 in Jiangsu, PRC, he went to Taiwan for secondary and tertiary education. In 1961, he flew to the US to start his Master of Fine Arts at Hawaii University, and then pursued a PhD at Wisconsin University. He started his employment in Hong Kong Repertory in 1983 and continued as Artistic Director until 1998. *The Merchant of Venice* was his first Shakespearean production in Hong Kong, but before that he had already been involved in Shakespearean productions as Producing Artistic and Administrative Director for Colorado Shakespeare's Festival starting 1976. Unlike Zhang who admitted she could not read English (and therefore original Shakespeare), Yang is confident of his competence[14] in English, which he claims is comparable with celebrated Shakespearean literary translators such as Zhu Sheng Hao, Fang Ping etc. Being a director, translator and scholar, he has watched over 200 Shakespearean productions,

---

12. The first Cantonese production in 1964 at Chinese University of Hong Kong was presented in selective acts, but not as a complete translation.
13. See Yang,"The Shakespearean Productions," 78–88.
14. Fong, *Interviews on Theatre Directors in Hong Kong*, 60–63.

including Zhang's production, and over 75 of which were from the Royal Shakespeare Company.

Cognitive and Behavioral Conditions

Style of Yang's production

When he took the helm at Hong Kong Repertory Theater, *The Merchant of Venice* was his second Shakespearean production[15] and the theatre's fifth Shakespearean production. Building on his previous experience in directing *Taming of the Shrewd* in Hong Kong,[16] he translated *The Merchant* on a similar pattern, rendering all verse passages into rhymed verses and all prose into prose. The quality of his translation has improved recently, judging from audience and critical reaction. Yang's Shakespearean productions belong to the Western style, as his directorial concept has been to bring the original Shakespeare with fine detail to the public.[17] He also brought along three American designers responsible for costumes, lighting and scenery to work on his production. It should be noted that his creativity is not compromised by other constraints, especially budget, which he describe as "handsome." With such plentiful resources and talents, he hopes that the Hong Kong audience were able to appreciate the first "carefully mounted Shakespearean production whose acting, directing, scenery, costumes, accessories, and lighting were of the same standard as those seen at a major theatre company of the Western world."[18] Remaining faithful to the original was one of the characteristics of this production, so faithful that only the last scene from Act 3 has been deleted, rendering it a 3 hour performance in total.

> Against the idea of Sinicized Shakespeare, he said:
>
> I am not going to produce a Peking Opera style Shakespearean production just because I am Chinese. I don't need to work on face masks, broad sleeves, drum rolls. I only have to give full play to Shakespeare's script, to work out the best production. No need to use 'gimmicks' to appeal to the crowd, no need to make a difference in intention . . . think few Shakespearean

---

15. Yang's first Shakespearean production in Hong Kong was *Taming of the Shrew*, followed by *The Merchant of Venice*, *Much Ado about Nothing*, *King Lear*, and *Midsummer Night's Dream*.
16. See Yang, *The Latest Scene and Trend of Shakespeare*, 75–80.
17. Ibid.
18. Yang, "Shakespeare at Hong Kong Repertory Theatre," 80.

productions allow Sinicization. If we Sinicize a Shakespearean production successfully, that is equivalent to murdering Shakespeare—although this view may seem conservative.

Yang's Middle-of-the-road Interpretation

Aware of the Victorian and contemporary interpretations of the play, Yang admits that his production is "quite traditional in design" and the interpretation of Shylock and Antonio "very middle of the road"—neither portraying Shylock as a villain nor Antonio as a blameless hero.

> While the theme of racial prejudice will be highlighted here and there, there is no attempt to make this production a pro-Semitic piece. If we can accept the "way of the world" and the imperfection of humanity, where the Christians are as despicable and admirable as the Jews, then we are closer to the proper blend of beauty and ugliness which is the dominant concept in the shaping of this production.[19]

How was this "middle of the road" interpretation brought to the audience? In the brief synopsis laid out in the house program, the words Jew or Jewish appears twice, while no mention is made of the Christian identity of Antonio or his friends being Christian. Without being "pro-Semitic," the synopsis describes Shylock as "pitiful," one who "fails to kill his enemy, loses all his money, destroys his daughter's respect for him in the meantime, and has to be further humiliated by the sentence of the enemy." Yang did not explicitly spell out the humiliation, but this became clear when the audience screamed out at the sentence, "He must presently become a Christian," after which a necklace with a cross pendant was then imposed on the "pitiful" Shylock.

Translation Profile

Daniel Yang, the director, visualized the play as a comedy which has its tragic moments. The comic tones were set out through light-hearted background music. Adopting a "middle of the road" strategy, Shylock was a man in black long robes, donning a typical Jewish hat.

---

19. Cited from the house program of this production at the Hong Kong Repertory Theater archive.

Biblical references were translated faithfully rather than being domesticated or omitted, showing the consistency of the director's "faithful" strategy.[20] The allusion to Jacob's story in Act 1, which is normally deleted to shorten the play was left intact. Names such as Abraham, prophet from Nazareth and God were translated in accordance with the normal Bible translation. The name of Daniel, the biblical prophet used to describe Portia in the court scene, however was not translated according to the Protestant or Catholic translation convention. The name was transliterated as "但尼歐." When asked about why this name was not translated according to biblical tradition, Yang, whose name is also Daniel, could not, however, recall the reason, but he insisted that he knew his own name's biblical roots.

Being "faithful" does not mean the director's translation is literal. In the following two instances, modification is detected that gives a shift in meaning or a different emphasis.

I hate him for he is a Christian

我恨他，因為他基督徒的信仰

Back translation: I hate him, because of his Christian faith.

Stylistic modulation is detected, from Christian as a noun to Christian faith as a noun. Such a shift reduces the personal conflict between Shylock and Antonio, emphasizing instead the ideological differences between Shylock's and Antonio's faith. (Act One)

Therefore, Jew, though justice be thy plea, consider this, that, in the course of justice, none of us should see salvation ... No one shall see salvation (in Portia's mercy speech)

因此猶太人，請你想一想，雖然你的堅持是執行王法，但執行王法的過程中，沒有一人能得救進天堂。

Back Translation: Therefore Jew, consider this, though exercising the rule is your plea, but in the course of executing nation's rule, no one can be saved and enter heaven. (Act Four)

Semantic modulation/explicitation is used to render "should see salvation" as "should be saved and enter heaven" in order to make the

---

20. It should be noted that translation studies in recent years have gradually shifted from an emphasis on producing "faithful" translations of a source text, to a focus on social, cultural and communicative practices and the relationship between translation products and other socio-cultural factors. In my research, "faithful translation" does not mean literal, word-for-word translation, as the following paragraph shows, because that kind of translation is simply next to impossible in a theatrical setting. "Faithfulness" here should be understood in the thematic sense but not the semantic sense.

audience understand the concept of salvation better. Explication is also seen in the rendition of "mercy is . . . an attribute to God" to "mercy . . . represents God's lenience."[21]

This conversion requirement is further reinforced and developed on the stage, where the Christian Venetian citizens at the court nodded at the verdict to express their appreciation.

To intensify the "pitiful outcome," Shylock, upon receiving the verdict, was pushed to the ground by Gratiano who asked him to kneel and beg for the duke's pardon. The audience responded to the scene with laughter. When the Duke spared his life, the audience again laughed at the comedic tone of the Duke. Upon receiving the pardon from Antonio who required him to become a Christian, he twisted his Jewish hat, and when the guard put on the cross necklace on him, he grabbed the cross pendant tightly to signify his anger. He left the stage in despair, with his body lowered, and loud cries were heard when he entered back stage. According to Yang in the interview, this was a scene to show his Old Testament dignity. But instead of showing sympathy, the audience responded with bolts of laughter, which could be an expression of disagreement or ridicule.

Laughter was also provoked when Gratiano spoke the following lines in a comic way:

> I have a wife, whom, I protest, I love:
>
> I would she were in heaven, so she could
>
> Entreat some power to change this currish Jew. (Act IV)

The trial scene provoked laughter from the audience throughout. The play, being set as a comedy, did invite laughter even during scenes with tension.

Yang in the house program commented that he was well acquainted with the Victorian interpretations of this play, where Antonio is idealized as a supreme example of male friendship and Renaissance nobility. At the same time, the house program recognises the contemporary interpretation of Antonio as a homosexual who could not stand losing his lover Bassanio to a woman. Ralph Berry's interpretation of Antonio was also cited, as a "neurotic gambler" who plays to lose the emotional sensation of being overwhelmed. Having access to these interpretations, Yang maintained his unique view of the characters. In the interview, Yang described Antonio as a "generous" man whom he would like to befriend with, and rejected the idea that he was homosexual. This was shown in the last scene when the lonesome Antonio, seeing his best friend was married, was invited by Bassanio and Portia to join their company.

21. The source text is 慈悲⋯代表上帝的寬宏大量.

When asked in the interview about his view of the forced conversion, Yang did not hesitate to show his disapproval of this forced act, which explains his sympathy and sympathetic treatment of Shylock:

> That (forced conversion) appears to me very cruel, so in my performance Salanio, one of the Jews, put a cross on his neck, and had him to kneel down to beg for the duke's pardon. When he turned around and saw the cross, he was totally ruined, totally beaten, this is Old Testament dignity. The Christians were too harsh on him . . .

Yang then related this forced conversion to the history of China where foreign missionaries came to distribute flour and sugar as a bait for Chinese in poverty. "This for them was well-intentioned, but it was also a form of colonialism . . . powerful nations brought religion to poor people in a half-coercive way . . . uneducated Chinese came to churches for two bags of flour, but they were half-hearted at churches and were not genuine believers. They believed because they could get flour, do you understand? This is just like the case of Antonio . . . from his (Antonio's) Christian point of view it was something like a mercy, but in my view this merely added to the suffering of the Jew, so the cross that was forced upon him brought him more pain."

Yang's interpretation could be traced back to his religious experience—he has renounced Catholicism and sees rituals as a burden, although he denies that there is a connection between the two. As a non-believer reading Shylock's conversion as an equivalent to colonialism, and equating the situation with the colonial invasion of Chinese soil, it is not difficult to understand why his sympathy is skewed towards the converted, and not the converter.

Yang's thoughts underlying the interpretation process will be studied in more detail in the Chapter 6.

Cognitive and Behavioral Effects

Although being described as "pitiful" in the house program, Shylock was not treated as a tragic figure in the play. Being faithful to the original, Yang deleted only Act 3 Scene 5 regarding the conversation between Jessica, Lorenzo and Lancelot, which was often left out in other productions. Laughter from the audience echoed on and off. Even during the elopement scene which was not designed to be "comic," laughter broke out when Jessica said, "After tonight I will not be his daughter."

Even during the most dramatic speech "Hath a Jew no eyes," the audience was able to laugh when Shylock replied to Salarino's question "what's that [pound of flesh] good for?" with "To bait fish withal." Despite Yang's efforts to show the tragic outcome for Shylock through gestures such as clutching the cross and falling down, a comic tone was set at the outset, prompting laughter from the audience at every scene. Yang explained in the interview that this was not his intention, but the audience read the signs differently beyond his control, and the laughter was "silly," "nervous laughter."

Socio-cultural Effects

Being the first large-scale Cantonese Shakespeare play of an international standard, *The Merchant* set the standard for later productions. This production was put on to celebrate the inauguration of Ko Shan Theatre, a new theatre in Kowloon. The Urban Council of Hong Kong co-organised a Shakespeare Festival to celebrate this occasion, inviting over 10 amateur troupes to perform without charge scenes from Shakespearean plays, Elizabethan music etc. Because of the high publicity of the Shakespeare Festival, *The Merchant* caught the attention of the mass media and the public, as well as the attention of the theatre circle.

Being the first full-scale production of *The Merchant*, one could see the trajectory of how the interpretation of Yang, especially with his sympathetic treatment of Shylock, came to impact later performances e.g. the 2010 production, directed by a previous actor of the 1984 production, i.e., Ko Tinlung.

The use of props (like the sword of the Moroccan prince to symbolize his Islamic faith, and the gesture of crossing oneself before Antonio's intended execution), also inspired the stagecraft in *The Merchant* in 2010, which will be discussed later.

Bearing in mind that Daniel Yang's production in Hong Kong and Zhang Qihong's production in Beijing both took place in the early 1980s, how did the geographical and ideological differences between the two places impact on the transmission of the religious content of the play? Comparison of Zhang's and Yang's translations alerts us to how sensitive a translation can be to its particular socio-political context. The two plays were both staged at roughly the same time. Although both productions were put on by two well-resourced theatre companies where finance was less of an issue, the difference in political climate, the director's preference and the audience reception created two vastly different renditions. While both Zhang's and Yang's directorial intention was to introduce the "original," "quintessential"

Shakespeare to the audience, the two productions shown in different parts of China in the same era were subject to different environmental factors and constraints. Hong Kong, a British colony in the eighties, did not suffer from the immense distortion of cultural landscape brought about by the Cultural Revolution which ended in 1976. Christian schools set up by missionaries flourished in Hong Kong and were much sought after as "brand-name" schools. People were free to engage in religious activities and discussions during the sensitive times encountered by their Mainland counterparts. The 1980s was also a period when Hong Kong became "a platform for cultural interaction through the contribution of overseas directors" mostly hailing from the US or the UK, whose adaptations favored cultural co-existence and diversity above homogeneity. Audiences in Hong Kong were free from the Marxist ideology that dominated arts circles on the Mainland.

The Merchant of Venice in 2000

Socio-cultural conditions

Translated plays are an important source of inspiration for the drama scene in Hong Kong. According to Jessica Yeung's survey in 2008, over 900 Western plays have been translated and performed in Hong Kong since 1962. So much so that Hardy Tsoi once observed that the theatre in Hong Kong had become "impotent after being 'breast-fed' under British colonialism for the past century, and therefore many artists urged that theatre in Hong Kong should go back to its original aim of reflecting our society, exerting a social function."[22]

In the post-colonial period, literature in Hong Kong, including drama, has carved out its identity between the two colonizers, i.e. Britain and Mainland China. But the identity is unique, neither Mainland China nor British nor Taiwanese.[23] There is a drive to assert that Hong Kong is "different" from other Mainland cities. Although Jack Shu denied that his production is a reflection of the times, the issue of identity had been especially popular in the lead-up to the handover in 1997. In 1994, Hong Kong Hamlet, a comedy first performed during the Fringe Festival, describes the life of a young Caucasian called Hamlet Hamlet who lives in Hong Kong. Hamlet Hamlet recently came back to Hong Kong from Canada and mourns the death of his expatriate father. He then discovers that his Hong Kong Chinese mother is about to remarry to a Chinese family friend who has strong pro-Mainland

---

22. See Li, "Chinese-Speaking Theatre In Perspective," 310–323.
23. See Chen, "Postcolonial Hong Kong Drama Translation," 39–58.

China views. It is described as a drama of "neo-realist savagery, lust and straightforward bad public relations."[24] Through the eyes of a Caucasian, Hong Kong Hamlet describes a double dilemma. On one hand, the expatriate Hamlet feels unease in Hong Kong; on the other hand, the Chinese Hamlet feels uneasy about the change of governance.[25]

In the pre-handover period, theatres and films on the issue of identity were rife. A number of the leading Cantonese theatre companies used adaptation as a method of reflecting the socio-political situation in this period. High Noon Productions indigenized *Cyrano de Bergerac*; Kit Mang Drama has a Cantonese production of *Death in Venice*; the Academy of Performing Arts has produced a Cantonese *Twelfth Night*; the Sand and Bricks Company has turned Kafka's Metamorphosis into a study of a Hong Kong family in the midst of political upheaval; the Hong Kong Federation of Students has sponsored a play that orientalized *A Tale of Two Cities*, substituting two Asian metropolises for London and Paris. In some cases, the Western original has been used as a mirror and a commentary on the post-handover conditions.[26]

For example, in November 1997, four months after the hand-over, a musical called *My Fair Lady* was performed, which was full of nostalgia for the British colonial rule. In this adaptation of Bernard Shaw's play (1916), where a Chinese flower girl To Lanheong fell in love with a Chinese professor at the University of Hong Kong, translator Rupert Chan added an additional line, "I am grateful to you for teaching me the British style, which has transformed me into an upper-class person." Chan later admitted that most people in Hong Kong resonated with this line on the last day of colonial rule, i.e. 30th June 1997.

The search for identity was intensified when Hong Kong was hardly hit by the Asian economic crisis from 1998 onward. The technology bubble that burst in 2000 added to the uncertainty of the post-colonial city which used to pride itself on its status as a financial hub. The economic depression has left Hong Kong in a state of vulnerability and lack of confidence compared to the robustness and stability of the colonial days. Commentators further argue that Hong Kong is in a dilemma of "nationalization" versus "localization" post-1997, which weakens the sense of local identity. If nationalization is in the ascendant, Hong Kong's status might be reduced to that of another

---

24. See *Fringe '94*. Hong Kong: Hong Kong Festival Fringe, 1994, 19.
25. See MacKenzie, "Questions of Identity in Contemporary Hong Kong Theater," 203.
26. Ibid.

Mainland city. If localization is promoted by the Hong Kong government, it might be read as a threat to China.[27]

The search for a unique Hong Kong identity is compounded by the change in language policy where three-quarters of the secondary schools in Hong Kong have to use mother tongue rather than English as the medium of instruction upon the implementation of mother tongue policy in 1998. This paved the way for a more colloquial register in this local production in 2000. After the enormous success of *The Merchant* in Hong Kong and China and in the early eighties, the next production that came on their heels was on a much smaller budget and scale and was put on by an amateur troupe in Hong Kong in 2000, named Ding Theatre. Quite unlike the production in 1984 where the script was translated by Mandarin-speaking Daniel Yang, this script was colored by colloquial Hong Kong expressions. Additionally, unlike the previous production where the director doubled as the translator, Jack Shu the translator was asked by the director Chris Shum to translate the whole text. The translation reflected the voices of both translator and director, who came to a consensus on what was to be retained and what omitted.

About the Director and Translator

Chris Shum graduated from Hong Kong Baptist University, majoring in Chinese Literature, followed by a Master of Philosophy degree at the School of Education at University of Hong Kong. He has been a renowned and award-winning lyricist for musicals, plays, movies and TV dramas. Occasionally, he directs plays as an amateur. Recently he has been involved in translating plays, such as Alan Ayckbourn's *Communicating Doors* (2009), and *Love Letters of Shakespeare* (2012).

Shu was the fellow schoolmate of Shum and graduated Bachelor of Arts, majored in English Literature and minored in translation. He graduated from Hong Kong Baptist University with a Master of Philosophy degree in 1996 under the supervision of Simon Chau, a Shakespearean scholar in Hong Kong. Shu had been a secondary school teacher in liberal arts and was actively involved in drama education in his different positions as adjunct lecturer at Hong Kong Arts Center and recently assistant professor at Open University of Hong Kong, where he designed undergraduate courses on drama education. He gained his PhD at Warwick University. He was an executive member of the Ding Troupe when he was commissioned to carry out the translation.

---

27. So, "One country, three systems?," 235–53.

Cognitive and Behavioral Conditions

The Merchant of Venice was chosen by the troupe in 2000 that season because they were considering staging comedies. In two separate interviews with translator Shu and director Shum, both said that they had received their first impression of *The Merchant* by reading the story in primary school materials.[28] Shum, recalling his early impressions, found the story interesting based on the impression formed earlier, and hence selected it for the season. Since the story of the pound of flesh was included in the primary school education curriculum, people brought up in the 1970s are familiar with the play, according to Shu.[29]

Shu's translation is a product of negotiation between director and translator. Both agreed on the treatment of religious material, and Shu was left alone to translate the play text. The director commissioned Shu for the translation work because he had confidence in the translation competence which Shu had shown during college days, Shum also highly commended his translation of *The Merchant* as "one of the best" he had read. Both the translator and the director became the agents in the process of selective appropriation,[30] where the elements of racial and Judeo-Christian conflict were suppressed in the narrative, as the textual analysis will show in the later section.

While translating, Shu deliberately did not read other Chinese translations to prevent himself from being influenced by them. He translated *The Merchant of Venice* based on used Barron's edition of 1985, and referred to dictionaries for Shakespearean plays as well as to the modern English version. He did a search on the religious conflict between Christians and Jews, but decided not to incorporate this because the audience in Hong Kong might not understand.

The set-up of Ding Theatre as an amateur troupe is worth our attention as it contributed to the dynamics of the translation process that gave rise to the treatment of religious material in the text. In Shu's translation, it is not just the identity of Christians that is not mentioned, Shylock's nationality is not named either. Shu explained in an interview that this was

---

28. Shu said in the interview that he watched the story of "a pound of flesh" in Education Television in Hong Kong, an educational channel for primary school students. Shum said he remembered the story was published in English materials when he studied at primary school.

29. Shakespeare was introduced into the secondary school curriculum in Hong Kong in 1882, which tended to generate a favorable reception towards Shakespeare. Shakespeare was a compulsory part of English in Hong Kong public exams between 1950 and 1968. See Wong, "Shakespeare in Hong Kong," 1995.

30. See Baker, *Translation and Conflict*, 72.

a market-driven decision rather than one arising out of self-censorship or political concern.

> We (myself and director, Chris Shum Wai Chung) discussed together how to proceed. Ding Troupe at the time was considering which Shakespearean play to stage in that season, and we finally chose this play. But we came up against a thorny issue during the translation process. Besides the rich religious culture (embedded in the original play), I and people in Hong Kong generally are not familiar with the Judaic culture or religious conflicts. We decided that the religious elements, or religious conflicts which do not constitute the core of this play, will be subdued in order to guarantee box office and cater to a bigger market. Perhaps this [religious conflict] is what Shakespeare wanted to emphasize in his time, but most people in Hong Kong are not interested. Therefore we had better reduce it and focus on the characters.

From the above interview, it seems possible to apply Lefevere's translation theory on the relationship between ideology and patronage on the one hand and the image of translated literature on the other. With an amateur troupe, which is not government-funded unlike the Hong Kong Repertory Theater, income from ticket sales is an important criterion in ensuring that the production can break even. But is the above reason cited by Shu the only or major reason for reducing the religious dimension? Additionally, in a theatre production, the director almost without exception has the final decision on the translation of the script. Without the approval or endorsement of Shum, the reduction could not take place. So why would Shum initiate this reduction in the first place? As my interviews with Shum and Shu show, such reduction is more a theological decision than a business decision. I will discuss this later in this chapter and in Chapter 6.

Translation Profile and Treatment of Religious Material

While the narratives in the original Shakespeare are basically retained in this production, the identity "Christian" was omitted throughout the play, and Shylock was described as an "alien," instead of having his Jewish identity asserted as seen in Zhang's production in 1980. The religious conflict between Jews and Christians has been replaced by a conflict between an "outsider" and a "local." In the various speeches where Christian identity was originally Shylock's reason for bearing a grudge, and where the Jewish nation was being scorned, a shift of identity took place from Judeo/Christian to Outsider/Local. In line with Zhang's translation, Shylock hated Antonio not for being

CASE STUDIES OF *THE MERCHANT OF VENICE* IN HONG KONG 167

a Christian but for being generous without charging interest. This is most clearly expressed in the following Shylock's soliloquy:

> 夏洛克：[旁白]你睇下佢樣衰到？成隻烏龜咁耷頭耷腦！我最憎佢哋啲本地人，懶好心，借錢俾人又唔收息，做壞個市仲懶得戚。我知，佢哋自居地頭蟲，睇唔過眼我哋班過江龍。有次喺總商會佢當眾奚落我，踩我盤生意，話我放貴利鬧我賤，侮辱我啲血汗錢。你話如果俾我促到佢把柄，我唔同佢算番筆舊帳我塊面放去邊！

> Shylock:[Aside] Look at him, like a tortoise with sloppy ears and brains! I hate these locals, who pretend to be kind by not charging interest, lowering the market rate. I know, they think they are local bugs and despise outside "dragons." In the chamber of commerce he rails at my business, my usances, insults me and my hard-earned moneys. If I catch him, where is my dignity if I do not ask him to repay his deeds. (Act 1 Scene 3)

In Shylock's most telling and emotive speech "hath not a Jew eyes," Shu retained the emotion while replacing all the references to Jews with "outsiders."

> 愛嚟吊魚都好呀！就算吊唔到魚，都唔駛吊住我鋪報仇癮！佢侮辱我九十幾次，咒住我發達，趁我損手爛腳嗰陣諦我，到我賺得幾個崩就嚟挖苦我，搞亂我檔攤，離間我同朋友嘅感情，仲喺我啲對手面前搧風點火，佢為咩要咁做啊？就係因為我係外江人！外江人同本地人有咩分別呀？外江人冇眼耳口鼻㗎？外江人冇手冇腳，冇知覺冇感情㗎？我哋食垃圾大㗎？刀槍不入㗎？睇醫生唔駛打針食藥㗎？我哋冬天唔凍夏天唔熱㗎？你攞針吉我我唔流血，你唧我我唔笑㗎？你攞毒藥毒我唔死，你得罪我我唔會報仇㗎？你哋教我嘅嘢我會學以致用！唔止呀，仲會青出於藍㗎呀！

> Shylock: To bait fish withal: if it will feed nothing else, it will feed my revenge. He has disgraced me over 90 times, and hindered me from making money, laughed at my losses, mocked at my meagre gains, thwarted my bargains, cooled my friends, heated my enemies; and what's his reason? I am an outsider! How different is an outsider from a local? Have outsiders no eyes, mouth or nose? Have outsiders no hands and legs, senses? Do we eat rubbish? Are we unharmed by weapons? Are we immune from medication? Are we not warmed and cooled by the same winter and summer? If you prick us, do we not bleed? if you tickle us, do we not laugh? if you poison us, do we not die? and if you

wrong us, shall we not revenge? The villainy you teach me, I will execute, and it shall go hard but I will better the instruction.

(Act III Scene 1)

Under Shu's rendition, Shylock was a "wai-jiang lao 外江佬," a Chinese expression that literally addresses a person on the other side of the river, or *jiang*. Antonio himself is the "ben di ren 本地人," or local. The story is still set in Venice, but religious identities were removed.

The translation "wai-jiang lao" brings out the "otherness" of being a Jew. At the same time, "lao 佬" is of a low register used in colloquial Cantonese but not in written Chinese. Shylock was addressed in 13 occasions as "Wai-jiang lao," two occasions as "Wai-jiang Xia 外江夏" (surname of Shylock's Chinese name). It is only in his soliloquy that that he addresses himself as "Wai-jiang ren 外江人," where "ren 人" is a neutral title that stands for person. His daughter Jessica was addressed as "Wai-jiang xiao jie 外江小姐" (Miss Outsider). The linguistic analysis above demonstrates the use of register to signify his less dignified status in this production. Wai-jiang lao can also be interpreted as applying to the Mainland Chinese businessmen who since the 90s had an investment interest in Hong Kong: people in Hong Kong were threatened by their investment activities in ramping up property prices and share prices.

There was another reason for weakening the cultural identities of the protagonists. Shu explained that reducing their racial and religious conflicts could lower the cost of otherwise elaborate costumes. While the play is still set in Venice, and the content stays close to the original narrative structure, the troupe did not incur expense on using elaborate costumes, but opted for the basic Western dress.

As all Christian references are omitted, the Christian term "mercy" which appears in Portia's "mercy speech" was transmitted into the Buddhist and Confucian discourse.

Consider the following example:

> 仁慈之心並唔係勉強得嚓嘅。慈悲心好似天降嘅甘霖，會祝福兩種人，一種係施者，一種係受者。但擁有至高無上嘅力量，比皇冠更加顯出帝皇嘅尊貴，比權杖散發出更加懾人嘅威力。慈悲心係一種屬於天神嘅素質，而當人類將仁慈同公義結合嘅時候，人就超凡入聖。因此，夏洛克，雖然你一心維護公義，但係同時請你考慮，仁義兩存先至係至高境界。

The heart of kindness is not strained, it drops as the gentle rain from heaven. It gives blessings to two types of people—one that gives and one that takes. It possesses the mightiest power and it becomes the throned monarch better than his crown, the force mightier than the staff. Mercy is an attribute of heaven's God: when human beings combine both kindness and justice, humans will be like consecrated like saints. So, Shylock, although you plead justice, but please consider, the co-existence of kindness and justice is the highest realm. But if you insist, then this strict court of Venice must needs give sentence against Antonio.

The original lines emphasized the "highness" of mercy above justice. In the target text, having been removed from the Christian discourse, "when mercy seasons justice" is translated into a Confucian term *renyi liangcun* 仁義兩存 which upholds both values of *ren* 仁 (kindness) and *yi* 義 (righteousness). It is this co-existence, the harmonic relationship between the two values, that is being upheld by Portia in order to convince Shylock the "Other." The mitigation of justice in the original line "I have spoke thus much To mitigate the justice of thy plea" is fully integrated into the Confucian system of equilibrium.

Shu deleted Shylock's "forced conversion" as a requirement for his release in the trial scene, which is not surprising after he deleted all Christian and Jewish references in the text. The deletion seemed "natural" in order to maintain consistency. But after entering into dialogue with Shum and Shu regarding their faith, I believe that the deletion may point towards ideological conflicts below the surface- it reflects the selective attention the translator gives to the text.

I now give excerpts from my interview with Shu to demonstrate the ideological conflicts in the translation process.

> Interviewer: When I watched Zhang Qihong's version of *The Merchant of Venice* (1980), I found striking similarities between her treatment of religiosity and yours. Both versions deleted the forced conversion of Shylock.
>
> Shu: I deleted it?
>
> Interviewer: Yes.
>
> Shu: Oh, (I did not realize) I so disliked that part! I forgot I deleted it, although I found this (forced conversion) ridiculous.
>
> Interviewer: I thought, may be you took reference from Zhang's version.
>
> Shu: Why did I delete it? I really disliked this part. Why? There are several conditions required of Shylock (in the trial scene).

First is to hand over his estate. Secondly is the forced conversion. I think, did Shakespeare intentionally put the line here to show how unreasonable this is. How can it be. I don't know. If Christians so emphasize love, equality of all humans and empathy, why would they force people, using legal means to enforce conversion? This is simply a forced act, not to move people with love. I did not consider whether this is a satirical approach. But the logic is unreasonable. May be I have considered Shylock's feelings. He was left with nothing, and was deprived of his faith. He was forced to believe in Christianity, a religion he so hated. I think Shylock probably said, why don't you take my life? May be this was not a mature decision. He hated them, but (Christians) forced me to comply with these "wise" ways. If you force me to turn to Christianity, will I comply? This is hardly acceptable.

In a separate interview, Shum's answers to the cutting of religious content echoed with Shu's, that there are two aspects which are particularly difficult to translate: first, the Jewish identity, second, the Christian references. "People from Hong Kong are not a particularly religious fanatics," said Shum. But beneath the surface, during the interview Shum revealed his "other reason" in terms of his resistance to religion. Religious experience is in fact a decisive factor in the "untranslation" of religious content. When both the director and translator are theologically aligned on the irrelevance of religious content, its omission of which is inevitable. This relationship between one's theology and the translatability of religious concepts will be studied in more detail in Chapter 6.

No reviews of this play have been published to date, which made it difficult to analyze its impacts, whether socio-cultural, cognitive or Behavioral. As a post-colonial production where Cantonese is showcased to counter the trend of Mainland colonization, the frequent use of colloquial Cantonese did set the production apart from its predecessor in 1984, which was translated by a Mandarin-speaking director. While the socio-cultural effects of an amateur production are relatively limited, its use of Cantonese script as a way of creating the Hong Kong identity was echoed in later productions, as in the next case shows.

The Merchant of Venice in 2010

During the period from 30 October to 7 November 2010, six performances of *The Merchant of Venice* were staged in Hong Kong by Chung Ying Theatre Company. Over 4,800 people watched the play, a high turnout by the standard of a big city. According to my interviewee director Ko Tinlung, he believed that this adaptation should be "a definitive version that should serve as a reference point for future productions to come—if there are future productions of *The Merchant*, people will ask: will your production fare better than this one by Chung Ying? I am very confident of that, because of my clear briefing with the actors. The comedic effect is attained, and the inner psychology [of characters] is exposed."

About the Translator

Rupert Chan graduated from the University of Hong Kong in the early seventies where he studied English and comparative literature. His passion for and engagement with drama began in secondary school during which he had his first taste of acting and dramaturgy. Upon graduating from university, the opportunity came for him to write, direct and perform a play for his church which hoped to convey religious messages through drama. To date, he has translated six Shakespearean plays[31] for different theatre companies, and *The Merchant* was his sixth. He was baptized, upon "mature consideration" as a Catholic during his matriculation in 1967. He was Assistant Registrar at the University of Hong Kong before retirement.

---

31. His portfolio includes *Hamlet, Titus Andronicus, The Two Gentlemen of Verona, The Twelfth Night* and *The Midsummer Night's Dream*.

172 SHAKESPEARE FROM PAGE TO STAGE, FROM WEST TO EAST

Figure 4.1 House programme of *The Merchant of Venice* in Hong Kong in 2010, directed by Ko Tinlung.

About the Director

Ko Tinlung began his studies at the department of sociology at the Chinese University of Hong Kong in 1976. Having graduated from university, he taught in a secondary school and later became an actor with Chung Ying Theatre Company since 1981, a government-funded theatre company in Hong Kong, and joined Hong Kong Repertory Theater (HKRT) in 1983. He was an artistic director in HKRT from 1990-1993 and joined Chung Ying as artistic director in 1993 to the present. His first part in a Shakespeare play was Bassanio in *The Merchant of Venice* directed by Daniel Yang in 1984. His drama training was mostly gained on-the-job upon graduating from university, though he had been writing plays since secondary school. In 1987 he was in New York for a year on a scholarship, and served as assistant director on some Broadway shows.

Socio-cultural Conditions, Including Same-Sex Issues

More than a decade into post-colonial rule, the theatre scene is still free from intervention by the government. Very little evidence of political interference is seen in the arts, although the issue of interference was a worry that plagued playwrights a decade ago. The artistic director of Chung Ying Theatre Company, Ko Tin-lung, hoped that the government would "tolerate different opinions, to give artists space and freedom. Only in that way will creativity and development not be stifled." Anthony Chan Kam-kuen, head of directing and script writing at the Hong Kong Academy for Performing Arts, speculated that artists would "retain their freedom so long as they do not maliciously attack the authorities."[32]

Since Antonio is portrayed as a homosexual in this production, a brief sketch of the social acceptance of homosexuality in Hong Kong is given here. As early as 1993, the Hong Kong Arts Center offered a season of gay film and theater. Starting in 2005, the International Day Against Homophobia (IDAHO) has been organized annually in Hong Kong. The first Gay Pride Parade was held on 13 December 2008. In November 2012, a number of well-known artists[33] supported the Pride Parade, with the largest ever attendance (2500) since its inception.[34] While the legislative council voted down motion to conduct public consultation on Sexual Orientation Discrimination legislation in November 2012, the expression of homosexuality has been allowed in drama circles since the colonial times. The past colonial and present administration are tolerant towards artistic expressions of sexuality as long as the themes are not anti-government.

---

32. See MacKenzie and Arthurs, "Together Again," 75.

33. Popular singer Ho Wan Sze admitted her homosexual orientation for the first time at the parade.

34. According to the organizer, the parade totalled 4,000, but according to the police, the number peaked at 2,500.

Cognitive and Behavioral Conditions, Including the Translation Process

Unlike *The Merchant* under the direction of Yang in 1984, who did not communicate with actors and actresses on the mode of performance, Ko Tin-lung's production reflected a high degree of collaboration with performers, who had an input regarding how a line should be said, rather than merely executing the lines. Such a collaborative translation mode gives rise to interactive dialogue. More importantly, director Ko sees the play as both a tragicomedy (from Shylock's point of view) and a comedy (as regards the rest of the characters), this is reflected in his choice of music, and the tone adopted by the performers. The blend of comedic and tragic stage effects gives a whole new dimension to the rendering and perception of the religious content, as will be shown in a later section.

Rupert Chen, the translator, had already worked with director Ko Tinlung on several productions before. In this production, Chen was asked to translate the whole play, with the help of some commentaries and a Chinese translation provided by the theatre company, while it was Ko's decision what to leave out. Ko saw how important it was for their interpretation and stage performance that actors and actresses should fully understand the script. The cast were given Chen's full translated text to read before Ko gave his own interpretation in a briefing. Unlike most directors, who simply deleted the lines themselves without further consultation, Ko would at times split the actors into different groups and asked them to act out different interpretations, should there be disagreements. The final decision whether or not to cut lay in the hands of the director and the actor/actress who would act out that line. The translator was not usually involved in such decisions, but would participate in the first recital of script, and in the rehearsal of the whole play. In spite of the apparent downgrading of the translator's role, Chan is highly respected by Ko given his high cultural capital and Ko's regard for Chan's research on the play's background. In the pre-performance seminar in September 2010, Chan was enlisted as one of the main speakers sitting next to Ko to introduce the historical background of the play. Ko also invited Chan to brief the audience on Ko's interpretation of certain Shakespeare scenes. *The Merchant* was Chan's most satisfying translation because he was able to translate the whole text. In the end, 45 minutes of the original translation were deleted, the deleted lines being those deemed redundant, uninteresting or those requiring high processing efforts (e.g. allusions) to the audience.

To avoid being influenced by other Shakespearean productions, director and actors/actresses refrained from watching any particular adaptations until the final rehearsal. While Ko used to act the part of Bassanio under the directorship of Daniel Yang, he reckoned the interpretation of this version as purely his own, without taking reference from Yang. But, as the textual analysis below will show, the similarities in their interpretation invite speculation that Ko did follow the interpretation of Yang at some points.

The idea of producing *The Merchant of Venice* came when the troupe was considering putting on a classic for the season. Chung Ying's strength is in producing comedies, and it had in the past staged Midsummer Night's Dream and Twelfth Night. In fact, *The Merchant of Venice* was Chung Ying's first stage production, but it was then acted in English by Caucasians. Staging *The Merchant* in Cantonese became a natural decision in that season in post-colonial Hong Kong, since local productions are increasingly encouraged as a post-colonial response to reassert the city's identity.

Translation Profile

In terms of lexicon, the translation is faithful to the English script. Biblical references are mostly retained, and Daniel is transliterated in line with the Christian Bible. Certain Christian terms are explained to cater to the mass audience. Your prophet the Nazarite (in Act I Scene 3) was rendered as Jesus your prophet the Nazarite. Daniel was originally translated as Daniel the most righteous judge, but later the director deleted the modifier to keep it concise. But much of the adaptation, especially the religious content, lies not in the lexicon but in the mise-en-scene. Consider the following "hath not a Jew eyes" speech in Act 3 by Shylock. It is not recited as a soliloquy, but addressed to Salarino and Salanio and interspersed with gestures from both. The actions and tone of characters are shown in brackets.

愛嚟做魚餌釣魚囉；如果餵唔倒俾人食，可以餵飽我嘅復仇之心。佢羞辱過我，阻止過我賺成五十萬，恥笑過我蝕本，譏諷過我嘅盈利，藐視我嘅民族，破壞我嘅交易，潑我朋友冷水，煽動我敵人搧風點火 —— 佢為咗乜嘢理由咁做呢？因為我係個猶太人。猶太人冇眼嘅咩？猶太人冇對手、冇五臟、冇四肢、冇感覺、冇情義、冇血氣嘅咩？之唔係食同樣嘅食物，揸咗同樣嘅刀槍會受傷，患同樣嘅病，用同樣嘅藥醫番好，一樣感覺得倒冬暖夏涼，同一個基督徒冇分別咩？如果你用利器拮我，我地唔會流血嘅咩？如果你啷我，我地唔會笑嘅咩？如果你落毒毒我，我地唔會死嘅咩？如果你欺負我，我地唔會報仇嘅咩？如果我地其他一切都似足你，咁呢一樣都一樣似你啫。如果有個猶太人欺負個基督徒，佢點樣以基督徒寬恕精神回應呀？報仇囉。如果有個基督徒欺負個猶太人，佢點樣照基督徒嘅榜樣作出忍耐精神嘅回應呀？報仇吖嗎！你教咗我有仇不報非君子，我會有樣學樣照做，唔青出於藍，道高一尺魔高一丈，點算係高材生呀。

To bait fish withal (said slowly, seriously. He then climbs up the stairs and stands alongside Salanio and Salarino): if it will feed nothing else, it will feed my revenge. He hath disgraced me, and hindered me half a million; laughed at my losses, mocked at my gains, scorned my nation, thwarted my bargains, cooled my friends, heated mine enemies; and what's his reason? I am a Jew. (Salarino spits on Shylock.) Hath not a Jew eyes? Hath not a Jew hands, organs, dimensions, senses, affections, passions? fed with the same food, hurt with the same weapons, subject to the same diseases, healed by the same means, warmed and cooled by the same winter and summer, as a Christian is? (Salarino takes out his knife, but Salanio holds him and says, No! Both of them rush down the flight of stairs.) If you prick us, do we not bleed? if you tickle us, do we not laugh? if you poison us, do we not die? and if you wrong us, shall we not revenge? If we are like you in the rest, we will resemble you in that. If a Jew wrong a Christian, what is his humility? Revenge. (Both go up the stairs, Salarino takes out his knife again) If a Christian wrong a Jew, what should his sufferance be by Christian example? Why, revenge. You teach me that, a revenge not taken is not the mark of a gentleman:[35] as virtue rises one foot, vices rise ten.

Unlike Yang who took the middle-of-the-road line in his portrayal of Christian characters, the hypocrisy and arrogance of Christians were highlighted in Ko's production. This arrogance was in a stark contrast to the humane portrayal of Shylock on the other hand. The relationship between Shylock and his daughter Jessica was an intimate one. Jessica addressed him as "Papa," which was absent from the English script. Rather than being stern towards Jessica, Shylock smiled from time to time. Jessica showed struggle in her face when saying the lines "To be ashamed to be my father's child! But though I am a daughter to his blood, I am not to his manners" (Act II Scene 3) "I have a father, you a daughter, lost" (Act II Scene 5) when she decided to run away with Lorenzo. In Act II Scene 6, just before leaving home, she expressed her regret and said, "Papa . . . " to an empty house. In the conversation between Jessica and Lorenzo in Act V, the translator added a line which is shown below in italics to show Jessica's struggle in converting to Christianity.

Lorenzo:

---

35. A Chinese proverb, meaning the righteous takes revenge.

> In such a night
> Did Jessica steal from the wealthy Jew
> And with an unthrift love did run from Venice
> As far as Belmont.
> *She betrayed her father and her faith.*[36]

Jessica's face darkened her face when she heard the added line. The line was added because the director interpreted Act V Scene 1 as a portrayal of Jessica's struggles. Ko said that at the start actors and actresses had a hard time acting out the scene as they did not understand the purpose of those lines. But after it had been explained to them that this scene was about Jessica's dilemma in running away from her Judaic belief and from her father, the performers acted the lines differently.

The Jewish identity is The Jew: rather than being addressed as *You Tairen* 猶太人, a neutral form of addressing, is addressed by Gratiano, Salanio and his servant Lancelot as *You Tailao* 猶太佬, where "lao 佬," is of a lower register than "ren 人."

The director was aware of the various interpretations put upon the conversion of Shylock. He took the line of interpretation that Antonio's demand for Shylock's conversion arose out of good intentions. In order to relay such intentions, Gratiano spoke with sympathy the following lines:

> I have a wife, whom, I protest, I love:
> I would she were in heaven, so she could
> Entreat some power to change this currish Jew. (Act IV)

Antonio and others made the gesture of crossing oneself when Shylock said "I am content," to show their genuine forgiveness towards Shylock. Shylock, still kneeling down, begged others in a pitiful manner to let him go. His state of despair as expressed in his face and his body gesture (kneeling, rather than standing) successfully won him sympathy from the audience, as will be shown later.

The relationship between Antonio and Bassanio—ambivalent, if not brotherly, in the original script—was interpreted as one of homosexuality. Such a relationship weakens Antonio's Christian image, as one who sacrificed not unconditionally but out of his love for Bassanio. The director arranged for Antonio to kiss Bassanio in his "profession of love" speech before his execution. At the curtain call, Antonio was holding hands with Bassanio

---

36. The source text for this line is: 背叛了父親和她的宗教.

to thank the audience, not Bassanio with Portia. One audience noted in a post-performance review:

> In addition, I was shocked at the homosexual relationship between Antonio and Bassanio. In the past, I thought Antonio's sacrifice for Bassanio was out of pure friendship. But now, I realized that pure friendship cannot drive them to this point. Shakespeare looks at and understands the existence of the homosexual love. I think this is the approach by the bard—reflect life through comedies.

Treatment of Religious Material

The religious theme in this play was clearly brought out, and this has much relevance to the cognitive aspect, and the interpretation of the translator and the director. Ko has expended effort in ensuring that actors and actresses understand his interpretation, and has striven to bring the fine details to the audience. All the major speeches of Portia and Shylock that contain Christian vocabulary and theology are retained and rendered faithfully from the source text. The synopsis shown in the promotional poster and house program shows the Judeo-Christian conflict as central to the play, which writes,

> A story set in Venice, Italy, during the Middle Ages. To help his friend marry a lady, Antonio, a merchant, borrows money from a Jewish moneylender named Shylock. Shylock hates Antonio's Christian identity and from past experience makes an unusual demand: if Antonio is not able to pay the debt at the specified time, one pound of flesh meat will be taken from him. However, Antonio is unable to pay the debt on time.

Only two lead male characters, Antonio and Shylock, are mentioned in the synopsis, without any mentioning of Portia, who is the title character of two Cantonese opera versions on the Mainland.

The decision of the director, not the translator, plays an important role in delivering the visual and audio effects to enhance the religious experience of the audience. In the pre-performance seminar, Chan said that the director has the ultimate authority, while his job is to "obey." In the casket scenes, the Prince of Aragon, a Spanish city, donned a costume with a red cross, highlighting the fact that he is from a Catholic nation. When the Prince of Morocco was choosing a casket, he took out a crescent-shaped instrument to symbolize that his country of origin was Islamic. Images were added by the director here and there without distorting the original play script. The choice of costumes used by Christians and Shylock left an impression on the audience. Antonio's and Bassanio's youthful and elaborate costumes demonstrated their nobility of bourgeois: they were generous and playful; Shylock's crooked back, as well as his dark costumes, communicated a dark and oppressed impression. The background music was at times melancholic, adding to the tragic undertones of the play.

Both the director and translator agreed on a main line of interpretation: Shylock intended a gesture of friendship through the lending contract, without any intention of claiming Antonio's pound of flesh. It was simply a joke. But later, when his daughter Jessica ran away with Lorenzo, and took his money, Shylock turned cruel and was filled with hatred. This was a desire for revenge and not necessarily related to Antonio's religion. This interpretation is similar to Yang's interpretation in his 1984 production, during which Ko, acting as Bassanio, was given briefing as to Yang's interpretation. However similar the interpretations are, Ko insisted that his interpretation came from his own ideas and not from Yang.

In line with this interpretation, Shylock was portrayed at the outset, without making extensive changes to the script, as a caring father through the addition of bodily gestures. For example, he kissed Jessica goodbye, called her "good daughter," talked to her gently, and reminded her to put on more clothes in the cold weather. "If he did not love his daughter he did not need to be so upset over her elopement." Ko explained.

The humane portrayal of Shylock contrasted with the satirical treatment of Christians in the play. In Act I, Shylock was pushed by Antonio to the ground when Antonio approached him for money. Antonio kicked Shylock's feet when he was lying on the ground. Antonio spat on Shylock's face while he was speaking to him. When Shylock finished his speech, Antonio again spat on Shylock.

The spitting gesture recalled one of the spitting of Antonio's friends Salanio and Salarino on Tubal, a Jewish ally of Shylock in the opening pantomime of Yang's production in 1984. Ko might have been inspired by Yang's treatment, but he insisted in his originality in that mise-en-scene.

In fact, such treatment reflects the theology of the translator and the director. Chen remarked in my interview, "Christians like to say how forgiving and merciful they are, how they treat Jews nicely, but what they did is the opposite. Jews are oppressed, spat upon and despised. Shylock's daughter ran away. Shylock got what he deserved, but when he lost at the trial, all his estate was confiscated and he was forced to adopt another religion. I am sympathetic towards him. Christians were not consistent in their profession—took away his daughter, pursued a rich heiress."

As a Catholic, Chan disagrees with Protestantism in terms of its exclusivity of other religions, as the quote below shows:

> I came across Judaism, Christianity and Catholicism, upon comparison, I found that Catholicism is the most encompassing of all, that's why I chose to believe in Catholicism, which is more inclusive than Judaism and Christianity, the latter reacts against Catholicism due to many historical reasons, Christians were persecuted. Catholics and Buddhists have a lot in common . . . religions need not be mutually exclusive.

Ko asserted his resistance to religion, including Christianity, since his youth. Although Ko and Chan differ in their religious choice, one being an atheist and the latter being a Catholic, both showed resistance to Protestantism. Even though Chan is a Catholic, he did not hesitate to admit that some Christians are hypocrites. It is reasonable to assume that the negative depiction of Christianity in this production could be traced back to the unsatisfactory religious experience of both.

In the trial scene, Shylock cried out upon hearing the verdict: "I am very content." An additional gesture was added, in that Antonio made the gesture of crossing oneself, symbolizing the forgiveness of God. The duke was seen lifting up Shylock's body. This was a collaborative decision by the actors and the director. Ko's interpretation of the "forced conversion" is that the Christians hoped to convert Shylock for his own good, not out of revenge. Despite holding to his own interpretation, he asked the actors during rehearsals to perform using two approaches: in one version, which is (the director's) interpretation, the Christians' intention in requiring Shylock's conversion was to save his soul. In the other version, they acted as the conversion requirement was out of revenge.

The Universal Theme of The Merchant

Despite the visibility of the religious material retained in the play, Ko believes that the central message is mercy.: He believes that the play is not about Judeo-Christian conflicts, but ultimately about "belief and prejudice," a theme that can be applied to Islam and other religions. "In the contemporary world, Muslims and Christians are in enmity. So I think Shakespeare is universal. If you believe in something, prejudice will be generated against non-believers." Mercy is the solution to prejudice, "if you could make concessions, show mercy, others will not repay evil for evil, but yield to each other. However strong you are, you still need mercy, otherwise there will be no end of disputes."

Cognitive and Behavioral Effects

The portrayal of Shylock and of Christians stimulated the audience to rethink the issue of racial and religious conflict. From the theatre reviews posted on websites by the audience in Hong Kong, it seemed to be generally agreed that different religions should retain their own dignity and ideals. One pointed out that the speech of "hath not a Jew eyes" set against the backdrop of the flight of stairs successfully created the tension. [37] One blogger who had left the church since graduation from school commented that the play added to his resentment towards Christians, who were hypocritical.[38]

The audience from Mainland China[39] who watched the performance were deeply inspired by the religious conflicts depicted. Some of them reviewed their previous understanding depicted in secondary school course books of Shylock as a villain, and showed sympathy towards Shylock, as the following quotation of Respondent 123 shows:

> Shylock was severely insulted and spat upon, he was pushed to the ground by the angry Antonio, and was later deprived of his Judaic roots . . . Shylock was in fact a man of flesh and blood, of rich emotions.

The treatment of Shylock can be seen as effectively communicated from page (i.e. the director's interpretation of the text) to stage, as most reviews showed sympathy towards Shylock. Changing attitudes to the money-lending business enabled the audience to accept Shylock. The business of money-lending has a long history in China. Money-lenders, classified under the category of merchants, used to be the second lowest in the social strata.[40] But contemporary China is characterized as a "socialist state with Chinese characteristics," i.e. it is a socialist country with a capitalist ideology. One respondent's sympathy towards Shylock was connected to his/her

37. See Harry's theatre review. Web. November 2010. <http://hk.myblog.yahoo.com/fridaystage/article?mid=980>

38. See Chan, Review on *The Merchant of Venice*, Web. 8th November 2010. <http://www.facebook.com/home.php?#!/note.php?note_id=456257622143&id=585841136>

39. Based on the theatre reviews of 75 freshmen coming from Mainland China enrolled in an Arts and Cultural Education Programme in the academic year 2010–2011 run by the Center for Holistic Teaching and Learning at Hong Kong Baptist University.

40. The four main categories, in the order of social status in China, are the literati, craftsmen, merchants and peasants.

recognition of capitalism: "He is simply a pioneer of capitalism, a person who knows how to make money with money. Shylock's case is realistic and reasonable in today's society. He used his capital to obtain reward—this is just, reasonable and legal." Apparently, the younger generation in this capitalist economy have been liberated from the Marxist interpretation of Shakespeare that viewed Shylock as an exploiter.

Christian hypocrisy, which was also highlighted in this production, was successfully conveyed to this Mainland group studying in Hong Kong. The reviews show that following the play, the audience mostly held a biased view of Judeo-Christian conflict, with the oppression of Jews being cited in many reviews. Only one respondent mentioned that this conversion means "comedy" to Christians. It can be seen that the prevalent ideology among them, representative of the younger generation Mainland Chinese, is one of scepticism towards Christians and Christianity. Mixed feelings from the audience can be seen towards Antonio the Christian. While a minority of reflections give Antonio a positive marking, whether as a "大善人" (great kind man), "仁慈、不計較利益" (kind and non-profiteering) "豪爽"(generous) or "天使般"(angelic), and view his sacrifice to Bassanio as "touching." But the majority of reflections on Antonio's characterization fasten on his humiliation of Shylock, including spitting, kicking and pushing him to the ground. The Christian interpretation of Antonio as a depiction of Christ did not occur in any of the reflections. As the respondents were originally educated in atheist Communist China, under the prevalent ideology, it is not surprising that a number of respondents showed antagonism towards Christianity. Anti-Christian sentiment was noted, and Christianity is still associated with the West and Western civilization, as shown in the expression used, "Western Christianity." Their pre-understanding, or biased view of Christianity, created further prejudice of this religion as they watched the conversion scene, and they developed a negative view of Christian mercy. As Chan the translator highlighted the hypocrisy of Christian mercy in the play: this induced a similar view in the audience, where the "mercy speech" was seen as an irony satirizing Christians. "The Christians who always preach mercy in front of Jews did not practice their mercy," as one respondent commented.

What respondents found most impressive in the play, whether scene or gesture or character, were the conversion scene, the scene where Antonio pushed Shylock to the ground in Act 1 when he asked him to lend money, and the gesture of spitting on Shylock. One respondent noted that at the conversion scene nearly the whole audience cried out with "Oh" and sighed to express their disapproval. Others mentioned the crooked back of Shylock throughout the play and the sympathetic undertone it induced. Clearly, the director's sympathetic treatment of Shylock as a tragic figure and a kind father, and his reading of the play as a tragicomedy, influenced the reception of the audience who viewed it as a problem play.

Thus shows that the force of the adaptation is most effectively achieved by semiotic, rather than lexical means. Without changing the words on the script, the director effectively converts his audience to his interpretation.

Socio-cultural Effects

Since this was one of the biggest Chinese Shakespeare productions in Hong Kong in recent years, the heightened religious undertones portrayed in *The Merchant* in 2010 which attracted critical acclaim seems to suggest that there indeed is an interest among the audience in religious matters on stage, rather than the common misconception that audiences in Hong Kong find religious matters irrelevant in their life. In fact, the anti-Christian sentiment after watching the show as seen in certain blog reviews by members of the Hong Kong audience simply illustrates the fact that religion does matter to them, because the Christian hypocrisy highlighted in the production reminds these people of the days when they were nurtured under Christian education, an educational system institutionalized in the colonial era. The high attendance figures at this production should give confidence to future directors who may be wondering about the marketability of religious plays in Hong Kong.

While it will take time for the above socio-cultural effects in Hong Kong to be assessed, one thing is certain and can be quantified. Among the audience was a group of Mainland young adults, totaling over a hundred, who studied at the foundation program of Hong Kong Baptist University. They had been taught by director Ko Tinlung in the classroom and were then taken to watch his production. Their reviews show that they underwent an irreversible hermeneutical shift—breaking free from the textbook interpretation of Shylock as a villain and Antonio as the hero, as the aforementioned analysis shows. These students, as they returned to the Mainland upon graduation, would question and challenge the traditional interpretations, and would no longer view or direct Shakespeare the same way they did before.

Conclusion

In this chapter, I have shown the varying interpretations, translations and adaptations of the religious dimension of three productions in Hong Kong in the chronological order. Quite unlike their Mainland counterparts, the directors in Hong Kong tend to pride themselves on conforming to the "original intent" of Shakespeare. When Daniel Yang directed *The Merchant* in 1984, this "original intent" meant conforming to Western standards. He brought along with him three Americans responsible for design and scenery, and expressed his intention to bring "a carefully mounted Shakespearean production whose acting, directing, scenery, costumes, accessories, and lighting were of the same standard as those seen at a major theatre company of the Western world." [41] Ko Tinlung, his successor, also reckoned in the interview that his version, close to the original intent of Shakespeare, should be the "definitive" version for later productions to follow. The Western-style productions under study—both Yang's and Ko's—represent a close approximation to Shakespeare's scripts with minimal alterations in terms of narrative. It may be surprising to learn that both Ko and Yang strive to stay close to the original intention of the author amidst the trend of postmodern interpretations, where the concept of original intention is abandoned. This, I would argue, is a postcolonial response as a way to "mimic" the colonizers, and the religious content is thus retained, albeit subject to various manipulations according to the directors' directorial and theological presuppositions. But one striking similarity upon comparing the directorial treatment and audience reception in Hong Kong with their Mainland counterparts is that both parties are moving towards a more sympathetic treatment towards the oppressed. Ethnic oppression is condemned; while at the same time there is a move away from the concept of a stark opposition between good and evil. In Hong Kong, that kind of sympathetic treatment came earlier in the 1980s under the directorship of Yang, but the audience then was not yet ready for his interpretation, as manifested by the "stupid laughter" encountered during the performance. In the productions in 2010 in Hong Kong and Shanghai, the audience and the directors are both on the same page—they are aligned in this sympathetic attitude and in a pluralistic understanding of characters as rounded and not flat. Such reception and directorial treatment marks a postmodern, post-Holocaust response superseding the binary oppositions (good versus evil, hero versus villain) in previous productions. It also reflects the impact of globalization where such postmodern interpretations, in the form either of articles or various recent film productions of *The Merchant*, are readily available online (e.g. Wikipedia, Youtube) and pass quickly to the new generations in Hong Kong and China.

In the next chapter, I will look at a recent adaptation of *The Merchant* in Taiwan, which represents a final strand in the quest for a fuller

---

41. Yang, "Shakespeare at Hong Kong Repertory Theatre," 80.

understanding of the translatability of the religious dimension in Greater China across different time periods and regions.

5

The Merchant of Venice in Taiwan—*Bond* in 2009

Background

BOND, STAGED IN TAIWAN in 2009, was the first commercial public production and adaptation of *The Merchant of Venice* to be performed there. Accordingly, in this chapter I will give close examination only to this production, under Chesterman's modified model. Before 2009, *The Merchant* had been performed only in Taiwan universities,[1] either as a full performance or as an excerpt. Unlike the situation in China and Hong Kong where the story of the bond of flesh was widely known through school education[2] and through the popular reception of Lin Shu's adaptation, the Taiwanese were banned from reading the play until the 1970s. In Taiwan as much as in China, the popularity and reception of a Shakespearean play was influenced by political factors. When Kuomintang (KMT) retreated from Mainland in 1949 and ruled over Taiwan, as a newly established political regime, it maintained strict political control characterized by executions without trial, long prison terms for political dissidents, suppression of any gatherings including religious ones.[3] The martial law in force since the Taiwan Nationalist government's accession to power in 1949 banned the import of pre-1949 books from China to prevent the infiltration of the communist viewpoint into Taiwan audiences.[4] Taiwan Shakespearean scholars were

---

1. The more well-known stage production of *The Merchant of Venice* was staged in 2001 at the National Taiwan University.

2. In China and Hong Kong, the trial scene was taught in the secondary school curriculum. In some secondary school textbooks published in the Mainland, the part on forced conversion was omitted. See Chapter 3, section 3.2.1.1 for more details.

3. See Chou, *Contemporary Religious Movements in Taiwan*, 56.

4. See Chen, *Shakespeare in Taiwan*, 111.

forced to develop their own brand of Shakespeare criticism. *The Tempest* was banned by Chiang Kai-shek, then President of Taiwan, who read it as a usurpation plot. In 1968, Shakespeare's *Othello* was banned from staging by the police, because they considered that the usurpation in *Othello* might affect the military unity. It was later approved only when Othello was adapted to a non-military personnel, and the deputy commander became his secretary.[5] *Hamlet* was allowed, because Claudius' usurpation was read as equivalent to Mao Zedong's usurpation of Chiang's government. Hamlet's revenge was seen as analogous to Chiang's mission to regain China from the Communist rule. Similarly, *The Merchant of Venice*, under the influence of Marxist interpretation during Mao Zedong's rule in China, was not fully accepted by Taiwan audiences.[6] *The Merchant of Venice* was not performed under Chiang Kai-shek's rule. At that time, books from abroad had to be vetted for their ideology.[7] It was only in the 1970s that the ban on *The Merchant of Venice* was lifted.[8]

Interpretation of Shakespeare in Taiwan under the martial law was laden with Confucian ideology, the predominant line of interpretation in keeping with the political socio-cultural environment in Taiwan in the 1970s, which emphasized "Chineseness" through imposition of Mandarin and Chinese culture by way of the education system.[9] It was only with the lifting of martial law in the 1980s that saw new forms of drama and indigenous culture flourished. In 1981, an agency for culture, known as the Council for Cultural Planning and Development (Wenjianhui 文建會) was established under the Executive Yuan of the government, marking an important milestone in the recognition of Taiwan's indigenous culture. Bangzi Opera Troupe, the troupe behind *Bond*, is now under the auspices of CCPD. Before the lifting of martial law in 1987, the "Chinese concept" was the predominant culture. After 1987, native Taiwan culture gained momentum, creating a culture that is "sinicized, indigenized, popularized, delicatized, sanitized, diversified, modernized."[10] In 1988, the censorship requirement applying to play scripts was lifted, which saw the flourishing of traditional drama forms such as Peking Opera, representing the "Chinese culture," and other forms such as *gezi xi* 哥仔戲, representing the "nativist" or "Taiwan" culture.

5. See Bai, "*Shi xue, yi shi xing tai ji zan zhu ren yu fan yi*," 113.
6. Chen, op.cit. 112.
7. Ibid, 117.
8. Ibid, 122.
9. See Brown, *Is Taiwan Chinese?*, 2004.
10. Su, "The Effects of Cultural Policy," 78.

Such developments set the stage for the popularity of a series of Shakespearean adaptations, such as Wu Hsing-kuo (吳興國)'s adaptation of *King of Desire* 慾望城國 (*Macbeth*), a Peking Opera production, and *Revenge of the Prince* 王子復仇記 (*Hamlet*) by Peking Opera. The purpose of these new drama forms was to "borrow Western classics in order to complement the weakness of traditional Chinese dramas, i.e. the philosophical aspect, and to encourage a renewed performance through an alienated theme."[11] The use of Western themes and styles to revitalize a weakened literature echoes with translation scholar Even-Zohar's poly-system theory[12]. This describes situations in which translations can be innovative and contribute to the building up of new repertoires: when a literature is weak and/or peripheral within a larger group of literatures, and when a literature contains a vacuum or finds itself in a state of crisis or at a turning point.[13] Bangzi Opera, like other traditional forms of opera, was a peripheral form in need of revitalization, and this is where Shakespeare came to the rescue.[14]

Socio-cultural Conditions

Religious Diversity in Taiwan

Compared with its colonial counterpart Hong Kong, Taiwan has a longer history of Christianity which can trace its roots to the Dutch colonial period starting in the 1620s, that saw the first Dutch missionary sent by the Reformed Church in 1627.[15] These missionaries set up churches, schools, hospitals, campus ministries, publishing houses, among others. People in Taiwan have enjoyed religious diversity except during the period of Japanese occupation (1895-1945) during which Shintoism was enforced among the people. After the lifting of the martial law, the Taiwan government no longer suppressed any religious activities, cults or gatherings, including Falun

11. Ibid, 79.

12. Poly-system theory points out the distinction between primary and secondary forms of literature, where the former represents the canonized form of literature accepted by the community as part of the historical heritage. While the theory has been criticised by translation scholars such as Edwin Gentlzer, it has proven to be particularly relevant to China. See *Chung Wai Literary Monthly*, Vol. 30, No. 3, August 2001; Shuttleworth, "Polysystem Theory," 176–179.

13. Hermans, *Translation in Systems*, 190.

14. Another important Western adaptation that revived audience's interest in Bangzi Opera is *Chinese Princess Turando*, an adaptation of *Turandot* staged in 2000, which toured worldwide and captured a large number of young audiences and media coverage.

15. See Lo, "Taiwan, Hong Kong, Macau," 173–183.

Gong. Four main Buddhist groups existed alongside Christian churches and have enjoyed a large following.[16] Today, on the streets in some well-known night markets in Taipei, fortune-teller booths can be seen alongside food stalls, a scene not unlike the Temple Street in Hong Kong. In this religiously diverse place, a person can worship the Buddha, Matsu 媽祖 (Goddess of Sea in the Daoist tradition) and Guanyin 觀音 at the same time, showing their syncretic nature.[17] A strong Christian influence can be seen in Taiwan, with over one million Christians and nearly 4,000 churches in a population of 23 million.[18] The founding father of Taiwan, Dr Sun Yatsen and his wife, his successor Chiang Kaishek and his wife, past president Lee Tenghui (1988–2000) and current president Ma Yingjiu (2008-) are all Christians. Not only did Christian churches establish their presence through providing social services and education from primary to tertiary level, they also participated actively in the democratic movement. For instance, the Presbyterian Church in Taiwan (PCT), Taiwan's largest denomination, issued political statements that called for social and political reform—"Statement on Our National Fate (1971)," "Our Appeal (1975)," "The Human Rights Declaration (1977)." Church leaders also took a strong stance against the recent proposal of marriage equality bill to legalize same sex marriage. Thus, against a religiously diverse environment in Taiwan, the removal of religious discourse in *Bond* deserves our attention. As the next chapter will show, the suppression of the religious dimension reflects not only socio-cultural conditions, but also the individual translator's theological conflicts.

Ethnic Tensions and Identity

Bond addresses issues in identity and ethnic prejudices faced by Taiwanese. The Judeo-Christian conflict in *The Merchant* is instead replaced with a conflict between the natives and outsiders as ethnic conflicts are an ongoing issue in Taiwan. After being colonized or dominated successively by the Dutch (1624–1662), the Japanese (1895–1945) and the Nationalist Party, or Kuomintang (KMT) 國民黨,[19] people in Taiwan developed a strong

16. See Chou, *Contemporary Religious Movements in Taiwan*, 56.
17. Qu, *Religion and Society*, 41–44.
18. Chou, *Contemporary Religious Movements*, 56.
19. KMT treated Taiwan as a colony by implementing the martial law, restricting basic human rights of Taiwanese including freedom of speech. Among the restrictive measures is the imposition of the Mandarin language and Chinese culture through the educational system, censoring drama productions, amongst others. The purpose of such military ruling is to suppress resistance to KMT's regime. For further discussions on the identity issue of Taiwan, see Brown, *Is Taiwan Chinese?*, 2004.

anti-foreign sentiment towards outsiders and a search for their own identity. While Taiwanese recognize the Chinese culture, they have developed a bonding and cultural impulses with their island that distinguishes themselves from Mainlanders. Taiwanese, also known as *bensheng ren* 本省人 (those who are from within the province), refer to those whose ancestors came to Taiwan before 1895 when the Japanese colonial government prohibited further immigration from China. They are contrasted with *waisheng ren* 外省人 (lit. those who are from outside of the province), who are Mainlanders who came to Taiwan with the Nationalists between 1945 to 1949 and their children born and bred in Taiwan. As such, the dichotomy between Taiwanese culture and Mainland culture (Zhongyuan culture 中原文化) is formed. Apart from the Mainlanders and Taiwanese who share the Han culture, another distinct ethnic group is the Aborigines, or the mountain tribes (yuanzhumin 原住民), who are largely ignored in the political sphere. [20]Many Taiwanese see themselves as forming a nation different from the Chinese, other Taiwanese consider that they are a part of the Chinese nation, but reject being subsumed under China. Taiwan-born Mainlanders, on the other hand, carry a sense of "rootlessness" and cannot identify themselves as either Taiwanese or Chinese.[21] Taiwan, under the influence of Dutch, Spanish, Han-Chinese, Manchurians, and Japanese who once occupied the land, have formed a distinct culture and identity very different from their Mainland counterparts. The Japanese occupation in World War II, in particular, has left an indelible mark on the identity of the Taiwanese, and they found themselves having nothing in common with the Mainland Chinese who took over the island after the war.[22] Other factors that contributed to the emergence of a sense of group identity included, firstly, the island's geographical separation from the mainland (travel between China and Taiwan being banned before 1987), secondly, the nationalist party's efforts at promoting a Mainland high culture at the expense of the native culture of Taiwan, and also the language and cultural policies, amongst others, enforced in Taiwan that institutionalized differences between the two communities.[23] The division between Mainlanders and local Taiwanese was felt in the Christian churches in Taiwan, where the Presbyterian Church in Taiwan (PCT), Taiwan's largest denomination, represented the interests

20. Brown, *Is Taiwan Chinese*, 9–10.
21. Wachman, "Competing Identities in Taiwan," 61.
22. Ibid, 44.
23. Ibid, 62. Regarding the language policy, mandarin is promoted as the dominant language by the nationalist party, and it was not until recent years that Taiwanese became popular. Cultural policies under martial law included promotion of "Chineseness": its subsequent relaxation in the 1970s encouraged a more diversified culture.

of the Taiwanese, whereas the churches that came to Taiwan from Mainland after 1949 represented the interests of Mainlanders.[24] PCT supported the notion of an independent Taiwan, which was heavily criticized by the churches and denominations of Mainlanders.[25] Set against the background of this deep division among different ethnic groups, *Bond* shifted the focus of the play from religious conflicts to ethnic conflicts.[26]

Homosexuality

While Taiwan shares a cultural heritage with Mainland China, its political and geographical separation from China has generated a unique identity that results in a vastly different social acceptability of homosexuality. Under the Nationalist rule which asserted family values using the Confucian model, public discourse on homosexuality was non-existent in the 1950s.[27] Reports of homosexuality in the 1980s were suppressed and negative, when the medical description of homosexual relations was "abnormal" and a form of "mental illness."[28] Discussion of same-sex relationships was deleted in the Chinese translation of *The Color Purple*, illustrating the conservatism of publishers in that period.[29] It was only in the 1990s when Taiwan's homosexuals protested against prejudice that hostility was reduced. Public discussion of homosexuality flourished especially after the lifting of martial law in 1987, and since then has undergone dramatic changes, from a negative description to a socially acceptable one.[30] During the rule of Chen Shuibian 陳水扁 (2000-2008),[31] there were discussions on the legalization of gay marriage. *The Wedding Banquet* 喜宴, a Taiwan-produced film in the 1990s, which is about the story of a bi-sexual man who came out after the wedding, won popular and critical acclaim not just in Taiwan but internationally. At

---

24. For an overview of Taiwan's history of Christianity, see Lo, "Taiwan, Hong Kong, Macau," 173–183.

25. Ibid.

26. The emphasis of ethnic issues in Taiwan's Shakespeare productions is not an entirely novel idea. Wu Hsing-kuo's Tempest (2004) attempted to highlight the conflict and division of each ethnic group in Taiwan, where Prospero represents KMT in the post-martial period and Caliban represents the aborigines. See Huang. "Performing Shakespeare in Contemporary Taiwan," 2012.

27. See Damm, "Same Sex Desire and Society in Taiwan," 67–81.

28. Ibid, 71.

29. See Lee, "Translators as Gatekeepers," 2010.

30. Damm, op.cit. 67.

31. Hogg, "Taiwan move to allow gay unions" *BBC News World* edition 28 October 2003. Web. 1 June 2014.

present, the acceptability of homosexuality in Taiwan is much higher than in Mainland China. Starting from 2003, attendance at the lesbian, gay, bisexual and transgender parade has been on the rise. In 2009, the parade attracted over 20,000 participants, the highest attendance of the kind in Asia.[32] In 2013, a "marriage equality" draft bill was proposed to give legal recognition to same-sex marriage and pluralist families. Once accepted, Taiwan will become the first Asian city to legalize same-sex marriage.[33] The altered view of homosexuality in Taiwan explains the shift of characterization in Bassanio and Antonio, which will be discussed later.

Cognitive and Behavioral Conditions

This production (the Bangzi Opera Adaptation) brought together Shakespeare scholars and Chinese literary scholars as well as theatre practitioners from Taiwan and Mainland China. *The Merchant of Venice* was translated in 2005 by Perng Ching Hsi. Based on this translation, Perng worked with Chen Fang, a Chinese studies professor at National Taiwan Normal University, to adapt the existing translation for Bangzi Opera. Chen has expert knowledge in traditional Chinese drama and is the adviser for the Bangzi troupe which, in the interests of enlivening this operatic format, hopes to inject Western artistic material like Shakespeare. It was a time when the audience's interest in traditional drama, characterized by fixed themes, moralized narrative and stereotyped characters, had been on the decline. However, adapting a Western drama into a traditional drama does not happen only at a linguistic level, because arias, dance and gestural movements are an important part of the success of the traditional drama. The opportunity for a collaborative translation came about when Chen was approached by the troupe for advice on the choice of dramas which would appeal to a mass audience. Chen, who had attended Perng's Shakespeare lectures for three years, introduced Perng to the troupe. *The Merchant of Venice* was chosen instead of other Perng's work such as *Hamlet*, as the complexity of the character could hardly be portrayed in traditional Chinese drama, which is characterized by single-sided characterization. For this adaptation, Perng, the original translator, decided what to keep and what to leave out. Using the existing translation as a blueprint, Chen, who was familiar with the style of Bangzi opera and its prosodic requirements, converted certain speeches into arias, and modifies the speeches to make them conform to the tonality of Chinese drama. After re-arranging and

32. Hou, "Promoting Rainbow Pride in Formosa," 6 August 2010.
33. Engbarth, "Taiwan Lawmakers Push Marriage Equality Bill," 30 Oct 2013.

re-writing, the two translators discussed the dialogue between the characters, the emotional register of the speeches, and the category to which each character belonged.[34] The performance script was improved with the input of director Lu Poshen 呂柏伸 who commented on theatrical design and the gestures and movements of characters appropriate to the script, and with the input of Daniel Yang, who made suggestions on the speeches. A briefing was then arranged by Perng to teach them how this play should be understood in modern terms. Chen taught the troupe the characteristics of this adaptation, which is promoted as yu sha ju 豫莎劇, a combination of Bangzi and Shakespearean theatre. It is Perng's interpretation, rather than the director's, that defined the line of interpretation of the troupe.

From this account of the translation process, it can be seen that the translators, renowned scholars, who are in Bourdieu's terms, with a higher cultural capital than the director, set the translation approach to be followed by the director, rather than the other way round as seen in most productions. Accordingly, the interpretation of the translators, rather than of the directors, calls for further examination in this study to shed light on their translation decisions.

Adapting Shakespeare to traditional Chinese drama, i.e. Sinicization of Shakespeare is not a totally new concept. Using Shakespearean themes can on the one hand enliven traditional dramas. This can be seen in Wu Hsing-kuo's *Kingdom of Desire* (1986), a Peking Opera production of Macbeth, Wang Jiaming's *Titus Andronicus* (2003), a Taiwanese Little Theatre version, and *The Tempest* (2004), a fusion of Shakespeare text and Peking Opera directed by Wu Hsing-kuo. Furthermore, Perng believed that taking advantage of the universal recognition of Shakespeare could save the troupe from heavy publicity costs. Adapting for a Bangzi opera poses numerous challenges for professional translators and actors. In traditional Chinese opera, the protagonists are stock characters who are either good or evil. However, the complexity of Shylock as a comic and tragic figure defies any easy classification. Perng noted in my interview:

> He[Shylock] is not just sheng 生 (male lead), jing 淨 (stout and often tempestuous male), or chou 丑 (clown), but all three in one—a first in Yuju 豫劇. Whoever plays him, then, has to cross the boundary of character categories (kua hangdang 跨行當),

---

34. Characters in traditional Chinese drama are categorised into four types, namely: "Sheng 生, Dan 旦, Jing 淨, and Chou 丑." Every type has its specific facial makeup and decoration. "Sheng" is the positive male role, "Dan" is the positive female role, "Jing" is a supporting male role, often tempestuous with striking character and "Chou" is the clown or negative role.

which poses a formidable challenge to actors trained in the strictest confines of role types.

A briefing of the cast was therefore arranged by Perng to teach them how the play should be understood in modern terms.

As this production focused on the ethnic conflicts rather than the religious conflicts, how have the identities of characters become? The play is vaguely set in the Northern Sung Dynasty 南宋 (960–1126AD), and Xia Luo 夏洛 (Shylock) becomes a *Dashiren* 大食人 (Saracen), of Arabian origin instead of a Jew. It was set in the Northern Sung Dynasty because the then capital was Kai Feng 開封 in Henan Province, the province where Bangzi Opera 梆子戲 originated and became popular. Kai Feng was also the city where the well-known court stories of Judge Bao 包青天 were set in the period.[35] Antonio, or An Yuan Wai 安員外, represents the insider from the Middle Kingdom, i.e. China. Why then was Shylock represented as *Dashiren* and not a Jew? The answer is that no Jews were recorded in the history of China until after the Sung Dynasty. On the other hand, historical records show that *Daishiren* from Persia had constant trade with Mainland Chinese in the period between 968–1116AD. In Chen's first translation draft, Shylock belonged to an ethnic minority group *Qi Dan* 契丹. After the first meeting involving translators, directors and the production crew, *Geng Yuqing* 耿玉卿, a renowned Bangzi Opera dramatist in Mainland China and adviser to the troupe, objected to this idea for fear of disrupting harmony among ethnic groups if this ministry group were specifically mentioned in the drama. He suggested that the ethnic reference should be removed from the script: hence the introduction of *Dashiren*, which does not belong to any existing ethnic group in the Mainland. This shows that, despite the liberal creative environment in Taiwan, its adaptation strategy could not be totally independent of the socio-cultural environment in the Mainland.

As Perng noted in the interview, such sensitivity to racial conflict takes into account likely audience reception and the social relevance of the play. He explained the Chinese way of treating a foreigner, where "On the one hand, treat them warmly and courteously; however, if they compete with local interests, be suspicious of them, even jealous, or hate them." This is reflected in the existence of different clan groups in Taiwan, such as the Guangdong Clan Group, whose distinct dialect and costumes may preclude outsiders from joining. When Chen Fang brought in the Saracens, extra research effort had to be made to find out their practice in the use of

---

35. I interviewed Chen Fang, co-translator of *Bond* on 18 December 2011 in Macau. Also see Chen's elaboration of her translation strategies in Fang, "Bonding? What Bonding?," 63–83.

money and costumes. Perng described ethnic conflicts as "ridiculous and demeaning," as seen in the perceived threat faced by indigenous Hokkien speakers and the nickname of the Hong Kong-born Taiwan President Ma Yingjiu as "Hong Kong Feet." Accordingly, *Xia Luo* was given sympathetic treatment: "Care has therefore been taken to give the underdog a louder voice in this adaptation."[36]

It should be noted that, while ethnic issues are highlighted in the play to give it social relevance, they are only part of the reasons behind the adaptation of the religious dimension. Much of the characterization has to do with the theology of Perng, which will be discussed in more detail in Chapter 6.

Translation Profile

The adaptation weaves the three sub-plots in *The Merchant* to thread through the play, i.e. the courtship between Bassanio and Portia, the "pound of flesh" bond between the Shylock and Antonio, and the commotion over the loss of the ring by Bassanio. All these plots relate to the common theme—the bond—which is the main focus of this adaptation. In order to highlight the main theme, some less relevant story lines are curtailed or deleted, including the condensation of the scenes on the choice of caskets, the sub-plot of Jessica and Lorenzo along with their elopement, and Lancelot and his father Gobbo along with their clowning.

The theme of *Bond* is emphasized through the repetitive use of "ring"—two in the Chinese character "yue 約," and one on the hand of Portia. The three thematic "bonds" are featured in the description in a prominent place in the poster. The disyllabic term, *Yue* 約 (contract) *Shu* 束 (restriction), was separated by a stroke /. This separation highlights the contract (i.e. *yue*) of the flesh on one hand, and the bondage (i.e. *shu*) of marriage. The adaptation is promoted as *yu sha ju*, a combination of Bangzi and Shakespearean theatre, a new theatrical form that increases its appeal to a young audience.

The original five-act play is rearranged into eight scenes: The Caskets, The Loan, Bonding of Love, The Disguise, The Debate, The Sentence, Offering Thanks and The Bargain. After the rearrangement, some speeches are delivered in a different context. The speech "Hath not a Jew eyes" originally in Act III is postponed to the law court just prior to the legal proceedings take place. Many speeches are condensed in order to accommodate arias, while passages relevant to the three main storylines are retained or lengthened. For example, in scene 7 where Master An (Antonio) keeps pressing

36. See Perng, "Bonding Bangzi and the Bard," 135–156.

Master Ba (Bassanio) to present Murong Tian (Portia) with the ring as a token of appreciation, the speech becomes an aria involving several singers, duets and choruses.

Treatment of Religious Material

With the adaptation of the Judeo-Christian conflict into one between Saracen and Cathayans, other biblical references were domesticated. Portia was not called Daniel the biblical prophet for her wise judgment, but "an excellent judge," a "great judge." The Christian spirit that the Duke showed towards Shylock in pardoning his life in Act IV scene 1: 364 was referred to as the "Cathayan principle of forgiveness."

Not only was the Judeo-Christian conflict in "Hath not a Jew eyes" were domesticated into the target culture, the speech was also lengthened, part of it being sung in arias.

安員外: 請聽我說，好心的夏老闆－

（唱）多年縱橫在商場，

情知賺賠是尋常。

時運不濟身惆悵，

容我設法作補償。

大發善心功無量，

寬延數日美名揚。

夏洛： 哈！你現在知道我是「好心的」夏老闆啦？你曾經－

（唱）三番兩次無理取鬧，

阻我買賣散錢鈔。

出言譏諷是非挑，

盆盆冷水當頭澆。

千方百計擋財寶，

幸災樂禍把我嘲。

莫怪老夫錙銖較，

禍福皆由你自招。

點點滴滴恨多少，

報應分明在今朝。

（白）哼！你曾經害老夫損失了幾千兩的雪花銀！還到處挑撥是非，在生意場上孤立老夫。你有甚麼理由這樣做呢？只因為我是個大食人。哼！大食人跟中原人有甚麼不同？大食人就沒有手腳、沒有感覺、沒有慾望嗎？大食人不跟中原人吃同樣的東西、生同樣的疾病？大食人－

（唱）大食人平白也會知飢飽，
受欺也會怒火燒。
大食人病痛也要用良藥，
被刺也會魂魄消。
大食人天公地道向誰討？
（白）此仇不報，哼！
（接唱）叫老夫如何發付這滿腹牢騷？！

An: Hear me, good Master Xia-
(sings)
As an old businessman, I know so well
You win some and you lose some—a common tale.
It's my ill fortune that my luck's been bad,
Allow me to find some means to pay my debt.
Please demonstrate your mercy generous,
And grant me a reprieve of several days.

Xia: Ha! Now you call me *good* Master Xia! You used to –
(sings)

Thwart bargains that I made, with efforts mad—
By giving money out with open hand,
Urge enemies against me, spurn me too;

Laugh at my losses, hold me in disdain.

If I dispute now over small details,

Know that you have deserved my fullest spite!

Little by little my large hatreds grew,

Till the time for retribution has arrived.

(says) Humph! You have caused me to lose many a thousand taels of shining silver! You stirred up trouble for me and isolated me in the business world. And what's your reason? Just because I'm a Saracen! Humph! What's really the difference between a Saracen and a Chinese? Has not a Saracen hands, or feet, or feelings, or passions? Is he not fed with the same food, subject to the same diseases, as a Chinese is?

(sings)

Likewise we know when we feel hunger pangs;

When bullied and berated, we're enraged;

When sick, we too, need aid of medicine;

When stabbed, we bleed and die just like you do;

Ah, when can Saracens have their just day.

(speaks) If I do not avenge myself on you,

(resumes singing)

Oh, how can I unload the cargo of this grief?[37]

Xia Luo's speech, followed by an aria, became a more emotionally charged and appealing utterance than it would have been in purely spoken form. An aria, sung slowly but sympathetically, balanced the revengeful emotions built up in the speech. Columnist Frances Kai-Hwa Wang commented that the aria was particularly "lyrical" in this ancient Chinese context.[38]

Following the verdict whereby Xia Luo was required to surrender half of his estate to the state, and half to Antonio, Antonio, showing "mercy," asked that he be assimilated to the Chinese Han culture as a Cathayan and drop his "exotic costumes." Just before he replied "I am content," Xia Luo delivered this emotionally charged aria which does not exist in the original Shakespeare text:

---

37. All the back translations in this chapter are translated by Perng Ching-Hsi in Perng. *Bond*, translated from Ching-Hsi Perng and Fang Chen, *Yue/Shu* (約/束) (Taipei: Student Book).

38. Wang, "Lessons from Taiwan Bangzi Company." 10 May 2011.

夏洛：唉！（旁唱）離絕城、到中原、越過千山和萬水，

白手起家、謹小慎微。

晝夜不休心勞瘁，

外地經商能靠誰？

年年繳納苛捐雜稅，

人前人後把小心賠。

身為異族非同類，

遭受排擠淚暗垂。

忍氣吞聲等機會，

好容易——今朝終於辨是非。

我只道十拿九穩萬事備，

磨刀霍霍爐火炊。

誰知曉風雲變色成譎詭，

煮熟的鴨子啊、撲喇撲喇喇喇展翅飛。

三倍的銀兩好實惠，

親手推卻悔難追。

高利放貸功虧一簣，

樂極竟然也生悲。

精打細算全枉費，

完美的合同與願違。

事到如今知難退，

老夫唯有賠本歸。

[Aside]:
To China's land I come from distant home,
Both mountains and wild rivers have I crossed.
From rags to riches, I've been scrupulous,
While <u>toiling</u> day and night with little rest:
A foreign businessman is all alone.

Each year I heavy taxes surely pay;

To everyone I must bow humbly down.

An alien, not equal looked upon,

I <u>wept</u> in silence when I was <u>abused</u>,

And <u>swallowed insults</u> biding still my time,

Believing that the moment had arrived,

And that, today, I'd finally be revenged.

My knife was sharp, my stove was full of fire.

How could I know that tables turn so fast,

This crisp-cooked duck away flies on singed wings?

Three times the principal a bargain was.

I pushed it away; now too late for regrets.

My schemes fell sadly short of true success;

And greatest pleasure now brings greatest grief.

Wasted are my careful calculations!

A perfect written bond now binds its scribe.

What can I do, but thus embrace defeat,

Return a total bankrupt to my home.

Such form of forced conversion from a Saracen to a Cathayan is a provocative act to the Taiwanese audience, which reminds them of their colonial past especially with regards to their unwilling assimilation or conversion to the Chinese identity over a Taiwan identity when the Kuomintang (KMT) took over Taiwan in 1945. The KMT Party imposed cultural assimilation through such practices as the Mandarin-only policy which remained in effect until 1987 when the martial law was lifted. The Taiwanese identity remains so strong that assimilation to the Mainland identity seems impossible. Emotive words like "wept in silence," "abused," "toil," "swallowed insults," which are totally absent in Shakespeare's Shylock, expose the human side of Xia Luo. He also mentions the humiliation he suffers as an outsider, and the institutional injustice he encounters as a foreign businessman required to pay heavy taxes.

Traditional Chinese dramas are also characterised by their Confucian undertones. To be consistent with the bonding theme, the loss of the ring was dramatised as a breaking of bond. Qualities of loyalty and righteousness, two important Confucian values, were emphasised in the arias. In Portia's Mercy Speech, which brings out that the quality of mercy is an attribute of God, and prayers are needed to elicit mercy, a Christian interpretation would render it an allegory of the contrast between the old law and the New Testament, a dichotomy between Judaism which upholds the old law and Christianity post-Easter. While the dichotomy of law and mercy is retained in *Bond*, allusions to the Chinese classics are added to conform to the operatic style. Confucian ideas of "kindness" or "good will" and "righteousness" are embedded in the speech, as are Buddhist karmic teachings like "Good repays good" that had a widespread influence among Chinese audiences. Murong (Portia) pleads for forgiveness and mercy from Xia Luo by referring to these qualities as embedded in age-old Chinese traditions without mentioning them as attributes of God.

慕容天: (唱) 大慈大悲天下本，
猶如雨露降凡塵。
善有善報古明訓，
典冊記載言諄諄。
柳毅傳書成合巹，
漂母一飯值千金。
一念之間懷惻隱，
結草含環報深恩。
寬容大度留分寸，
得饒人處且饒人。
即便訴求要公允，
法理人情宜酌斟。
顧全仁義盡本分，
勸君三思存哀矜。

Murong Tian: (sings)
The basis of all humanity is mercy;
It droppeth as the gentle rain from heaven.
<u>Good deeds are ever recompensed with good,</u>
As witnessed truthfully in history.
The message of Liu Yi is marriage bliss.[39]

39. It refers to a traditional Chinese story where Liu Yi forgoes his civil exam to save the humiliated princess by sending letters to her palace. They were happily married

Her bowl of rice makes rich a washerwoman.[40]

Even beyond this life, a moment of

Commiseration can be deeply felt.

Be tolerant, and be magnanimous;

Forgive where mercy seems to have a case.

For even if your suit is just and right,

It's well to weigh humanity with law.

Consider both of <u>justice and good will</u>.

I entreat you this: think thrice, be merciful.

Gender and Sexuality Issues

The relationship between Bassanio and Antonio, deemed as ambiguous by the translator, was played with ambiguity. With more and more stage performances and films of *The Merchant* played in terms of homosexuality, the translator proposed to take his cue from Trevor Nunn's film version where Portia is seen doing nothing to stop Shylock's first attempt to cut flesh from Antonio, implying her willingness to see Antonio out of the way through jealousy. The death of Antonio, whom Bassanio claimed was as dear to him as his own life and whom he would give up the world to save, would mean that no one could be her rival for Bassanio's love. This insight was then communicated to the director and actors at the briefing. In the production, Shylock, with trembling hands, tried to stab Antonio. He then retreated his footsteps and consulted his peers, who nodded. It was only at his second attempt that Portia intervened. Their ambiguous relationship can be seen in the aria sung by Antonio below and the weeping Bassanio.

安員外：唉。寥寥數言罷了，我已然作好準備。

賢弟啊—

（唱）我運數已定結難逃，

命懸一線如紙鷂。

巴山夜雨空憑弔，

置酒相待隨風飄。

---

afterwards.

40. An allusion to the story of a woman who, while washing clothes by the river, fed a starving student with rice who did not have food to eat.

四顧茫然仰天笑,

甘願為弟把心掏。

從此徘迴黃泉道,

也免得落拓潦倒、晚景淒涼、苦受煎熬

勸賢弟你不必自責懊惱,

對弟妹也莫要隱瞞分毫。

義結金蘭對天表,

兄弟一場生死交。

巴公子:(唱)大哥為我難周全,

小弟揮淚愧無言。

雖然新婚多繾綣,

難忘結拜在當年。

膠漆相投情匪淺,

悲憤無已問蒼天。

(白)唉!

(接唱)悔不該娶親貝芒縣,

驀然平地起波瀾。

何惜嬌妻共家產?

恨只恨不能代兄赴黃泉!

Master An (Antonio):
The fate predestined I cannot escape
And like a kite my life hangs by a thread
Our time together's now a thing of the past
Our merry moments blown off by the wind
Surrounded by the dark, I laugh toward heaven
Content to pray for you with all my heart (weeping)
I'll henceforth roam that undiscovered hell
From poverty and loneliness set free
Dear brother, grieve not that I die for you

> Nor anything conceal from your brothers and sisters
> Our bond of brotherhood the heavens see
> For such a bond I'll sacrifice my life
>
> Master Ba (Bassanio): (in tears)
> Brother!
> Ah, what a sacrifice you've made for me
> There's nothing I can say through tears and shame.
> Despite my deep attachment to my bride
> How can I forget our former oath
> We met—became such bosom friends
> I charge the heavens with my bitter grief
> Myself I hate, that cannot die for you.

They hold hands, kneel down and embrace each other. The spotlight was then cast on Murong Tian, who now played the judge. She put her hand on her mouth upon seeing their intimacy, and sang the following aria (which has no basis in Shakespeare's script) with great sadness:

> 慕容天: (旁唱) 原指望月老已將紅繩繫,
> 正慶幸終身有託情不移。
> 如今是難捨難分賢棠棣,
> 似拋卻信誓旦旦的結髮妻。
> 霎時間五味雜陳偷眼覷,
> 顧不得冷言冷語反唇譏。
>
> I thought in heaven was our marriage made
> That in his never-changing love I'd trust
> Inseparable from his sworn brother now
> He's spurned a wife
> to whom he promised love
> conflicting feelings swiftly surge to me
> I must respond to this sarcastically.

The ambiguity of the sexuality of Antonio had perplexed Zhu Haishan who played Antonio in *Bond*. The issue of gender was complicated as Zhu is an actress who usually played male parts in other Bongzi productions.

The ambiguity made her conscious of the minor details. The first thing "he" glanced at when "he" entered Murong Tian's place was not Murong, but the furniture. Zhu explained, "If I am a lady who likes Bassanio, then I should take a close interest in how this woman [Portia] looks. Is she attractive? Why did he choose her but not me? But now that I am a man, whoever my brother Bassanio loves, she is a woman, whether she is beautiful or not."[41]

Racial Issues

The translator originally proposed an intermission after the stabbing scene to allow time for the audience to reflect, which was later countermanded by the director who considered that a pause at such a an emotionally charged moment would subvert the emotional impact on the audience. Lu arranged for two Saracens, of the same ethnic group as Shylock, to nod their heads, thus giving Shylock the green light to cut Antonio's flesh. Perng explained in an interview that this represented a form of peer pressure from an ethnic group: "When they are irritated, can you not kill [Antonio]?" This ethnic peer pressure can be seen in an earlier act. When Xia Luo was offered monetary compensation to spare Antonio's life, one of the Saracens patted his shoulder, and they both shook their heads, showing disapproval of this offer. Xia Luo, instead of making a cruel face, showed hesitation from time to time in his need to obtain support from his ethnic group. The character of Xia Luo became more complex, in that his attempt to cut Antonio's flesh was prompted by his peers. He made the move for fear of being alienated by his ethnic group, even though he personally felt able to forgive Antonio and let him go. In the overseas performance, his "otherness" was also symbolized when he addressed Portia in English "Of course!" after she came to chair the legal proceedings:

> 慕容天：您提告的案件確實不尋常，但也合乎律法的規定。以案論案，這也不能怪罪於你。
>
> Portia: This is a strange suit you bring
> Yet from a legal standpoint
> The law cannot impugn you for proceeding.
>
> Xia Luo: Of course! [in English]

At another point, she said, "Right on!," which gained a laugh from the audience.

41. See Zhu Haishan, *Ambiguity*, in the house programme of *Bond* (2009).

Semiotic Features

One major difference between staging Shakespeare in traditional Chinese opera and in spoken drama is the important role that music plays in the former. *Bond* enlisted an ensemble involving 14 different Chinese musical instruments, together with a cello. The use of a three-stringed organ *Da San Xian* 大三弦 in certain arias effectively emphasized the cruelty of Xia Luo. On the other hand, the sound of *Guzheng* 古箏, an ancient musical stringed instrument resembling a piano, served to bring out the collegiality of Portia's house. *Erhu* 二胡, a two-stringed instrument, demonstrated the emotions of Portia over the choice of a husband. The rubbing of the strings of the *Pipa* 琵琶, another two-stringed instrument, reinforced the tension of the court scene.[42] Each character was given a distinct voice by the music director to promote recognition by the audience.

The costume design of the major characters in Bangzi Opera presents another major challenge. The costume of Xia Luo, being a Saracen from the Arab world, reflects a blend of styles from Persia, Assyria and the *Miao* 苗 ethnic minority group in China in order to highlight his "otherness." Indian embroidery is used to strengthen this "other" identity. In the court scene, Murong's costume carries the pattern common among the Miao ethnic group to bring out her gentleness, creating a counter-balance to Xia Luo.[43]

Cognitive and Behavioral Effects

Audiences in Taiwan and the US gave generally positive feedback on the adaptation of religious conflicts. An American English literature professor who watched the performance in the US commented that when the parties involved are Saracen and the Cathayan, such treatment offers Westerners "a certain exotic flavour," but also "limits the deeper resonances of the historical religious (and economic and social and national) conflict between Christians and Jews." While Wang Haining, who played Xia Luo, is capable of shifting between roles in order to convey Shylock's complexity, the commentator felt that this adaptation renders Shylock less complicated. Xia Luo, who posed as a funny, moustache-twirling villain, and who occasionally cracked jokes and even cited common English expressions such as "okay," is viewed by the audience as one at whom "we can far more easily laugh and in whose downfall we can more thoroughly rejoice."[44]

---

42. See Zhang Ting Ying's notes in the house programme of *Bond*, 2009.
43. See Lin Heng Zheng's notes in the house programme of *Bond*, 2009.
44. Jones, "Bond, Shakespeare's *Merchant of Venice* in Mandarin Chinese," 7 May

Socio-cultural Effects

While some commented on the over-simplification of the plot by omitting the Judeo-Christian conflicts from the script, the production nonetheless gained critical acclaim internationally. Two scenes, "the debate" and "the sentence" of *Bond,* were premiered at Greenwood Theatre, King's College London on 11 September 2009 (as part of the program of "Local/Global Shakespeare," The Fourth British Shakespeare Association Conference, from 11-13 September 2009). The 15-strong delegation, including performers, director and translator, was supported by the British Council, CCPD and the Ministry of Foreign Affairs of Taiwan, and Imperial College. What distinguished this tour from other worldwide tours of the troupe is that they were performing at a prestigious British Shakespeare Association Conference. Beatrice Lei, convener of the National Taiwan University Shakespeare Forum, noted the significance of this production in the academic arena: "In the past, such [cross-cultural] productions have generally been part of various arts festivals, playing before people who are open to all kinds of innovation. This time, we will perform before Shakespeare scholars, people who uphold an academic tradition."[45] The performance won the applause of hundreds of attendees from twenty nine countries, many of them Shakespearean scholars. Wang Haining, Bangzi Opera Diva, captivated the 300 plus audience with her exceptional performance of Xia Luo. The performance was followed by seminar discussions the next day, which saw unanimous commendation of the production. Wang Haining demonstrated how she could shift from a male voice to a female voice. This was highly commended by theatre professor Alan Read of Imperial College. Beatrice Lei, the driving force behind the London tour, described the show as a piece of "successful cultural diplomacy."

Riding on the success of this "cultural diplomacy," the production continued to exert its cultural influence, building on its academic-practitioner alliance—and reached a wider audience during its US tour including three universities and the conference of Shakespeare Association of America in Seattle, Washington with the generous grants from the Taiwanese government, the Taiwan Embassy, and US universities. All performances were offered free to the public. In Scranton alone, the performance attracted nearly 1,800 people in the community. Keith Jones, a professor of English and Literature, remarked, "I was frantic to see it; having seen it, I find that

---

2011.

45. Bartholomew, "The Bard—Henan Style," 10 Oct 2011.

my frantic state should have been upgraded to hysterical. It was amazing. Missing it would have been deeply regrettable."[46]

The new theatrical expression significantly raised the profile of the troupe and of the Bangzi operatic form. Some commented that the Henan-originated Bangzi Opera had found its aesthetic foothold in Taiwan, while others asserted that this production represented a form of "reverse Orientalism," interpreting and defining Shakespeare from the Bangzi perspective.[47] Daniel Yang,[48] adviser to the production, wrote that the elegant arias in *Bond* should be modified so that they could be used in Peking Opera, alongside other drama forms. This production further proves how translation and adaptation can sustain and revitalize the life of a weakening, peripheral literature. By adapting a play of high cultural capital (e.g. a Shakespearean play), a traditional drama is preserved and is capable of exerting influence in the global arena.

Conclusion

In this chapter, I have sought to show, by way of textual analysis, the adaptation strategy for processing the religious dimension in this traditional operatic version in Taiwan. I have shown that the decision to cut or suppress does not always come from the director who usually holds the ultimate authority in a production. This case represents a collaborative approach where the decision on adaptation is distributed among the director (who holds less cultural capital) and the two scholarly translators. Additionally, some parallels can be drawn in terms of untranslatability of the religious material between *Bond* and the Cantonese operatic production *For the Heiress' Hand*. Such untranslatability is the result of various circumstances—culturally, replacing the Christian discourse with Confucian/Buddhist discourse and local folk tales fits better with the norms and expectations of a traditional Chinese opera. While Shakespeare's name and fame is utilized in promoting the productions to ensure a handsome box office success, the producers in both cases have the agenda of fostering an appreciation of traditional Chinese culture among the local and global audiences. Christian discourse, which is considered foreign to the general public, is therefore displaced. Having said that, it is interesting to note that both operatic versions are under a certain degree of foreign influence, such as the use of foreign musical instruments or musical piece, and the occasional use of

46. See Keith Jones, 9 April 2010.
47. See Chen, *Bonding?*, 80.
48. See Yang, "Preface," i-vii.

English expressions (e.g. "Okay" as in *Bond*). However, such foreignness is only expressed through the semiotic features without manifesting itself ideologically. Thematically, each of these productions chooses to highlight a theme that is, in their judgment, appealing to their respective target audiences at the expense of the religious dimension. In *Bond*, it is the ethnic tensions; in *For the Heiress' Hand*, it is the traditional ethos of zhen-shan-mei (truth, kindness and beauty). I have thus shown, in this case study, that stage performance is indeed a highlighting act as proposed by Gadamer, where all performance is interpretation and all interpretation is highlighting. In circumstances of religious freedom and diversity, the loss of the religious dimension in this case is not a result of political censorship or self-censorship, but the result of highlighting. When the translation agents choose to highlight issues of identity, ethnicity and sexuality, the religious dimension is inevitably suppressed. The untranslatability of the religious dimension in this religiously diverse place reminds one of the suppression in the case of the Hong Kong production, when the Christian theology in the play ran counter to the director's belief system. This alerts one to the deep seated roots of the untranslatability of the religious discourse in *Bond*. In the next chapter, I will study the impact of these directors' theological positions on the translatability of the religious dimension.

Figure 5.1 Photo of Shylock (left) with Portia (right) at the trial scene in *Bond* 約/束, 2010 in Taipei. (Source: Taiwan Bangzi Company 台灣豫劇團)

Figure 5.2 Poster showing the major characters of *Bond*. (Source: Taiwan Bangzi Company 台灣豫劇團)

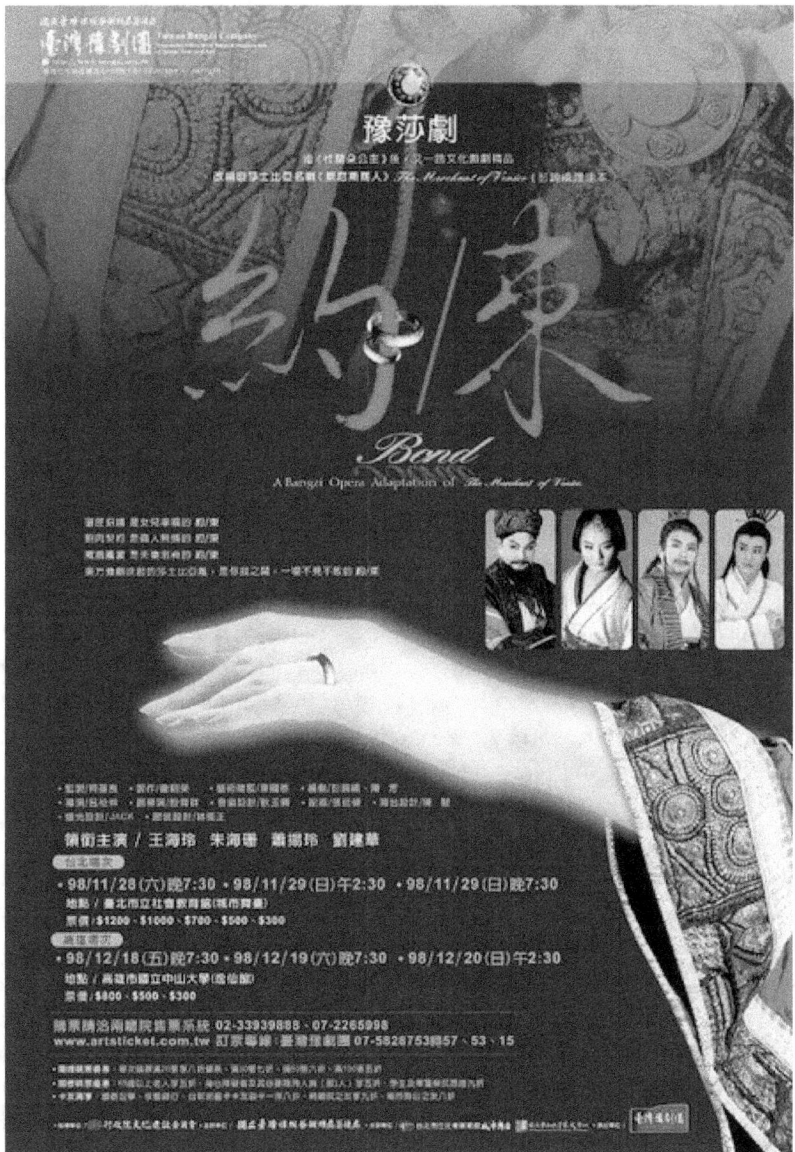

Figure 5.3 Poster of *Bond* 約/束 staged in 2009 in Taipei, featuring the ring on Portia's hand, signifying a marriage bond. (Source: Taiwan Bangzi Company 台灣豫劇團)

6

The World behind the Text— Pre-understanding of Directors and Translators

THE CASE STUDIES IN the previous chapters shed light on how the different conditions, i.e. social, cognitive, behavioral, shaped the translation of the religious dimension in a particular Shakespeare play. The cognitive conditions, which include the hermeneutics of these translation agents merit further examination. In the literature review in Chapter 1, I have shown that Chinese translation scholars such as Martha Cheung draw attention to the practice of ideological manipulation by translators in their reduction of Christian references. These studies, however, are solely based on the prevalent ideology of the Chinese society, without investigating the translator's theological discourse. This methodology is inadequate to explain why, in some of the case studies where religious freedom prevails, the religious dimension is still not translated. For example, why would the director and translator agree to suppress the religious content in *The Merchant* in 2000 in Hong Kong? Why should Perng, a Christian himself, be uninterested in showcasing the religious dimension in *The Bond* in Taiwan? Why was there a suppression of religious content in later performances of the Beijing-based Weinisishangren amidst the religious fever of the 1980s?

This research gap prompted me to investigate what part was played in the decisions about translation by the worldview of the agents concerned. In this chapter, I present an account of the directors' and translators' thought processes in adapting and translating religious materials in *The Merchant of Venice* for the Chinese stage. A phenomenological approach was employed to illustrate how the preconceptions, or pre-understanding in Heidegger's terms, and religious experiences and concepts of these directors and translators shaped their directorial interpretation and translation strategies.

There are a few terms that deserve further clarification. I define *religious experience*, a term coined by William James,[1] as the internal process triggered "by a religious encounter either mentally or physically which bears significant religious consequences."[2] Such experience is more closely related to emotion and feeling than are religious concepts, which are used to refer to values and ideas of religious importance that result from particular experiences or traditions.[3] *Pre-understanding* can refer to the prejudices of a translator, or to the preconceived meaning of a concept (e.g. mercy, sympathy for the Jews). It can also be the previous version of a play—or a theory or model regarding the play—which appeals to a translator. In Ricoeur's hermeneutical terms, I am investigating the "world behind the text" as articulated by and filtered through individual artists and performers that gives rise to the image of translated literature. Eleven translators and directors who were involved in the making of *The Merchant of Venice* in Mainland China, Hong Kong and Taiwan were interviewed and the transcripts analyzed using the method of Interpretative Phenomenological Analysis (IPA), developed by Jonathan A Smith.[4] This is a methodology which has its roots in phenomenological philosophy and stands within a tradition of qualitative research. The works of Husserl, Gadamer and Ricoeur provide important insights into the study of phenomenological psychology, which draws on Husserl's concept of lifeworld—the world we concretely live in. A phenomenological approach in psychology helps one to see how meaning is created by understanding how people perceive the world they live in. It places a strong emphasis on human experience as a topic in its own right; it is concerned with meaning and the way in which meaning arises in experience, and it focuses on the understanding of meaning in context (historical, cultural and personal).[5] Its emphasis on meaning-making implies a close connection with cognitive approaches in psychology, but it differs from mainstream psychology (which is concerned with a positivistic, quantitative approach in data collection) by employing in-depth qualitative analysis. There is no definite way of doing such qualitative analysis, but I engage in a detailed examination of the participant's lifeworld and attempt to explore

---

1. See James, *The Varieties of Religious Experience*, 489.
2. See Yao and Badham, *Religious Experience in Contemporary China*, 14.
3. Ibid.
4. See Smith, et al, *Interpretative Phenomenological Analysis*, 2009.
5. Langdridge, *Phenomenological Psychology*, 9.

personal experience through interviews, amongst other methods.[6] IPA is probably the most widely known approach to phenomenological psychology.[7] Given its concern with hermeneutics and the interpretation of human experience, IPA is appropriate to the present study and can help us understand what gives rise to the meaning of certain theological concepts created by the directors and translators whose work is under review, and what experiences shaped their perception of different characters and of the plot. While IPA is widely used in the field of health science and education, its application in the field of arts and literature is, I believe, innovative—its originality lying in the application of IPA to an unforeseen area, i.e. arts and culture.

The technique, as can be seen from the interviews, is extended to apply to dramatists and actors. Unlike "real-life" subjects (e.g. patients) in the areas of health and science whose description of lifeworld experience is based on the physicality of flesh and blood, these represent a radically different hermeneutics in making meaning on stage, as will be illustrated in the following section. The originality also lies in the intercultural, highly inter-disciplinary nature of the application of the methodology. It extends the study of the Shakespeare's religious language from the Western traditions to the subtle differences within the eastern traditions, including those of Hong Kong, Taiwan and Mainland China. Each of these has its particular political and social peculiarities—emphasized where the interviewees come from diverse cultural backgrounds and disciplines.

Method

The present study particularly focuses on how interviewees perceive religious concepts in *The Merchant of Venice* and on the interaction of theatre with the religious contents of the play. Acquaintance with interviewees' worldviews can help one understand the translatability of religious concepts in *The Merchant of Venice*. The research program is a qualitative one which included voice recordings of interviewees and directors who had been involved in the production and translation process during the thirty year period between 1980 and-2011. Semi-structured interviews were conducted to tease out the factors contributing to the adaptation or loss of religious material. Where possible, both the director and the translator for the same production were interviewed, as in the two productions of *The Merchant of Venice* staged in Hong Kong in 2000 and 2010, and *The Bond* staged in

---

6. See Smith and Osborn, *Qualitative Psychology*, 53–80.
7. Ibid, 55.

Taiwan. A total of 9 interviews were then transcribed, and later studied line by line according to the IPA method. They were triangulated with the published reflections written by the same directors about each of the relevant productions. The religious experience and theological understanding (including pre-understanding) of these agents emerged as the main themes in explaining the adaptation of religious language in their productions. This finding confirms the hypothesis that the translatability of religious concepts is dependent largely on the hermeneutical process of the translator.

Procedure

Interviews lasted between 50 and 90 minutes. Questions that were asked in the semi-structured interview were as follows:

- Before your translation / production, did you read or watch other versions of *The Merchant*?
- Describe your translation and interpretation processes.
- What do you think of the treatment of Shylock and his forced conversion in the trial scene of *The Merchant*?
- What do you think of the characters in the play?
- Do you have a religious background? Since when have you held religious views?

The interviews were audio-recorded and transcribed with the consent of the interviewees. IPA involves a detailed study of the transcripts line by line. The use of left and right hand margin codes was followed,[8] whereby left hand codes highlight any important keywords or themes. Such units were then put in the right hand margin and categorised as "experiential claims" and "objects of concern." After identifying initial themes, I looked for any connections between them, i.e. a cluster of themes which, when taken together, became a number of major overarching or superordinate themes. A table of themes was then produced showing the themes that occurred most frequently and which best described the experience under investigation. In the final analysis, the transcript was examined again using the features of the lifeworld. A lifeworld, according to interpretative phenomenological psychologists, comprises four essential features: temporality (the experience of time), spatiality (the experience of space), embodiment (the experience of one's own body), and intersubjectivity (the experience of relationships with

---

8. See Smith and Osborn, *Qualitative Psychology*, 53–80.

other people).⁹ These features are examined because they are important in reflecting the degree of importance the agents attach to certain aspects of their lifeworld. As shown in the interviewee's transcript, one aspect (e.g. embodiment) of the lifeworld that was emphasized by the interviewee would be translated on stage.

Since the interviews were originally conducted in Chinese, the transcripts were translated into English using formal equivalence. That is, rather than showing the interviewee as speaking in idiomatic English, the transcripts retained the syntax and collocations of Chinese language, which explains why certain quotations sound grammatically odd when translated back into English. Words in [] were added in the transcript to indicate that such content was presumably intended by interviewees but not explicitly spelt out in the conversation.

Ethical Issues

Participants were informed of the topic of research, the researcher's name and her affiliations. They signed a form of informed consent, in which the name of the supervisor was also given should they need to direct further queries. Since the interviews touched on participants' conceptions on religious issues, and could generate sensitive data regarding their personal views, ethical approval was obtained in 2010 through the university research ethics committee.

Findings

Behavioral aspects of the productions, such as the length of preparation, attendance at the shows, the *modus operandi* among actors, directors and translators, were discussed in the previous chapter. In the findings that follow, I will focus on the interpretative aspects, that is, what drives the interpretation of the play that the agents finally adopt.

Three superordinate themes emerged from the analysis: 1) Religious experience; 2) Theological concepts; 3) Directorial approach and interpretation.

The following table shows the themes and subthemes of each superordinate theme category developed in the analysis. These themes explain the meaning-making process of the play's religious content, and hence its translatability. The first main theme to be discussed is one's religious experience,

---

9. Dahlberg et al, *Reflective Lifeworld Research*, 45–69.

which often shapes one's theological position or ideology (Theme Two), as the analysis below shows. The agents' theological positions on the religious dimension of the play in turn give rise to interpretations which reflect their directorial approach or translation strategy. It should be noted that not all the interviewees have religious experience, especially those living in an atheist environment. For these interviewees, their "world behind the text" will start from Superordinate Theme Two.

Theme Table. Religious Experiences

Table 6.1 Theme Table on Religious Experiences

Superordinate Themes	Sub-themes
1. Religious experiences	i. Faithful
	ii. Doubtful/ Leaver
	iii. Anti-religious
2. Theological and religious concepts	i. Forgiveness
	ii. Mercy
	iii. Conversion, mission and freedom of religion
	iv. View of religious issues in the play
3. Directorial treatment	i. Impression of the Jews
a. Characterisation and generic decision	ii. Impression of Christian characters
	iii. Genre
b. Directorial approach	i. Director emphasis
	ii. Social relevance
	iii. Catering to audience expectation
	iv. Universal Shakespeare

Theme 1: Religious Experiences

Believing

Among the transcripts studied, five showed that the interviewees have had some contact with Christianity. The religious experiences of all the directors under study show a surprisingly intricate relationship with their inclusion or exclusion of religious content in the play. While one might have assumed that practicing Christians would keep the religious content intact in the production, the outcome may be different. Perng Ching Hsi's translation is a case in point. Perng, was converted to Christianity a decade ago. He had been reading the Bible before his baptism: his wife took him to morning devotions every day and read devotional materials. "For the three to four years before baptism, I followed my wife in listening to sermons and reading the Bible. We went for morning devotions together every day, and read the devotional books entitled "huangmogancun (荒漠甘泉)" But in the production, all the religious content was changed to a focus on ethnicity. Besides the need to conform to the theatrical conventions of traditional Chinese theatre, this decision could be traced back to his dissatisfaction with the idea of Christian "mercy" displayed in the play:

> Originally, [Portia said that things done] according to the law were not good. But you [Portia] are a Christian, you also work according to the law. If this condition is changed, he [Shylock] will be set free, rather than having Antonio to get all the money. Shylock [, on the other hand,] gets nothing. I [Antonio will be the one who] help you manage the remaining penalty to be handed to your Christian son-in-law, but only Christians have it [the money]. *If this is performed from Christian point of view, this has to be changed.(emphasis added by myself)*

The above quotation implies that by omitting the religious dimension and highlighting the ethnical dimension, Perng sought to protect Christians from being labelled as unforgiving and unmerciful. This is related to his life transition (temporality) as a Christian. He understood Christianity and the Bible not through his own intellectual pursuit, but through relating with others (intersubjectivity)—through relating to the church community, through spending time and being influenced by his Christian wife who is a cell group leader in his church, through relating to God in morning devotions. Therefore, while he sees the Christians in the play as "unforgiving," his understanding of Christianity is different from what is depicted in the play. In fact, Perng never shied away from professing his Christian faith throughout this interview, and through the articles he wrote on the Christian dimension in *Measure for Measure*. [10] He unconsciously developed an interest in the theme of forgiveness in Shakespeare's plays after he became a Christian (temporality). When asked if his Christian faith had any relationship with his interest in the theme of forgiveness in

---

10. Perng, "The Title of a Problem Play: Measuring a Play," D5.

this and other Shakespearean plays, he reckoned this was a good question he had never thought of:

> Good question! I have not noticed this. I have not thought about this issue. It happened roughly the same time (when I was baptized). Before my baptism I read the Bible extensively. My wife brought me to morning devotions. I am not totally familiar with the Bible, but for three to four years before baptism, I had Bible reading and listened to sermons together with my wife.
>
> I think the two issues [turning to Christ and having this interest in forgiveness] come together.

Before the interview, I showed him a Christian course of study that I wrote. Perng showed pleasure in knowing me to be a Christian, and he then identified himself as a Christian likewise who regularly attends Bread of Life Christian Church in Taipei (台北靈糧堂). Throughout the interview, his speech was peppered with Christian terminology or statements drawn from Christian theology, such as "human beings are weak, because all have sins," "[as a Christian] I was saved very late." He revealed to me after the interview that he hoped his son, now a Jew, would be converted to Christianity one day, and he was keen to introduce to me his Christian student who is doing mission work in China. Perng is the only practicing Protestant Christian among all my interviewees, but no trace of Christianity is visible in this stage production despite his faithful rendition of the printed version. His religious experience is one of the reasons underlying his stance, which will be further illustrated below.

What makes him so passionate about the theme of forgiveness? He cited one incident that happened more than a decade ago, when his Greek colleague was complaining about different matters to the department head and to the dean. The colleague was so angry that he did not speak to him for a year. In 2000, he and his wife prayed for this matter daily while residing in Chicago as a visiting scholar. One year later, he introduced to this colleague of an upcoming Greek show. After watching the show, the colleague reconciled with him. "I think the Holy Spirit is working, that's why he forgives [me after the show]."

Rupert Chan, who translated the script for the 2010 production, considered himself an "average" Catholic Christian, and his whole family were baptized and read the Bible. But since it was the director Ko who gave the main interpretation to the actors, Ko's theology carried more weight in deciding the approach to religious content. He should be classified as an "anti-religious" type, which I will show as follows.

Anti-religious

"I studied in a Catholic secondary school, but I resisted religion from an early age. I had to pray Holy Mary prayers, and this went on into secondary school. Why so many rituals? Why force me to recite [prayers]? So I resisted these religious rituals. I read the Bible, Buddhism scriptures, mantras... I like reading Buddhist scriptures. There are a lot of controversies in the Bible. There used to be female popes. The Bible talks about how the Jews should read the Old Testament. The book *The* Da Vinci Code tells us that there is a woman in the Last Supper... I enjoy alternative readings—for example, the view that there is a gap in Jesus' life—his deeds during and beyond age twenty were not mentioned. Someone surmised that he had gone to Tibet."

The above interview excerpt from Ko shows that he enjoys reading alternative, unorthodox readings about different religions, and has developed an egalitarian approach to different traditions, without submitting to any hierarchy. However, he does not reject religion unthinkingly, but his rejection is related to his past (temporality), on the ground that rituals such as prayers form a restriction on his personal space (spatiality). Showing resistance to religion does not make Ko filter out all the references. But he read the play from an anti-religious perspective, and he returned to the notion of Christian hypocrisy throughout the interview. He also considered that Christians showed extreme prejudice against Shylock. However, the converse, i.e. Shylock's hatred against Christians, was not mentioned throughout the interview. The sympathy shown to the Jew was not matched by sympathy towards the Christian merchant. This will be discussed as a sub-theme later.

Doubtful/Leaver

Chris Shum's degree of faith is considered to fall into the doubtful category. As the excerpts from the interview cited in Chapter 4 show, he was doubtful whether God exists, and or why the Virgin Mary is a virgin. He considered his baptism as a Catholic a "stupid" move, and as he continued to question his faith, he decided to cut out the religious content in the play. He states:

> I became a Catholic and innocently got baptized due to something that happened. I was stupid, there was no need to be baptized. I was baptized when I was a working adult. But if I am a nice person, I think that God will [save me], and that [salvation] does not necessarily require baptism, which is only a ceremony... why it [Christianity] is a Jewish tradition... I

know of Catholics who are not pious; some are fraudulent in the name of religion; for them religion is only an outer shell. But I also know some good Catholics, ones who did not just pay lip service. I think religion is not [important], so I did not include religious content in the play. Also, I don't think it [God] exists, [even when one becomes a Christian], so what?

Shum explained in the above quotation how his past (temporality) gave rise to his decision to omit the religious dimension. His interpretation of the religious dimension as a peripheral theme in the play is related to his encounter with both false and genuine Christians (intersubjectivity), which made him think that religion is not important at all in shaping good character. In the end, religion to him is like a shell, a metaphor which describes its emptiness and voidness (spatiality). His rejection of religion came to a point where he described religious people as "stupid," not only himself, but also those who professed their faith.

Shum mentioned that "something that happened" in the past (temporality) that led him to consider baptism. So, in a follow-up interview,[11] I asked him to elaborate his past religious experience that led him to this decision, in a hope to unpack his disdain for Christianity and thus the elimination of Christian references in his production. He explained that, since his secondary school years, he had been an apprentice of a Catholic veteran director, anonymized as M, only to be disappointed by his "hypocritic" and "shameless" character. Not only did M cheat his money without repaying the loan, he also lacked sympathy towards his family ordeal. However, this director M was, and still is, serving the Catholic Church by teaching pre-baptismal preparation classes, which he attended in the nineties and became his Godson. He became so disappointed to a point that in 2003, he nearly wrote to the Catholic Church to cut off this Godfather-Godson relationship. This incident, together with other rumors he heard about the hypocrisy of some Christian leaders, changed his perception of Christian church and Christians. "I am not saying that the church must be bad, but I won't think that just because you are a Christian worker will mean you are good—it's just a job. Catholics are like that, not to mention Christians! So I think, the doctrine is meaningless, what I trust is the wisdom [in that religion].

Throughout the interview, he took a utilitarian view of religion and use metaphors such as *banghui* 幫會 (Mafia), or *shengyi* 生意 (business) to describe the nature of Christian churches. "I think Christian churches are a kind of business, some have conscience running the business, selling products that are pure, some leverage on brandnames such as celebrities

---

11. A second interview was conducted on 12th June 2014 in Hong Kong.

to help build up the brandname of a church, some add more preservatives [in this product], some add less. Some even cook it with dirty oil recycled from kitchen waste. The church is just God's spokesperson in the secular world, so one has to be smart to discern what is true and what is false." His past dissatisfactory religious experience has a bearing not just in his faith, but also in his interpersonal relationship, because he decided not to trust what people said about their ideals or beliefs, rather he will observe their deeds. The Christian identity to him is meaningless, so is the doctrine, as he confessed in the aforementioned quote. As such, the omission of these unimportant references from the performance text is not surprising.

While Chris Shum did not openly say that he left Catholicism, and only considered that he is not "devout," Daniel Yang, on the other hand, admitted that he is no longer a Catholic. He spoke of his religious experience after being asked where his Christian knowledge came from, for instance, his view on missionary enterprise. When he spoke at length of the missionary enterprise in the early twentieth century China as an act of colonialism, this prompted my interest to enquire what shaped his religious views:

> Later I lost my passion [for Christianity]. In the past I thought that going to Sunday mass was a spiritual pleasure, I liked the Catholic rituals, but later I didn't feel that this was a spiritual pleasure, it was a burden. I went to mass every week and had to go for confession before receiving the bread, I felt this as a burden, so I didn't want to, and then I gradually didn't attend, and I didn't go any more. Sometimes I still go [to church], [but I am] not a devout Christian [or] a devout catholic, not any more. My daughters are Christians, I sometimes went with them to the church in US. Both of my daughters are very devout, so on Sunday when I visited their church, I quite liked the environment, but since our daughter left us, I no longer have the urge to go to church. But in fact, I remember there was a year when I was the visiting professor at National Taiwan University, which was close to where I was baptized, so I sometimes went there, but I am no longer a Catholic.

In the above quote, Yang talked about his past in an embodied sense (embodiment). He used "burden" as a metaphor to describe the unease he had while attending Mass. His body was situated in a ritualistic space (spatiality) that happened weekly (temporality). Going for confession, a ritualistic encounter with the priest (intersubjectivity), did not give him relief but added to his burden. This burden was temporal (temporality), as it disappeared along with his passion. Yang mentioned how his motivation to attend the church services was related to the company of his daughters (intersubjectivity), but such motivation was also temporal (temporality) because it went away with the departure of his daughters. The environment (spatiality) played a part in affecting his religious experience—apparently, he enjoyed the church environment better in the company of his daughters, and he reminisced his old college days (temporality) when he worshipped at a church near National Taiwan University.

Yang had distanced himself from the Catholic community, and without the religious passion, he spoke of the social service done by Christian missionaries as both an act of kindness and an act of invasion. He believed that those who came to church in the early twentieth century had a utilitarian purpose, rather than being true believers. Yang's notion of mission and conversion will be teased out further in the following theme.

Theme 2: Theological and Religious Concepts

Forgiveness

Forgiveness is the theme that Perng most wanted to communicate in the play (and in other Shakespeare plays). When asked why he chose to adapt *The Merchant* into Bangzi Opera, Perng brought up the topic of forgiveness and spoke at length. He admitted that he liked the theme of forgiveness, being "very willing to advance the idea of forgiveness," and he confirmed that this was related to his faith. Perng stated:

> In the past 10 years, I have worked on the theme 'forgiveness' in Shakespeare's plays, *this is related to my faith* (my emphasis). I think forgiveness is hardest. Hardest. Not only to forgive others is hard, to accept forgiveness is also hard. I accept others' forgiveness, what does it mean? It means I am in the wrong, I beg your pardon. I forgive you means I am standing at a higher [moral] position, despite this I still am reluctant to do this [forgive]. So forgiveness is hard for both sides. Why do I need your forgiveness? I am not wrong at all.

He admitted that, well before he became a Christian, God already gave him the passion to work on the theme of forgiveness, hence he translated *Hamlet* before he became a Christian. Other later commissioned works include *Winter's Tale* and *Cardenio*, all relating to this theme.

As illustrated above, "forgiveness" is a theme that he brought up on his own—it was not the interviewer who asked him about it, he introduced the theme in order to explain his reason for adapting *The Merchant of Venice*. In fact, the word "forgive" or "forgiveness" recurs again and again in the above excerpt, and it is striking to see Perng using strong words such as "hard," "hardest" and short simple sentences such as "I beg your pardon. I forgive you" to illustrate the big theme of forgiveness. How he understands forgiveness affects his interpretation of sympathy for the Jews and the depiction of the Christian characters. To Perng, forgiveness is not practiced by the Christian characters in *The Merchant*. To him, forgiveness should be unconditional. He continues:

> Portia said, you have evidently attempted to take the life of a Venetian citizen, so your life is in the hands of the Duke—I cannot forgive you. Then the Duke said, in order to show that the Christian's spirit is different, I forgive you before you ask. Very good, but several lines later, Antonio said, you are forgiven after fulfilling these conditions. The Duke said, he must do it: otherwise, I am going to change my mind. Is this forgiveness? His action appears magnanimous at the beginning, i.e., I forgive without asking you to kneel, but later on new conditions are added, making it a conditional forgiveness—this is not forgiveness.

Since in his view forgiveness is not shown by Christians, I asked, why did he decide to adapt *The Merchant* if his central purpose is to promote the theme of forgiveness? He admitted that by showcasing the unforgiveness of the Cathayans, he could show importance of forgiveness and what it would be like in its absence.

Forgiveness is a vital keyword or theme that recurs throughout the interview with Perng. From the sympathetic treatment given to Shylock in the trial scene, one can see that it is the "unforgiveness" of Christians that Perng and Lu are interested in.

When Daniel Yang was asked for his opinion of Antonio's pardon as an act of forgiveness to Shylock, he did not elaborate on his idea of forgiveness as much as Perng, but he did show his view that this forgiveness, in the form of conversion, was "a cruel act." He saw this conversion as an act of colonialism. Underlying Yang's sympathetic treatment of the Jew was his disagreement with this act of conversion, which will be discussed as a subtheme later. Ko and Chan did not bring up the theme of forgiveness in the semi-structured interview. Rather, they introduced the concept of mercy, which will be discussed below.

Mercy

Is mercy shown by Christians in the play?

Ko reckoned that "belief and prejudice" is the main theme of the play, and that belief leads to prejudice: the better way is mercy. More specifically, Ko referred to Christian belief as leading to prejudice against the Jews, since he considered that the Christians had gone to the extreme in (mis)treating the Jews without mercy. Rupert Chan agreed with Ko's interpretation, and both of them cited the loss of Shylock's property and even his daughter to Christians. "The Christians exaggerated [their mercy]: saying how to forgive, how forgiving they were in their treatment of the Jews . . . but it was a different thing in practice. Jews were persecuted in such a way, as if chasing the dog into a lane, this is tragic [of Shylock]. His daughter was taken away, he was discriminated against for his whole life, although he was only asking for what was his due. In court he lost the case, his property was confiscated, and he was forced to adopt another religion."

The sympathy towards the Jew, the moneylender, shown by the director and translator from Hong Kong is connected with the city's status as a capitalistic financial center. Chan, as quoted above, believed that Shylock was only asking for "what was his due." In Hong Kong, financial companies that lend money at high interest abound: they advertise their services on television during primetime, whereas the money-lending profession was abhorrent in Shakespeare's time, or under the Marxist ideology.

On the other hand, Yang thought that mercy was truly shown in the mercy speech. When asked if he agreed with some scholarly reviews which argue that the mercy speech by Portia is not genuinely about mercy, he said, "I think these scholars have nothing to do, this is rubbish, I think it is a sincere speech, she means it. I don't think that he [Antonio] is hypocritical, no, that's rubbish, many scholars have nothing to do, I laughed at these reviews . . . " Here, one can see that Yang who is sympathetic to Shylock holds a balanced view towards the Christians, that is, he is not discrediting them as completely hypocritical. In his view, there are both good Christians and bad Christians in the play. The result of this balanced portrayal of Christians is less sympathy towards the Jew.

However, Chris Shum and Jack Shu are not totally aligned in their reading of mercy in the 2000 production. Chris is unimpressed with the vengeance on Shylock, rather than sympathizing with his loss following the trial.

> Shylock deserves this, the conditions he set out are stupid . . . it is he who set out the conditions, one who was oppressed and despised . . . I think he really deserves this. Some say this is due to the low esteem among ethnic groups, [for instance], I was once oppressed, but now I oppress you. But if I come to ask your help,

do you take this chance to oppress me? He has this thought and was oppressed . . . doesn't this serve him right? Is this mercy?

Mercy, in Shum's view, is lacking on the part of Shylock, not of the Christians. Shum's ethical stance is clearly shown in the above quote—he clearly disapproves of Shylock's vengeful act, and that one who was oppressed should not retaliate with oppression. The adjective "stupid" appears again, this time being used to describe Shylock's insistence on the bond. In an earlier excerpt, I have shown that Shum discredited those who look "stupid" (i.e. Christians who are pious). Stupidity, in his view, seems to be an unforgivable quality, which this explains his treatment of Shylock as a villain.

But Shu the translator thinks differently—he sympathizes with Shylock in view of the unmerciful attitude of Christians: "Shylock said, you (Christians) often talk about mercy, but how can this (treatment of the Jews) be considered mercy? How is love being manifested? Is this play a piece of irony against what Christian said about helping the Jews?"

In the hierarchy of a stage production, director Chris Shum had the ultimate authority in deciding the final product over Jack Shu, who did not participate in the rehearsals or discussion after he submitted the translated text to Shum. The end result is a comedic treatment of the Jew that follows Shum's interpretation.

Conversion, Mission, and Religious Freedom

How was the "forced conversion" of Shylock understood? Basically almost all the interviewees found this unacceptable. As Chapter 3 shows, Zhang Qihong and Jack Shu considered it so unreasonable that they deleted this condition of "forced conversion." Jack Shu found this conversion unreasonable for two main reasons: firstly, conversion is now enforced, not out of love or conviction? Secondly, (from Shylock's perspective) he had to abandon his Judaic faith and adopt a faith that he hated.

Both Zhang and Shu omitted the part unconsciously, and could not recall that such deletion did actually take place until I mentioned it to them. Shu said, "Oh, [I did not realize] I so disliked that part! I forgot that I deleted it, although I found this [forced conversion] ridiculous."

While Shu used "ridiculous" to describe the conversion scene, Zhang used the word "meaningless." Zhang found the forced conversion unreasonable because she believed in "freedom of religion." She commented:

Maybe I deleted it, I think it's meaningless. Believing [in a faith] or not is not the issue. It does not mean you can [force someone] to be a Christian. Maybe I found it meaningless and did not retain that part. The other thing, I believe, relates to one's freedom. Shylock has his freedom to believe in Judaism.

"Freedom" is a recurring keyword used by Zhang in the interview. As a reputable director, Zhang is known for her way of breaking free from existing frameworks, making bold attempts to carve out a new style of Chinese Shakespeare, rather than "walk in the shadow of predecessors."[12] Her personal sense of "freedom" is connected with the importance she attaches to respecting the freedom of others to choose their religion.

Ko, Yang and Perng acknowledged the good intentions of Christians in wanting to save a soul through conversion, but once again their sympathy is skewed towards the Jew who lost his faith. This led, in varying degrees, to a sympathetic treatment of Shylock in their productions. When I asked the two Christian translators, namely Perng and Chan, how they felt towards this scene, Perng expressed his unease as a Christian at seeing Christians imposing their doctrine by force, "I feel unsettled [about forced conversion], [the situation] is similar to the Crusades, don't you think? I should put it like this, if the scene is set 400 years ago, I can accept that this is mercy. But 400 years later, in the environment of religious freedom, I feel that this is not right."

Rupert Chan's sympathy towards the Jew comes from his theological rejection of forced conversion, which implies that salvation is not from God but by man.

> This [forced conversion] to him [Shylock] is a cruel punishment. The Jews never acknowledged the New Testament, never acknowledged Jesus as the Messiah, they are still waiting for their Messiah, the Messiah mentioned in the Old Testament. To force them to believe in Jesus is a great penalty . . . they [Christians] believe that they are the ones to save [a soul], i.e. salvation is [made possible] through human beings." His sympathy is echoed by Ko who believes that forced conversion is a false way for Christians to spread Christianity, "Why did Shakespeare write this [about forced conversion]? I think the theme is belief and prejudice—Christians have gone to an extreme [in prejudice against the Jews].

Yang, who took a sympathetic view of Shylock, described the act as "very cruel" and linked the idea of conversion with colonial expansion.

12. See Zhang, *The Artistic Ideas of Director*, 1988.

Yang tried to make him appear pathetic when a cross was forced on him. "From his [Antonio's] stance there is good intention, but we see this as making the Jews suffer even more. So when this thing [the cross] is placed on his body the pain is even greater, I think it's rather cruel, it's very cruel, and Shylock had to bear this, and didn't break down, he cried when he left, not crying on the spot, this is his dignity." In conclusion he said "The Christians were too harsh on him."

In the above quote, Yang talked about the cross in the embodied sense (embodiment). It is perhaps suggestive that the personal burden he mentioned in connection with attendance at Catholic Mass in his college days is translated into a physical cross laid on Shylock, i.e. a burden. Yang's unique religious experience is translated not through verbal means, but through a metaphorical object.

This burdened experience of the Christian faith has left its traces in Yang's unfavorable view of the missionary enterprise, which to him is little different from colonialism. The colonizing image of missionaries in China becomes a pre-understanding of his reading of the forced conversion scene. Yang reckons that mission work among the poor especially in century China is no different from forced conversion, as he explains in the following quotation: "This [forced conversion] made me think of one thing, in the nineteenth-century late Qing government, China suffered a lot of calamities and became very poor. Missionaries come, from their point of view this is an act of kindness, but the Chinese don't necessarily feel that way! There are many who convert to Christianity, but I think this is half coercion. This is a kind of colonialism."

View of Religious Issues in the Play

How do the agents view the religious dimension in the play? Do they attach importance to it or dismiss it as irrelevant? For different reasons, agents such as Ni Huiying and Chris Shum, who totally omit any trace of Christian identity, do not see religion in the play as relevant. As discussed above, Shum's view of the irrelevance of religion is linked to his faith. Ni Huiying sees religious issues in the play as no different from ethnic conflicts, and with a limited performance time of just over two hours, religious references that require a lot of effort in explanation need not be included. For Shum and Perng, who shift the focus from religious issues to ethnic issues, what makes the latter become the central themes is their social relevance. Perng disapproves of the ethnic competition in Taiwan, as shown in the following remark:

When Ma Yingjiu [president of Taiwan] came forward for presidential election, people described him as 'Hong Kong feet', because he was born in Hong Kong . . . I think such [ethnic] competition is ridiculous and demeaning." Similarly, Shum opined that if he were to stage the play again, ethnic conflicts between Hong Kong and Mainland should be the main theme of the production, given the current conflicts in Hong Kong.

The interviews show that for the directors who view the social relevance of the play as important to their choice of staging *The Merchant*, there is a tendency to emphasize ethnic issues and subdue religious issues, reflecting the relatively low social relevance of religion in Greater China. This will be discussed further in the following sub-theme.

Theme 3: Directorial Approach and Interpretation

Characterization and Generic Decision:
Impression of the Jews

What is it that determines the director's choice and adaptation of religious materials in the play? I have shown in the previous two themes how religious experiences and theological positions form the "world behind the text." The pre-understanding of directors and agents of translation also derived from their reading of previous translations or versions of this play, and from reviews and scholarly research. In three of the productions under study, sympathy for Jews emerged as a recurring theme.

Perng admitted that, of all the versions that he watched, it was Trevor Nunn's version of *The Merchant* that made the deepest impact on him. He later passed on his sympathetic attitude towards Jews to the director and actors, which resulted in a positive portrayal of Shylock in the court scene. The quotation that follows is a good illustration of Perng's interpretation under the influence of Nunn's version.

The murderer [Shylock] in Nunn's version could not kill: [at his first attempt], [he] retreated, then muttered "Courage" the second time, then "Kill," and he said, no. This [scene] is more complicated. First, Shylock's character is manifested. On the surface, he [Shylock] said I hate you, I kill you, but killing is not that simple, it needs a lot of courage. Second, why didn't Portia stop him at the first attempt? She watched and stood still [Interviewer: She wants him to die], but why want him to die? [Interviewer: she is afraid that Antonio would steal her husband]. Yes, this becomes more complicated. This scene has not changed Shakespeare [his text], no words added [to the text], [the text] depends on your performance. Director Lu Poshen agreed that Perng's briefing had some degree of influence on his directorship. He attached more emphasis to describing "human nature" in the production. I shall illustrate this emphasis on human nature in another sub-theme.

Daniel S. P. Yang, who directed The Merchant in 1984 in Hong Kong, also revealed in the interview his sympathy towards the Jew. "In the first session when I talked about directorial concept, I mentioned, very specific[ally], this is the view I am taking, I am sympathetic to Shylock." He told the actors, according to the interview, that in *The Merchant* "the most important thing is how to treat Shylock as a character." Why is he giving Shylock sympathetic treatment? I suggest this is related to his religious experiences as a church leaver, the burden that he encountered as a Catholic, which in the end led him to this line of interpretation. He believed that the actors did not have the sophistication in Shakespearean studies that he had.

Yang's sympathetic treatment, unlike Zhang Bowen's, did not lead his audience into a sympathetic attitude towards Shylock. "Sympathy" was a recurring word in his interview: he wanted to "tell the audience specifically that Jews in Christian society are mistreated. Shylock said clearly in the script, you kick me, you call me cur, this is what he said, I think (what he said) is true, Jewish people are mistreated, for sure." Such sympathetic treatment is also mentioned in his reflective article in 1988,[13] in the course of which he cited the history of the suffering Jews from the Middle Ages to the Renaissance period, "because they were associated with Judas who betrayed Christ."[14] He admitted in the same article that his interpretation was not "middle of the road." On the other hand, it was not his intention to go overboard, as had happened in other post-Hitler productions.

Underlying this sympathetic treatment is the notion of Old Testament dignity, a theme particularly featured in Daniel Yang's production. He defined this Old Testament dignity in his 1988 article[15] in the words "Shylock should lose the battle at the end of the trial scene with dignity, not with humiliation." In the interview, he cited Old Testament dignity as his main line of interpretation, "when Salerio one of the Jews put a cross on his neck, made him kneel to beg to the duke, he turned around, saw this cross, totally ruined, totally beaten, he should cry but not cry, I let him go out and cry, this is Old Testament dignity, Christians are too harsh with him." In Yang's view,

---

13. See Yang, "Working with RSC Actor Tony Church on the Role of Shylock," 53–62.

14. Ibid.

15. Ibid.

Shylock is a proud and stubborn man who will not show any signs of defeat in front of his victors.[16] In the production, he turned this Old Testament dignity into a dignified, silent exit without words, where the Christians in the play are to "hold their victorious cheers until Shylock is out of sight—in order to maximize the effect of this silent exit . . . ," thus creating a "quite powerful and effective" result.

In Ko's production Shylock is prominently featured as a kind father who loves his daughter. This interpretation and characterization was in fact first seen in Yang's 1986 production. Yang wrote in his article,[17] that Shylock intended the bond as a "merry bond," not a "pre-meditated, vicious scheme." He intended only to humiliate Antonio by making him, a rich and influential merchant, sign "such an insulting bond." But he, after learning of Jessica's elopement with the Christian playboy Lorenzo, became so deeply hurt that he decided to insist on the bond. That his daughter gave away his late wife Leah's turquoise ring for a monkey was a cruel blow to him.

This line of interpretation continued in the production of Ko Tinlung in 2010: he had previously acted as Bassanio in Yang's 1986 production. Ko cited a similar interpretation in the interview and in a pre-performance seminar on 18 September 2010, where it was the elopement of Jessica that provoked Shylock. But when I asked Ko if that was what he inherited from Yang's production in which he acted Bassanio, he denied this and said that the director did not give that interpretation. Yang, on the other hand, told me that this was the groundwork he laid in his production.

Not all directors or translators in this post-Holocaust period showed the same sympathy for the Jews, nor did all directors cameo under the influence of previous versions. In her article[18] Zhang Qihong cited an English film version of *The Merchant* in the 1940s as one source of inspiration. The film is set almost like a tragedy, depicting Shylock as the person who takes revenge on behalf of his nation. But Zhang strove to strike a different style from previous film-makers or directors or, in her own words, not to "walk in the shadow of predecessors." She disagreed with this sympathetic treatment, which is like giving "a sacred halo to Shylock, which is totally different from Shakespeare's original depiction of Shylock." The inspiration she got from this previous version was not to follow suit, not to "mystify Shakespeare or deify him" and never to put Shakespeare on a pedestal. Rather, she was inspired to demystify Shakespeare by bringing him to the "soil of China, [so that Shakespeare can] befriend the mass public." Remember that

---

16. Ibid.
17. Ibid, 57–58.
18. Zhang, "Some Points in the Process of Implementation," 280–287.

Zhang attaches much importance to the issue of "freedom," or spatiality, in her lifeworld. The metaphors that she uses in describing her introduction of Shakespeare, such as "soil," "ivory tower," "walk in the shadow," are all connected with space. Breaking free from a shadow or pre-set space is of paramount importance in her lifeworld.

Though Zhang emphasized that her portrayal of Shylock breaks free from previous productions, her interpretation is controlled by the prevalent Marxist ideology. Zhang sees Shylock as the representative of the feudal system, and to her the major conflicts are between the feudal moneylender and the emerging capitalist, i.e. Antonio. In the interview Zhang describes him as a greedy, selfish man.

Zhang's interpretation of Shylock as a villain is carried through to the Cantonese operatic version by Ni Huiying, who acted the part of Portia in Zhang Qihong's production. In the interview, she described Shylock as a calculating, cold-blooded man who wants to take Antonio's life. "This money slave sees money as larger than his life. When the duke ordered the confiscation of his property, Shylock said, Oh, I would rather you took a pound of my flesh. This is a graphic depiction of his character."

Impression of Christian Characters: Negative and Hypocritical

Christian hypocrisy is commonly mentioned by directors and translators. Some of the hypocrisy is exemplified by the way Christians treated Shylock. Rupert Chan said:

> In our play this (Christian hypocrisy) is illustrated. Christians like to brag, how merciful they are, e.g. how they treat the Jews, but their actions are not consistent. The Jews were persecuted in such a way that they bit back. They are very tragic. His daughter was taken away, and he was despised all his life, he only asked for what was due to him. He lost the case in court, and had his property confiscated, he had to convert to another religion. Tragic. I don't think Christians are [remarkable], they were insincere, persuaded (Jessica) to run away, wooed as a rich woman. In the case of Antonio, he looks like a good man, but he treated Shylock like a dog, and had an inexplicable hatred towards [him].

Chan sees this Christian hypocrisy as a common theme across other Shakespeare's plays, and this comes from his reading of Shakespeare as one who disapproves of Puritans: "Shakespeare thought that they [Puritans) are hypocrites, they speak pious words, but in their hearts they are very cruel ... In Shakespeare's plays there are a lot of implicit criticisms of Puritans ... the criticisms of Christians can be considered as a way of criticising Puritans."

To reinforce this negative impression, Chan, a Catholic, cites his personal experience which led him to the view, after comparing different religions, that Protestantism is less pluralistic than Catholicism. "I think Catholicism is most tolerant. Besides its own religion, Catholicism tolerates Judaism and Christianity, more than Protestantism [tolerates other religions]. It (Christianity) is very much against Catholicism. This has its historical roots, because Protestants were persecuted [by Catholics]. Catholicism has a lot of common ground with Buddhism. Recently, a Zen Buddhist came to Hong Kong for a retreat that took place in Wu Kai Sha Youth Village, and among the participants were Catholic nuns. Religions need not be mutually exclusive." Here, Chan is referring to the exclusivity of Protestantism, on which Ko was in agreement: "Why did Shakespeare introduce [the forced conversion]? I think the theme is belief and prejudice—Protestants have gone to extremes [in their prejudice against the Jews]"

The above quotation shows that the negative impression of Christians, which is rooted in the agents' unsatisfactory experiences with Christianity, had a bearing on their construction of Christian identity and Shylock's character in the production.

Others derived their impression of Christian hypocrisy from the way Christians converted Shylock by force. Jack Shu, who translated the 2000 production, commented, "If Christians put so much emphasis on love, equality of mankind, empathy, why do they force people to do certain things, i.e. use legal force to convert people? This is force, not love."

Similarly, Perng held a negative impression of Christians in the play, which later turned to a sympathetic treatment of Shylock. The omission of Christian identity in this operatic version, it seems to me, is related to Perng's unease as a Christian when he saw that Christians are portrayed as hypocrites. Perng said, "He [Shylock] insists on the bond, because this Christian has treated him badly in the past, spat on him, said he is a dog, and said, lending me money is like lending to an enemy, I [Antonio] will continue to spit on you when I see you again. *Such a reaction [is] from a Christian!* (my emphasis added) So, Shakespeare doesn't just criticize Jews, he also criticizes the Christians' hypocrisy." In Perng's experience of life, the Christian attributes which he observed in the real world were different from those of the Christians portrayed in Shakespeare. So in the line "Such a reaction from a Christian!," he tries to draw a line between the fictional Christians and real-life Christians, who in his experience are merciful rather than hypocritical.

Not only did Perng criticize Antonio's hypocrisy, his impression of Portia is that she is a "shrewd" lady, one who is jealous of Bassanio's intimate friendship with Antonio. This may be related to his exposure to Trevor Nunn's portrayal of Portia, which was cited by Perng as his source of inspiration for this production. He recalled that in Nunn's version, Portia did not intervene at Shylock's first attempt to stab Antonio, she just watched and stood still, because she was afraid that Antonio might steal her husband. In the interview, Perng elaborated on his impression of Portia as an unmerciful Christian, who appeared to give Shylock the right to decide whether or not to enforce the bond, although in the end he lost everything by insisting on the supremacy of law. Portia was another hypocritical Christian, who on one hand stressed the importance of mercy in the "mercy speech," but on the other hand she as a Christian also enforced the law without showing mercy to Shylock. Perng's conclusion is that *"if the play is performed from a Christian point of view, this scene has to be changed."*(my emphasis)

Both good and bad

Yang in the house program of the 1984 production said that he took a middle of the road position on Antonio. This neutral treatment can be traced back to his impression of Christians in the play—he sees them as both good and bad. "I think in the play there are both good Christians and bad Christians, Salerio and Solanio are so-so Christians, they are not perfect example of citizens in Venice, they are Christians, and looked down on the Jews, their [contempt of Jews] is worse than Antonio's, well that's Christian. But in the production none of the Christian characters are remarkable." His balanced view of Christians in the play gives rise to a balanced approach in his adaptation process. He truly admires Antonio's generosity, but disapproves of his discrimination against Jews. He also admires the wit and beauty of Portia, so in Yang's interpretation not all Christians are hypocrites, there are both good and bad Christians.

Genre

Directors and translators who worked for the productions in either Hong Kong, Taiwan or China have indicated their awareness of the differing interpretations of the play, whether as comedy or tragicomedy. Some of them decided to make it a comedy despite the overwhelming sympathy for the Jews post-Holocaust. Zhang saw it as a romantic comedy, despite her prior research on the varying interpretations of the play as a tragedy and as a comedy. She showed her independent thinking and strove to move on from her previous acceptance of the reading of Heinrich Heine, an eighteenth century writer who saw Shylock as a tragic figure.[19] What underlay her insistence on maintaining the play as a comedy was her determination to bring Shakespeare's original intention to the audience, which overcame her respect for tradition.[20] "Is it the purpose of Shakespeare's comedy to make people cry, to let the audience sympathise with this 'bloodsucker'—the moneylender?" This respect for Shakespeare's authorial intention is seen in the interview: "If this motif was not written (by Shakespeare), then why should you as director or actor impose your views on Shakespeare? I don't know whether Shakespeare, now in the 'yellow spring underworld',[21] agrees or not. If [we are] to respect the writer's right, we should not impose on him what he did not write." Here, I can see that Zhang's creative freedom is still bound by tradition. While trying her best not to walk in the shadow of others, her respect for tradition prevents her from making abrupt changes to the plot.

Along with Chris Shum and Jack Shu, Yang also views this as a romantic comedy, but with serious moments especially Shylock's forced conversion. Ko, however, sees the genre as more complicated, which arises from his theological position in regard to the concept of mercy. That is, Shylock is a tragic figure ill-used by unmerciful Christians. "I say, mainly it is a comedy, because of its structure with a happy ending. But not for Shylock, for him it is a tragicomedy. To Christians it is a comedy. To Jews it is a tragicomedy. Knowing that it is a comedy, one can decide on the comic moments." Ko then cites examples where comic moments can be seen in the play, e.g. the scene when Shylock learnt from Tubal of his daughter's elopement.

Accordingly, the way in which the directors interpret the genre of the play leads to different degrees of translatability of the Judeo-Christian conflict and the religious element. Zhang, who wants to be true to Shakespeare's comic treatment, in the end suppresses the religious conflict, and highlights what is "true, kind and beautiful" instead. Ko and Chan, who see the complexity of the genre, give full play to the conflicts between the two parties and highlight the multifaceted nature of human beings, both of Shylock and of Antonio.

---

19. Ibid.
20. Ibid.
21. This is a Chinese expression that means the underworld where the dead lives.

Directorial Approach and Emphasis

What themes are being emphasized in these productions? As Gadamer says, performance is interpretation—the decision as to which themes to highlight is not arbitrary, but traces its origin to the agents' ideology or theological position. The highlighting of certain themes such as feminism or humanism will inevitably lead to the suppression of other themes such as religion. In the house program of the play, Perng mentions that he sees the main theme of the play as encompassing three main bonds—the selection of the husband of Portia, who is under a contract set by her late father requiring her to marry the one who chooses the right casket; the bond between Antonio and Shylock, and the marriage bond between Bassanio and Portia. So the concept of bond and covenant naturally appears in the interview, and his reading of the characteristics of a human bond is under the influence of his Christian theology.

> I grasped the theme [bond], because several incidents occurred surrounding the covenant. This covenant has two sides, either to protect you or to bind you. If there is not a slash / [in the title of the play] between the two words 约 (covenant) 束 (translation: bondage), people tend to think of it as constraint. But this covenant 约 and bondage 束 has two sides. *The positive side of a covenant is that it is the covenant between God and human beings. But human covenants also have this kind of issue.* (italics added by myself).

"This issue" refers to the construction that human beings impose on a bond. One can see that although the religious material is lost in the production, the Christian interpretation has left its footprint in the translator's emphasis.

Female directors, such as Zhang Qihong and her successor Ni Huiying, put the emphasis on the female character Portia and portrayed her as the title character. In the interview, Zhang admitted her affection for this character. Zhang's pursuit of women's liberation can be seen in the quotation below:

> I like Portia, the new female, very much. As a director, I like freedom, I like her courageous, clever arrangement which frees her from her bondage. She dresses as a male in order to be a lawyer and strike down the greedy and selfish Shylock: what he can request is only a pound of flesh, neither more nor less. I think this shows Shakespeare's passion for women in the Renaissance

period and his respect for female dignity. He commends women's liberation as reflected in Portia's wisdom.

It is worth noting that the keyword "freedom" appears again in the quotation above. In her lifeworld, "freedom" seems so indispensable that it becomes a reason for her fondness for the character Portia who knows how to free herself from the bond.

Ni Huiying likes this play because "Portia is the cleverest woman in Shakespeare's plays." But beyond her fondness for this female character, the interview shows her intention of promoting the Chinese heritage and national identity. This can be seen in the following quotation in which she hails the humane Chinese culture and criticizes the shortcomings of the Western belief system. "The Western legal system has its shortcomings—according to the rule-based Western culture, this bond is reasonable, because it is signed on mutual consent. However, this bond is unethical in Chinese culture, especially as it concerns the taking of life. Thus, it is necessary to consider a cultural exchange between the East and the West for the development and enhancement of human thinking." The assertion of Chinese heritage can be similarly found in Zhang's production, as she hoped to blend the uniqueness of Chinese aesthetics into the Western-style spoken drama. She says, "I name Shakespeare as God (Shangdi), I invite God (Shangdi) to Mainland China. In order to showcase him to Chinese audiences, I need to make Shakespeare attractive to the Chinese: it should be innovative, but not just to put something over, and to let a Chinese audience watch something foreign. Foreign [plays] can be given a Chinese aesthetic touch. I think Chinese art forms, especially our folk songs, are more aesthetic, dynamic, and visual. I mean to make a difference in this area, not to walk in others' shadows." Zhang's assertion of national identity, and her determination to make a difference by indigenising a foreign product supplies, in my view, the motivating force to create her unique Chinese Shakespeare which refuses to import any foreign religious content into the local production.

One common theme underlying the above two productions by Zhang and Ni is the acknowledgement of the good as opposed to the evil. Good is exemplified by Antonio's good deeds while evil is represented by Shylock's cruelty and greed. Zhang's emphasis of one theme over another is rooted in her ideology. Zhang said *The Merchant of Venice* touches on the issues of Israel, racial conflict, and religious conflict. They are not easily "touchable"' The word "untouchable" has a context wider than the "sensitivity of religious matters under Communist rule: the repetition of the word "conflict" points to the negative connotation this word has in the post–Cultural Revolution period that is still full of conflicts and power struggles—hence the shift to the perennially popular theme of good and evil instead. Such highlighting, in Gadamer's terms, is most obvious in Ko's directorial emphasis, which is on belief and prejudice. As a result, the religious conflicts that arise due to different belief systems are highlighted in the production.

Social Relevance

Zhang Qihong, Perng, and Shum all agree that a production should be relevant to society, i.e. they all attach importance to the social function of a play. Coincidentally, their productions all have their religious content removed, in order to highlight themes that are socially relevant. This is related to the history of church-state relations in China, where the church's influence in the social sphere is restricted by the government.[22] The social relevance of churches or other religious organizations is comparatively weaker than their Western counterparts. Zhang believes that, in today's society, Antonio's good character is much needed, although she does not relate this good character to Christianity, as shown in the quotation below:

> Interviewer: Do you think *The Merchant* is relevant to today's society?
>
> Zhang: Yes, the relevance is strong. We need honest merchants, qualities such as truth, kindness and beauty are always needed. *The Merchant's* humanistic spirit, the desire for freedom, true friendship . . . Antonio is such a kind person who helps his friends. I think there are not many of these people nowadays. I think it is necessary, very necessary.

Perng believes that the ethnic issues portrayed in *The Merchant* are relevant to Taiwan's situation, and that highlighting what is socially relevant can draw in an audience. The quotation that follows illustrates the plot's relevance to a Taiwan audience.

> Interviewer: This adaptation from religious to racial conflict—is it related to Taiwan's situation?
>
> Perng: Yes, I think it is related. For any theatre to succeed, the audience should be a contemporary: if the audience don't watch then it's a failure, e.g. if an audience came round to it only after 50 years. Shakespeare has its appeal because the issues talked about are important. Is this play appealing to a

---

22. For a comprehensive historical overview of the state-church relationship in China, see Ying, *Church-State Relationship in Contemporary China*, 1999.

> Taiwan audience? I think yes, that's why people go for it. The story itself attracts people. But we still want to consider where the "outsider" stands" [in Taiwan], because this [ethnic conflict] is a continuing problem since the National party took over in the past 20–30 years . . .

The above quotation serves to illustrate that while attaching importance to the social function of a play is not the single or predominant factor in shaping the religious dimension of a play, this factor, when combined with a conflicting ideology, eventually leads to a non-religious interpretation and translation of the play.

Catering for audience expectations

Not all productions are made to satisfy market expectations. Zhang Bowen's Shylock in 2010 was an amateur production, offered to audience free of charge. Without relying on ticket sales as the production's source of income, the team decided to retain the religious content irrespective of the audience's taste.

Bowen Zhang said, "We are all amateur, non-professional [actors]. If we were profit-making, we certainly would not work on this theme. This play is certainly not a commercial production. Few will be willing to buy tickets [for this play]—maybe only a small number, certainly not a good number." Again, this decision was not purely a market decision—it was also a theological decision. In her production, Shylock was portrayed as an oppressed figure following the dramaturge's theatrical experience as an actor in a play about Jewish suffering. The following interview excerpt shows how one's pre-understanding of *The Merchant* is shaped by previous versions:

> Originally, I told Liu Lei [the dramaturge who brought this production to China] that I was not interested in this serious production. I thought it was all about words. Besides. I am not interested in religion. But in a production I am one of the cast. Shanghai and Hamburg are sister cities. In Shanghai there is a Jewish museum. In this production a director from Hamburg was invited to Shanghai to recruit actors, and that is why I was contacted. During the rehearsal of the show, which was about how the Jews suffered in the Second World War, how they were persecuted . . . the Jewish museum used to be a refugee site for these Jews. They rehearsed for a day. We watched their performance in November 2009, we felt particularly moved. I suddenly found the relationship between the Jews and us . . .

Zhang Bowen's initial indifference to religion is typical of the attitude of Chinese audiences. However, the above interview shows that one who is originally uninterested in religion can change their attitude if given some priming that provokes an interest in religion or in Judeo Christian relations.

The need to conform to the theatrical conventions of traditional Chinese operas as a way of catering to audience taste helps to explain the omission of religious content in Perng's translation. In the interview, Perng's sees the success of adaptation of Shakespeare plays in the following two ways: "firstly, whether we can capture Shakespeare's spirit. What to keep, what to leave out, everyone's view is different. Secondly, the arias must be sung well. Peking Opera should be in the Peking Opera tradition, Cantonese Opera in the Cantonese tradition. If those who know Peking Opera point out that the performance is not conforming to tradition, or has many flaws, then whether it is a Shakespearean adaptation is not important."

He further explained that Chinese traditional operas should be set in a particular period. However, it would be difficult to find a period in China when such religious conflict occurred. The decision to shift from religious to ethnic issues, he admitted, took audience expectations into account, in the sense that audiences would find it irrelevant if the play was about religious conflicts which are non-existent in Taiwan.

Are religious conflicts totally non-existent in Taiwan? In the 1970s, in an attempt to promote Mandarin as the national language, the Nationalist government had tried, without success, to ban the use of the Taiwanese dialect Bible which is a collaborative project translated by the Bible Society, the Taiwan arm of United Bible Societies and the Catholic Church in Taiwan. Similarly, the Nationalist Party has interfered with the establishment of the New Testament church since the 1970s. During the Japanese occupation (1895–1945), Shintoism was enforced among the people in Taiwan, all Western missionaries were expelled, and churches, Christian schools and seminaries were closed down or taken over. Thus, religious oppression did exist in Taiwan, but for a limited period before Perng became a believer and thus he had no any direct experience in such persecution. One can see that the decision not to highlight religious conflict in *Bond* is not purely sociological (i.e. conforming to the socio-cultural conditions), it also reflects the individual theology of the translator.

Universal Shakespeare

Shum mentioned that "Shakespeare timelessness," a notion which he picked up from Daniel Yang, serves to justify his approach not to set his production within a historical period. Hence the use of modern clothing (e.g. suits) by the characters. Without a historical background, religious and racial issues that were difficult to approach were cut by the director. Shylock was no longer a Jew, but contextualised as an outsider.

Shum explained his directorial approach based on "Shakespeare timelessness" as follows:

> I think *The Merchant of Venice* has two issues that are difficult to approach. First, he Jews, difficult to talk about that [in theatre]—should we [adapt to] the Chiu Chow people?[23] At the time of the show ethnic conflicts were not that serious, now the [equivalent of the] Jews would be the people from the north [i.e. Mainland], but there wasn't such [conflict] at the time, so I didn't talk at this level. Second, in terms of Christianity, in Hong Kong, if you talk about religion, they are not fanatical about religion, not like in religious Ireland where people give thanks over meals. But I think that's crazy, we describe them as 'Jesus youth 耶青'.[24] They hold their faith to a fanatical degree. We say this is 'Jesus youth behaviour 耶青行為'. This term has been current in [Hong Kong] for the past 3-4 years. [It means] Have faith to an extent where you give thanks as you wake up . . . so I thought [to myself], how can we get rid of this way of thinking? I wondered about setting the scene back in the Cretaceous period, i.e. before the Jurassic period. But I decided that this wouldn't work—did the contract mentality in *The Merchant of Venice* exist in that period? No, so [we] changed the Jews to "cross-the-river dragon 過江龍,"[25] decided by me and Jack Shu.

The above quotation shows that underlying this notion of Shakespeare's timelessness is the director's personal attitude towards faith. He doubted the interest of the audience in religious matters, but at the same he had already labelled those pious Christians who gave thanks in Ireland and Hong Kong as "crazy." So even when he was directing the play in a

---

23. Chiu Chow 潮州, or Chao Zhou in Mandarin, is an affluent province in Southern China which is a breeding ground for numerous well-known merchants, who came to Hong Kong to set up businesses. For instance, tycoon Li Kashing originates from Chiu Chow. Thus people from Chiu Chow, who are reputed for their business acumen, can be considered as a contextualised equivalent of the Jews in the play.

24. "Ye Ching 耶青" is a derogatory term for young adults who fervently follow Jesus. The term bears the same pronunciation of another term in Chinese—young coconut.

25. "Cross -the-river dragon 過江龍" refers to a foreigner who enters the foray with the locals. He or she may be a prominent figure in his homeland and is in pursuit of a new foothold in another country.

religious environment, his dislike for Christianity would still preclude him from retaining the religious dimension. Shakespeare's timelessness is just a theory to justify his suppression of religious themes as well as making other adaptations.

From the interviews, Shakespeare's timelessness is implied in other productions, but may not be a notion as specifically spelt out as in Shum's transcript. In Zhang Qihong's production, which subdued religious content, she introduced a scene in which the ghost of a Chinese moneylender of the Ming Dynasty had a dialogue with Shylock. "My idea is that a person like Shylock can exist in China, or anywhere else in the world. He does not belong to a particular nation." Not only Shylock should be universalized, but Shakespeare as well: "The works of the great playwright Shakespeare belong not only to the United Kingdom, but to the whole of humankind." Indeed, her universalizing strategy in conformity with market expectations by focusing on universal themes such as truth and beauty eventually contributes to the reduction of the religious dimension, as the following quotation shows: "Audiences in China, particularly in the eighties, are not interested in issues in Israel, or racial and religious issues. Whether Shylock merits sympathy, and what kind of sympathy, has its historical background and relates to his race's humiliation. I think the focus should be kindness and evil, the praising of truth, benevolence and beauty. [As for] selfishness and greed—this can be found in any country."

Ko, while agreeing that Shakespeare is universal, did not think that this timelessness could be applied to *The Merchant*, and tried to direct the play as if in Shakespeare's time, i.e. the Elizabethan period. He reasoned that "Shakespeare is universal, its period can be changed, but in my view, *The Merchant's* period should not be changed. The original period should be maintained. If we change the period, a lot of issues become hard to explain. In which modern period should we set it? If not Venice, but set it in China, have we seen *Judeo-Christian conflict* in China (emphasis added by myself)? There isn't much [conflict] between the Chinese and the Jews, so the answer is no. Set it in China Town? No way. Set it in contemporary Venice? Contemporary Venice is *not like that* [without Judeo-Christian conflicts]" (emphasis added by myself)." As I reflect on the above quotation more deeply, I conclude that the decision not to contextualize based on "Shakespeare timelessness" is a theological one, because ultimately Ko sees the theme of Judeo-Christian conflict as one not to be suppressed. Other directors such as Ni Huiying have contextualized the play to a Macanese setting, and it still appealed to the audience. Why then can one not set it in China, or contemporary Venice, by adapting the religious dimension? Ko clearly wanted to highlight the theme of religious conflicts, and hence his decision not to contextualize the play.

Conclusion

I have subjected these interviews to a phenomenological approach in order to make sense of the interviewees' lifeworld, and how this lifeworld impacted on their interpretation of the religious dimension, and their subsequent directorial treatment and characterization. The interview excerpts show that certain features of their lifeworld which they deem important—be they spatiality, temporality, embodiment or inter-subjectivity—manifest themselves in the script or on the stage. The most obvious examples can be seen in Yang's burden translated into a cross forced upon Shylock, and Zhang's emphasis on freedom which led her unconsciously to remove the forced conversion which went against her perception of religious freedom. In phenomenological psychology, pre-understanding can be understood along the social dimension, the cognitive dimension and the emotional dimension.[26] The interview excerpts show that these directors and agents of translation often derive the meaning of religious concepts from their pre-understanding, including their own religious experiences and their exposure to previous versions of the play. Such experiences may affect them socially, for instance making them view Christians as hypocrites, while some experiences may affect them emotionally. One can recall how Zhang Bowen's sympathy for the Jews was stimulated by a previous production in which she played a part. The cognitive side of pre-understanding informs us that some concepts are developed in a pre-conscious and pre-reflective way,[27] and this is illustrated by the way Shu and Zhang read "forced conversion" in the play. So unconscious was their rejection of the concept that they could not recall having omitted the relevant lines, and both came to the conclusion that the omission might have been as a result of their ideological conflict.

The above analysis also shows that the adaptation of the religious dimension rests primarily upon the directors' own religious experiences and theological position. Aesthetic concerns and market expectations, while still contributing to the treatment of the religious dimension, are not the determining factors. Echoing Gadamer's view that every performance is an interpretation, I suggest that the decision to translate or not translate the religious dimension is a theological decision. The decision as to which themes to highlight is more theological than market-oriented. Given the relatively small

26. Dahlberg et al, *Reflective Lifeworld Research*, 129–134.
27. Ibid.

Christian population in Greater China, the director or translator can easily do away with all Christian discourse in the script without affecting market expectations. And yet, in some productions, the theme of religious conflict is not only retained but is highlighted—with some explanatory material, for instance in Zhang Bowen's production, by relating the persecution of the Jews to Chinese suffering in order to make the audience understand.

The above analysis also shows that the relationship between the translatability of the religious dimension and the agent's theology is not a straightforward one. For instance, among our interviewees are two ex-Catholic Christians, Shum and Yang. Shum omitted all Christian references because they were "unimportant" to the main theme, while Yang used 'Old Testament dignity" as the main theme, illustrating Shylock's tragic character. Ko, with his anti-religious mentality, did not view religious issues as a peripheral theme, but centerd on the theme 'belief and prejudice', portraying Christians as the ones who create prejudice. As the story of the agents' religious experiences unfolds in the interviews, it is possible to see the complexity behind their directorial treatment, which is rooted in their unique encounter with Christianity.

Another interesting observation is that while these interviews show how their interpretation is grounded in history, i.e. their reading might be influenced by previous versions, in the end each reading is also a present activity. It is true that pre-understanding has an influence on present interpretation, but interpretation is also more open to the otherness, i.e. new experiences, just as Gadamer has said, " The author, because of the many experiences he has had and the knowledge he has drawn from them, is particularly well equipped to have new experiences and to learn from them."[28] For example, revelation of the relationship between Chinese and Jews totally transformed Zhang Bowen's interpretation of the Judeo-Christian conflicts. Zhang Qihong is a good example of showing that interpretation entails two horizons. The one who strove to liberate herself from the traditional baggage of post-Holocaust interpretation, is still succumbing to the then prevailing Marxist interpretation.

As mentioned above, the translatability of the religious dimension is a complex subject. It is now time to examine the translatability issue in our next, concluding chapter.

---

28. Gadamer, *Truth and Method*, 355.

7

The Problems of Translating Religious Language in Plays

AT THE BEGINNING OF the book, I asked questions about the translatability of religious language. The complexity of theatre translations requires a sophisticated model. This chapter, departing from the conventional way of approaching these questions from the semantic or linguistic perspective, uses a ground-breaking approach by drawing on Ninian Smart's model of the seven dimensions of religions as mentioned in Chapter 1. I approach translatability not only on the reader level, but also on the audience level; not only on the linguistic aspects on the page, but also the semiotic aspects on the stage; focusing not only on the effects at the receiving end, but using the hermeneutics of translation agents as the start point of the translatability issue.

Smart's seven dimensions are

- doctrinal and philosophical
- mythic and narrative
- ethical and legal
- emotional and experiential
- social and institutional
- ritual and practical
- material.

In the section that follows, I seek to illuminate the areas that are untranslatable, and the areas that are translatable, in a play with religious concepts. Biblical translators tend to agree on the notion that "all translations fail" and that no translations are adequate to suit all purposes.¹ But to what extent are religious texts not translatable? To answer this question, the notion of translatability should be set in a wider context. While conventionally it refers to the translatability of concepts from one language to another, I would like to widen its scope to cover the transfer of ideas from page to stage, and from directors and translators to the audience, owing to the intersemiotic nature of this transfer.

Taking together the findings of the textual analysis of translated scripts and the data collected from interviewing directors, agents of translation and from the reflective journals and reviews of individuals, the doctrinal dimension presents one of the biggest challenges in the translation process.

Untranslatability of Doctrinal Dimension

One should recall in Chapter 1 the untranslatability of "Dasein" and the proposition of Schleiermacher that philosophical words should not be domesticated but should be translated in a philosophical discourse. Here I shall borrow thoughts from Alasdair MacIntyre² on the problems of translating from one tradition into another. Basically, he believes that adequately expressing the convictions, presumptions and beliefs embedded in the discourse of some traditions is so difficult so that speakers of English should be wary of ever thinking that we can translate another's discourse simply by matching words and phrases in their language with words and phrases in the English language. Stephen Foul in his article³ "Could Horace Talk with the Hebrews?" makes two supplementary points: first, that "our contemporary moral discourse is a minefield of incommensurable disagreements . . . because we, as the liberal heirs of the Enlightenment, lack the skills for rationally supporting our own moral discourse, much less adjudicating between conflicting discourses," and second, relating to the illusion that people have regarding the common ground, "fostered in part by the fact that we wrongly assume that because we use the same words we are talking about the same thing," e.g. a term such as "justice": "each tradition invokes different (sometimes irreconcilable) convictions and presumptions when using the term."

Turning to the subject matter of the book, Portia's mercy speech was substantially reduced in a few productions, with a consequent loss of the balance between mercy and justice. This is a telling example of MacIntyre's

---

1. See Norton, "Confessions of the Perplexed," September 2013.
2. MacIntyre, *Whose Justice? Which Rationality?*, 1988.
3. Fowl, "Could Horace Talk with the Hebrews?," 1–20.

notion of untranslatability. Ni Huiying reduced it because the Chinese culture has a different notion of justice—the saying of "the law takes account of humanity 法律不外乎人情" aptly illustrates that this is why the directors view the bond of contract as so unreasonable that it could not occur in Mainland China. Mercy, no longer an exclusively Christian concept in modern English, cannot be translated and understood in a way that involves the forgiveness of wrongdoings in a Christian sense. Mercy from the Christian tradition embedded in Portia's speech in Elizabethan England can only be understood in the Chinese tradition as the equivalent of compassion, or the Buddhist notion of compassion (慈悲, *ci bei*), which does not specifically point to the forgiveness of sins. Thus, the word 慈悲, *ci bei* is used in most Chinese translations, or "仁 ren," the Confucian notion of kindness, in other versions. Although "仁 ren," being upheld as the universal virtue that makes men fully and perfectly human, is often seen as the equivalent of the Christian virtue agape, "仁 ren" has a human-centerd-ness that does not offer explicitly heaven's love for man as a model for imitation, unlike the Christian teaching of love which is rooted in God's love for man through the revelation of Jesus Christ. "仁 ren" is primarily concerned with relationships between men and the perfectibility of the human nature. The tensions between God-centerd mercy and human-centerd "仁 ren" inevitably lead to the loss of the Christian dimension in this human-centerd cultural tradition.[4] Accordingly, total cultural equivalence in the doctrinal/philosophical dimension is as unachievable as equating apples with oranges.

With the few exceptions from Mainland China where director Zhang and producer Ni appear to imply that mercy is shown to Shylock by the major characters, all others in their reading of *The Merchant* have expressly said that mercy is not shown by Christians. This is an apt illustration of the fact that the interpretation and the translatability of theological concepts change across cultures. Ni Huiying, as an actress in Zhang's 1980 production, inherited Zhang's Marxist interpretation of the play—Shylock being an exploiter and manipulator of capital does not deserve mercy. However, across the straits and the border, directors and translators in Hong Kong and Taiwan see mercy differently. They agree with Shylock because they consider that mercy is not shown to him. On the one hand, they recognise that mercy on condition of conversion is intended for the good of Shylock; on the other hand, they disapprove of this kind of conditional mercy, which in essence is not mercy at all. This overwhelmingly sympathetic treatment underpins their theological understanding of God's unconditional mercy to

---

4. For a comparison between the Confucian values and Christian thoughts, see Julia Ching, "I-Confucianism: A Philosophy of Man," In Whitehead and Shaw , *China and Christianity: Historical and Future Encounters*, 8–34.

humankind which does not require Christian conversion in salvation. One recalls Chris Shum's comment in the interview that "if I am a good person, I think, if God exists, even if I am not baptised I will still [be saved]." The notion of conditional mercy, i.e. belief in Christianity leading to salvation, is not translatable by either believing directors/translators or non-believers. Daniel Yang, educated in the US, shows a similar resistance to such conditional mercy—he reckons that the requirement to confess sins before participating in the Eucharist is too big a burden. The US educated Perng, a practising believer, rejects the idea of conditional forgiveness, because the imposition of conditions on Shylock as a way of pardoning his sins is no forgiveness at all. When the notion is met with resistance from the agents of translation, it is hardly surprising that the audience could not comprehend Christian mercy, writing it down as hypocrisy, as in Ko's production.

This leads one to another untranslatable notion cited by Portia—salvation. Whether in the 1914 translation by Laura White or in the recent Chinese stage translations, the notion is either cut or subdued (e.g. translated as "live" in White's version). There is resistance to this Christian notion of salvation in the prevailing socio-cultural climate of Greater China. The three great traditions in China—the Confucian, Daoist and Buddhist—do not require salvation through conversion, but salvation through self-achievement, i.e., good deeds, good karma and ritual practices (such as chanting Buddhist mantras). It is not difficult then to understand Chris Shum's emphasis on being a "good person" as a condition for salvation, rather than conversion.

This leads one to the next issue for discussion: why has the notion of Christian conversion been mostly left untranslated or deliberately cut out? Conversion is not celebrated in Chinese culture which emphasises the harmony of different thoughts, as manifested in the teaching "harmony with a difference 和而不同," a Confucian philosophy that is conducive to pluralistic thinking. In China and elsewhere in Asia, people live under a pluralistic tradition[5] where different religions co-exist without excluding others. The history of the Jews in China is a good example: as early as the Ming Dynasty, Jews were allowed to maintain their faith and tradition, and to worship in their synagogues, without being required to convert to the prevailing religions. In the Chinese Rites Controversy in the seventeenth and eighteenth centuries, the Jesuits argued for the maintenance of ancestral rites as a legitimate practice of Chinese culture, whereas the Franciscans and Dominicans argued against such practices as idolatry. Judith A.

---

5. For a review of the different religious traditions, see the works of Francis Clooney and Paul Knitter on comparative theology and interreligious dialogues, as shown below: Clooney, *The New Comparative Theology*, 2010). Knitter, *Jesus and the Other Names*, 1996.

Berling shows that Chinese thinking about religious diversity is shaped by nationalist concerns, as can be seen from the proposal by Protestants, in response to the anti-Christian movement of the 1920s,[6] that churches should find a way to honour ancestors and the lunar calendar. Even in present-day China, one can see Christians visiting Buddhist temples and worshipping ancestors, wearing both the cross and Buddhist pendants, submitting themselves to a variety of deities belonging to the same or different religions. The notion of being faithful to one God, i.e. the requirement of conversion, or discarding their original traditions quickly and abruptly, as in the conversion of Shylock, is one major obstacle for non-believers and new believers in the Chinese tradition. To the Chinese, this is equivalent to the loss of cultural identity and is culturally and even politically inappropriate.[7] I say this on the basis not only of mission reports and observations but also from my personal conversion experience—moving from the worship of deities of various religions to a position of understanding the exclusivity of Christian conversion, which happened to me only several months after professing the Christian faith.

The disapproval of forced conversion in the play is a mirror of the historic event in China when missionaries were allowed to engage in evangelism after the defeat in the Opium War. Although Christian activities flourished in the trading ports which allowed missionary access, this was a form of "forced conversion," where conversions took place when the missionary enterprise is supported by military force. There was a general consensus among missionaries including Gutzlaff, Pierce and Nevius that it was acceptable to Christianise China through military force. It is because of the memory that Western missionaries were involved in military aggression that the three-self church movement in China was formed to foster church growth from within China rather than relying on external force. Wang in his book *China's Religious Issues and Religious Policies*, which expounds the Communist Party's position on missionary enterprise, commented that "those hailed as Gospel ambassadors mostly sided with their governments which invaded China, and served as a tool of imperialistic forces towards the Chinese."[8] A parallel between the forced conversion in

---

6. See Berling, "Why Chinese Thought on Religious Diversity is Important?," 27–37.

7. A detailed, systematic, empirical study of religion and religious experience in contemporary China shows that in the culture of China, people take a syncretic attitude towards other faiths. For instance, 25 percent of the self-styled Christians surveyed admitted that they had prayed to non-Christian gods. See Yao and Badham, *Religious Experience in Contemporary China* ,70–95.

8. See Wang, China's Religious Issues and Religious Policies, 172.

The Merchant of Venice and the forced conversion in China's history can be drawn—while conversion serves the well-meant purpose of salvation: the end does not justify the means.

Sudden change of identity is not an accepted process in Chinese culture. The conversion of Shylock is not only a change of faith but a forced assimilation into Christian culture, a forced sacrifice of the Jew's cultural heritage. In China, not only does one rarely see forced religious conversions, but the forced assimilation of non-Han Chinese to the Chinese culture rarely occurs. The Daoist philosophy of non-violence and non-coercion, plus the Confucian emphasis on harmony, are influential in shaping a harmonious strategy of assimilation. There have been periods in, for example, the Yuan and Qing Dynasties, during which the Han Chinese were invaded by other tribal groups (i.e. Mongols for Yuan and Manchurians for Qing): these saw a sudden, drastic imposition of the other traditions, which eventually met with resistance leading to revolution. One can recall that in *Bond* a Mainland adviser asked for a change in the ethnicity of Shylock from *Qi Dan* 契丹 group, an existing ethnic group, to Saracen (no longer present in China) as a way of maintaining harmony among ethnic groups. This and this illustrates the present-day strategy that embodies the non-violent, harmonious philosophy of the Chinese tradition. Among the majority of directors who showed disapproval of the condition of "forced conversion," Jack Shu and Zhang Qihong unconsciously deleted that condition; whereas those who disapproved of forced conversion, but retained it in the plot, showed a sympathetic attitude towards Shylock, i.e. the over-translation of one in suppression of the other.

The dilemma of the doctrinal dimension reminds one of Jan Assmann's arguments mentioned in Chapter 1 that religions are not translatable.[9] But further analysis of religious discourse shows that translatability does exist in some dimensions of religion, as will be illustrated with reference to other case studies later.

In the following section I shall illustrate by means of the issue of identity the difficulty of translating the social dimension.

---

9. Jan Assmann wrote, "if all religions basically worship the same gods there is no need to give up one religion and to enter another one. The possibility only occurs if there is one religion claiming knowledge of a superior truth. It is precisely this claim that excludes translatability." See Assmann, "Translating Gods," 31.

Untranslatability of the Social Dimension

In this book *Whose Butterfly?* William Sun asserted that, in the view of a Chinese audience, a Jew is no different from the average Westerner, who is considered the Other. This partly explains why, in *Bond* and the 2000 production in Hong Kong, neither the Christian nor the Jewish identity is translated, as these identities represent the Other. But equally worth looking at is the fact that in a number of cases, the Christian identity is suppressed, whereas the representation of the Jewish characters remains (albeit weakened), as in Zhang Qihong's production. Even in the Cantonese operatic version *Tianzhijiaonv* 天之驕女 where one would expect the Other identities to be completely untranslated in order to conform to theatrical conventions and the audience expectation of a traditional opera, Shylock is still a Jew who dons Jewish costumes, while Antonio is no longer represented as Christian. This hybridity in the maintenance of one identity but not of another can be traced back to Lin Shu's adaptation—one of the first published translations of *Tales from Shakespeare* in 1904. The influence of his hybrid translation can be seen in Bao Tianxiao's version which was published a decade later. William Sun might have wished to amend his statement if he had read these early Shakespeare translations in that the Jewishness might have been distinguished from the Other as represented by the rest of the Western characters. The migration of Jews to China dated back to the Ming Dynasty: they integrated and assimilated into the Chinese culture gradually while maintaining their ethnic identity. In addition, the Jews were seen as Christ-killers and were the subject of prejudice and persecuted in Europe for centuries partly owing to their different religious beliefs. The Chinese, however, did not carry the same historical baggage as Europeans. Imperial China never subscribed to any single religion, never was "Christianized," which prevented the Chinese from harbouring a similar prejudice against the Jewish diaspora. In a way, the Chinese could identify themselves more with Jews than with Christians, because, like the Jews, the Chinese were under the domination of the West in two World Wars, which gained the support of some Protestant churches. The writings of the Communist Party about their religious policy shed light on their anti-Christian sentiment. Robert Morrison, a Christian missionary and Bible translator hailed in the West as one of the first and greatest missionaries to China, was on the contrary labelled by the government as a spy because he translated for the East India Company which was involved in opium trading to China. An opium merchant was even invited to chair Morrison's Education Committee (馬禮遜教育會). The German missionary Charles Gutzlaff, who was hired by an opium trader as translator, was later accused by the Chinese government as providing intelligence for the British military forces.[10] Christian missionaries, because of their direct and indirect involvement with the imperial powers, created an association between Western imperialism and Christianity. The Chinese can find resonance in the situation of the Jews, who were similarly persecuted by Christians. That is, the Jews became a familiar Other, rather than the foreign Other whose foreignness was resented. The critical period of the opening up of China to the world was the early part of the twentieth century and the early 1980s and this coincided with the start of the major Christian missionary effort. It is to this period that the suppression of Christian identity can be traced. This alerted me to the potentially disruptive force that Christianity might represent. As Martha Cheung pointed out, omissions reveal as much as they conceal.

In both Zhang's and Ni's production, with the omission of Christian identity, especially as regards Antonio, comes the consequent omission of the conflicts involving Jews and Christians, as seen in the modification of Shylock's "hath not a Jew eyes" speech. (See Chapter 3, Section 3.1.3) The speech is modified so that the Christian prejudice and revenge against the Jews is not mentioned. In the end this change gave a more favorable portrayal of Antonio, the great hero. Shylock remains a villain, whether he is a Jew (in Zhang's production) or not a Jew (in Ni's production). Why can't a character be a hero and a Christian at the same time? This relates to their humanistic reading of Shakespeare—they are of the view that Shakespeare highlights the good qualities of mankind, which are universal and can be found throughout humanity. The social dimension of religious conflict and the complexity of characters are not brought out in these two productions: What remains is the characteristic good versus evil narrative which is the norm in conventional theatres in China. While critics mostly attribute this omission of the social dimension to market concerns (i.e. in order to appeal to a non-religious audience), I would see it as an indication of the lack of social function of Christian churches in Mainland China. While churches in Mainland China can operate under the banner of religious freedom, their social influence is still limited by the authorities, who interfere with church affairs through the Religious Bureau.[11] This can be explained by the dominance of Confucian ideology throughout Chinese history which insisted upon political control being in the hands of the secular authorities. Clerical power is subordinate to secular power, and as a consequence, institutional religions have a relatively weaker role than Confucianism in the

---

10. See Wang, *China's Religious Issues*, 166–168.

11. For a comprehensive historical overview of the state-church relationship in China, see Ying, *Church State Relationship*, 1999.

educational or moral system.[12] The failure to convey the social dimension in Hong Kong, as in Shum's omission of all Christian and Jewish identity, has less to do with the social function of the church, which still has influence in the areas of education, healthcare and social service, thanks to colonial rule which allowed missionary establishments. The suppression in Shum's case, or the Christian hypocrisy highlighted in Ko's play, is more related to the individual's anti-religious theology, which ironically, in Ko's case is the result of the colonial enterprise, as seen in the enforced rituals which were unwelcomed by missionary school students.

In the next section I discuss the translation of other narratives in the play.

Untranslatability of Narrative Dimension

Modern productions of this play typically last 2½ hours, which means that certain narratives cannot be included. Among the commonly deleted plots are the elopement of Lorenzo and Jessica, the story of Jacob and Laban cited by Shylock to justify his money-lending business, the allusions to Old Testament Daniel and Hagar's offspring. What is the result when certain narratives are untranslated? Omission of the elopement will render Shylock a more cruel figure, who is seemingly blindly insistent on the bond. The rebellion of Jessica and her subsequent conversion to Christianity after marrying the Christian Lorenzo offers an important motive for Shylock's outrage and justifies his reaction. He has lost a daughter to a Christian, one who in Elizabethan times would have been prejudiced against Jews. The conversion of his daughter to Christianity seems to foreshadow the inevitable conversion of the father, unwillingly and abruptly, not out of his own choice but imposed by the duke. The omission of these two motifs eventually leads to the untranslatability in another dimension—the social, especially since their interfaith love and marriage would be disapproved of by Jewish society. Another story—that of Jacob and Laban, a long passage—is commonly deleted. Accordingly the tensions between Antonio the Christian and Shylock the Jew over the interpretation of the same sacred text (Genesis 25–35) are left out. However, directors who have decided to skip such narratives simply think that there is too much for an audience to take in. They make the assumption that an audience would not be interested in the religious dimension of the play, which could hardly be explained within a short time-frame. Ko's production in 2010 which retains the above narratives, however, demonstrates that the religious dimension does have a market. What is it then

---

12. See Chou, *Contemporary Religious Movements in Taiwan*, 37–75.

that makes the other directors lose confidence in the inclusion of important narratives? Economic concerns are one contributing factor, but interviews show that what lies beneath the surface is their own theology and religious experience. Under the Communist regime and trained in the USSR, Zhang Qihong and her successor Ni Huiying, did not see religion as an important issue in the play, or simply viewed it as equivalent to an ethnic issue. On the other hand, Chris Shum attributed this deletion to his religious "revelation" that God might not exist after his baptism. That is, Chris attempted to translate his religious experience to the audience through untranslation of the religious content of the play. In the following section, I illustrate how translation of the experiential dimension can be achieved.

Translatability of Emotional and Experiential Dimension

Religious language often contains emotive statements, which can hardly be clearly verified. Statements such as "God is love," "I am the way, the truth, the life" have emotive qualities which may be understood differently by religious and non-religious communities. In this play, certain speeches by Shylock are particularly laden with emotion. When the emotions are translated from the page to the stage, the effectiveness of translations hinges on more variables than when translated in print. When Shylock said in the speech "Hath not a Jew eyes?," some translations have provoked more emotion than others. The translatability of emotion is dependent on the genre in which the play is set, the characterization, the mise-en-scene and the performance of the actors. Ko's production offers a most powerful delivery of the speech, which is made possible through a combination of the above variables. The play is set as a tragicomedy instead of a pure comedy. Shylock is portrayed as a kind father through the mise-en-scene well before this speech. Antonio's prejudice and aggression towards the Jew are highlighted. The director gave Shylock a sympathetic treatment which was communicated effectively to the actor through briefings and a collaborative directorial approach. Such translatability did not occur only in this production, but was strengthened longitudinally—Ko inherited the vision of Daniel Yang in the eighties when he was cast as Bassanio in Yang's production. Yang insisted on a sympathetic treatment for Shylock and the portrayal of Old Testament dignity in his character. In fact, Ko surpassed his predecessor Yang in this transmission of sympathy towards the Jews.

It may be recalled that in Yang's production, while he tried to give a sympathetic treatment to the Jew, the audience engaged in bouts of laughter at the forced conversion scene. This again boils down to the above variables—the director sees Antonio as a generous man, the play is set as a comedy, the tensions between Shylock and Antonio are not highlighted. The director adopts an authoritative directorial approach, there is an absence of actor participation in the directorial process. These factors may help to explain why Yang's vision of a sympathetic Jew was not effectively communicated, giving rise to what Yang described as the "stupid laughter" of the audience when the cross was forced upon Shylock (See, Chapter 4, Section 4.4.2).

Another interesting area of study is how the religious experience of directors and translators is communicated and translated to the audience. Conditioned by their own pre-understanding, these agents are not only translating the religious content of the play, but also their preconceptions, their experience in interacting with Christianity, and their emotional baggage. In *Shylock*, sympathy towards the Jew was effectively translated not only through mise-en-scene, but through the inclusion of the history of Jews in Shanghai during the world Second World War period. This was an outcome of Zhang's exposure in her acting career to an earlier play centerd on the persecution of the Jews in World War II and their life when they found refuge in Shanghai—an experience which brought home to her that the history of Jewish persecution had relevance in China.

Another example is Ko's production. Director Ko's unhappy experience of being forced to recite prayers in school as a child, and translator Chan's unique pre-understanding of the exclusivity of Protestantism encouraged them to read their impression of Christian hypocrisy into the play.

The fact that the agents in three out of seven productions implied that the Christians in the play were hypocrites alerted me to cross-cultural differences in the interpretation of hypocrisy. Some of these differences relate to their past unique experience with Christians, but, as MacIntyre[13] has suggested, the term "hypocrisy" invokes a different set of responses across cultures. Confucian philosophy centers on a whole person approach to the morality of human beings. Consistency of words and deeds is an important criterion for being a righteous man.[14] Thus it is hardly surprising that Perng and Chan, being Christian believers themselves, expressed their disapproval of the behaviour of Christians, citing the example of Antonio spitting on Shylock's robes. Sometimes, the religious experience can be

13. Fowl,"Could Horace Talk with the Hebrews," 1–20.

14. There are numerous teachings in the Book of Analects which emphasize actions and deeds over words. For instance, 先行其言而後從之 (He acts before he speaks, and afterwards speaks according to his actions) , 君子恥其言而过其行 (The superior man is modest in his speech, but exceeds in his actions), 君子欲讷于言，而敏于行 (The superior man is reserved in speech but forward in action).

translated through the untranslation of the Christian elements. This oxymoron should be understood from the way in which Chris Shum omitted the Christian content owing to his doubt whether God exists. His post-conversion doubt and his unhappy encounter with hypocritical Christians in his unique religious experience led him to delete all Christian discourse from his production.

Translatability of the Ethical Dimension

In an earlier section, I mentioned that theological concepts such as mercy and justice cannot be completely translated, because each tradition has its own reading of the same term. I also mentioned that the contract of the pound of flesh does not fit with the Confucian emphasis on humanity. However, one should not deduce from this is that the ethical dimension has no common ground and cannot be translated. Quite the contrary: one learns from the study of ethics that certain ethical principles are universal, for example murder, rape, and behaviours that inflict harm on human beings. Other principles are culturally bound and can change over time, such as marriage and gender issues. Going back to the theology of mercy above justice, a major theme in the play from a Christian perspective, one could find an equivalence in Chinese culture. In China this notion is not an especially religious one, but it is embedded in the Confucian way of thinking—*Dezhu Xingfu* 德主刑輔, i.e. virtue as primary, punishment as supplementary.

As a way of governance current even in present day China, the principle can trace its roots back to Confucius, who in the *Analects*, in the politics section 《論語.為政》recommended that a country should be ruled by virtue (以德治國), emphasizing the priority of virtue over punishment—first education, then penalty.[15] This notion was challenged during the Qin Dynasty when the concept of legalism took center stage, but that phase was short-lived as the use of rigid rules and punishment met with resistance in society and even an uprising of the people. The Chinese principle of mercy over justice was revived in the Han Dynasty through the Confucian political figure *Dong Zhongshu* 董仲舒, who proposed 貴德賤刑 "treasuring virtue over penalty." His recommendation of a Confucian way of governance was supported by the then Emperor *Han Wudi* 漢武帝, who, building on the

15. The Analects Book II talks about the importance of governing by virtue. Chapter 3 says: 子曰：道之以政，齊之以刑，民免而無恥。道之以德，齊之以禮，有恥且格。 1. The Master said, "If the people are led by laws, and uniformity is enforced by punishment, they will try to avoid the punishment, but will have no sense of shame. 2. "If they are led by virtue, and uniformity is enforced by the rules of propriety, they will have a sense of shame, and moreover will become good."

above framework, developed other principles such as 大德小刑, 前德後刑 (major on virtue and minor on punishment, first virtue then penalty). These became the mainstream principles of governance in the succeeding dynasties and up to the present day.[16] Han Wudi believed that moral education could persuade the people to accept the feudal system. But he reckoned that mere education without punishment cannot consolidate the social order, and thus it is only when moral education is supplemented by punishment that the country can be governed effectively.

In most versions of Portia's mercy speech, the Christian vocabulary is erased, and there is thus a dilution of the Christian theology of mercy versus justice, but the emphasis on compassion and mercy is still recognizable throughout the different versions.

The translatability of the above concepts serves to challenge MacIntyre's point that translation is not possible due to irreconcilable presumptions and convictions across cultures. The challenge is cogent because different cultures do share a certain common ground in terms of ethical tradition, whether it is mercy above justice in Christian terms, or virtue over law in Chinese traditions.

Such translatability of ethics without mentioning Christianity reminds us of the notion of "non-religious interpretation of Christianity" by Dietrich Bonhoeffer. Yang Huilin argues that against the background of atheist Mainland China today which has long undergone ethicization, a non-religious interpretation of Christianity serves as "a point of entry for cogitation" regarding Chinese-language Christianity.[17] In view of the indifference of German church leaders towards the persecution of the Jews by the Nazi state, Bonhoeffer struggled to understand the identity of Christianity. "What is bothering me incessantly is the question what Christianity really is, or indeed who Christ really is, for us today."[18] He criticizes the church for failing in its mission to the modern world because it fails to separate the message of Christ from religious trappings. God was used as a metaphysical *deus ex machine* by the church, which promotes a retreat into subjectivism and away from the world rather than facing the challenge of the gospel. In a secular age, when the metaphysical God becomes more and more irrelevant to everyday life, he argues that Christianity's identity is a problem because "a mature world is actually more godless, and perhaps for

16. It should be noted that despite the prevalent Confucian ideology, the legal framework from the Han Dynasty onwards has been somewhat legalistic, putting more emphasis on authority and obedience.

17. See Yang, "Ethicized Chinese-Language Christianity and the Meaning of Christian Ethics," 68–84.

18. See Bonhoeffer, *Letters & Papers from Prison*, 277.

this reason it is perhaps nearer to God than the world before maturity."[19] The non-religious interpretation of Christian concepts thus allows the gospel to address humans in a secular age without their having to become 'religious', because Christ met humans at the center of their lives and activities, in joy and in sufferings, not just as a response to man's inner state of despair and anxiety or to matters of death and guilt. The non-religious interpretation of Christian ethical concepts by Chinese directors and translators while still retaining the essence of these ethical qualities serve to remind us that in an atheist society, the Christian attributes are still comprehensible and translatable without being "religious."[20]

Translatability of Social Dimension

In the previous section, we have seen the difficulties in translating the social dimension. But not all aspects of the social dimension are untranslatable. It is true that religious identity is not translated in some versions, but one of the play's themes (ethnic tensions) has been maintained in most versions whether they have been de-Christianized or not. This is because the theme of ethnic conflict and competition has its relevance in society across time and cultures. Whether it is across the different ethnic groups within China or outwith China, ethnic tensions still exist. In Europe where there is a long tradition of association of church and state, where religious identity may not be easily separated from ethnic identity, there used to be a high percentage of Christians in Europe and Jews were equated as followers of Judaism, but this is not the case in China. Perng in the interview particularly commented on the competition among the different ethnic groups in Taiwan, including those from Hakka, Fujian, indigenous Taiwan and Hong Kong. Then again, Zhang Qihong's and her successor Ni Huiying's productions became the exceptions in that the social dimension of ethnic conflict was subdued, highlighting the "truth, benevolence and beauty" of humankind under a humanistic interpretation. Recall that in chapter 3 we noted that actor Wang Jingyu who was cast as Shylock pointed out that such reduction is a post-Holocaust response so that Jews would not be depicted as villains. "We assume that, if Shakespeare were still alive, he with his

---

19. Ibid, 362.

20. Bonhoeffer connects religion with individualism and a metaphysical system According to him, both aspects of religion are problematic because individualism promotes a retreat from the world, and religion's attempt to provide a secure metaphysical explanation of salvation enables people to escape the challenge of the gospel. See de Gruchy, "Introduction," 1–43.

humanistic spirit would probably not highlight the Jewishness of Shylock and go on to humiliate him."[21] Zhang's successor Ni Huiying pursued the main theme of zhen-shan-mei 真善美 (truth, benevolence and beauty) so far that she changed Shylock to a Macanese who no longer represented the ethnic minority in the play. What lurks behind such untranslation of the social dimension is not just a post-Holocaust response, because as Zhang has pointed out Chinese audiences in that period were generally indifferent to Jewish-Christian conflicts, but a response to the needs of the Chinese people right after the Cultural Revolution, the period when this production was staged. Human conflicts and power struggles were such a part of everyday life over the decade from 1966 to 1976 that people were tired of the conflict theme. In my interview with Zhang, she asserted that issues off religious and ethnic conflict are "untouchable" and that the audience would not be interested. When I asked her what made it "untouchable," Zhang did not answer the question directly but pointed to her decision to prioritize the theme of Portia's brilliance in a relatively brief production (See Chapter 6. Theme Three for details).

From the above discussion, it is clear that the predominant adaptation strategy is a response to social issues in China, where the social function of theatre is highly regarded. In addition, emphasis on other social issues such as the portrayal of Portia as the title character in Zhang's production under a feminist interpretation, or of a homosexual relationship between Antonio and Bassanio, may seem to have no direct relationship with the suppression of the religious dimension. But such suppression comes about when other social issues are highlighted. Some of the audience, for example, were struck by the implication that Antonio's sacrifice was not out of pure brotherly love. Respondent 65 said, "In addition, I was shocked at the homosexual relationship between Antonio and Bassanio. In the past, I thought Antonio's sacrifice for Bassanio was out of pure love. But now, I realize that pure love could not motivate them to this point. Shakespeare looks at and understands the existence of homosexual love." Perhaps it was the website of the production, which read: "Is the bond of flesh driven simply by pure friendship?" that sensitizes the audience to the issue of homosexual love displayed by Antonio.

21. See Wang, "Debates on the Characterization of Shylock," 62.

Translatability of the Ritual, Practical, and Material Dimension

What are the material and ritual dimensions of religion? The material aspect includes the religious symbols, costumes, architecture that are visible, whereas the ritual aspect entails the practices of the religion, including festivals and worshipping rituals. But the translatability of the material is dependent not only on the vision of the director and whether he sees religion as important or unimportant, but is also on the financial budget of the play. Amateur productions such as Shylock in Shanghai (2010) and *The Merchant* in Hong Kong (2000) could only afford the making of contemporary rather than period costumes. Ko's production is an excellent example of how a combination of an adequate budget, his strong vision of the play (emphasizing "belief leading to prejudice"), and his effective communication with the actors, led to a high visibility of the religious dimension. Through the use of Jewish robes with a distinctive red hat marking Shylock's Jewishness, an elaborate stage setting that transported the audience into the Elizabethan era, and the bright colors of the costumes worn by the major Christian characters—all these highlighted, the differences between the two parties. Of the audience reviews received, some particularly pointed to the Vitruvian Man painting in center stage, its rotation synchronized with the motion in the court scene highlighting the tensions between the Jew and Christian. Respondent 29 wrote:

> The (painting of) Vitruvian Man, situated in the middle (of stage), was rotating. The two faces portrayed in the painting were facing each other. When Shylock said in despair, "I am content," the middle painting did not move. When Shylock exited, the middle painting rotated again. The two faces in the painting faced towards each other.s

Shylock as a representation of the patriarchal figure in the Jewish tradition was translated differently in different versions. In Ko's production, bodily gestures such as Shylock's caring goodbye kiss to Jessica communicated a sympathetic, feminine side of the Jewish father. Among the most impressive item respondents noticed were the scene where Antonio pushed Shylock to the ground in Act 1 when asking for a loan, and the gesture of spitting on Shylock. Others mentioned the hunched back of Shylock throughout the play which gained him a sympathetic audience. These examples illustrate the fact that the physical bodies were used as "sites of translation" (in Smart's terms) to engender a sympathetic attitude towards the Jew. Although the physical objects referred to are not particularly religious objects, yet this physical dimension is capable of heightening religious awareness.

While the ritual dimension is not prominent in the original script, Antonio's act of making a trinity cross to show forgiveness to Shylock (in the court scene when he said "I am content") is an effective way in drawing the audience's attention to the religious dimension in the play. References to festivals such as Ash Wednesday are often deleted, as there is no scope in a performance to introduce explanations of such rituals to the audience.

In Daniel Yang's production, a big cross pendant was forced upon Shylock at the court scene to signify forced conversion. However, from the audience response which showed laughter rather than sympathy, it appears that the translatability of the material dimension to the audience is uncertain, as I have shown in earlier sections. The translatability of one dimension of religion is interwoven with that of another. This is hardly surprising because all the seven dimensions proposed by Smart are not completely independent of each other, but have a mutual inter-relationship with.

In summary, this section serves to illustrate the fact that religious language, when broken down into various dimensions, has different degrees of translatability. Even for the most recondite doctrinal aspects, translatability depends on the particular religious view that one holds. Theological terms that appear to me untranslatable owing to my exclusivist approach to Christianity can still be translatable to communities who adopt a pluralistic view.

In the next section, I will discuss how translatability of the religious dimension can change across time and cultures.

Translatability across Time

In the previous section, I have examined which aspects of Shakespeare's religious language can and cannot be translated. Is this translatability a static or a dynamic process? From the case studies considered, which span a time frame of thirty years, and range across cultures from Mainland, Hong Kong to Taiwan, one can see that translatability of the religious dimension is a dynamic process. What was not translated in the early eighties, i.e. the Christian identity and also the forced conversion in Zhang Qihong's production, became visible and explicit in the 2010 Shanghai adaptation known as *Shylock*, because directors found that religion was not a sensitive issue any more. What was untranslatable to the audience in the early eighties in the emotional dimension, i.e., the emotions triggered by the forced conversion scene in Hong Kong, became translatable thirty years later in Ko's production. The nervous, stupid laughter in Yang's 1984 production at the conversion scene was no longer seen in later productions, but was replaced by a sympathy for Shylock and criticism of the Christian merchant. This translatability occurred through a variety of factors: paralinguistic features such as a synopsis of the play printed in the house program and mise-en-scene; a more collaborative directorial approach and actor involvement; and increased interest in the Other cultures in the context of globalization.

On the other hand, can what is translatable then or now become untranslatable in the future? Consider the ethical dimension. The main theme of "truth, benevolence, beauty" in the Beijing production in 1980, and in the Cantonese operatic version produced by its successor was, not explicitly featured in other productions, which had a focus on ethnic tension and sympathy for the Other. As noted above, ethical values can evolve over time. The Christian ethical values that are important traditionally, e.g. "mercy seasoned with justice" in the mercy speech, are facing a paradigm shift too. In today's society and in Christian circles, the banner of "all you need is love" is being upheld, giving rise to an overwhelming, one-sided emphasis on compassion rather than a balanced approach between mercy and justice. This accounts for the shift in focus of the latest director's interpretations, which are skewed towards showing compassion to the oppressed Jew.

This line of interpretation is not only a post-Holocaust response, but reflects a heightened awareness of social justice in the global arena, as exemplified in the Occupy Movement, where the oppressed group that represents 99 percent of the world population protested against the 1 percent of corporations and powers-to-be which control most global wealth and resources.[22] The more the theme is shifted towards the issue of social justice and equality, the beautiful qualities of Antonio as a sacrificial, generous, genuine friend, and the wisdom of Portia who liberates Antonio from a dire situation will be increasingly suppressed, as these Christians are seen as the oppressors of the Jews. That can be seen already in *Bond*, and may continue to be seen in future productions. As Jonathan Norton has pointed out, a translation that might serve the purposes of a particular group well may become inadequate in addressing the needs of a dynamic community.[23]

Translatability across Cultures

When one talks about the translatability of the religious dimension in China, the general focus, as seen in scholarly research, is on censorship, power and

---

22. For a theological reflection of the Occupy Movement, see Rieger and Kwok, *Occupying Religion*, 2012.

23. See Norton, "Confessions of the Perplexed," 2013.

politics.[24] The case studies in my research offer a new perspective that liberates the translatability issue from the current focus on power and politics—a focus which derives from the trend towards cultural materialism in literary studies. Instead, I claim that religious experience plays an important role in the translatability of the religious dimension. In twenty-first century China, the theatre translations under study show that it is not Mainland China that suppresses the religious dimension—in fact, *Shylock* (2010) is one of the few among the recent productions in the Greater China region which preserve the religious identities and the controversial conversion scene. On the other hand, it is the productions in Taiwan (*Bond*) and Hong Kong (*The Merchant of Venice* in 2000) that suppress the religious dimension, although these are places where a higher degree of religious freedom is experienced compared to Communist Mainland China. It was the religious experience and post-conversion doubt of Shum that led him to remove the religious dimension: whereas for *Bond*, it was the absence of religious conflict among the audience, and the desire of the translators to protect Christians from being seen as hypocritical—among other factors—that induced the decision to omit.

But that is not to say that censorship is not at work—a Mainland music director exercised his influence over the Taiwan production by his advice not to depict Shylock as originating from an existing ethnic group契丹 to avoid possible racial conflict. In the current vogue for globalized Shakespeare production, the power of decision is distributed among parties from several regions working on a production. Suppression does not necessarily come from within the host culture. It can come from outside.

So what kind of force is paramount in translating or displacing the religious dimension in Shakespeare—the political, the economic, the religious or the cultural? How do these forces interact with one another?

From the current body of research it has been said that in stage translation market concerns and thus audience expectations reign supreme. As Susan Bassnett puts it, the main factor that shapes stage translation is "the size of the audience and the price they are willing to pay for the tickets" and "certainly not the ethics of translation." Thus the texts are "cut, reshaped, adapted, rewritten and yet still described as 'translations.'"[25] In today's market-driven economic climate, one would have expected that economics would be the main force behind the displacement or adaptation of the religious dimension. The case studies offer a fresh insight, suggesting that economic concerns and audience expectations are only superficial reasons

---

24. Martha Cheung is among the few who has written on the translatability of religious material in China. See Cheung, "The Discourse of Occidentalism?," 127–149.

25. See Bassnett, "Translating for the Theatre," 102.

for omitting religious references. Consider first the Sinicized Shakespeare versions by Zhang (*Tianzhijiaonv*), Ni (*Haomenqianjin*) and Perng (*Bond*). Why, given that there had to be cuts because of the limited time-frame, were other plots prioritized over religious references? The directors or translators, in general, believed that religious issues were not the main focus of the production. Perng offered the explanation that Sinicized Shakespeare plays should conform to the theatrical conventions of traditional Chinese operas and the taste of the audience: in other words it was the foreignness of the religious dimension that called for excision. It seems to be that in traditional Chinese operas, the Confucian political theology becomes so dominant that it excludes other types of interpretative framework.[26] When these traditional operas are set in ancient China, which is much more rooted in Confucian ethics than modern day China impacted by Western ideals and institutional religions such as Buddhism, little wonder that these Sinicized Shakespeare plays are produced under a Confucian interpretative framework.

However, instead of viewing the suppression purely as a displacement by economic or cultural forces, one should also consider the inclusivistic theology behind such a decision. In *The New Comparative Theology*, Kristin Beise Kiblinger proposed that in the older sort of inclusivism or pluralism, "claims of distinctiveness are easily dismissed and particularities of language are not taken seriously, because various expressions can all be seen as inadequately approximating the same experience."[27] This is so because traditional inclusivists look for similarity, interpret others in "the home system's terms and impose home tradition-influenced categories as though they are universally valid,"[28] such that the foreignness is minimized and is no longer recognized as such. In the Sinicized versions of *The Merchant*, foreignness is minimized to facilitate the promotion of Chinese culture—as Ni Huiying commended the superiority of Chinese culture as a humane approach to interpreting law and justice.

Will the foreignness of the religious dimension be perennially assimilated into the traditional art forms or traditional interpretative framework? Kiblinger pointed out that, in the newer type of inclusivism

---

26. For most of Chinese history, the Chinese society is dominated by Confucian ideology which insisted upon secular control of political power. Clerical power is subordinate to secular power, and as a consequence, no other religions can rival Confucianism. Institutional religions have a relatively weaker role than Confucianism in the educational or moral system. However, such dominance of Confucianism is challenged by the impact of modernisation and importation of Western values. See Chou, *Contemporary Religious Movements in Taiwan*, 37–75.

27. See Kiblinger, "Relating Theology of Religions and Comparative Theology," 21–42.

28. Ibid.

and pluralism, people do not see others as "anonymously practising the home tradition or doing in their way what we do in ours," but will find ways to value differences. Accordingly, the "differences and particularities of religious language and their contexts are studied in depth to learn the grammar from a native speaker's point of view rather than writing off the distinctiveness of others' expressions as something that could be quickly translated to the home system's language."[29] Yang Huilin noted that such interpretative change is taking place in China. While in the past, the most direct guides for Western thinking in the Chinese cultural context are perhaps Confucianism, Buddhism, or Daoism, nowadays they may be the existential experiences of contemporary people.[30]

In today's theatrical circles, there is a growing trend to introduce foreign elements into traditional operas. In *Bond*, common English expressions such as "okay" are added to bring freshness to the old forms. Preserving the religious dimension, especially the Christian dimension, as a way of "valuing the differences" can be achieved if society gradually adopts the later form of inclusivism. On the other hand, the preservation of the religious dimension in Chinese theatres can be achieved if Christianity, which is still considered a foreign force from the West, is gradually accepted as part of the Chinese culture.[31] Such indigenization is happening, as seen from the religious experience of the Chinese people where Christian faith and practice already exerts an influence on Chinese culture and other religions. For example, according to research on religious experience in China conducted between 2004–2006, 3 percent of Buddhists and 4.8 percent of Daoists say they have prayed to or worshipped the Christian God.

In other non-Sinicized versions of *The Merchant*, one can still see the influence of this ideological force over and above other forces. Consider

29. Ibid.

30. Yang Huilin believes that such a hermeneutical shift is already taking place in China: Once personal existential experience becomes the basis for interpreting outside thinking and cultures, the so-called accommodation in the history of the spreading of Chinese-language Christianity no longer resorts to the concept mechanisms of traditional culture, and is able to understand "the other" as its otherness instead of as a "projected other," and to interpret Christianity with the consciousness of difference instead of melding it into the traditional interpretive framework. If one looks at the development of Christianity in the mainland of China since the 1980s, such a shift in hermeneutical grounds is, in fact, already taking place. See Yang, "Ethicized" Chinese-Language Christianity and the Meaning of Christian Ethics," 76.

31. Yang Huilin reminded us that although Christianity already plays an extremely important role in the Chinese people's religious beliefs, its legitimacy in the Chinese cultural context has never been truly resolved. To understand the contextual interpretation of Christianity in the Chinese cultural context and its problems, see Yang, "Inculturation or Contextualization," 7–32.

the productions by Shum (2000), Yang (1984), Ko (2010), Zhang Qihong (1980) and Zhang Bowen (2010). In the interview, Chris Shum pointed out that it is not the directorial techniques that shape the production, but the vision of directors. What is central in this "vision" is the director's theology. In his theory of the field of cultural production, Pierre Bourdieu would argue that the retention or displacement of the religious dimension is the result of a struggle between various poles—for example, whether *The Merchant* was staged as a comedy versus a tragicomedy, whether the play is geared towards faithful rendition or the market, whether the play attaches importance to aesthetics at the expense of social or political relevance, or whether it is staged in a mainstream or avant-garde theatre. The resultant dynamism "is the outcome of the field being the site of conflict between translating agents whose translation decisions are the result of their allegiance to either the field of theatre or literary production or the dictates of their respective markets." [32] In the translation of the religious dimension of the play, I would agree with Shum's argument that it is the "vision" of the director that shapes the final product. Ko sees the main theme of *The Merchant* as "belief and prejudice": therefore in his production issues of religious conflict must not be overemphasized, and the burden and blame of religious prejudice is shouldered by Christians, not Jews. Shum is a doubter who questions the existence (and importance) of God and religious matters and expends efforts to do away with the religious dimension. Yang is an ex-Catholic Christian who sees religious conversion as an imperialistic act, hence his sympathetic treatment of Shylock. Zhang Qihong firmly believes in the humanistic qualities of "truth, benevolence, beauty" through a humanistic lens, and accordingly downplays the religious dimension of the play. Bowen, directing in Communist China thirty years after Zhang Qihong's production, was so touched by Jewish resilience that she kept the plot intact in spite of the low interest in religious matters in China. Since religious topics are never mainstream, popular themes in Hong Kong or Mainland China, and since the Christian population (if Susan Bassnett is correct) does not exceed 10 percent in either place, one would have expected all these productions to have substantially reduced the religious dimension.

After the religious tone is set, then how much to cut, how much to retain, and how the characters are realised is the result of a struggle among the above factors mentioned. In the productions of Yang and Ko, there is an aim to appeal to the aesthetics, i.e. to give a faithful rendition of the original intention of Shakespeare, and this accounts for the retention in large part of the religious theme. Shum is attracted the other way, seeing social and

---

32. Hanna, "Towards a Sociology of Drama Translation," 82–83.

political relevance as important to the success of the play, and the religious part is cut (note his argument that people in Hong Kong are not as religious as people in Northern Ireland). Perng too, has his translation skewed to make it socially relevant to the Taiwan audience, although his published version of *The Merchant* aims at a faithful rendition including footnotes to the biblical allusions. Ko and Zhang Bowen set the play as tragicomedy, and the sympathetic treatment of the Jews is explicitly communicated to the audience. At the other end of the spectrum is the comedic production of Yang and Zhang Qihong, where the audience laughs at Shylock's conversion during the trial scene.

What is the strength of the political factor in this struggle and how does it interact with other factors? While scholars such as Andrew Chesterman in his causal model of translation argues that socio-cultural forces are at the top of the hierarchy of conditions that shape a translation, I would offer a slightly different perspective, in that the socio-cultural and political conditions interact with the ideology of translating agents, rather than being the overmastering force that decides the image of translated literature. Except in the extreme case of the Cultural Revolution, when all Shakespeare plays were prohibited, the ideology or theology of the individual agents can sometimes buck the trend of the predominant socio-political ideology. This insight can be traced to the first productions of *The Merchant*, in which the missionary Laura White's version, elaborating on the religious dimension of mercy and justice, offered a stark contrast to her contemporaries who suppressed the Christian values of the play. In my view, therefore, socio-political forces at most run alongside, rather than being the predominant factor, in shaping the religious dimension in the text. Sabrina P. Ramet's theory on the interaction between religion and politics can be used to understand this phenomenon.[33] Amongst the seven dimensions of such interactive relationship, Ramet pointed out that in the ideological dimension, the religious doctrine can be shaped by the political ideology, while at the same time the former can foster ideological transformation. In the values system dimension, both spheres can interact at the personal, social or transcendent levels.

From the above case studies, one can see that the religious dimension in a secular play or text is not a stable concept. It is a fluid dimension subject to destabilization by varying forces, which will be discussed in the following section.

The translatability of religious language is of a fluid nature when it comes to a secular play, and even more so a problem play. As stated in Chapter 1, a sacred text commands authority from translators because

---

33. See Ramet, "Sacred Values and the Tapestry of Power," 7–19.

they have a divine source of inspiration: accordingly. A religious language within sacred texts seldom remains untranslated due to its divine quality. Religious discourse in a secular play, however, does not enjoy the same a quality of divine revelation. Quite often religious references are employed in literature or performance not just to strengthen faith-based communities but to challenge existing religious practices, such as taboos, exclusions, ossified institutions and rituals, or propose new ways of thinking. In *The Merchant of Venice*, issues of religious and ethnic conflict are problematic in the source culture. However, the religious references may be suppressed when the above issues are not considered relevant or important in the target culture, i.e. these issues are not presented a problem to the target audience. In *The Merchant of Venice*, Zhang Qihong and Ni Huiying did not see Judeo-Christian conflict as the main theme of the play. Contrarily, Ko Tinlung particularly took the view that belief leads to prejudice, and chose to highlight the Judeo-Christian conflicts. This is because he believed that such conflicts can be universalized to different religions and ethnic groups, be they Muslims or Christians. Religious references that are not translatable in one version may be translatable in another, due to the fluidity and unstability of this dimension in a secular text.

Contribution of this Study

What is the contribution of this study of the translatability of religious language in literature? From the study, I conclude that neither politics nor power is the deciding factor in shaping the translator's image, whether in terms of literature or performance. The manipulation school emerged as a breakaway from the pure aesthetics approach in translation studies when scholars such as Andre Lefevere and Theo Hermans saw it as necessary to situate translation in socio-cultural and political conditions. The "power turn," as characterized by Maria Tymoczko and Edwin Gentzler, further inspired scholars to take into account the power of translation to effect change, and to participate in political and ideological struggles. However, from the case studies above, it is time to strike a balance between the different turns in translation studies. The predominant socio-political environment has a bearing on the way in which the audience respond to the play, but on the other hand the theology and religious experience of directors and translators can create a different trajectory that defies the prevailing assumptions. Ignoring the importance of their theological position may easily lead to the premature conclusion that the omission of religious references is tied to the oppressive political environment, when in fact it is the directors'

THE PROBLEMS OF TRANSLATING RELIGIOUS LANGUAGE IN PLAYS   269

independent theological choice to leave it out. Laura White's translation as early as 1914 shows that one's theological position is an important contributing factor to the way religious language is being retained or adapted in spite of a hostile environment. Chris Shum's production in 2000 in Hong Kong is another case in point: his omission is a theological decision in spite of the religious freedom in Hong Kong. On the other hand, the retention of religious references may not be in line with the predominant political environment. One example is Zhang Bowen's 2010 production in Shanghai. The keeping of religious language was a daring attempt which was liable to alienate an audience generally indifferent to religious conflict. Nevertheless the effort to challenge market expectations under an atheist regime has born fruit—the show is still running year after year since its premierè in 2010. I conclude that the translatability of the religious dimension in literature is a fluid, unstable concept, subject to the interaction of the socio-cultural environment and one's theological or ideological position, as my modified translation model in Chapter 1 suggests. The case studies show that the ideology of the individual agent can be so strong a determining factor that it creates a unique adaptation, counter to the predominant trend. This is hardly surprising, because an agent's theological position, conditioned by his/her religious experience, can be vastly different from the norms and expectations of society at large. The conversion experiences of people in atheist countries bear witness to this.

What insights could the hybrid, intercultural Shakespeare bring to Western theatre, and in what ways could the latter be enriched by it? Shakespeare used to be seen as a colonial force whereby schools included Shakespeare in their education curriculum to further colonial ends. In contrast, in the context of globalization, a Chinese perspective can give renewed insights to productions in the West. For example, in Zhang Qihong's production one religious identity (i.e. Christianity) was suppressed in order to downplay the religious conflicts in the play, but Zhang explained that in her interpretation the conflicts were peripheral to the plot—an embodiment of the Confucian philosophy to attain harmony. In similar vein, her successor Ni Huiying tried to paint the merits of Chinese culture through showing the unreasonableness of the contract of the pound of flesh, which could not be depicted in Chinese culture because of its inhuman nature. Her portrayal of Shylock is one of a villain, which defies the post-Holocaust sympathetic treatment. It is a portrayal in the spirit of her predecessor. The villainous portrayal underpins not only Shylock's character, but also the nature of the contract –inflexible, inhuman and rule-based, rather than the human-based as is the core value of Confucianism. Truth, benevolence, and beauty are the three values that both Zhang and Ni give special emphasis to the core values of this play. The villainous portrayal of Shylock, the emphasis on these core values, plus the relegation of religious conflict to the background, together constitute a form of the "harmonious treatment" of the play. This treatment serves to balance off the overwhelmingly sympathetic portrayal of Shylock and consequently serves to introduce an unsettling tone by underpinning the Judeo Christian conflict.

Traditionally, Chinese dramas attach more importance to on-stage visuals and actor performance than to dialogue. When Shakespeare plays are adapted to the Chinese dramatic conventions, the productions in China, Hong Kong and Taiwan become visually rich, sensational and colorful. How does that impact on the reception of the religious dimension in the play? In Ko's production, gestures such as spitting on Shylock, his kissing the daughter, and the imposing position of Antonio, intensified the performance and these actions did make an impression on the perception of sympathetic treatment by the audience, as seen from their reviews. In *Bond*, the arias of Xia Luo intensified the sympathy, while the acrobatics performed by Xia Luo sharpened to the comedic tone of the play. Enhancing staging effects does not necessarily require enormous production costs. In the production of *Shylock* in Shanghai in 2010, the amateur directors employed three different actors to play the role of Tubal, rather than following the original production with only one actor throughout. In the casket scene, Zhang Qihong set an example for future productions to follow when she employed three dancers dressed in corresponding colors (representing gold, silver, and lead) to bring in three boxes, intensifying the economic symbols represented by the gold, silver and lead caskets.

In post-colonial Hong Kong, the directors exhibited a form of post-colonial 'strategic alliance' with the source culture, to borrow a term used by Gilbert Fong in Hong Kong Drama Review (2006). Hong Kong seldom shows resentment against its previous colonizer, i.e. the United Kingdom. Rather, it has benefited from importing from the West *inter alia* the systems of education and law and order. Thus, Hong Kong in the post-colonial period has never experienced a revolutionary phase—at most it went through the stage of rediscovering its identity, i.e., the second stage in creating national identity after colonization, according to Frantz Fanon.[34] In accordance with this strategic alliance, many translated plays in Hong Kong emphasize their closeness to the source text, i.e. Shakespeare. They are also more influenced by Western interpretations than their Mainland counterparts, e.g. Ko and Yang, who adopt sympathetic treatment as their main line of interpretation. And it is trying to showcase an authentic

---

34. See Fong, "Self Identity in Suspense," 4–5.

Shakespeare that gives rise to the retention of religious references, setting these productions apart from the Mainland ones.

What are the future prospects for the translatability and reception of the religious dimension in Chinese Shakespeare? I can foresee a parting of the ways in both these respects, on the Mainland and Taiwan on one hand and Hong Kong on the other. In China, there is a spiritual awakening which followed the Cultural Revolution; and this so-called religious fever (宗教熱) is still current. Statistics for the total number of Christians in the Mainland are hard to come by, as official statistics only record the numbers attending services at registered churches. According to the figures of Operation World, the current Christian population is estimated at over 105 million. Queues for baptism and for attending worship services can be seen from time to time, especially during festivals. Yang Fenggang, a renowned researcher in the field of Chinese religion, was recently quoted to the effect that China is on its way to be become the largest Christian nation in the world, with an estimated 160 million Christians by 2025.[35] He attributed the religious fever to the "socialist religious economy based on atheist Communist ideology,"[36] prompting individuals to seek solace from different religious practices and sects, whether the recognized religions, or quasi-, or pseudo- ones. Increasing religious supply, therefore, is one of the options proposed by Yang[37] in this shortage economy, despite the ongoing crackdown by the authorities on religious activities and venues. In this unstable milieu, religion in literature is one safe way to satisfy the overwhelming religious demand. In fact, the study of religion as a part of culture has been vibrant since the 1990s,[38] and new religious journals are being launched. Yang is insightful in pointing out the importance of the cultural approach to religious research: when religion is studied as a cultural phenomenon, "its ideological incorrectness becomes un-important and its scientific incorrectness obscured." Moreover, the cultural approach makes "religious research more wide-reaching and consequently academically rewarding" Scholars, atheist or not, can ride on this religious fever by publishing articles on religion and its relationship with culture and literature. Yang further points out that, since the 1990s, several major universities have established departments of religious studies, including Peking University, Renmin University of China, Fudan University, and Wuhan University. This is in line with my observation that new books on

---

35. Phillips, "China on Course to Become 'World's Most Christian Nation'",. 30 May 2014.

36. See Yang, *Religion in China*, 156–157.

37. Ibid, 156.

38. Ibid, 55.

Bible stories and Christian art are coming on to the market every year. For example, a book entitled "An Introductory Course of Biblical Culture" was published in 2012 by Shanghai Foreign Language Education Press. It is a course book for university students and used at China Ocean University and Hebei Normal University for five years before its publication.

In the context of globalization, the Confucian ideal which used to be the prevailing interpretative framework in Mainland China and Taiwan, is gradually losing its dominance. The process of modernization, alongside the processes of urbanization and commercialization, has deeply challenged the Confucian value systems. In particular, the Confucian sense of community and kinship which take priority over individual interests is being destroyed by the tendency towards individualism and the accompanying sense of alienation occurring in these Chinese societies especially among the younger generation.[39] While the Confucian ideology constitutes the main interpretative framework among the Mainland and Taiwan directors and translators whom I interviewed (i.e. Zhang Qihong, Ni Huiying, Perng Ching Hsi), it is losing its dominance among the younger generation, as such, this may become a point of entry for the revival of the Christian dimension in the play.

I have adduced evidence to show that in the early eighties the religious dimension was displaced in *The Merchant of Venice*. But the staging of *Shylock* by a group of young dramatists (born after 1980s) in Shanghai recently is indirect testimony to the continuation of religious fever, which permits the translatability of the religious dimension in literature.

Can the same phenomenon be predicted in post-colonial Hong Kong? Here the picture is less clear, in terms of interest in the Christian dimension in literature. Hong Kong, with its 150-year colonial history, followed a different trajectory in that Christian education made its entry through the colonial powers. Before the New Secondary School Curriculum took effect in 2012, students from Christian secondary schools were forced to take religious studies in the O-level exam. From my observation as the alumnus of a missionary school, I saw classmates showing so much resistance to this imposition that they decided to throw away the Bible immediately after the public examination. The history of missionary establishment in Hong Kong began under colonial rule in 1842, when Western missionaries came to establish stations, providing social services and education. By the 1970s, forty percent of schools in Hong Kong were either Protestant or Catholic. By 2005, the Protestant churches ran to over 630 schools, 116 nurseries

---

39. For a comprehensive analysis of the impact of modernisation on the traditional Chinese/Taiwanese society, including changes in their worldviews, see Chou, *Contemporary Religious Movements*, 37–75.

and more than 20 theological seminaries and Bible colleges, exerting a disproportionate degree of influence in areas of education and social service, given the only 5 percent of the population are Christians.[40] With such a long history of missionary establishment, in an environment with a high degree of religious freedom, the religious deficit as seen in Mainland China does not apply here. Against this post-colonial background, one can understand the divergence as exhibited in the case studies in Hong Kong. There are directors who want to form a 'strategic alliance' with the source culture, emphasising the authenticity of their Shakespeare productions, and retaining the religious aspects. On the other hand, there are versions which deliberately cut out the religious dimension, due to ideological considerations, and as a way of satisfying the expectations of an audience which is mainly non-Christian.[41]

What about Taiwan? Since the withdrawal of martial law in 1987, religious freedom as part of the constitution has become more fully operative in Taiwan. There is now a state of religious oligopoly, whereby the society is dominated by a select few religions which are privileged over others. Phenomenal growth in the Christian population has been reported in recent years: the latest estimate from Operation World puts the total at around 1.3 million, or 5.82 percent of the whole population. Does this necessarily bode well for interest in religious literature, and thereby its translatability? Postcolonial Taiwan has been distinguished by its unique national identity and a long-standing tradition of indigenous literature. Accordingly, its Chinese Shakespearean productions are often characterized by an appropriated, contextualized Shakespeare, such as Wu Hsin-kuo's *Tempest*, rather than an emphasis on reproducing an authentic Shakespeare with whatever religious dimension it happens to have. Yet this may not spell the end of the representation of religious dimensions in future Shakespearean plays in Taiwan. From *Bond*, I detect an ambition on the part of the production team, comprising Western-educated academics, to showcase their national treasure to an international audience. *Bond* received many credits for its elaborate costumes and sensational performance when staged in the US and London, but was criticized for its simplification of the plot and the characters because of its suppression of the Judeo-Christian conflict. In the post-colonial era, the colonized still privilege Western products over local products: thus overseas recognition for a theatre production bodes well for its local reception. As

40. See Lo, "Taiwan, Hong Kong, Macau," 183–189.

41. There are over 320,000 Protestant church members in Hong Kong, according to the statistics published by Hong Kong Church Renewal Movement in 2009 which surveyed 1,142 churches (91.4 percent) in Hong Kong. This accounts for 5 percent of overall population.

dramatists become increasingly aware of this, the religious dimension may be revived in the future as a postcolonial move to gain recognition, both locally and internationally.

Is Translation Conversion?

The ancient philosopher Cicero, along with the post-modernist Derrida[42] and contemporary translation scholars such as Douglas Robinson, have proposed that translation is conversion. How should we understand conversion in the first place? While some from Judaic or Christian traditions propose a radical change to reject evil and have a new relationship with God, others see conversion as a more gradual process. Rambo Lewis proposes a holistic model of conversion that should have the following four components in order to reflect the richness and complexity of the subject: cultural, social, religious, personal.[43] With the different possible meanings and components of conversion, the process of conversion exhibits similarities with the process of negotiation as Batairwa Paulin suggests, during which the convert "discerns and chooses between the essential and the accessories," decides which must be taken off to accommodate and which has to be put on, which concessions are allowed and which are prohibited in order to be classified as a conversion.[44] Similarly, in the context of translation, some references are kept, some are left out. But even when they are converted to a different tradition (i.e. words with Buddhist or Confucian connotations), even when certain narratives are prohibited (i.e. forced conversion), in this negotiation process, some core universal values, such as compassion and mercy, are still inherent in the story. Translation of the religious dimension is like negotiating between the boundaries of the two cultures. From the cases that we see, the conversion process is more a

---

42. See Derrida, "What is Relevant Translation?," 174–200 for Derrida's elaboration on translation as conversion.

43. Rambo Lewis proposes a holistic approach to conversion. The cultural component constructs the intellectual, moral, and spiritual atmosphere of life. Sociologists consider social conditions at the time of conversion, important relationships and institutions of potential converts, and characteristics and processes of the religious group to which people convert. Psychology considers transformation of the self, consciousness, and experience, in both objective and subjective aspects. Scholars of religion focus on transcendence, inquiring into the religious expectations, experiences, and worldviews of converts. He also distinguishes five types of conversion, involving apostasy, or intensification of one's faith, or affiliation to a new group, or a transition from an ecumenical institution to another, or a transition from one tradition to another. See Lewis, *Understanding Religious Conversion*, 1993.

44. See Paulin, "Conversion as Negotiation," 1 June 2013.

partial conversion than a total conversion, for example in Zhang Qihong's production, taking off the Christian identity (religious dimension) of the characters and the related Christian festivals (cultural dimension) but retaining their merciful traits (personal dimension).

Douglas Robinson in *The Translator's Turn* reminds us that the translation process is not simply a transmission of information, but involves "converting the target language reader to his or her reading of the source language text,"[45] and "doing something to the target language reader."[46] Conversion occurs when the target language reader is persuaded to agree with the translator about the source language text, and to agree with the source language writer about the world. As can be seen from the different case studies, directors or translators have their own theology or ideology that leads them to the filtering or shaping of religious discourse. He or she then converts his or her view about religion—including religious freedom, salvation and religious conflict—into a production, whereby audience members are persuaded to agree with the new play text, then agrees with the world of Shakespeare and, later, to undergo a transformation of themselves. Such transformation is achieved not by reading the text in print, but by responding to drama, whose expressive function intersects with its instrumental function. Accordingly, conversion is compounded by the instrumental power of theatre. For instance, those who watched Ko's production in 2010 tended to agree with the sympathetic treatment of the Jew in Shakespeare. Some even said that they hated Christians all the more because of their "hypocrisy." Theatre, with its historical connections as a site of religious rituals in both East and West, assumes the role of a quasi-sanctuary. The capacity of translation as conversion in theatre, epitomized in Raymond William's description of' the instrumental function of dramatic forms, "complicated as it is by delay, by the unevenness of change, and by the natural variety of responses to change, only some of which achieve adequate communication, the outline surely exists, in which we can see drama, not only as a social art, but as a major and practical index of change and creator of consciousness."[47] Theatre theorist Erika Fischer Lichte in her work *The Transformative Power of Performance* testifies to the fact that transformation of an audience took place in a performance where spectators were not "presented with a distinct object to perceive and interpret; rather, they were all involved in a common situation of here and

---

45. See Robinson, *The Translator's Turn*, 213.
46. Ibid. 212.
47. See Williams, *The Long Revolution*, 271–299.

now, transforming everyone present into co-subjects."[48] Spectators can become so involved in a performance that they are not passive observers who simply absorb the interpretation of the artists. In one experimental performance she watched in 1975, she concluded that understanding the artist's actions was less important than the experiences the artist had on stage under the influence of the audience, "the central concern of the performance was not to understand but to experience it and to cope with these experiences."[49] The audience is thus capable of being transformed from being a spectator to an actor, from being a receiving object to an experiencing and acting subject.

The discussion of translation and conversion at the conclusion of this book leads one back to the discussion of hermeneutics at the beginning. Ricoeur's proposition is that the interpretation of a text culminates in the self-interpretation of a subject, that understanding the text is not an end in itself; ultimately the goal is to mediate the relation to the self, i.e. self-understanding.[50] The directors and translators whom I have interviewed have been converted one way or another in the interpretation of the text—some against the Chinese culture of religious diversity, some became sympathetic to the persecuted and oppressed, some became more appreciative of the Confucian ethic that does not agree with the literalness of the bond, some were drawn to the humanist qualities of mercy and sacrifice, some became displeased with Christian hypocrisy. When Shakespeare's text written some four hundred years ago is translated into contemporary Chinese, translation is not purely a linguistic process, but an adaptation or appropriation that reflects a hybrid of two cultures, a Jewish moneylender with a Chinese shadow, a Venetian merchant showing Confucian and Buddhist mercy. Thus I conclude that the translatability of a religious text should not be defined by linguistic or semantic criteria, but should be viewed in the context of a broad range of religious dimensions. The often untranslated doctrinal or ethical aspect of the religious language should not make us neglect the translatability of other dimensions that a religion can offer, be they social, narrative, material, emotional and experiential and ritual. From the cases I have examined, I propose a new way of looking at the (un) translatability issue of the religious dimension. Rather than following the "sociological turn" or "power turn" in translation studies (i.e. considering the translations merely under the socio-political framework), I also investigate the theology or the ideological discourse of the translating agents. One can see that the deciding

---

48. Fischer-Lichte, *The Transformative Power of Performance*, 17.
49. Ibid.
50. See Ricoeur and Thompson, *Hermeneutics and the Human Science*, 142–143.

factor for such translatability is often an interaction between the religious and political spheres. Religion has such a unique and powerful role in shaping a piece of literature that a mere cultural, social or political approach can hardly do justice to its translatability. When such religio-political interaction involves competing values, i.e. when one's theology or ideology differs from the predominant state ideology, religious values play a more decisive role in translatability or untranslatability than socio-political factors. This can be illustrated by the cases where, in places of religious freedom, the religious dimension is suppressed (as in *Bond* in Taiwan and *The Merchant* in Hong Kong directed by Shum in 2000); or in places of relatively restricted religious freedom, the religious dimension is retained (as in *Shylock* in Shanghai). As Ramet reminds us, religion is probably the "single most powerful source of values," and even the state can rarely compete with religion in terms of the intensity of its authority for society as a whole.[51]

51. See Ramet, "Sacred Values and the Tapestry of Power," 11.

Bibliography

Works Cited

Appiah, Kwame Anthony. "Thick Translation." *Callaloo* 16.4 (1993) 808–19.
Armstrong, Gareth. *A Case for Shylock: Around the World with Shakespeare's Jew*. London: Nick Hern Books, 2004.
Assmann, Jan. "Translating Gods: Religion as a Factor of Cultural (un)Translatability." In Sanford Budick and Wolfgang Iser, Eds. *The Translatability of Cultures: Figurations of the Space between*. Stanford, California: Stanford University Press, 1996.
A.Ying (QianHengCun), Ed. 4 vols. *Wan Qing Wen Xue Cong Chao: Translations from Foreign Literature*. Shanghai: ZhongHua Shuju,1961.
Bai, Liping 白立平. "Shi xue, yi shi xing tai ji zan zhu ren yu fan yi 詩學、意識形態及贊助人與翻譯:梁實秋翻譯研究". PhD diss. The Chinese University of Hong Kong, 2004.
Baker, Mona. *Translation and Conflict: A Narrative Account*. Oxon: Routledge, 2006.
Bao Tianxiao 包天笑. The Lawyeress 女律師. *Female Students Periodical* 女學生. Shanghai Chengdong Nuxueshe 上海城東女學社, 1911.
Bartholomew, Ian. "The Bard—Henan Style." *Taipei Times* 7 Sept 2009. Web. 10 Oct 2011.
Bassnett, Susan. "An Introduction to Theatre Semiotics." *Theatre Quarterly* 10.38 (1980) 47–55.
———. Lefevere, André, Eds. *Translation, History and Culture*. London, 1990.
———. "Translating for the Theatre: The Case Against Performability." *TTR (Traduction, Terminologie, Redaction)* 4.1 (1991) 99–111.
———. "The Translation Turn in Cultural Studies". In Susan Bassnett and André Lefevere, eds. *Constructing Cultures*. Clevedon, 1998.
Bassnett, Susan, and Harish Trivedi, eds. *Postcolonial Translation: Theory and Practice*. London: Routledge, 1998.
Berling, Judith A., "Why Chinese Thought on Religious Diversity is Important?" In *Religious Diversity in Chinese Thought*, edited by Perry Schmidt-Leukel and Joachim Gentz, 27–37. New York: Palgrave Macmillan, 2013.
Brown, Melissa. *Is Taiwan Chinese? The Impact of Culture, Power, and Migration on Changing Identities*. Berkeley: University of California Press, 2004.

Cai Yuanpei 蔡元培. *Cai Yuanpei Quanji* 蔡元培全集第三卷 [Collection of Cai Yuanpei's essays Volume 3]. Zhejiang: Zhejiang Jiaoyu Chuban she, 1997, pp. 30–35.

Chan Tak-hung, Leo. *Twentieth Century Chinese Translation Theory.* Philadelphia: Benjamins, 2004.

Chang, Namfung. "Censorship in Translation and Translation Studies in Present-Day China." In *Translation and Censorship in Different Times and Landscapes*, edited by Teresa Seruya and Maria Lin Moniz, 229–40. Newcastle: Cambridge Scholars, 2008.

Chau, Simon 周兆祥. *Han yihamuleite* 漢譯哈姆雷特 [Studies on the Chinese Translation of Hamlet]. Hong Kong: Chinese University Press, 1981.

Chen Fang. "Translating Theatre: *The Merchant of Venice* as 'Shake-*xiqu*.'" *Journal of Theatre Studies* 8 (July 2011) 59–90.

Chen Hong Shu. "Translation and Manipulation: From Cuore to Xin's Journal About School Life." PhD diss. National Taiwan Normal University, 2010.

Chen, Chapman. "Postcolonial Hong Kong Drama Translation." In *Beyond Borders—Translations Moving Languages, Literatures and Cultures*, edited by Pekka Kujamäki et al., 39–58. Berlin: Frank & Timme, 2011.

Chen, Fang. "Bonding? What Bonding? On Bond, a Yuju Adaptation of *The Merchant of Venice*." *Taipei Theatre Journal* 14 (2011) 63–83.

Chen, Shu-fen. "Shakespeare in Taiwan: Struggle for Cultural Independence from Mainland China and Euro-America." PhD diss., University of Manchester, 1999.

Chesterman, Andrew. "A Causal Model for Translation Studies." In *Intercultural Faultlines*, edited by Maeve Olohan, 15–28. Manchester: St. Jerome, 2000.

Cheung Pui-Yiu, Martha. "The Discourse of Occidentalism? Wei Yi and Lin Shu's Treatment of Religious Material in Their Translation of Uncle Tom's Cabin". In David Pollard, Ed. *Translation and Creation-Readings of Western Literature in Early Modern China, 1840–1918*, 127–49. Amsterdam: Benjamins, 1998.

———. "Re-reading of Lin Shu's and Wei Yi's translation of Uncle Tom's Cabin." 從話語的角度重讀魏易與林好合譯的《黑奴籲天錄》. *Chinese Translators Journal* 24.2 (March 2003).

Chia, Adeline. "Cantonese Twist for *The Merchant of Venice*." *The Straits Times*, 22 Nov 2007.

Ching, Julia. "I-Confucianism: A Philosophy of Man." In James Whitehead, Yu-Ming Shaw, Eds. *China and Christianity: Historical and Future Encounters*. Notre Dame, IN: University of Notre Dame Press, 1979, pp.8–34.

Chong, Y. Y. *Study of the Phenomenon of Authoritativeness in the Chinese Translations of the Protestant Bible.* 基督教聖經中文譯本權威現象研究. Hong Kong: International Bible Society, 2000.

Chou, Kai-Ti. *Contemporary Religious Movements in Taiwan.* Lewiston: Mellen, 2007.

Chow, Alexander. *Theosis, Sino-Christian Theology and the Second Chinese Enlightenment.* New York: Palgrave Macmillan, 2013.

Clooney, Francis. *The New Comparative Theology: Interreligious Insights from the Next Generation.* London: T. & T. Clark, 2010.

Coghill, Nevill. "The Theme of The Merchant of Venice." In *Twentieth-Century Interpretations of The Merchant of Venice: A Collection of Critical Essays*, edited by Sylvan Barnet, 108–12. Twentieth Century Interpretations. Englewood Cliffs, NJ: Prentice-Hall, 1970.

Cohen, Paul. *China and Christianity*. Cambridge: Harvard University Press, 1963.
Compton, Robert. "A Study of the Translations of Lin Shu." PhD Diss. Stanford University, 1971.
Copeland, Rita. *Rhetoric, Hermeneutics, and Translation*. New York: Cambridge University Press, 1991.
Covell, Ralph R. *Confucius, The Buddha, and Christ*. Maryknoll, NY: Orbis, 1986.
Crosby, Kate. "What Does not Get Translated in Buddhist Studies and the Impact on Teaching." In *Translation and Religion*, edited by Lynne Long, 41–53. Topics in Translation. Buffalo, NY: Multilingual Matters, 2005.
Cross, F. L., and Livingstone, Elizabeth, eds. *The Oxford Dictionary of the Christian Church*. 3rd ed. New York: Oxford University Press, 1997.
de Gruchy, John. "Introduction." In *Dietrich Bonhoeffer: Witness to Jesus Christ*, 1–43. Minneapolis: Fortress, 1991.
Dahlberg, Karin, Nancy Drew, and Maria Nystrom, eds. *Reflective Lifeworld Research*. Lund: Studentlitteratur, 2001.
Damm, Jens. "Same Sex Desire and Society in Taiwan." *China Quarterly* 181 (March 2005) 67–81.
Deacon, David, Pickering, Michael, Golding, Peter, and Murdock, Graham. *Researching Communications: A Practical Guide to Methods in Media and Cultural Analysis*. London: Bloomsbury Academic, 1999.
DeGroot, J. J. M. *Is There Religious Liberty in China?* Berlin: Reichsdruckerei, 1902.
Ding Dagang 丁大剛. "Laura M. White's Translation of *Silas Marner*". *The Reconstruction of Classics: Studies on Literature Translation from the Perspective of Religions Conference*, 231–40. Shanghai Normal University, Shanghai, June 2014.
Diu Zefang 刁澤放. YitiaoBugaiGequdeweiba- tan kewenweinisishangrendez-uihoushanjie 一條不該割去的尾巴-談課文威尼斯商人的最後刪節 [A Tail that Should Not be Cut Off—On the Omission in *The Merchant of Venice*] *Zhongxueyuwenjiaoxue* 中學語文教學 [Secondary School Language Pedagogy] 5 (2005) 40.
Donovan, Peter. *Religious Language*. London: Sheldon, 1976.
Engbarth, Dennis. "Taiwan Lawmakers Push 'Marriage Equality Bill.'" *Interpress Service News* 30 Oct 2013.
Fairclough, Norman. *Critical Discourse Analysis: The Critical Study of Language*. London: Longman, 1995.
———. *Language and Power*. 3rd ed. New York: Routledge, 2015.
Fang Ping, trans. *Weinisishangren*. 威尼斯商人 *[The Merchant of Venice]*. Shanghai: Ping Ming Chubanshe. 1959.
———. "Lun Xia Luoke 論夏洛克 [On Shylock]." *WaiguoWenxueYanjiuJikan* 外國文學研究 *[Foreign Literature Studies Collections]* 1979, pp. 213-233.
———. trans. *XinShashibiyaQuanji* 新莎士比亞全集 [New Shakespeare Translations]. Shijiazhuang: Hebei Education [HebeiJiaoyu], 2000, p.5.
Fawcett, Thomas. *The Symbolic Language of Religion: An Introductory Study*. London: SCM, 1970.
Fischer-Lichte, Erika. *The Transformative Power of Performance: A New Aesthetics*. Translated by Saskya Iris Jain. London: Routledge, 2008.
Fringe '94. Hong Kong: Hong Kong Festival Fringe, 1994.
Fong, Gilbert 方梓勳. "Xijujiayuxijufanyi: CaoYu de rou mi ouyu you li ye 戲劇家與戲劇翻譯:曹禺的柔蜜歐與幽麗葉 [Dramatists and Drama Translation: Romeo

and Juliet by Cao Yu]". In 中大學者論曹禺 [*Chinese University Scholars on Cao Yu*], edited by Tian Benxiang & Liu Jiming Eds.Zhong Da XuezheLun Cao Yu. Tianjin: Nankai University Press.1992.

———, ed. *Xianggang hua ju fang tan lu.* 香港話劇訪談錄 [Interviews on Theatre Directors in Hong Kong.] Hong Kong: Xianggang Xiju Gongcheng, 2000.

———. Xuanzhi de ziwo renting- xianggang xiju fanyi de beihou 懸置的自我認同 - 香港戲劇翻譯的背後 [Self Identity in Suspense- Behind the Drama Translations in Hong Kong]. *Hong Kong Drama Review* 6 (2006) 4–5.

Fortosis, Steve. *Multilingual God.* Pasadena, CA: William Carey Library, 2012.

Fowl, Stephen E. "Could Horace Talk with the Hebrews? Translatability and Moral Disagreement in MacIntyre and Stout." *Journal of Religious Ethics* 19.1 (1991) 1–20.

Francisco, Jose Mario C. "Translating Vice into Filipino—Religious, Colonial and Nationalist Discourses on Sloth". In *Translation in Asia: Theories, Practices, Histories*, edited by Ronit Ricci and Jan Van der Putten, 104–18. Manchester: St. Jerome, 2011.

Gadamer, Hans-Georg. *Truth and Method.* Translated by Joel Weinsheimer and Donald G. Marshall. New York: Crossroad, 1991.

Gallagher, Aoife. "Pasternak Hamlet: Translation, Censorship and Indirect Communication." In *Translation and Censorship: Patterns of Communication and Interference*, edited by Eiléan Ní Chuilleanáin, Cormac Ó Cuilleanáin, and David L Parris, 119–31. Dublin: Four Courts, 2009, pp

Gentzler, Edwin. *Contemporary Translation Theories.* New York: Routledge, 1993.

Hanna, Sameh Fekry. "Towards a Sociology of Drama Translation: A Bourdieusian Perspective on Translations of Shakespeare's Great Tragedies in Egypt." PhD. Diss. University of Manchester, 2006.

Harrison, Victoria. "Metaphor, Religious Language, and Religious Experience." *Sophia* 46 (2007) 127–45.

Hassel, R. Chris. *Shakespeare's Religious Language: A Dictionary.* London: Thoemmes Continuum, 2005.

Hawthorn, Jeremy. *A Glossary of Contemporary Literary Theory.* London: Arnold. 1992.

He, Qi-xin. "Shakespeare through Chinese Eyes." PhD diss., Kent State University, 1986.

Hermans, Theo. *Translation in Systems: Descriptive and System-oriented Approaches Explained.* Manchester: St Jerome, 1999.

Hogg, Chris. "Taiwan Move to Allow Gay Unions." *BBCNews World Edition*, 28 October 2003.

Hou, Chengnan. "Promoting Rainbow Pride in Formosa: A Study on the Media Strategies Model of the LGBT Rights Movement in Taiwan." Paper presented at the annual meeting of the International Communication Association, Singapore. 6 August 2010.

Hu Shi 胡適. "Jianshe de wenxue geming lun. 建設的文學革命論 [The Making of a Theory of Literary Revolution]". In *Hushi Xueshu Wenji Xinwenxue yundong*, 40–54. Beijing: Zhonghua shu ju, 1993.

Hu Wei Min 胡偉民. "Notes on Directing Twelfth Night in the Form of Shaoxing Opera." In 中國莎士比亞研究會 [Shakespeare Association of China]. In *Shakespeare in China*, 128. Shanghai: Shanghai Literature and Art Press, 1987.

Huang Guming 黃谷明. *Weinisi Shangrenrenwusuozao zhongtuxian de jidujiaoqinghuai* 威尼斯商人人物塑造中凸现的基督教情怀 [The Christian Dimension

Embodied in the Characterization of The Merchant of Venice] *Journal of Huangshi Institute of Technology.* 2007 Dec, p.54.

Huang Zicai 黃梓材." Zhengjiaofenquanlun 政教分權論" [On the Separation of Church and State], *Wanguogongbao* 196 (May 1905) 14–15.

Huang, Alexander, "Shakespeare on the Chinese Stage 1839-2004: A History of Transcultural Performance". PhD diss., Stanford University, 2004.

———. "Lin Shu, Invisible Translation and Politics." *Perspectives: Studies in Translatology* 14 (2006) 1.

Huang, Yahui. "Performing Shakespeare in Contemporary Taiwan." PhD diss., University of Central Lancashire, 2012.

Hui Ji 惠紀. "Discussions on the Directorship of *The Merchant of Venice*." In *Shakespeare Research*, 302–6. Hangzhou: Zhejiang People's Press. 1983.

Hunter, Jane. *The Gospel of Gentility: American Women Missionaries in Turn-of-the-Century China.* New Haven: Yale University Press, 1984.

James, William. *The Varieties of Religious Experience.* London: Collins, 1960.

Jeffner, Anders. *The Study of Religious Language.* London: SCM, 1972.

Ji Chengzhi 紀乘之. *GuZhongyi Yi WeinisiShangren* 顧仲彝譯威尼斯商人 [Translation of *The Merchant of Venice* by GuZhongyi] *Wenxue Pinglun* 文學評論 1.2 (1934) 307–16.

Johnston, David. *Stages of Translation.* Bath, England: Absolute Classics, 1996.

Jones, Keith. "Bond, Shakespeare's *Merchant of Venice* in Mandarin Chinese." *Bardfilm: The Shakespeare and Film Microblog.* Blogger 9 April 2011.

Kiblinger, Kristin Beise. "Relating Theology of Religions and Comparative Theology." In *The New Comparative Theology: Interreligious Insights from the Next Generation*, edited by Francis Clooney, 21–42. London: T. & T. Clark, 2010.

Kirk, Peter. "Holy Communicative? Current Approaches to Bible Translation Worldwide". In *Translation and Religion*, edited by Lynne Long. Buffalo, NY: Multilingual Matters, 2005.

Kittel H., and A. Poltermann. "German Tradition" In *Routledge Encyclopedia of Translation Studies*, edited by M. Baker, 418–28. London: Routledge, 1998.

Knitter, Paul. *Jesus and the Other Names: Christian Mission and Global Responsibility.* Oxford: Oneworld, 1996.

Komonchak, J.A., M. Collins, and D. A. Lane, eds. *New Dictionary of Theology.* Dublin: Gill and Macmillan, 1987, pp.650–652.

Krebs, Katja. *Cultural Dissemination and Translational Communities: German Drama in English Translation, 1900–1914.* Manchester: St. Jerome. 2007.

Kwok Pui-lan. *Chinese Women and Christianity 1860-1927.* Atlanta: Scholars, 1992.

Lai, John T.P. "Institutional Patronage-The Religious Tract Society and the Translation of Christian Tracts in Nineteenth-Century China." *The Translator* 13:1 (2007) 53.

———. "On the Translation Strategies and Styles of the Three Chinese Translations of *Pilgrim's Progress*" 〈論《天路歷程》三個漢譯本的譯詩策略與風格〉. *Bianyi lunching* 編譯論叢 4.1 (2011) 73–97.

Lamb, Charles and Mary. *Tales from Shakespeare.* New York: Crowell, 1878.

Langdridge, Darren. *Phenomenological Psychology: Theory, Research and Method.* Essex: Pearson, 2007.

Lee, Adele."'Chop-Socky Shakespeare'?!: The Bard Onscreen in Hong Kong." *Shakespeare Bulletin* 28.4 (2010) 459–79.

Lee, Elaine Tzu-yi. "Translators as Gatekeepers: Gender/Race Issues in Three Taiwan Translations of The Color Purple." Unpublished PhD diss., University of Newcastle-upon-Tyne, 2010.

Lefevere, André. *Translation, Rewriting and the Manipulation of Literary Fame*. London: Routledge, 1992.

———. "Why Waste Our Time on Rewrites? The Trouble with Interpretation and the Role of Rewriting in an Alternative Paradigm." In *The Manipulation of Literature: Studies in Literary Translation*, edited by Theo Hermans, 215–43. London: Croom Helm. 1995.

———. "Chinese and Western Thinking on Translation." In *Constructing Cultures*, edited by Susan Bassnett and André Lefevere, 12–24. Buffalo, NY: Multilingual Matters, 1998.

Legge Helen. *James Legge, Missionary and Scholar*. London: Religious Tract Society, 1905.

Leung, Beatrice and Chan Shun-hing. *Changing Church and State Relations in Hong Kong, 1950-2000*. Hong Kong: Hong Kong University Press, 2003.

———."China's Religious Freedom Policy: The Art of Managing Religious Activity." *China Quarterly* 184 (2005) 894–913.

Li Weimin 李偉民. *ZhongguoShashibiya pi ping shi* 中國莎士比亞批評史 [History of Critique of Chinese Shakespeare]. Beijing: Zhongguo xi juchu ban she, 2006, p.37.

Li Zehou 李澤厚. *ZhongguoSixiangshilun*. 中國思想史論 [History of Chinese Thoughts] Hefei: Anhui wenyichuban she, 1999, pp.193,316.

Li Ziyun. "Women's Consciousness and Women's Writing." In *Engendering China: Women, Culture, and the State*. Christina K. Gilmartin, Ed. Cambridge: Harvard University Press, 1994, p. 299.

Li, Ruru. *Shashibiya: Staging Shakespeare in China*. Hong Kong: Hong Kong University Press, 2003, p.17.

———. "Chinese-Speaking Theatre In Perspective: A Symposium." *Asian Theatre Journal* 22.2 (2005): 310–323.

Liang Shiqiu trans. 梁實秋譯. *Weinisishangren* 威尼斯商人. Taipei: Yuan Dong tushu gongsi, 1968, p.6.

———. *Liang Shiqiuwenxuehuiyilu*. 梁實秋文學回憶錄 In Li Zhao Ed. *Lu Xun / Liang Shi qiu lun zhan shi lu*. 魯迅/梁實秋論戰實錄 [Debates between Lu Xun and Liang Shiqiu] Changsha: Yuelushushe: Hunan sheng xinhuashudianjingxiao, 1989, p.367.

———. *Shashibiyalunjinqian* 莎士比亞論金錢 [Shakespeare on Money]. In Li Zhao Ed. *Lu Xun / Liang Shi qiu lun zhan shi lu*. 魯迅/梁實秋論戰實錄 [Debates between Lu Xun and Liang Shiqiu] Beijing: Hua ling chu ban she, 1997, pp. 626–631.

———. *Wenxue piping bian* 文學批評辯 [Talks on Literary Criticism]. Beijing: Hua ling chu ban she, 1997, pp.133–134.

———. *yashe sanwen* 雅舍散文 Beijing: Wenhua yishu chubanshe,1998, p.81.

Lichte, Erika Fischer. *The Semiotics of Theatre*. Bloomington: Indiana University Press. 1992.

Lin Kehuan 林克歡. "LixiangGuodu de Guangmang: WeinisiShangrenGuanhou 理想國度的光芒:威尼斯商人觀後" [The Light of the Ideal Dimension: Post-Performance Reflections on *The Merchant of Venice*]. *Beijing Yishu* 北京藝術 [*Peking Arts*] 1(1981): 22–24.

Lin Shu, Wei Yi trans. 林紓、魏易譯. *Yinbian Yanyu* 吟邊燕語. Beijing: Shangwu Yin Shu Guan, 1981, pp.1-2.

Lindsay, Jennifer. *Between Tongues: Translation and/of/in Performance in Asia*. Singapore: Singapore University Press, 2006.

Ling. *Shanghai kaiShashibiyayanjiubaogaohui*. 上海開莎士比亞研究報告會. [Report on Shanghai Shakespeare research]. Wenyiyuebao. 文藝月報 May 1955.

Liu Bin 劉斌. Cong XialuokeXingxiangKanShashibiya de zhongzuqishi 從夏洛克形象看莎士比亞的種族宗教歧視 [Shakespeare's Racial and Religious Discrimination From Shylock's Image.] *Journal of Yunnan Normal University* 2000.9, p.81.

Liu Xiaofeng 劉小楓. *Zhengjiuyuxiaoyao* 拯救與逍遙 [Salvation and Easy Wandering]. Shanghai: Shanghai Renminchubanshe., 1988, p.176.

Liu, Yi 劉義. "Religious Freedom Grounded in the Ideology and Political Implementation in Late Qing and Early Republican Period—focusing on activities of Christian Churches 清末民初思想與政治實踐中的信教自由-以基督教會的活動為中心 (1900-1917)". In Wu Ziming 吳梓明, Wu Xiaoxin 吳小新, Eds. *Christ and Chinese Society* 基督與中國社會. Hong Kong: Chinese University Divinity School of Chung Chi College, 2006, pp. 247-270.

Lo Lungkwong. "Taiwan, Hong Kong, Macau". In Peter Phan, Ed. *Christianities in Asia*. Malden, MA : Wiley-Blackwell, 2011, pp.173-189.

Losonsky, Michael. Humboldt. On Language, On the Diversity of Human Language Construction and its Influence on the Mental Development of Human Species. CUP, 1999, p.46

Luo Lie 羅列, "The Construction of Translation Literature and Feminist Discourse - The Translation and Construction of Portia's Image in Early Twentieth Century China ", *Journal of Translation Studies* volume 11 (1) (2008): 105-132.

MacIntyre, Alasdair. *Whose Justice? Which Rationality?* Notre Dame, IN: University of Notre Dame Press, 1988.

MacKenzie, Clayton G. "Questions of Identity in Contemporary Hong Kong Theater." *Comparative Drama*. 29. 2(1995): 203.

———. Arthurs, Moira. "Together Again, Theatre in Postcolonial Hong Kong." *Comparative Drama*. 37.1(Spring 2003): 75.

Mackerras, Colin. *The Chinese Theatre in Modern Times*. London: Thames and Hudson, 1975.

Mak, George K.W. 'Laissez-faire' or Active Intervention? The Nature of the British and Foreign Bible Society's Patronage of the Translation of the Chinese Union Versions' *Journal of Royal Asiatic Society*, Series 3, 20, 2 (2010) pp.167-190.

Malcolm, Cheryl Alexander and Malcolm, David. "(Re) Locating The Jew in Tadeusz Slobodzianek's *Citizen Pekosiewicz*: His Sad and Instructive History". In Sabine Coelsch-Foisner, Holger Klein, Eds. *Drama Translation and Theatre Practice*. Frankfurt; New York: Peter Lang, 2004.

Mao Zedong 毛澤東. Mao Zedong ZhuzuoXuanji Di Sanjuan 毛澤東著作選集第三卷 [Selected Works of Mao Zedong Volume 3.] Beijing: Renmin Chu ban she, 1991.

McFague, Sallie. *Metaphorical Theology: Models of God in Religious Language*. Philadelphia, Pa.: Fortress Press, 1982.

Meng Xianqiang 孟憲強. *zhongguoshaxuejianshi*. 中國莎學簡史 [Shakespeare in China-A Brief History]. Changchun: DongbeiShifanDaxue Chu Banshe, 1994.

Meng Zhao Y, Li Zaidao, eds. 孟昭毅, 1946-; 李載道, *ZhongGuo Fan Yi Wen Xue Shi* 中國翻譯文學史 [The Literary History of Chinese Translations]. Beijing: Beijing Da xue chu ban she, 2005.

Milton, John. "Translation Studies and Adaptation Studies", in *Translation Research Projects 2*, Anthony Pym and Alexander Perekrestenko eds.Tarragona: Intercultural Studies Group, 2009. pp. 51–58.

Monteiro, Maria Goreti. "Choosing Not to Translate – Zero Translations in the First Portuguese *Robinson Crusoe*" In Anthony Pym, Miriam Shlesinger, Zuzana Jettmarova, Eds. *Sociocultural Aspects of Translating and Interpreting*. Amsterdam, Philadelphia: J. Benjamins, 2006, pp. 65–74.

Morrison, Robert, trans. *Yesu jilishidu wo zhu jiu zhe xin yi zhao shu.*[Bible. New Testament] China, 1813.

Ng Tzeming, Peter 吳梓明. "Xianggang Zongjiao de Shehui Jiaose: yige Zongjiao Shehuixue de Lilun tanjiu." 香港宗教的社會角色：一個宗教社會學的理論探究 [The Role of Religion in Hong Kong Society: A Religio-Sociological Theoretical Study] In Peter Ng ed. *Zongjiao shehui jiaose chongtan* 宗教社會角色重探. [Revisiting the Role of Religion in the Society.] Hong Kong: Chinese University of Hong Kong. Centre for the Study of Religion and Society, 2002, pp. 3–20.

Nida, Eugene. *God's World in Man's Language*. New York: Harp Brothers, 1952.

———. *Toward a Science of Translating: with Special Reference to Principles and Procedures involved in Bible Translating*. Leiden: Brill, 1964.

———. *Customs and Cultures: Anthropology for Christian Missions*. South Pasadena, CA: William Carey Library, 1975.

Norton, Jonathan. "Confessions of the Perplexed: An Historian's Worries about Translating Traditional Texts." Paper presented at The Signs of the Times: Exploring Translation of the Bible and Other Texts Conference, Heythrop College, London, September 2013.

Paulin, Batairwa K. "Conversion as Negotiation: Christian Responses to Ancestor Related Practices". Paper presented at 15th Academic Seminar of Fu Jen Catholic University Religious Department, Taipei, 1 June 2013.

Pavis, Patrice. "Problems of Translation for Stage: Intercultural and Post-Modern Theatre." In *The Play Out of Context: Transferring Plays from Culture to Culture*. Translated by Loren Kruger. Edited by Hanna Scolnicov and Peter Holland, 25–44. Cambridge: Cambridge University Press, 1989.

Perng, Ching-hsi. "Bonding *Bangzi* and the Bard: The Case of *Yue/Shu* (*Bond*) and *The Merchant of Venice*". In *Shakespeare in Culture*, edited by Biqi Beatrice Lei and Ching-Hsi Perng, 135–56. Taipei: NTU Press, 2012.

———. "Wentiju de Juming wenti. 問題劇的劇名問題：量度一齣戲" [The Title of a Problem Play: Measuring a Play]. *Ming Pao Daily News* 明報 27 May 2011: D5.

Pfister, Lauren. *Re-thinking mission in China: James Hudson Taylor and Timothy Richard*. Cambridge: North Atlantic Missiology Project, 1998.

Phillips, Tom. "China on Course to Become 'World's Most Christian Nation' within 15 years." *Telegraph* 19 April 2014.

Pines, Yuri. "Chinese History Writing Between the Sacred and the Secular". In *Early Chinese Religion, Part One: Shang Through Han (1250 BC—220 AD)*, edited by John Lagerwey and Marc Kalinowski, 315–40. Handbook of Oriental Studies. Section Four: China 21–1. Leiden: Brill, 2009.

Pollard, David. *Translation and Creation: Readings of Western Literature in Early Modern China, 1840-1918*. Philadelphia: Benjamins, 1998.
Qian Zhongshu 錢鍾書, *Lin Shu de Fanyi* 林紓的翻譯 [Lin Shu's Translations]. Beijing: Shangwu Yin Shu Guan, 1981.
———. "The Translations of Lin Shu." In *Twentieth-Century Chinese Translation Theory: Modes, Issues and Debates*, edited by Leo Tak-hung Chan, 104–15. Benjamins Translation Library. Philadelphia: Benjamins, 2004.
Qu Haiyuan 瞿海源, 宗教與社會 [*Religion and Society*]. Taipei: NTU Press, 2002.
Rambo, Lewis R. *Understanding Religious Conversion*. New Haven: Yale University Press, 1993.
Ramet, Sabrina P. "Sacred Values and the Tapestry of Power: An Introduction." In *Render Unto Caesar: The Religious Sphere in World Politics*, edited by Sabrina P. Ramet and Donald W. Treadgold, 3–20. Washington, D.C. : American University Press, 1995.
Raphael, Vicente. *Contracting Colonialism: Translation and Christian Conversion in Tagalog Society under Early Spanish Rule*. Ithaca: Cornell University Press, 1988.
Reiss, Katharina. "Text types, Translation Types and Translation Assessment." Trans. A.Chesterman. In *Readings in Translation Theory*, edited by A. Chesterman, 105–115. Helsinki: Finn Lectura, 1989.
Reventlow Henning, Graf. *Authority of the Bible and the Rise of the Modern World*. London: SCM, 1984.
Ricoeur, Paul. "Existence et hermeneutique." In *Le Conflit des interpretations*. Paris, 1969. Cited in George Steiner, *After Babel*. Oxford: Oxford University Press, 1975, p. 313.
———. "Preface to Bultmann." In *The Conflict of Interpretations*, 381–401. Translated by Don Ihde. Evanston: Northwestern University Press, 1974.
———. *The Symbolism of Evil*. Translated by Emerson Buchanan. Boston: Beacon, 1967.
———. *Time and Narrative*. Vol. 1. Translated by Kathleen McLaughlin and David Pellauer. Chicago: University of Chicago Press, 1984.
Ricoeur, Paul, and John Thompson, eds. *Hermeneutics and the Human Sciences*. Cambridge: Cambridge University Press, 1981.
Rieger, Joerg, and Pui-lan Kwok, eds. *Occupying Religion*. Lanham, MD: Rowman & Littlefield, 2012.
Robertson, Roland. *The Sociological Interpretation of Religion*. New York: Schocken Books, 1970.
Robinson, Douglas. *The Translator's Turn*. Baltimore: Johns Hopkins University Press, 1991.
Sanneh, Lamin, *Translating the Message: the Missionary Impact on Culture*. Maryknoll, N.Y.: Orbis Books, 1989.
Schleiermacher, Friedrich. "On the Different Methods of Translating." In Lawrence Venuti, Ed. *The Translation Studies Reader*. New York: Routledge 2004, p.49.
Shen Lin. "What use Shakespeare? China and Globalization" In *Shakespeare in Asia*, edited by Dennis Kennedy and Yong Li Lan, 219–20. Cambridge: Cambridge University Press, 2010.
Shen Yanbing, "Thoughts about the Past Year and Plans for the New." *Fiction Monthly* 12 (December 1921). Cited in Shen Lin, "What Use Shakespeare? China and

Globalization." In *Shakespeare in Asia*, edited by Dennis Kennedy and Yong Li Lan, 219–220. Cambridge: Cambridge University Press, 2010.

Shuttleworth, Mark. "Polysystem Theory." In *Routledge Encyclopedia of Translation Studies*, edited by Mona Baker, 176–79. Routledge: New York & London.

Simpson, Paul. *Language, Ideology and Point of View*. London: Routledge, 1993.

Smart, Ninian. *The World's Religions*. Cambridge: Cambridge University Press, 1998.

Smith, Jonathan A., and M. Osborn. "Interpretative Phenomenological Analysis." In *Qualitative Psychology: A Practical Guide to Methods*, edited by J. A. Smith. London: Sage, 2003.

Smith, Jonathan A., Paul Flowers, and Michael Larkin. *Interpretative Phenomenological Analysis: Theory, Method and Research*. Los Angeles: Sage, 2009.

So, A. Y. "One country, three systems? State, nation, and civil society in the making of citizenship in the Chinese triangle of Mainland-Taiwan-Hong Kong." In *Remaking Citizenship in Hong Kong: Community, National and the Global City*, edited by A. S. Ku and N. Pun, 235–53. Oxford: Routledge Curzon, 2004.

Song Lihua 宋莉華. Chuanjiaoshi hanwen xiaoshuo yanjiu. 傳教士漢文小說研究 [A Study on Chinese Fictions by Missionaries]. Shanghai: Shanghai Guji Chubanshe, 2010, pp.179–189.

Soskice, Janet Martin. *Metaphor and Religious Language*. Oxford: Clarendon, 1985.

Stiver, Dan. *The Philosophy of Religious Language*. Cambridge, MA: Blackwell, 1996.

Strange, William. *Authority of the Bible*. London: Darton, Longman & Todd, 2000.

Su, Katie. "The Effects of Cultural Policy on Drama in Taiwan after the Abolition of Martial Law 1987-1997." In *Transformation! Innovation? Perspectives on Taiwan Culture*, edited by Christina Neder and Ines Susanne Schilling. Wiesbaden: Harrassowitz, 2003.

Sun Huizhu. *Who's Butterfly?* Beijing: Commercial Press, 2009.

Tracy, David. *The Analogical Imagination: Christian Theology and the Culture of Pluralism*. New York: Crossroad, 1981.

Trible, Phyllis. *God and the Rhetoric of Sexuality*. Overtures to Biblical Theology. Philadelphia: Fortress, 1978.

Tsui, Jean Kam. "Rewriting Shakespeare: A Study of Lin Shu's Translation of *Tales from Shakespeare*" MPhil diss., University of Hong Kong, 2009.

Tu An, Fang Ping, Trans. 屠岸、方平譯. *Xin Shashibiyaquanji.* 新莎士比亞全集 [New Shakespeare's Works]. Taipei: Mao Tou Ying, 2000.

Tymoczko, Maria and Gentzler, Edwin, eds. *Translation and Power*. Amherst: University of Massachusetts Press, 2002.

Upton, Carole-Anne. *Moving Target: Theatre Translation and Cultural Relocation*. Manchester: St. Jerome, 2000.

Venuti, Lawrence, ed. *Rethinking Translation: Discourse, Subjectivity, Ideology*. London: Routledge, 1992.

———. "Translation as Cultural Politics: Regimes of Domestication in English." *Textual Practice* 7.2 (1993) 208–23.

———. *The Translator's Invisibility: A History of Translation*. London: Routledge, 1995.

Wachman, Alan M. "Competing Identities in Taiwan." In *The Other Taiwan: 1945 to the Present, edited by* Murray Ad. Rubinstein. Armonk, NY: Sharp,1994.

Wang, Frances Kai-Hwa. "Lessons from Taiwan Bangzi Company's Chinese Opera Adaptation of *Merchant of Venice, Bond.*" *Ann Arbor News*, 17 April 2011. Web. 10 May 2011.

Wang Jingyu 王景愚. "Guanyu Xia LuokeRenwuXingxiang de Zhengming" 關於夏洛克人物形象的爭鳴 [Debates on the Characterization of Shylock]." *WaiguoXiju* 外國戲劇 [*Foreign Theatre*] 1(1981): 61–62.

Yiman Wang. *Remaking Chinese Cinema: through the Prism of Shanghai, Hong Kong and Hollywood*. Honolulu: Univeresity of Hawaii Press, 2013, pp.82-112.

Wang Yiqun. "Shajuyanchuzaiwuoguowutaishang de bianqian 莎劇演出在我國舞台上的變遷 [The development of Shakespearean performances on the Chinese stage]," *ShashibyaZaiZhongguo* 莎士比亞在中國 [Shakespeare in China], p.92.

Wang Zuoan 王作安. *Zhonguo de zongjiaowenti he zongjiao zhengce* 中國的宗教問題和宗教政策 [China's Religious Issues and Religious Policies.] Beijing : Zong jiao wen hua chu ban she, 2002, pp.166–168,172.

Wen-shan Shih. *Intercultural Theatre: Two Beijing Opera Adaptations of Shakespeare*. PhD. Diss. University of Toronto, 2000.

White, Laura. "*Wan Rouji*. 剜肉記 [The Story of Shredding Meat]." *Nu Duo* 女鐸 4:5 (1915).

Williams, Raymond. *The Long Revolution*. New York: Columbia University Press, 1961.

Wong, Dorothy. "Shakespeare in Hong Kong: Transplantation and Transposition." MPhil. Diss. Hong Kong Baptist University, 1995.

———. "Situating in Another Context: Reading Shakespearean Productions and Hong Kong Theatre." *International Conference Shakespeare in China: Performance and Perspectives*. Shanghai: Shanghai Theatre Academy, 1999, pp. 27–40.

———. The "Cooking Stove" vs. the "Chinese Takeaway": The Intercultural Representation of Shakespeare on the Hong Kong Stage. *Shakespeare's World/World Shakespeares: The Selected Proceedings of the International Shakespeare Association World Congress, Brisbane, 2006*. Newark: University of Delaware Press, 2008, p.293.

Wong, Jenny. "Text of Submission or Text of Equality – Revisiting Gender-Biased Scriptures and Its Impact on Women's Role in Churches in Hong Kong" Conference Paper presented at Society for Study of Theology at York University, United Kingdom, 11 Apr–13 Apr 2011.

Wong, Lawrence. *Chong shi "xin da ya" : er shi shi ji Zhongguo fan yi yan jiu*. 重釋"信達雅": 二十世紀中國翻譯研究 [Re-interpreting Fidelity, Communicability and Elegance]. Shanghai: Dongfang Chu ban zhong xin, 1999.

Wong Man Kong. "Christian Missions, Chinese Culture and Colonial Administration: A study of the Activities of James Legge and Ernest John Eitel in 19th century Hong Kong." PhD. Diss., The Chinese University of Hong Kong, 1996.

Wu Furong 吳福榮. "WeinisiShangrenZuo Tan Hui San Ji 威尼斯商人座談會散記 [Post-Symposium Afterthoughts of *The Merchant of Venice*.]" *WaiguoXiju* 外國戲劇 [*Foreign Theatre*] 1(1981): pp. 54–57.

Wu Jiemin, Zhu Hongda, eds. 吳潔敏,朱宏達 *Zhu ShenghaoZhuan* 朱生豪傳. [Biography of Zhu Shenghao] Shanghai: Shanghai WaiyuJiaoyuChubanshe, 1990.

Xi Huiling. "Ba JiushiNian Dai ZhongguoNuxingXiezuoTezhengHuimou" 八九十年代中國女性寫作特徵回眸 [Review of the Characteristics of Feminist Writings in the 1980s and 90s.] *wenyipinglun* 文藝評論 [Commentaries on Literature and Arts] 5(2001): pp. 47–50.

Yao Xinzhong and Badham. Paul. *Religious Experience in Contemporary China*. Cardiff: University of Wales Press, 2007.

Yan Xiaojiang 嚴小江. *Liang Shiqiu Zhong Yong Fanyi Guan Yanjiu* 梁實秋中庸翻譯觀研究 [Research on Liang Shiqiu's Middle-Way Translation Strategies].Shanghai: YiwenChuban She., 2008.

Yang, Daniel S.P. *Jin san shi nian lai oumei shaju shangyan qingkuang he xin qushi*. 近三十年來歐美莎劇上演情況和新趨勢 [The Latest Scene and Trend of Shakespeare Performance in Europe and America in the Past Thirty Years]. *Nanguo xiju* 南國戲劇 [South China Theatre] April 1984, pp. 75–80.

———. "Working with RSC Actor Tony Church on the Role of Shylock." *On Stage Studies* 1988: 53–62.

———. "Xianggang huajutuan de shajuyanchu." 香港話劇團的莎劇演出 [The Shakespearean Productions of Hong Kong Repertory Theater.] *Xiju yishu* 戲劇藝術 [Theatre Arts], 2(1999): 78–88.

———. "Shakespeare at Hong Kong Repertory Theatre". In *Shakespeare in China: Performance and Perspectives*. Shanghai: Shanghai Drama Academy, 1999, p.80

———. "Preface" In Perng, Ching-Hsi and Chen Fang, Trans. *Bond, Yue/Shu* (約/束). Taipei: Student Book, 2009, pp. i-vii.

Yang Fenggang. *Religion in China: Survival and Revival under Communist Rule.* New York: Oxford University Press, 2012, pp.55, 156–57.

Yang Huilin. "Inculturation or Contextualization: Interpretation of Christianity in the Context of Chinese Culture". *Contemporary Chinese Thought*, 36:1 Fall (2004): 7–32.

———. "Ethicized Chinese-Language Christianity and the Meaning of Christian Ethics". *Contemporary Chinese Thought*, 36: 1 (Fall) 2004: 68–84.

Yang Tianhong 楊天宏. *Christianity and Modern China* 基督教與現代中國. Chengdu: Sichuan, Renmin Chubanshe, 1994.

Ye Xiaowen 葉小文. shehuizhuyiyuzongjiao de lishixinbian 〈社會主義與宗教的歷史新編〉 [New Collections on Socialism and the History of Religion.] *Zhongguozongjiao* 中國宗教 [Chinese Religion] 1(2002):13–15.

Yi Hongxia 易紅霞. "Shakespeare in Guangdong" in International Conference on Shakespeare in China- Performances and Perspectives: a collection of theses. Shanghai: Shanghai Drama Academy, 2007, pp.197–208.

Ying Fuktsang and Leung Kalun. 邢福增, 梁家麟. *Zhongguo jizu wenti* 中國祭祖問題 *Chinese Ancestor Worship*. Hong Kong: Alliance Bible Seminary, 1997, p.85

———. Dangdai Zhongguo Zhengjiao Guanxi 當代中國政教關係. [Church-State Relationship in Contemporary China]. Hong Kong: Alliance Bible Seminary, 1999.

———. "New Wine and Old Wineskin: An Appraisal on China's Religious Legislation and the Regulations on Religious Affairs." *CSRCS Occasional Paper no. 20.* Hong Kong: Centre for the Study of Religion and Chinese Society, Chung Chi College, The Chinese University of Hong Kong, 2006.

Zatlin, Phyllis. *Theatrical Translation and Film Adaptation: a Practitioner's View.* Clevedon; Buffalo: Multilingual Matters, 2005.

Zhang Beichuan and Kaufman, Joan. "The Rights of People with Same Sex Sexual Behaviour: Recent Progress and Continuing Challenges in China". In Geetanjali Misra and Radhike Chandiramani, eds.*Sexuality, Gender and Rights-Exploring Theory and Practice in South and Southeast Asia.* London: Sage, 2005.

Zhang Da Min 張達民. *WenxueQixiangyuXueshuJiaxiang – Ping Feng Xiang Yizhu de Xinyue* 文學氣象與假象-評馮象譯註的新約 (Literary Phenomenon and

Scholarly Illusion—Comments on Feng Xiang's Commentary on The New Testament). Hong Kong: Christian Times. 2010 Sep 26 – Oct 24.

Zhang Longxi 張隆溪. "Lun Xia Luoke 論夏洛克 [On Shylock]." *WaiguoXiju* 外國戲劇 [Foreign Theatre] 1:1981: 57–60.

Zhang Qihong 張奇虹. *Dao yan yishu gousi* 導演藝術構思 [The Artistic Ideas of Director]. Beijing: Zhongguo Meishu Xueyuan Chubanshe 中國美术学院出版社, 1988, p.1

———. "ZaiShijian He TansuoZhong De JidianTihui: ShitanWeinisiShangren De DaoyanChuli 在實踐探索中的幾點體會:試探威尼斯商人的導演處理 [Some Points in the Process of Implementation and Exploration—Discussions on the directorship of *The Merchant of Venice*.]" *ShashibiyaYanjiu* 莎士比亞研究 [Shakespeare Research]. Hangzhou: Zhejiang People's Press, 1983, pp. 280–287.

Zhang, Xiaoyang. *Shakespeare in China*. Newark, NJ: U. of Delaware Press.1996.

Zheng Tusheng 鄭土生. "Zhen-shan-meishiyongheng de zhuti 真善美是永恆的主題" [Truth, Goodness and Beauty are Eternal Themes] *Proceedings of 1994 Shanghai Shakespeare Festival*, 1994, pp. 149–62.

———. "ZhongguoShaxueJinkuang. 中國莎學近況" [Recent Situations of Chinese Shakespeare Scholarship].In MengXianqiang Ed. "ZhongguoShaxueNianjian 中國莎學年鑑." [Yearbook of Chinese Shakespeare Scholarship] Changchun: Northeast Normal University Press, 1995, pp. 310–314.

Zheng Zhenqiu 鄭振秋. *Xinju kaozheng bai chu* 新劇考證百齣 [Textual Criticism on a Hundred Spoken Drama Plays]. Shanghai: Shanwu yinshuguan, 1919, pp.1–29.

Zhu Jing 朱靜." 新發現的莎劇威尼斯商人中譯本:剜肉記 [New Discoveries of Chinese Translation of Merchant of Venice: The Story of Shredding Meat.]" *Chinese Translators Journal* 26:4 (2005): 50–54.

Zhu Shenghao 朱生豪. *Zhu Shenghao JiaShu* 朱生豪情書 [Letters by Zhu Shenghao]. Shanghai: Shanghai ShehuiKexueChubanshe 上海社會科學出版社, 2003.

———, trans. *Weinisi shangren* 威尼斯商人 [The Merchant of Venice.] Taipei: shijie shuju, 1996.

Online blog theatre reviews

Ni manyi ma—Xia Luoke. 你滿意嗎-夏洛克 [Are you content -Shylock]. Web.7 June 2010. http://cando360.com/

Qishimeiyouhuairen. 其實沒有壞人 [In fact there are no villains]. Web.1 June 2010. http://cando360.com/

He zhongguoren tan zongjiao-wo hen xinwei. 和中國人談宗教-我很欣慰 [Talking to Chinese about religion-I feel pleased]. Web.1 June 2010. http://cando360.com/

Harry's theatre review. Web. November 2010. http://hk.myblog.yahoo.com/fridaystage/article?mid=980

Bobby Chan. Review on *The Merchant of Venice*. Web. 8 November 2010. http://www.facebook.com/home.php?#!/note.php?note_id=456257622143&id=585841136

Performances (in chronological order):

Zhang Qihong 張奇虹, dir. Qin Zhongying 秦中英 trans. *The Merchant of Venice*. 威尼斯商人. China National Youth Arts Theatre 中國青年藝術劇院. VCD. Beijing, 1980.

Daniel S.P. Yang 楊世彭, dir. trans. *The Merchant of Venice*. 威尼斯商人. Hong Kong Repertory Theater. 香港話劇團. VCD. Hong Kong, 1984.

Chris Shum 岑偉宗, Jack Shu 舒志義 trans, *The Merchant of Venice*. 威尼斯商人. Ding Theatre. 丁劇坊. VCD. Hong Kong, 2000.

Chen Xinyi 陳薪伊, dir. Qin Zhongying 秦中英 trans. *For the Heiress' Hand*. 豪門千金. Guangzhou Cantonese Opera Troupe 廣州粵劇團. VCD. Guangzhou, 2007.

Lu Poshen 呂柏伸, dir. Perng Ching-hsi, Chen Fang 彭鏡禧, 陳芳 trans. *Bond*. 約/束. Taiwan Bangzi Company 台灣豫劇團. VCD. Taipei, 2009.

Zhang Bowen 張博文, dir. *Shylock*. 夏洛克. Reflecting Drama Studio. 心照工作室. VCD. Shanghai, 2010.

Ko Tinlung 古天農, dir. Rupert Chan 陳鈞潤, dir. *The Merchant of Venice*. 威尼斯商人, Chung Ying Theatre Company 中英劇團. VCD. Hong Kong, 2010.

The House Programme of *The Merchant of Venice*. 威尼斯商人. China National Youth Arts Theatre 中國青年藝術劇院. Beijing, 1980.

The House Programme of *The Merchant of Venice*. 威尼斯商人. Hong Kong Repertory Theater. 香港話劇團. Hong Kong, 1984.

The House Programme of *The Merchant of Venice*. 威尼斯商人. Ding Theatre. 丁劇坊. Hong Kong, 2000.

The House Programme of *For the Heiress' Hand*. 豪門千金. Guangzhou Cantonese Opera Troupe 廣州粵劇團. Guangzhou, 2007.

The House Programme of *Bond*. 約/束. Taiwan Bangzi Company 台灣豫劇團. Taipei, 2009.

The House Programme of *The Merchant of Venice*. 威尼斯商人, Chung Ying Theatre Company 中英劇團. Hong Kong, 2010.

www.ingramcontent.com/pod-product-compliance
Lightning Source LLC
Chambersburg PA
CBHW070837020526
44114CB00041B/1646